# Finding Out About

## A Cognitive Perspective on
## Search Engine Technology and the WWW

The World Wide Web is rapidly filling with more text than anyone could have imagined even a short time ago, but the task of isolating relevant parts of this vast information has become just that much more daunting. Richard Belew brings a cognitive perspective to the study of information retrieval as a discipline within computer science. He introduces the idea of Finding Out About (FOA) as the process of actively seeking out information relevant to a topic of interest and describes its many facets – ranging from creating a good characterization of what the user seeks, to what documents actually mean, to methods of inferring semantic clues about each document, to the problem of evaluating whether our search engines are performing as we have intended.

*Finding Out About* explains how to build the tools that are useful for searching collections of text and other media. In the process it takes a close look at the properties of textual documents that do not become clear until very large collections of them are brought together and shows that the construction of effective search engines requires knowledge of the statistical and mathematical properties of linguistic phenomena, as well as an appreciation for the cognitive foundation we bring to the task as language users. The unique approach of this book is its even handling of the phenomena of both numbers and words, making it accessible to a wide audience.

The textbook is usable in both undergraduate and graduate classes on information retrieval, library science, and computational linguistics. The text is accompanied by a CD-ROM that contains a hypertext version of the book, including additional topics and notes not present in the printed edition. In addition, the CD contains the full text of C. J. "Keith" van Rijsbergen's famous textbook, *Information Retrieval* (now out of print). Many active links from Belew's to van Rijsbergen's hypertexts help to unite the material. Several test corpora and indexing tools are provided, to support the design of your own search engine. Additional exercises using these corpora and code are available to instructors. Also supporting this book is a Web site that will include recent additions to the book, as well as links to sites of new topics and methods.

Richard K. Belew is a professor in the Computer Science and Engineering departments at the University of California, San Diego. He is an associate editor of the journal *Evolutionary Computation* and co-editor (with Melanie Mitchell) of *Adaptive Individuals in Evolving Populations* (1996).

# Finding Out About

A Cognitive Perspective on
Search Engine Technology
and the WWW

**RICHARD K. BELEW**
*University of California, San Diego*

CAMBRIDGE
UNIVERSITY PRESS

PUBLISHED BY THE PRESS SYNDICATE OF THE UNIVERSITY OF CAMBRIDGE
The Pitt Building, Trumpington Street, Cambridge, United Kingdom

CAMBRIDGE UNIVERSITY PRESS
The Edinburgh Building, Cambridge CB2 2RU, UK
40 West 20th Street, New York, NY 10011-4211, USA
10 Stamford Road, Oakleigh, VIC 3166, Australia
Ruiz de Alarcón 13, 28014 Madrid, Spain
Dock House, The Waterfront, Cape Town 8001, South Africa

http://www.cambridge.org

First published 2000

Printed in the United States of America

*Typeface* Minion 11/14 pt.      *System* LaTeX $2_\varepsilon$   [TB]

*A catalog record for this book is available from the British Library.*

*Library of Congress Cataloging in Publication Data*
Belew, Richard K.
   Finding out about : a cognitive perspective on search engine technology
and the WWW / Richard K. Belew.
      p.    cm.
   Includes bibliographical references and index.
   ISBN 0-521-63028-2 (hb)
   1. Search engines – Programming.   2. World Wide Web – Computer programs.   3. Web
search engines.   I. Title.
   TK5105.884. B45      2000
   025.04 – dc21                                                    99-087329

ISBN 0 521 63028 2 hardback

Cover art by Kim Itkonen www.seenhere.com

# Contents

# Figures

# Foreword

This is a book that I would like to have written. Like all good scientific accounts it has a story to tell, and it tells it in such a way that makes it possible for the reader and student to understand the more technical aspects of information retrieval (IR). The title *Finding Out About* is highly significant, signaling that the book is concerned with the "process of actively seeking out information relevant to a topic of interest." Every keyword in this quotation is important, and each corresponding topic is treated within the book. This is not to say that formal and mathematical aspects are not discussed; they are, but not without considerable motivation first.

From the preceding you may infer that I like the book, which is correct. For many years there has been a dearth of books in our field, especially a lack of textbooks. To a certain extent books in IR have started to fill gaps; however, there are still very few. This book is an excellent addition to that small number. As a textbook it provides many examples and exercises supported by software tools and data for experimentation. The emphasis is on system building and search engine construction rather than user modeling; this is a deliberate choice by the author.

One of the wonderful things about this textbook is that it considers information retrieval in the context of the Web. The history of our subject stretches back to before World War II (for example, the work of Fairthorne), and if you include manual systems (e.g., traditional libraries) then it goes back thousands of years. It is only in the last ten years that a new technology – the World Wide Web – has started to have an impact on people's information-seeking activities. It is not easy to introduce current technology meaningfully and successfully into scientific discussions about IR, but Rik Belew has done just that. Students will come to this book with quite a sophisticated knowledge of the Web and will not be disappointed. From the point of view of a teacher introducing the Web as a vehicle for experimentation, it is ideal. Another attractive feature from an experimental point of view is that email data are used as an example of data to retrieve from, again data with which students will be very familiar.

The intellectual thrust of this book is well rooted in the IR tradition; theory and experiments are developed and presented in tandem. There is one, perhaps unique, approach that is most welcome. Belew draws on the not inconsiderable intellectual tradition of artificial intelligence (AI). As he points out, AI and IR in many respects developed in parallel and are often concerned with similar problems, but there has been little communication between the two fields. Recently this has begun to change a little; in particular, the very strong experimental methodology and statistical approach to natural language processing in IR has been embraced by AI researchers. In the reverse direction, AI research in approximate reasoning and machine learning has begun to have an impact on IR. At each stage in the book, when possible, bridges are shown between AI and IR, which is very refreshing.

The book is primarily concerned with text retrieval; a document is a piece of text. Other forms of retrieval – image, speech and video – are not discussed to any extent. This is not a disadvantage! Many of the ideas and techniques developed for text retrieval readily transfer to other media, and in an introductory book concerned with presenting fundamentals there is no need to clutter the text with other media. Besides, there is not the same experimental backing for work done in other media.

The way the story of IR unfolds is fairly traditional, following the path of many a research paper and book in IR. After the overview (which every student should read), Belew introduces the nature of data and the tools to manipulate and represent them. He then quickly moves on to the weighting and matching schemes, using formal explanations when needed. I particularly like the way he refers to the earlier work of Zipf, Mandelbrot, and Swanson. We also get an elementary introduction to one of the key developments in IR: the vector space model pioneered by Salton and his coworkers.

We are now ready to think about retrieval performance, and Chapter 4, "Assessing the Retrieval," is devoted to just that. The difficult notion of relevance, its definition or lack thereof, is not shirked but taken head on. For example, and I quote: "For now, we simply observe that it seems quite likely that an assessment of a document's relevance depends greatly on the 'basket' of other documents we have seen." The student is left in no doubt that we are simplifying but not forgetting that we are doing so. This chapter introduces the basic IR experimental methodology with much clarity. There is an added bonus of a description of RAVe, a didactic tool that can be used by IR experimenters to collect large numbers of relevance assessments for an arbitrary document corpus. Both students and teachers will find this extremely useful.

The next chapter, entitled "Mathematical Foundations," signaling that it is likely to be more difficult, introduces a mathematical account of some well-known retrieval models: latent semantic indexing, clustering and multidimensional scaling, probabilistic retrieval, and Bayesian networks. The neat thing here is that common themes across models, such as dimensionality reduction, are highlighted. It is cheering to see the correct attribution being made to the early work of Maron and Cooper. Chapter 5 has a distinctive information science flavor about it. It begins with a discussion of bibliometric and citation analysis, but then explores the development of these ideas in the context of the WWW, showing examples of recent work such as that of Kleinberg. A particularly intriguing section is on discovering latent knowledge within a corpus. It illustrates how, as described in Swanson's work, a possible causal connection between magnesium deficiency and migraine can be made by searching the published literature in particular ways (very reminiscent of Lorenzo's Oil).

Finally, we come to one of the centerpieces of IR research: adaptive information retrieval. Relevance feedback has been one of the great success stories of IR, and in Chapter 7 Belew discusses it from a number of different points of view. Experienced IR researchers might read this chapter first! It has the flavor of a manifesto, bringing to bear on a uniquely IR success, ideas from machine learning but at all times concentrating on the IR issues. This is an exciting chapter, justifying Belew's claim that "FOA is an especially ripe area for AI and machine learning." The chapter ends with "But as AI has moved from a concern with manually constructed knowledge representations to machine learning, and as IR has begun to consider how indexing structures can change with use, these two methodologies have increasingly overlapped."

The last chapter, "Conclusions and Future Directions," reaches out into the future and makes good bedside reading.

C. J. "Keith" van Rijsbergen
University of Glasgow

# Preface

One of the things you learn from students is jokes:

> This guy is shopping in a grocery store in Cambridge, Mass. He
> finishes and lines up with a full basket under a big sign marking
> the aisle, "Express: 10 items or less." When he gets to the front
> of the line, the exasperated clerk says, "Look fella, I don't know
> if you're from Harvard and can't count, or MIT and can't read,
> but either way you're in the wrong line."

You probably have to have gone to school in Cambridge to really appreciate this joke. I never did, but I find it funny because it laughs at an important division between thoughtful people.

## Two Cultures

According to C. P. Snow, the world seems eternally divided into "two cultures, the 'literary intellectuals' and the 'scientists'" [Snow, 1961, p. 4]. Snow himself provides very few clues as to just how we might identify someone at one pole or the other. He suggests that the literate have the unfortunate tendency of falling into the "moral trap":

... which comes through ... insight into man's loneliness. It tempts one to sit back, complacent in one's unique tragedy, and let the others go without a meal.

He sees scientists and engineers, on the other hand, as optimistic, impatient do-ers! This leads him to hypothesize that "literature changes more slowly than science" (p. 9).[†] He also thought that, due to the forces of a "fanatical belief in educational specialization" and a "tendency to let our social forms crystallize" (p. 18), the gap between the two cultures was "... much less bridgeable among the young than it was even 30 years ago." He said this in 1959! Certainly these same forces have not helped matters in the intervening 40 years.

*Testable hypothesis*

But Snow's most important recommendation remains true:

There's only one way out of all this: it is, of course, by rethinking our education.... [Speaking especially of British education:] Somehow we have let ourselves the task of producing even a tiny elite educated in one academic skill. For 150 years in Cambridge it was mathematics: then it was mathematics or classics: then natural science was allowed in. But still the choice had to be a single one. (pp. 19, 21)

The premise of this text is that Finding Out About (FOA), the process of actively seeking out information relevant to a topic of interest, absolutely demands a wide-ranging attack by both literary and scientific disciplines. The kind of fractionation that Snow describes has boxed investigators from various disciplines into corners from which they each attempt to address a broad range of fundamentally interdisciplinary questions of *cognition*. FOA is only one such question, but the tension between computational and linguistic sensibilities has been manifest in this domain for an especially long time.

For example, as part of an early meeting of cyberneticists exploring the way that communication and computation might interact, Benoit Mandelbrot, an eminent mathematician and physicist (now most famous for his fractal landscapes), presented hypothetical models of language use that would explain a phenomeon known as **Zipf's law** (a topic discussed in this text, cf. Sections 3.2 and 5.1), claiming these models were analogous to *physical* systems with which he was familiar.

In reaction, A. S. C. Ross, a famous linguist of the 1950s, offered the following commentary:

> [Mandelbrot] states that 'language is a message intentionally produced in order to be decoded word-by-word'. Many schools of linguistic scholarship would reject such a view . . . .
>
> It is, indeed, important that there should be liaison between specialists in communications theory and philologists [linguists, esp. concerned with literature]. The gap between the two subjects is very wide, especially in matters of technique and one wonders what philologists are going to make of remarks such as 'Our model of language is fully analogous to the perfect gas of thermodynamics.'. . .
>
> [But] all statements of this kind really imply that the occurrence of a word at a given point in a text is a matter of chance and this is what philologists and students of literature will deny. If an English writer has to express the idea of TEAPOT – and whether he has to or not is not in the least a matter of chance – the probability of his using the word TEAPOT is unity and the probability of his using the word KETTLE is zero. . . . [Ross, 1953; special typeface not in original]

Mandelbrot's probabilistic models and statistics did not have much to say to at least this linguist.*

An optimist, however, could see a basic *complementarity* between statistical methods and the linguists' syntactic methods. FOA's statistical methods are good at semantics, knowing gross things about an entire document's <u>meaning</u> – what words <u>mean</u> in terms of how they relate to other documents in the corpus and to users' queries. It blithely throws away **noise words** like AND, OF, and THE, because they are assumed to say little about the document's content. Syntactic analysis captures the fine structure of individual sentences and depends critically on the same noise words to reliably anchor its parsing.† Corpus-based linguistics

The title of this textbook also makes cognitive aspirations. "Cognitive" stems from the Latin *cognitio*, referring to structure, building. We typically imagine cognitive structures to be within an individual's head.

---

\* Ross's comments are reminiscent of van Rijsbergen, p. 127 concerning the probability ranking principle!

But part of what is now known as the discipline of cognitive science is the realization that these representations can be built by many individuals as well as by one. Considering the World Wide Web (WWW) as a representation of knowledge is a topic considered further in Section 6.9.

I am personally drawn to the FOA problem because of the way it intermixes verbal and numeric sensibilities. To say that "literary intellectuals" are interested in language is almost tautological. But one of the major arguments put forward by this text is that many linguistic phenomena also have interesting statistical and mathematical properties. Computations involving these numbers are not only central to the engineering of effective search engines, but they portend fundamental insights into the new forms of communication emerging on the WWW.

Depending on your particular background, some of the techniques and perspectives discussed in this text will come naturally to you, and others will seem as if they are from a different planet. But if you apply some effort at understanding these foreign objects, you may just find out you have lots of new friends in the rest of the solar system. Literate people can learn new mathematical names to apply to their literature, and mathematicians can appreciate new features of the language going on about them.

## Typographic Conventions

Other authors who have attempted to discuss language, of course using language to do so, have recognized the confusion that can result as words are used in these two very different roles. Like many of them, I have chosen to use typography to help make this distinction. For example, many of the examples used throughout the text will be drawn from the area of ARTIFICIAL INTELLIGENCE, a subdiscipline of computer science. Terms like this, which are used as examples of lexical items rather than as part of the discourse between me (the author) and you (the reader), will appear as CAPITALIZED and in MONOSPACE FONT.

Second, **boldface** type will be used to flag especially important terms that help to define the FOA problem. For example, **domain of discourse** is the technical term used to describe ARTIFICIAL INTELLIGENCE, the subject matter of the documents we hope to find. These are collected at the end of each chapter, for purposes of review.

Third, the fundamental relation between something in the world and what we think it <u>means</u> is a pivotal issue of this book. But <u>about</u>-ness is also a natural, ubiquitous part of much of our communication, so much so that we will adopt the typographic convention of <u>underlining</u> words such as <u>about</u> and <u>meaning</u> in order to highlight and better appreciate their use.

Finally, authors are always faced with decisions as to which thing they must say first. Making the right decision keeps the story moving forward, while interjecting a digression can make readers lose their way. The WWW is most people's first experience with the **hypertext** alternative to this linear flow. Readers are given the choice points and the opportunity to construct their own *nonlinear* path through a text simply by clicking on links. Obviously such jumps are more difficult to accomplish in a printed text. In this text marginal notes[†] are used to point to tangential topics that a reader might choose to pursue. On the accompanying CD, clicking on the correlated anchor will lead to a brief discussion of this topic. Extra details or clarifications will be provided by footnotes, which are called out in text by asterisks.[*] Traditional numbered footnotes will be used to give URLs of Web sites discussed in the text.

Marginal notes

## Audiences

My interest in the topics discussed here goes back to my own dissertation. At that point I was primarily interested in machine learning techniques, and I learned just enough about free-text information retrieval to use it as a demonstration "domain" for the "connectionist" learning techniques I proposed (cf. Section 6.5.2). Since then, I have become increasingly interested in the issues surrounding FOA and have taught courses in Information Retrieval (IR) for many years, at the University of California in San Diego and the University of Wisconsin in Madison.

This book began as a series of lecture notes for these classes. In the first years, I used Keith van Rijsbergen's seminal text [van Rijsbergen, 1979]. (This book was already out of print when I first found it, but *van Rijsbergen's text*[1] has now been placed in its entirety on the WWW.)

---

[*] Footnote.

[1] http://www.dcs.gla.ac.uk/~iain/keith/

This text so influenced my thinking on this subject that it occupies a special relationship with *FOA*: I quote from it especially often, and I use the special referential convention of van Rijsbergen, p. iii. With Keith's permission, I include a complete copy of his hypertext on the FOA CD, and every reference to that text will allow you to click and go directly to the cited page.

Several other texts deserve special mention. The collection of chapters edited by Frakes and Baeza-Yates [Frakes and Baeza-Yates, 1992] provides an excellent introduction to many topics; Fox's chapter 7 in particular figures heavily in Chapter 2 of this text. Baeza-Yates and Ribeiro have recently edited another collection of very useful chapters [Baeza-Yates and Ribeiro, 1999]. As I was finishing work on this book, Manning and Schütze produced an excellent survey of corpus-based linguistic techniques [Manning and Schütze, 1999] that extends significantly beyond the basics provided in Section 6.3.2. Robert Korfhage has written a textbook that is especially useful from the perspective of library science [Korfhage, 1997]. I highly recommend *Readings in Information Retrieval*, edited by Karen Sparck Jones and Peter Willett [Sparck Jones and Willett, 1997], as a companion to this text. That collection pulls together many classic papers from IR's distant past, some of which are now hard to get. A supplement (available at the ***FOA Web site***[2]) links readings from that text as an adjunct to this textbook.

Because I teach primarily in a Computer Science department, the primary audience for this textbook is computer science students, both graduate and undergraduate, like those I have had the good fortune to meet in my classes. At the same time, I have tried to suppress technical details or explain them in ways that should make the most important themes accessible to audiences (e.g., linguists, library scientists) who are more comfortable with words than with equations. Search engine technologies are central to the FOA problem, but this text was designed to be accessible to those who write such computer programs as well as to those who do not.

Executable versions of all basic routines are available on the attached CD-ROM; current versions are maintained at the ***FOA Web site***[2]. Together with the test corpora and experimental data (queries, relevance assessments), students and teachers should be able to explore many

---

[2] http://www.cs.ucsd.edu/~rik/FOA

variations without changing any code. Source code for the routines is also provided for those programmers who want to modify or extend the basic functionalities.

Exercises are collected at the end of each chapter, but they are an admittedly uneven mix. They are intended as basic review exercises; some are more challenging than others. The primary assignments for my classes are a series of machine problems: extended programming assignments that cumulatively build all the parts of a basic search engine. The details of these assignments, as well as lecture slides, test questions, and so on, are available on the *FOA Web site*[3] to instructors who might be interested.

The first chapter of the text is designed to give any audience a broad overview of the basic questions underlying FOA and how they interact. The next three chapters cover the core issues involved in building and evaluating a generic search engine at a level appropriate to undergraduates. Chapter 5 collects several important topics that require more mathematical sophistication, and Chapters 6 and 7 consider extensions of the basic core material at a graduate level. Chapter 6 considers extensions of basic search technologies that use features of documents beyond keywords to draw more "artificially intelligent" inferences about them. Chapter 7 focuses on how one particular branch of AI, machine learning, has been used to automatically learn more about both documents and the users searching through them. Chapter 8 concludes with some looks into the most active development in FOA and a reassessment of fundamental issues that will be with us for the foreseeable future.

## Acknowledgments

I had the good fortune to have David Blair at the University of Michigan (in a single lecture!) make it clear that FOA isn't just an engineering problem, but important to anyone deeply interested in language. Mike Gordon (energized by that same lecture), Manfred Kochen, Bob Lindsay, Gary and Judy Olson, Ken Winter, and Maurita Holland were all in Ann Arbor, and they taught me more than I would really appreciate until years later.

---

[3] http://www.cs.ucsd.edu/~rik/FOA/

Keith van Rijsbergen's unswerving confidence has made this book possible. His book is where I began and the standard I have tried to maintain. Gerry Salton and Karen Sparck Jones have been generous and patient with me as they have been to so many others in the IR community. I thank Nick Belkin, Bruce Croft, Doug Cutting, Sue Dumais, Norbert Führ, David Lewis, Jan Petersen, and Steve Robertson for uncountable interesting SIGIR dinners. I am happy to acknowledge the influence of the industrious groups around Carnegie Mellon University and Just Research, led by Tom Mitchell and Andrew McCallum, especially on Chapter 7.

A summer of exciting conversation (1987) with Ed Hutchins and Don Norman of UCSD's Cognitive Science department helped me think more broadly about "parallel distributed processing" models of cognition, involving networks of *people* rather than neurons, as parts of social systems. I have benefited from a long, productive relationship with the editors and others working at *Encyclopædia Britannica*. I am grateful to have met Mortimer Adler (once!) and especially to have worked closely with Editor-in-Chief Bob McHenry and others at *Encyclopædia Britannica* in Chicago, Chris Needham (in London), and Bob Clarke, John Dimm, John McInerney, and Harold Kester in La Jolla. Over an even longer period, Jack Conrad, Dan Dabny, Andy Desmond, Peter Jackson, and Isabelle Moulinier of West Publishing have provided my second, extended experience with the highly edited WESTLAW corpus. I enjoyed a pleasant sabbatical at the University of Wisconsin in Madison, teaching with and learning from Jude Shavlik and Mark Craven. Paul Kube is, more than anyone else I know, comfortable in both of Snow's cultures (and several others as well); he has helped me sober and balance many aspects of this manuscript. I thank Kim Itkonen for turning my words about words into a wonderful image for the cover.

Most of my own research has been done in collaboration with students. Many of my thoughts about what I had done right and wrong with AIR were shaped in conversations with Dan Rose, concerning his thesis. I am also grateful to both Dan and Susan Gruber for their help in shaping very early drafts of all chapters. Brian Bartell asked hard questions about FOA from the beginning, and I have appreciated the pleasure of his collaboration ever since. John Hatton, Amy Steier, and Fil Menczer have all helped me explore aspects of FOA as part of their own research; Thomas Kammeyer, Chris Vogt, and Bryan Tower have all helped push various aspects of the FOA code base forward. I am also grateful to Apple Computer, *Encyclopædia Britannica*, and the National Science Foundation for funding various portions of our work over the years.

Chris Rosin and Terry Jones provided useful feedback on some chapters, and Marti Hearst (University of California, Berkeley) and Paul Thompson (University of Minnesota and St. Thomas University) used early drafts of *FOA* with their classes. I am grateful to David Tranah and Shari Chappell for their rescue of *FOA* at Cambridge University Press.

Will, Lee, Cori and Julie are my nearest and dearest family. Simply completing this book (finally!) is the best apology I can offer them. Beyond that . . . "Whereof one cannot speak, one must remain silent."

It is here where I must say that despite the best efforts of these many friends and colleagues, I know I haven't said it all, and that mistakes surely remain. I have written down those things I wish I'd known when I began my thesis, for use by students in the classes I teach. If it helps you avoid any of the mistakes it has taken me a decade to learn, it will almost have been worth it.

## TERMS INTRODUCED IN THIS CHAPTER

**domain of discourse**          **noise words**
**hypertext**                    **Zipf's law**

# 1

# Overview

"What's the final episode          "It's about nothing."
of 'Seinfeld' about?"

Finding Out About. Reproduced by permission of *The New Yorker**

## 1.1 Finding Out About – A Cognitive Activity

We are all forced to make decisions regularly, sometimes on the spur of
the moment. But the rest of the time we have enough warning that it is
possible to collect our thoughts and do some research that makes our

---

* Robert Mankoff, © *The New Yorker*, 26 January 1998.

decision as sound as it can be. This book is a closer look at the process of **finding out about** (FOA), research activities that allow a decision-maker to draw on others' knowledge. It is written from a technical perspective, in terms of computational tools that speed the FOA activity in the modern era of the distributed networks of knowledge collectively known as the World Wide Web (WWW). It shows you how to build many of the tools that are useful for searching collections of text and other media. The primary argument advanced is that progress requires that we appreciate the *cognitive* foundation we bring to this task as academics, as language users, and even as adaptive organisms.

As organisms, we have evolved a wide range of strategies for seeking useful information <u>about</u> our environment. We use the term "cognitive" to highlight the use of *internal representations* that help even the simplest organisms perceive and respond to their world; as the organisms get less simple, their cognitive structures increase in complexity. Whether done by simple or complex organisms, however, the process of *finding out about* is a very active one – making initial guesses about good paths, using complex sets of features to decide if we seem to be on the right path, and proceeding forward.

As humans, we are especially expert at searching through one of the most complex environments of all: *language.* Its system of linguistic features is not derived from the natural world, at least not directly. It is a constructed, cultural system that has worked well since (by definition!) prehistoric times. In part, languages remain useful because they are capable of change when necessary. New features and new objects are noticed, and it becomes necessary for us to express new things <u>about</u> them, to form our reactions to them, and to express these reactions to one another.

Our first experience of language, as children and as a species, was oral – we spoke and listened. As children we learn *Sprachspiele* (word or language games) [Wittgenstein, 1953] – how to use language to get what we want. A baby saying "Juice!" is using the exclamation as a *tool* to make adults move; that's what a word <u>means</u>. Such a functional notion of language, in terms of the jobs it accomplishes, will prove central to our conception of what keywords in documents and queries <u>mean</u> as part of the FOA task.

Beyond the oral uses of language, as a species we have also learned the advantages of *writing down* important facts we might otherwise forget.

Writing down a list of things to do, which we might forget tomorrow, extends our limited memory. Some of these advantages accrue to even a single individual: We use language personally, to organize our thoughts and to conceive strategies.

Even more important, we use writing to say things to others. Writing down important, memorable facts in a consistent, **conventional** manner, so that others can understand what we <u>mean</u> and vice versa, further amplifies the linguistic advantage. As a society, we value reading and writing skills because they let us interpret shared symbols and coordinate our actions. In advanced cultures' scholarship, entire curricula can be defined in terms of what Robert McHenry (Editor-in-Chief of *Encyclopædia Britannica*) calls ***"Knowing How to Know."*** [1]

It is easiest to think of the organism's or human's search as being for a valuable object, sweet pieces of fruit in the jungle, or (in modern times) a grocer that sells them. But as language has played an increasingly important role in our society, searching for valuable written passages becomes an end unto itself. Especially as members of the academic community, we are likely to go to libraries seeking others' writings as part of our search. Here we find rows upon rows of books, each full of facts the author thought important, and endorsed by a librarian who has selected it. The authors are typically people far from our own time and place, using language similar but not identical to our own.

Of course the library contains many such books on many, many topics. We must Find Out About a topic of special interest, looking only for those things that are **relevant** to our search. This basic skill is a fundamental part of an academic's job:

- We look for references in order to write a term paper.
- We read a textbook, looking for help in answering an exercise.
- We comb through scientific journals to see if a question has already been answered.

We know that if we find the right reference, the right paper, the right paragraph, our job will be made much easier. Language has become not only the means of our search, but its object as well.

---

[1] www.justanother.com/howtoknow

Today we can also search the **World Wide Web** (WWW) for others' opinions of music, movies, or software. Of course these examples are much less of an "academic exercise"; Finding Out About such information commodities, and doing it consistently and well, is a skill on which the modern information society places high value indeed. But while the infrastructure forming the modern WWW is quite recent, the promise offered by truly connecting all the world's knowledge has been anticipated for some time, for example, by H. G. Wells [Wells, 1938].

Many of the FOA searching techniques we will discuss in this text have been designed to operate on vast collections of apparently "dead" linguistic objects: files full of old email messages, CD-ROMs full of manuals or literature, Web servers full of technical reports, and so on. But at their core, each of these collections is evidence of real, vital attempts to communicate. Typically an **author** (explicitly or implicitly) anticipates the interests of some imagined **audience** and produces text that is a balance between what the author wants to say and what he or she thinks the audience wants to hear. A textual **corpus** will contain many such documents, written by many different authors, in many styles and for many different purposes. A person searching through such a corpus comes with his or her own purposes and may well use language in a different way from any of the authors. But each individual linguistic expression – the authors' attempts to write, the searchers' attempts to express their questions and then read the authors' documents – must be appreciated for the **word games** [Wittgenstein, 1953] that they are. FOA is centrally concerned with <u>meaning</u>: the semantics of the words, sentences, questions, and documents involved. We cannot tell if a document is <u>about</u> a topic unless we understand (at least something of) the semantics of the document and the topic. This is the notion of <u>about</u>-ness most typical within the tradition of library science [Hutchins, 1978].

This means that our attempts to engineer good technical solutions must be informed by, and can contribute to, a broader philosophy of language. For example, it will turn out that FOA's concern with the semantics of entire documents is well complemented by techniques from computational linguistics, which have tended to focus on syntactic analysis of individual sentences. But even more exciting is the fact that the recent

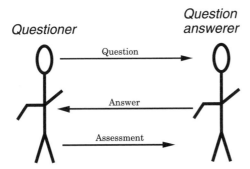

FIGURE 1.1 The FOA Conversation Loop.

availability of new types of **electronic artifacts** – from email messages and WWW corpora to the browsing behaviors of millions of users all trying to FOA – brings an *empirical* grounding for new theories of language that may well be revolutionary.

At its core, the FOA process of browsing readers can be imagined to involve three phases:

1. asking a question;
2. constructing an answer; and
3. assessing the answer.

This conversational loop is sketched in Figure 1.1.

## Step 1. Asking a Question

The first step is initiated by people who (anticipating our interest in building a search engine) we'll call **users**, and their questions. We don't know a lot about these people, but we do know they are in a particular frame of mind, a special cognitive state; they may be aware[†] of a specific gap in their knowledge (or they be only vaguely puzzled), and they're motivated to fill it. They want to FOA . . . some topic.

Meta-cognition about ignorance

Supposing for a moment that we were there to ask, the users may not even be able to characterize the topic, that is, to articulate their knowledge gap. More precisely, they may not be able to fully define characteristics of the "answer" they seek. A paradoxical feature of the FOA problem is that if users knew their question, precisely, they might not even need the search engine we are designing: Forming a clearly posed question is often the hardest part of answering it! In any case, we'll call this somewhat befuddled but not uncommon cognitive state the users' **information need**.

While a bit confused about their particular question, the users are not without resources. First, they can typically take their ill-defined, *internal* cognitive state and turn it into an *external* expression of their question, in some language. We'll call their expression the **query**, and the language in which it is constructed the **query language**.

## Step 2. Constructing an Answer

So much for the source of the question; whence the answer? If the question is being asked of a person, we must worry about equally complex characteristics of the *answerer's* cognitive state:

- Can they translate the user's ill-formed question into a better one?
- Do they know the answer themselves?
- Are they able to verbalize this answer?
- Can they give the answer in terms the user will understand?
- Can they provide the necessary background knowledge for the user to understand the answer itself?

We will refer to the question-answerer as the **search engine**, a computer program that algorithmically performs this task. Immediately each of the concerns (just listed) regarding the *human* answerer's cognitive state translates into extremely ambitious demands we might make of our *computer* system.

Throughout most of this book, we will avoid such ambitious issues and instead consider a very restricted form of the FOA problem: We will assume that the search engine has available to it only a set of preexisting, "canned" passages of text and that its response is limited to identifying one or more of these passages and presenting them to the users; see Figure 1.2. We will call each of these passages a **document** and the entire set of documents the corpus. Especially when the corpus is very large (e.g., assume it contains millions or even billions of documents), selecting a very small set (say 10 to 20) of these as potentially good answers to

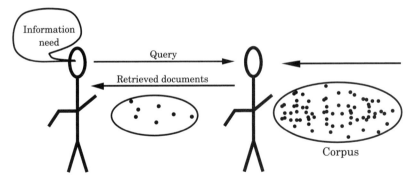

FIGURE 1.2  Retrieval of Documents in Response to a Query

be **retrieved** will prove sufficiently difficult (and practically important) that we will focus on it for the first few chapters of this book. In the final chapters however, we will consider how this basic functionality can be extended towards tools for "Searching for an education" (cf. Section 8.3.9).

## Step 3. Assessing the Answer

Imagine a special instance of the FOA problem: You are the user, waiting in line to ask a question of a professor. You're confused about a topic that is sure to be on the final exam. When you finally get your chance to ask your question, we'll assume that the professor does nothing but select the three or four preformed pearls of wisdom he or she thinks come closest to your need, delivers these "documents," and sends you on your way. "But wait!" you want to say. "That isn't what I <u>meant</u>." Or, "Let me ask it another way." Or, "That helps, but I still have this problem."

The third and equally important phase of the FOA process "closes the loop" between asker and answerer, whereby the user (asker) provides an assessment of how relevant they find the answer provided. If after your first question and the professor's initial answer you are summarily ushered out of the office, you have a perfect right to be angry because the FOA process has been violated. FOA is a *dialog* between asker and answerer; it does not end with the search engine's first delivery of an answer. This initial exchange is only the first iteration of an ongoing conversation by which asker and answerer mutually negotiate a satisfactory exchange. In the process, the asker may *recognize* elements of the answer he or she

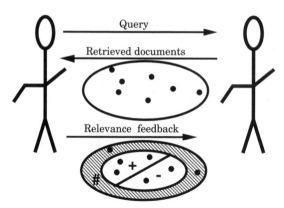

FIGURE 1.3 Assessment of the Retrieval

seeks and be able to reexpress the information need in terms of threads taken from previous answers.

Because the question-answerer has been restricted to a simple set of documents, the asker's **relevance feedback** must be similarly constrained; for each of the documents retrieved by the search engine, the asker reacts by saying whether or not the document is relevant. Returning to the student/professor scenario, we can imagine this as the student saying "Thanks, that helps" after those pearls that do and remaining silent or saying, "Huh?" or "What does that have to do with anything?!" or "No, that's not what I meant!" otherwise. More precisely, relevance feedback gives askers the opportunity to provide more information with their reaction to each retrieved document – whether it is relevant ($\oplus$), irrelevant ($\ominus$), or neutral (#). This is shown as a Venn diagram–like labeling of the set of retrieved documents in Figure 1.3. We'll worry about just how to solicit and make use of relevance feedback judgments in Chapter 4.[†]

What FOA data can we observe?

## 1.1.1 Working within the IR Tradition

If it seems to you that the last section has sidestepped many of the most difficult issues underlying FOA, you're right! Later chapters will return to redress some of these omissions, but the immediate goal of Chapters 2 to 4 is to "operationalize" FOA to resemble a well-studied problem within computer science, typically referred to as **information retrieval** (IR). IR is a field that has existed since computers were first used to count words [Belkin and Croft, 1987]. Even earlier, the related discipline of library science had developed many automated techniques for efficiently storing, cataloging, and retrieving *physical* materials so that browsing patrons could find them; many of these methods can be applied to the digital documents held within computers. IR has also borrowed heavily from the field of linguistics, especially computational linguistics.

The primary journals in the field and most important conferences[†] in IR have continued to publish and meet since the 1960s, but the field has taken on new momentum within the last decade. Computers capable of searching and retrieving from the entire biomedical literature, across an entire nation's judicial system, or from all of the major newspaper and magazine articles, have created new markets among doctors, lawyers, journalists, students, everyone! And of course, the Internet, within just a few years, has generated many, many other examples of textual collections and people interested in searching through them.

Other places to FOA IR

The long tradition of IR is therefore the primary perspective from which we will approach FOA. Of course, every tradition brings with it tacit assumptions and preconceived notions that can hinder progress. In some ways, an elementary school student using the Internet to FOA class materials is related to the original problem considered by library science and IR, but in many other ways it couldn't be more different (cf. Section 8.1). In this text, "FOA" will be used to refer to the broadest characterization of the cognitive process and "IR" to this subdiscipline of computer science and its traditional techniques. When we talk of the "search engine," this is not meant to refer to any particular implementation, but to an idealized system most typical of the many different generations and varieties of actual search engines now in use. If you are using this text as part of a course, you may build one simple example of a search engine.

Using Figure 1.4 as a guide, we'll return to each of the three phases and be a bit more specific about each component of our search engine. Here, finally, the human question-answerer has been replaced by an algorithm, the search engine, that will attempt to accomplish the same purpose. This figure also makes clear that the fundamental operation performed by a search engine is a *match*, between descriptive features mentioned by users in their queries and documents sharing those features. By far the most important kind of features are keywords.

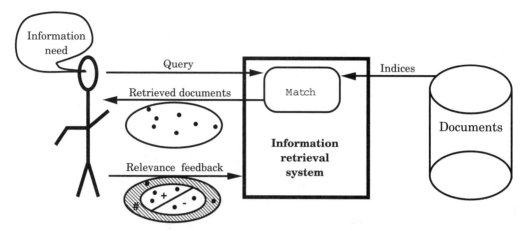

FIGURE 1.4  Schematic of Search Engine

## 1.2  Keywords

**Keywords** are linguistic atoms – typically words, pieces of words, or phrases – used to characterize the subject or content of a document. They are pivotal because they must bridge the gap between the users' characterization of information need (i.e., their queries) and the characterization of the documents' topical focus against which these will be matched. We could therefore begin to describe them from either perspective: how they are used by users, or how they become associated with documents. We will begin with the former.

### 1.2.1  Elements of the Query Language

If the query comes from a student during office hours or from a patron at a reference librarian's desk, the query language they'll use to frame their question is entirely **natural**, that most expressive "mother tongue" familiar to both question-asker and -answerer. But for the software search engines we will consider, we must assume a much more constrained "artificial" query language. Like other languages, ours will have both a meaningful **vocabulary** – the set of important keywords any user is allowed to mention in any queries – and a *syntax* that allows us to construct more elaborate query structures.

## 1.2.2 Topical Scope

The first constraint we can apply to the set of keywords we will allow in our vocabulary is to define a domain of discourse – the subject area within which each and every user of our search engine is assumed to be searching. While we might imagine building a truly encyclopedic reference work, one capable of answering questions <u>about</u> any topic whatsoever, it is much more common to build a search engine with more limited goals, capable of answering questions <u>about</u> some particular subject. We will choose the simpler path (it will prove enough of a challenge!) and focus on a particular topic. To be concrete, throughout this text we will assume that the domain of discourse is ARTIFICIAL INTELLIGENCE (AI). Briefly, AI can be defined as a subdiscipline of computer science, especially concerned with algorithms that mimic inferences which, had they been made by a human, would be considered "intelligent." It typically includes such topics as KNOWLEDGE REPRESENTATION, MACHINE LEARNING, and ROBOTICS.

Thus COMPUTER SCIENCE is a **broader term** than ARTIFICIAL INTELLIGENCE. This **hypernym** relationship between the two phrases is something we will return to later (cf. Section 6.3). For example, our task becomes more difficult if we assume that the corpus of documents contains material on the broader topic of COMPUTER SCIENCE, rather than just (!) ARTIFICIAL INTELLIGENCE. Conversely, the topics KNOWLEDGE REPRESENTATION, MACHINE LEARNING, and ROBOTICS are all **narrower terms**, and our task would, *caeteris paribus*,[*] be made easier if we only had to help users FOA one of them.

Constraining the vocabulary so that it is **exhaustive** enough that any imaginable and relevant topic is expressible within the language, while remaining **specific** enough that any particular subjects a user is likely to investigate can be distinguished from others, will become a central goal of our design. ROBOTICS, for example, would seem a descriptive keyword because it identifies a relatively small subarea of ARTIFICIAL INTELLIGENCE. COMPUTER SCIENCE would be silly as a keyword (for this corpus), because we are assuming it would apply to every document and hence does nothing to discriminate them – it is too exhaustive. At the

---

[*] (Assuming) all other things are equal.

other extreme, ROBOTIC VACUUM CLEANERS FOR 747 AIRLINERS is almost certainly too specific.

The **vocabulary size** – the total number of keywords – depends on many factors, including the scope of the domain of discourse. A typical language user has a reading vocabulary of approximately 50,000 words. Web search engines and large test corpora formed from the union of many document types may require vocabularies ten times this size. It is unlikely that such a large lexicon of keywords would be required for restricted corpora, but it is also true that even a narrow field can develop an extensive, specialized **jargon** or **terms of art**. In practice, search engines typically have difficulty reducing the number of usable keywords to much below 10,000.

### 1.2.3 Document Descriptors

We've introduced keywords as features mentioned by users as part of their queries, but the other face of keywords is as descriptive features of documents. That is, we might naturally say that a document is <u>about</u> ROBOTICS. Users mentioning ROBOTICS in their query should expect to get those documents that are <u>about</u> this topic. Keywords must therefore also function as the *documents*' description language. The same vocabulary of words used in queries must be used to describe the topical content of each and every document. Keywords become our characterization of what each document is <u>about</u>. **Indexing** is the process of associating one or more keywords with each document.

The vocabulary used can either be **controlled** or **uncontrolled** (a.k.a. **closed vocabularies** or **open vocabularies**). Suppose we decide to have all the documents in our corpus manually indexed by their authors; this is quite common in many conference proceedings, for example. If we provide a list of potential keywords and tell authors they must restrict their choices to terms on this list, we are using a controlled indexing vocabulary. On the other hand, if we allow the authors to assign any terms they choose, the resulting index has an uncontrolled vocabulary [Svenonius, 1986].

To get a feel for the indexing process, imagine that you are given a piece of text and must come up with a set of keywords that describe what the document is <u>about</u>. Let's make the exercise more concrete. You are the author of a report entitled USING A NEURAL NETWORK FOR

PREDICTION, and you are submitting it to a journal. One of the things this particular journal requires is that the author provide up to six keywords under which this article will be indexed. If you are sending it to the *Communications of the ACM*, you might pick a set of keywords that identify, to the audience of computer scientists you think read this publication, connections between this new work and prior work in related areas: NONLINEAR REGRESSION; TIME SERIES PREDICTION.

But now imagine that you've decided to submit the *exact same paper* to *Byte* magazine, and you must again pick keywords that have <u>meaning</u> to this audience. You might choose: NEURAL NETWORKS; STOCK MARKET ANALYSIS.

What is the **context** in which these keywords are going to be interpreted? Who's the audience? Who's going to understand what these keywords <u>mean</u>? Anticipating the FOA activity in which these keywords will function, we know that the real issue to be solved is not only to describe this one document, but to *distinguish* it from the millions of others in the same corpus. How are the keywords chosen going to be used to distinguish your document from the others?

It is often easiest to imagine keywords as independent features of each document. In fact, however, keywords are best viewed as a *relation* between a document and its prospective readers, sensitive to both characteristics of the users' queries and other documents in the same corpus. In other words, the keywords you pick for *Byte* should be different from those you pick for *Communications of the ACM*, and for deeper reasons than what we might cynically consider "spin control."

## 1.3 Query Syntax

Keywords therefore have a special status in IR and as part of the FOA process. Not only must they be exhaustive enough to capture the entire topical scope reflected by the corpora's domain of discourse, but they must also be expressive enough to characterize any information needs the users might have.

Of course we need not restrict our users to only one of these keywords. It seems quite natural for queries to be composed of two or three, perhaps even dozens, of keywords. Recent empirical evidence suggests that many typical queries have only two or three keywords (cf. Section 8.1), but even this number provides a great combinatorial extension to the basic vocabulary of single keywords. Other applications, for example, using a document itself as a query (i.e., using it as an example: "Give me more like this"), can generate queries with hundreds of keywords. Regardless of size, queries defined only as sets of keywords will be called **simple queries**. Many Web search engines support only simple queries. Often, however, the search engines also provide more advanced interfaces, including **operators** in the query language. Perhaps, because you have previously been warped by an exposure to computer science:), you think that sets of keywords might be especially useful if joined by Boolean operators. For example, if we have one set of documents about NEURAL NETWORKS and another set of documents about SPEECH RECOGNITION, we can expect the query: NEURAL NETWORKS AND SPEECH RECOGNITION to correspond to the intersection of these two sets, while NEURAL NETWORKS OR SPEECH RECOGNITION would correspond to their union.

The Boolean NOT operator is a bit more of a problem. If users say they want things that are *not* about NEURAL NETWORKS, they are in fact referring to the vast majority of the corpus. That is, NOT is more appropriately considered a binary, subtraction operator. To make this distinction explicit we will call it BUT_NOT.

There are other syntactic operators that are often included in a search engine's query language, but discussion of these will be put off until later. Even with these simple Boolean connectives and a keyword vocabulary of reasonable size, users can construct a vast number of potential queries when attempting to express their information need.

## 1.3.1 Query Sessions

As we consider the specific features of each query, it is important to remember the role these short expressions play in the larger FOA process. Queries are generated as an attempt by users to express their information need. As with any linguistic expression, conveying a thought you have can be difficult, and this is likely to be especially true of the muddled cognitive state of our FOA searcher. Users who are familiar with the special syntactic features of a query language may be able to express their need more easily, but others for whom this unnatural syntax is new or difficult will have additional difficulties.[†]

"Typical" users
have changed

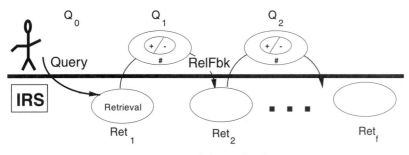

FIGURE 1.5  A Query Session

As with many of the idealizing assumptions we are at least tem-
porarily making, it is often simpler to think about only one iteration
of the three-step query/retrieve/assess FOA process at a time. In most
realistic situations we can expect that single queries will not occur in
isolation but as part of an iteration of the FOA process. An initial query
begins the dialog; the search engine's response provides clues to the user
about directions to pursue next; these are expressed as another query. An
abstract view of this sequence is presented in Figure 1.5. Note especially
the concatenation of a series of basic FOA three-step iterations. Data are
produced by the user, then by the search engine, and then by the user; this
constructs a very natural alternation of user–search engine exchanges.
Users' assessments can also function as their next query statement. This
can be achieved simply if we have some method for automatically constructing a query from relevance feedback. For example, if users click on
documents they like, the search engine can, by itself, form a new query
that focuses on those keywords that are especially associated with these
documents.

There are many such techniques for using relevance feedback from a
single query/retrieval, and there are many more things we can learn from
the entire query session. The full query session provides more complete
evidence about the users' information need than we can gain from any
one query. In fact, as will be discussed extensively in Chapter 7, there
exist algorithmic means by which the search engine itself might "learn"
from such evidence. Learning methods might even be expected to make
**transitive** leaps, from the users' initial expressions of their information
needs to the final documents that satisfied them.[†] (Of course, this transitive leap is only warranted if we are certain that users ended the session

Transitivity

satisfied and aren't just quitting in frustration!) For all these reasons, we must try to identify a query session's boundaries, that is, when one focused search session ends and the next session, involving the same user searching on a different topic, begins.

## 1.4  Documents

When "documents" were first introduced as part of the FOA process, it was as one of the set of potential, predefined answers to users' queries. Here we will ground this abstract view in practical terms that can be readily applied, for example, to the searches that are now common on the Web. Our goal will be to balance this practical description of how search engines work today with the abstract FOA view that goes beyond current practices to other kinds of searches still to come.

A useful working definition is that a document is a *passage of free text*. It is composed of text, strings of characters from an alphabet. We'll typically make the (English) assumption that uses the Roman alphabet, Arabic numerals, and standard punctuation. Complications like font style (italics, bold) and non-Roman **marked alphabets** that add characters like ä, ç, Ñ, and æ; and the iconic characters of Asian languages require even more thought.

By "free" text we mean it is in **natural language**, the sort native readers and writers use easily. Good examples of free text might be a newspaper article, a journal paper, or a dictionary definition. Typically the text will be grammatically well-formed language, in part because this is *written* language, not oral. People are more careful when constructing written artifacts that last beyond the moment. Informal texts like email messages, on the other hand, help to point to ways that some texts can retain the spontaneity of oral communication, for better and worse [Ong, 1982].

Finally, we will be interested in **passages** of such text, of arbitrary size. The newspaper example makes us imagine documents of a few thousand words, but journal articles make us think of samples ten times larger, and email messages make us think of something only a tenth that size. We can even think of an entire book as a single document. All such passages satisfy our basic definition; they might be appropriate answers to a search about some topic.

The length of the documents will prove to be a critical issue in FOA search engine design, especially when some corpus contains documents of widely varying lengths. This is because longer documents can discuss more topics, so they are capable of being <u>about</u> more. Longer documents are more likely to be associated with more keywords, and hence they are more likely to be retrieved (cf. Section 3.4.2).

One possible response is to make a simple but very consequential assumption.

**ASSUMPTION 1**    *All documents have equal <u>about</u>-ness.*

In other words, if we ask the (a priori) probability of any document in the corpus being considered relevant, we will assume that all are equiprobable. This would lead us to *normalize* documents' indices in some way to compensate for differing lengths. The normalization procedure is a matter of considerable debate; we will return to consider it in depth later (cf. Section 3.4.2).

For now, we will take a different tack toward the issue of document length, as captured by an alternative pair of assumptions.

**ASSUMPTION 2**    *The smallest unit of text with appreciable <u>about</u>-ness is the paragraph.*

**ASSUMPTION 3**    *All manner of longer documents are constructed out of basic paragraph atoms.*

The first piece of this argument is that the smallest sample of text that can reasonably be expected to satisfy an FOA request is a paragraph. The claim is that a word, even a sentence, does not by itself provide enough *context* for any question to be answered or "found out about." But if the paragraph has been well constructed, as defined by conventional rules of composition, it should answer many such questions. And unless the text comes from James Joyce, Proust, or Jorge Luis Borges, we can expect paragraphs to occupy about half an average screen page – nicely viewable chunks.

Assumption 3 alludes to the range of structural relationships by which the atomic paragraphs can typically be strung together to form longer passages. First and foremost is simple sequential flow, the order in which an author expects the paragraphs to be read. The sequential nature of traditional printed media, from the first papyrus scrolls to modern books and periodicals, has meant that a sequential ordering over paragraphs has been dominant. It may even be that the modern human is especially capable of understanding **rhetoric** of this form (cf. Section 6.2.3).

In any case, a sequential ordering of paragraphs is just one possible way they might be related. Other common relationships include:

- a *hierarchical* structure composing paragraphs into subsections, sections, and chapters;
- *footnotes*, embellishing the primary theme;
- *bibliographic citations* to other, previous publications;
- *references* to other sections of the same document; and
- *pedagogical prerequisite* relationships ensuring that conceptual foundations are established prior to subsequent discussion.

Of course each of these relationships has grown up within the tradition of printed publication. Special typographical conventions (boldface, italics, sub- and superscripting, margins, rules) have arisen to represent them and distinguish them from sequential flow.

But new, electronic media now available to readers (and becoming available to authors) need not follow the same strictly linear flow. The new capabilities and problems of traversing text in nonlinear ways – hypertext – have been discussed by some visionaries [Bush, 1945; Nelson, 1987] for decades. This new technology certainly permits us to make some traversals more easily (e.g., jumping to a cited reference with the click of a button rather than a trip to the library), but this same ease may make it more difficult for an author to present a cogent argument.

For now we will not worry about how arguments can be formed with nonlinear hypermedia. Assumptions 2 and 3 simply allow us to infer Assumption 1: If all the documents are paragraphs, we can expect them to have virtually uniform <u>about</u>-ness. These are also simplifying assumptions, however. In an important sense, a scientific paper's abstract is <u>about</u> the same content as the rest of the paper, and a newspaper article's first paragraph attempts to summarize the details of the following story. These issues of a text's **level of treatment** will be discussed later.

## 1.4.1 Structured Aspects of Documents

In addition to their free text, many documents will carry **meta-data** that gives some facts about the document. We may have **publication information**, for example, that this document appeared in this journal, in this issue, on this page. We are likely to know the author(s) of the document. Queries will often refer to aspects of both free text and meta-data.

**QUERY 1**   *I'm interested in documents <u>about</u> Fools' Gold that have been published in children's magazines in the last five years.*

The first portion of this query depends on the same <u>about</u>-ness relation that is at the core of our FOA process. But the last two criteria, concerning publication type and date, seem to be just the sort of query against structured attributes that database systems perform very successfully. In most real-life applications a hybrid of database and IR technologies will be necessary. (We distinguish between these techniques in Section 1.6.)

The most interesting examples concern characteristics that do not clearly fall into either IR or database categories. For example, can you define precisely what you <u>mean</u> by a "children's magazine" in terms of unambiguous attributes on which a database would depend? Consider another query.

**QUERY 2**   *What sort of work has K. E. Smith done on metabolic proteins affecting neurogenesis?*

Finding an exact match for the string K. E. Smith in the AUTHORS attribute is straightforward. But the conventions in much of medical and biological publication (as well as in some areas of physics) sometimes lead to dozens of authors on papers, from the director of the institute through all of the laboratory assistants. Although K. E. Smith might well fulfill the syntactic requirements of authorship on a particular paper, users searching for "the work of" this person might well have a more narrowly defined *semantic* relationship in mind.

## 1.4.2 Corpora

We have focused on individual documents, but of course the FOA problem would not interest us except that we are typically faced with a corpus of *millions* of such documents, and we are interested in finding only the handful that are of interest. The actual number of documents and their cumulative size will matter a great deal, as some of our IR methods have time or space complexities that make them viable only within certain parameters. To pick a simple example, if you are trying to find a newspaper article (you read it a few days ago) for a friend, exhaustively searching through all the pages is probably quite effective if you know it was in Friday's paper, but not if you need to search through an entire month's recycling pile! Similarly, a standard utility like the Unix `grep` command can be a practical alternative if the corpus is small and the queries simple.

## 1.4.3 Document Proxies

Do you remember the library's original card catalogs, those wooden, beautifully constructed cabinets full of rows and rows of drawers, each full of carefully typed index cards? The card catalog contained **proxies** – abridged representations of documents, acting as their surrogate – for the books it indexed. No one expected the full text of the books to actually be found in the drawers.

Computerized card catalogs are only capable of supporting a similar function. They do allow more extensive indexing and efficient retrieval, from terminals that might be accessed far from the library building. At the heart of this system is a text search engine capable of matching features of a query against book titles.[†] Just like with the original index cards, however, retrieval is limited to some proxy of the indexed work, a bibliographic citation, or perhaps even an abstract. The text of ultimate interest – in a book, magazine, or journal – remains physically quite distinct from the search engine used to find it.

Card catalogs were the first search engines

As computer storage capacities and network communication rates have exploded, it has become increasingly common to find retrieval systems capable of presenting the full text of retrieved items. In the modern context, proxies extend beyond the bibliographic citation information and subject headings we associate with card catalogs and include a document's title, an article's abstract, a judicial opinion's headnote, or a book's table of contents.

The distinction between the search engine retrieving documents and retrieving proxies remains important, however, for at least two reasons. First, the radically changing technical capabilities of libraries (and computers and networks more generally) can create conceptual confusion about just what the search engine is doing. While it has been possible for a decade or more to get the full text of published journal articles through commercial systems such as DIALOG and Lexis/Nexis, free access to these through your public library would have been almost unheard of until quite recently. In fact, most libraries did not even try to index individual articles in their periodical collections. Changing technical capacities, changes in the application of intellectual property laws, changes in the library's role, and resulting changes in the publishing industry are radically altering the traditional balance. Even when all new publications are easily available electronically, the issue of *retrospectively* capturing previously published books and journals remains unresolved.

Looking far into the future and assuming no technical, economic, or legal barriers to a complete rendering of any document in our corpus, there is still an important reason to consider document proxies. Recall that FOA is a *process* we are attempting to support and that retrieving sets of documents to show users is a step we expect to repeat many times. Proxies are abridged versions of the documents that are easier for browsing users to quickly scan and react to (i.e., provide relevance feedback) than if they had to read the entire document. If a document's title is accurate (if its abstract is well written, if its bibliographic citation is complete), this proxy may provide enough information for users to decide if it seems relevant.[†]

A misleading title, or did the document teach you something?!

## 1.4.4 Genre

A more subtle characteristic of documents that may need to concern us is their **genre** – the voice or style in which a document is written. You would, um, like, be pretty darn surprised to find stuff like this in a textbook, but not if it came to you over the phone. The genre of email seems to be settling somewhere between typical printed media and spoken conversation, with special markings of sarcasm:) and expletives #!?% common. Newspaper journalists are carefully trained to produce articles consistent with what newspaper readers expect, and their editors are paid to ensure that these stories maintain a consistent voice. Scientific journal articles are written to be understood by peers in the same field, according to standards that pertain to that community [Bayerman, 1988]. An important component of this audience focus is the **vocabulary choice** an author makes (cf. Section 8.2.1); stylistic variations and document structure may also differ. In a field like psychology, for example, it would be difficult to get a paper accepted in some journals if it is not subdivided into sections like Hypothesis, Methodology, and Subjects. Legal briefs are also written in highly conventionalized forms [Havard Law Review Association, 1995], and legislation is drafted to satisfy political realities [Allen, 1980; Goodrich, 1987; Levi, 1982; Nerhot, 1991].

In part, these variations in genre are difficult to detect because they remain consistent within any single corpus. That is, the typical email message would jump out at you as out of place if it appeared in your newspaper, but probably not if it were on the Letters to the Editor page. These examples highlight how much *context* <u>about</u> the corpus we bring with us whenever we read a particular document. They also foreshadow problems Web searchers are just beginning to appreciate, as WWW search engines include every document to which they can crawl, intermixing their very different contexts and writing styles. Without the orienting features of the newspaper's masthead, the "Letters to the Editor" rubric, or the purposeful selection of a tool that scans only Usenet news, the browsing users' abilities to understand an arbitrary document is diminished. Individual textual passages have been stripped of much of the context that made them sensible. As more and more of us generate *content* – in new hypermedia forms as well as traditional publications – that more and more of us retrieve, the range of genres we will experience can only increase, and our methods for FOA must help to represent not just the document but contextual information as well.

## 1.4.5 Beyond Text

Our definition of "documents" has hewn closely to the printed forms that still dominate the FOA retrievals most people now do. But print media are not the only form of answer we might reasonably seek, and we must ensure that our methods generalize to the other media that are increasingly part of the Net. Sound, images, movies, maps, and more are all appearing as part of the WWW, and they are typically intermixed with textual material. We need to be able to search all of these.

One reason for casting the central problem of this text as "finding out about" is that many aspects of multimedia retrieval remain the same from this perspective. We still have users, who have information needs. We can still reasonably use the term "document" to include any potential answer to users' queries, but now we expand this term to include whatever media are available. Most centrally, we must still characterize what each document is <u>about</u> in order to match it to these queries, and users can still assess how well the search engine has done.

At the same time, many parts of the FOA problem change as we move away from textual documents to other media. Most important is the increased difficulty of algorithmically extracting clues related to the documents' semantic content from their syntactic features. The primary source of semantic evidence used within text-based IR is the relative frequencies of keywords in document corpora, and a major portion of this text will show that this is a powerful set of clues indeed. We will also discuss the role other syntactic clues (e.g., bibliographic links) associated with texts can play in understanding what they are <u>about</u>. As we move to other media, the important question becomes what consistent features these new media have that we can also process to reliably infer semantic content. For example, what can we know <u>about</u> an image from the distribution of its pixel values? Do all SUNSETS share a brightness profile (dark below a horizontal line, symmetrically bright above it) that is reliable enough that this clue can be exploited to identify just these scenes?[†] If so, can this mode of analysis be generalized sufficiently to allow retrieval of images based on more typical descriptors such as CHILDREN FEEDING ANIMALS?

Signature of human culture?!

Even if we imagine that certain obvious, superficial aspects of some images may be extracted, our hopes must not blind us to the rich vocabulary that many images use every day. Consider a query like FIDELITY AS A POLITICAL ISSUE and consider Figure 1.6. Would any reasonable person claim that they could provide an *exhaustive* list of all the things these pictures "say"? Did you include the set of Hillary's jaw? The angle of Bill's gaze? The attitudes <u>about</u> divorce prevalent when the Doles' picture was taken and now? The tacit commentary by the editors of

FIGURE 1.6  Finding Out About **POLITICAL FIDELITY**[*]
Reproduced by permission of *The New York Times*

*The New York Times* produced by the juxtaposition of these two photos? Note also that this picture (and its selection for use in this text!) occurred

MONICA the
meme

years before anyone had even heard of Monica Lewinsky![†]

Figure 1.7 gives a second example. This is a photograph of a locking display case, containing a concert performance schedule. Pasted over the glass of the case is a sign, saying: "IGNORE THIS CALENDAR: THESE DATES ARE 3 YEARS OLD." But the photo also reveals a number of more subtle clues – that the key to the case has been lost (for three years!), that some frustrated teacher finally got tired of dealing with confused parents, that none of the school's administrators can think of a more imaginative solution.

These examples may seem far-fetched. But those of you old enough to remember the Cold War may also remember that there was an entire job category known as "Kremlinologist": someone expert at divining various power shifts among the Politburo based on evidence such as where various participants were placed within group photos! The conventional wisdom is that "a picture is worth a thousand words," and although some images may not require much explanation, others speak volumes. As we move from still images to *movies*, entirely new channels

[*] *The New York Times*, 15 Sept. 1996, Week in Review, p. 1.

FIGURE 1.7 Obsolete Concert Schedule

for <u>meaning</u> – conveyed with the camera's attentional focus, soundtrack, etc. – are available to a skilled director. Music itself has an equally rich but distinct vocabulary. The ability to easily record and transmit digital **spoken documents** (speech) makes this form of audio especially worthy of analysis [Sparck Jones et al., 1996].

As with text, music, film, and motion pictures all predate their representations on computers. The convenience and availability of all these electronic media make it more possible and even more important to analyze them.

Once again, text is an excellent place to begin. **Semiotics** is one label for the subfield of linguistics concerned with words as *symbols*, as conveyors of <u>meaning</u>. Words in a language represent a particularly coherent system of symbol use, but so do the symbols used by photo journalists, painters, and movie directors. The meaning of these symbols changes with time; recall the pictures of the Clintons and Doles, their interpretation at the time of publication, and their interpretation now. What these pictures <u>mean</u> is different if we ask <u>about</u> the original context of 1996 and its <u>meaning</u> now. And again, complex, shifting meanings are typical not only of images but of documents as well: Watson and Crick's publication of the DNA code in *Nature* in 1953 [Watson and Crick, 1953] was important even then, but what that paper <u>means</u> now could not have been anticipated.

Yet the prospects for associating contentful descriptors with images and even richer media are not quite as bleak as they might seem. In many important cases (e.g., the archives of news photos maintained by magazines and newspapers), images are accompanied by **captions**, and video streams with **transcripts**. This additional *manually constructed textual* data means that techniques for inferring semantic content directly from images can piggyback on top of text-based IR techniques. In conjunction with the machine learning techniques we will discuss (cf. Chapter 7), statistically reliable associations found in captioned image and video corpora can be extrapolated to situations where we have images without captions and video without transcripts.

In the interim, we will return to the narrower, text-only notion of a document with which we began and consider FOA solutions for this simpler (!) case.

## 1.5  Indexing

Indexing is the process by which a vocabulary of keywords is assigned to all documents of a corpus. Mathematically, an index is a *relation* mapping each document to the set of keywords that it is <u>about</u>:

$$Index \ : \ doc_i \ \stackrel{about}{\longrightarrow} \ \{kw_j\}$$

The inverse mapping captures, for each keyword, the documents it **describes**:

$$Index^{-1} \ : \ \{kw_j\} \ \stackrel{describes}{\longrightarrow} \ doc_i$$

This assignment can be done manually or automatically. **Manual indexing** means that people, skilled as natural language users and perhaps with expertise in the domain of discourse, have read each document (at least cursorily) and selected appropriate keywords for it. **Automatic indexing** refers to algorithmic procedures for accomplishing this same result. Because the index relation is the fundamental connection between the users' expressions of information need and the documents that can satisfy them, this simply stated goal – "Build the *Index* relation" – is at the core of the IR problem and FOA generally.

## 1.5.1 Automatically Selecting Keywords

We begin by considering the document at its most mechanical level, as a string of characters. Our first candidates for keywords will be **tokens**, things broken by **white space**. That is, each token in the document could be considered one of its keywords.

How good is this simple solution? Suppose users ask for documents <u>about</u> CARS and the document we are currently indexing has the string CAR. It seems reasonable to assume that users are interested in this document, despite the fact that the query happens to contain the **plural** form CARS while the document contains the singular CAR. For many queries we might like to consider occurrences of the words CAR and CARS, or even RETRIEVAL and RETRIEVE, as roughly interchangeable with one another; the suffixes do not affect <u>meaning</u> dramatically. And of course our problem doesn't end with plurals; we could make similar arguments concerning past-tense -ED endings and -ING participles.

This simple solution also depends too much on where spaces occur. Consider the German noun GESCHWINDIGKEITSBESCRANKUNG, corresponding to the English phrase SPEED LIMIT. In many ways, the fact that English happens to put a white space between the words while German does not is not semantically critical to the <u>meaning</u> of these descriptors or the documents in which they might occur. Such **morphological** features – used to mark relatively superficial, surface-structure features (such as tense or singular versus plural) – can be considered less important to the <u>meaning</u>. And differences between German and English are trivial when they are compared to Asian texts, where the relationship between *characters* and *words* is radically different.

What about **hyphenation**? Use of the word DATABASE, the phrase DATA BASE, and the hyphenated phrase DATA-BASE is highly variable, depending on author preference and current practice at the time and place of publication. Yet we would hope that all occurrences of any of these tokens would be treated as references to approximately the same semantic category. Similarly, we hope that the end-of-line hyphenation (breaking long words at syllable boundaries) would not create two keywords when we would expect only one. But simply adding "-" to the set of white space characters defining tokens would make CLINTON-DOLE and A-Z keywords, too!

Hyphenation is concerned with the situation in which a potential keyword is broken up by punctuation; what about those situations where a space also breaks up a semantic unit? SPEED LIMIT seems semantically cohesive, but what algorithm could distinguish it from other **bigrams** (consecutive pairs of words) that happen to occur sequentially? The problem only becomes that much more complicated if we attempt to consider longer noun phrases like APPLES AND ORANGES or BACK PROPAGATION NEURAL NETWORK, let alone more complicated syntactic compounds such as verb phrases, clauses, or sentences. Identifying phrases is an important and active area of research from the perspectives of both IR and computational linguistics.

Summarizing, we will take a token to be our default keyword because this is straightforward. More sophisticated solutions will handle hyphenation, multiword phrases, subtoken stems, and so on (cf. Section 2.3.1).

## 1.5.2 Computer-Assisted Indexing

The field of library science has studied the manual process of constructing effective indices for a very long time. This standard becomes a useful comparison against which our best automatic techniques can be compared, but it also demonstrates how difficult comparison will be. There are data, for example, that suggest that the capacity of one person (e.g., the indexer) to *anticipate* the words used by another person (e.g., a second indexer or the query of a subsequent user) is severely limited [Furnas et al., 1987]; we are all quite idiosyncratic in this regard. The lack of interindexer consistency among humans must make us humble in our expectations for automated techniques.

But manual and automatic indexing need not be viewed as competing alternatives. In economic terms, if we had sufficient resources, we could hire enough highly trained catalogers to carefully read every document in a corpus and index each of them. If we couldn't afford this very expensive option, we would have to be satisfied with the best index our automatic system could construct. But if we have enough resources to hire one or two human indexers, what tools might we give them that would make the most effective use of their time?

We seek methods that *leverage* the editorial resource, in the sense that this manual effort does not grow as the corpus does. How might editors and librarians guide an automatic indexing process? What information should this computation provide that would allow intelligent human readers the assurance of a high-quality indexing function? Chapter 7 will discuss ways that editors can **train** machine learning systems, and a number of analyses that are of interest to editors will be mentioned, especially in Chapter 6.

## 1.6  FOA versus Database Retrieval

Within the field of computer science, the subfields of databases and IR are often closely aligned. Databases have well-developed theoretic under-pinnings [Abiteboul et al., 1995] that have generated efficient algorithms [McFadden and Hoffer, 1994] and become the foundation for one of the most successful elements of the computer industry.

Both databases and search engines attempt to characterize a partic-ular class of queries by which many users are expected to attempt to get information from computers. Historically, database systems and theory have been perceived as central to the discipline of computer science, probably more so than the IR techniques that are the core technologies for FOA. Things may be changing, however.

The general public's discovery of the Internet and subsequent interest in search engines like Alta Vista, InfoSeek, and Yahoo! suggest that many users find value in the lists of Web pages returned in response to searches. These search engines are clearly doing an important job for many people. It is also a quantitatively different job from organizing their address book (or record collection or baseball statistics) *databases*. How are IR and database technologies to be distinguished?

To make the distinctions more concrete, let's imagine a particular information need and think about how both a database and a search engine might attempt to satisfy it. An example query might be as follows.

**QUERY 3**  *What is the best SCSI disk drive to buy?*

TABLE 1.1  Hypothetical Database

| Model number | Manufacturer | Vendor | Size (GB) | Interface | Price ($) | Speed (msec) |
|---|---|---|---|---|---|---|
| 123 | Seag | J&R | 2.4 | SCSI | 162 | 12 |
| 123 | Seag | Fry | 2.4 | SCSI | 159 | 12 |
| 456 | Metrop | A&B | 2.5 | IDE | ∅ | 12.5 |
| 789 | Seag | J&R | 1.5 | EIDE | 121 | 10.5 |
| . . . | | | | | | |

In the case of databases, strong assumptions must first be made about *structure* among attributes of individual records. Good database design demands that the fundamental elements of data, their format, and logical relations among them be carefully analyzed and anticipated in a **logical data model** long before any data are actually collected and maintained within a physical implementation. These assumptions allow specification of a syntax for the query language, strategies for optimizing the query's use of computational resources, and efficient storage of the data on physical devices.

Now let's assume that a logical data model has been constructed and that a large catalog of information from various hard drive manufacturers and vendors has been collated. We will also make the larger and problematic assumption that the users can translate the natural language of Query 3 into the somewhat baroque syntax of a query language such as SQL. The result of the database search might look something like Table 1.1.[†]

**NLP for databases**

Creating an example relation like this and populating it with a few instances is simple, but performing the necessary data modeling, collating the data from all of the manufacturers and vendors, and keeping it all up to date are much more daunting tasks. If the database catalog is out of date or missing data from important vendors, users might leave the database badly informed.

Now let's imagine using a search engine on the same query. When run against a UseNet news search engine like DejaNews, this query results in the retrieval shown in Figure 1.8 with the most highly ranked posting shown in Figure 1.9.

Users of this search engine will read <u>about</u> many issues *related* to hard disks, some of which may be *relevant* to their particular situation.

Matches **1-20** of **726** for search:  **best SCSI disk**

```
      Date    Scr        Subject            Newsgroup        Author
 1.  97/08/29 062  Re: IDE or SCSI?        comp.os.ms-windows. hima@ur
 2.  97/08/04 053  Re: switching from IDE t comp.unix.unixware. arthur@
 3.  97/08/28 051  Re: Sun SCSI and Linux   comp.os.linux.hardw tallpau
 4.  97/08/03 050  Re: switching from IDE t comp.unix.unixware. Larry F
 5.  97/08/02 050  Replace SCSI Disk on R3. comp.unix.sco.misc  ericl@m
 6.  97/08/21 049  FS: 486-100Mhz multimedi misc.forsale.comput tjioe@s
 7.  97/08/11 049  SCSI problems            comp.os.linux.hardw ///ax Z
 8.  97/08/03 049  Re: Which is Best: More  comp.os.linux.hardw o r c @
 9.  97/08/01 049  Best Scsi CDR for $300-$ alt.cd-rom          "Scott
10.  97/08/16 048  Re: IDE increases Interr microsoft.public.vi "Nolan
11.  97/08/16 048  FS:Micropolis 3243WAV dr rec.video.marketpla John Cc
12.  97/08/09 048  CDR Server --- Audio CD  hk.forsale          Mattgor
13.  97/09/01 047  comp.sys.apple2 Freq#8/1 comp.sys.apple2     nathan@
14.  97/08/31 047  Re: W95 vs. MacOS Micros comp.sys.mac.advoca dfield@
15.  97/08/27 047  miro configuration utili rec.video.desktop   Edy Gas
16.  97/08/05 047  [FOR SALE] Dual PowerPC  comp.sys.be.misc    "Frank
17.  97/08/04 047  Re: IBM OEM 0664-CSH and comp.periphs.scsi   Chuck 7
18.  97/08/01 047  error i kernel32.dll alt no.pc              Jorunn
19.  97/08/12 046  SUN SPARC 20 FOR SALE.   comp.sys.sun.hardwa power@i
20.  97/07/26 046  Re: Help: Replacing pri  comp.os.ms-windows. Christc
```

FIGURE 1.8  Results of SCSI Search of UseNet

Subject:       Re: IDE or SCSI?
From:          helpful@urban.or.jp (me @ my humble abode)
Date:          1997/08/29
Message-Id:    <3406f93a.50446926@nnrp.gol.com>
Newsgroups: comp.os.ms-windows.nt.setup.hardware,comp.windows.nt.misc
[More Headers]

On Thu, 28 Aug 1997 23:10:03 GMT, Michael Query <query@dpi.qld.gov.au> wrote:

>My question is, should I get another 2 Gb SCSI disk for putting the
>OS (NT 4.0 WS), software, etc on, or should I get an IDE disk for this?

Having played around with different conÆgsfor a while, I'd say go SCSI. I'd
do that even if I had to get a second SCSI controller.

(You'll ``hear''a lot of people arguing that IDE is good enough, but if you are
after overall improved performance SCSI is best.)

my 2Y.

FIGURE 1.9  A Relevant Posting

For example, does the "best" qualifier in Query 3 <u>mean</u> lowest cost, maximum capacity, minimum access time, or something else? Can users choose between IDE and SCSI, or are they restricted to SCSI? Depending on what kind of users they are, some of the information retrieved may be

TABLE 1.2  IR versus Database Retrieval

|  | *IR* | *Database* |
|---|---|---|
| **System provides** | Pointer to data | Data item |
| **User's query** | General | Specific |
| **Retrieval method** | Probabilistic | Deterministic |
| **Success criteria** | Utility | (Correctness) |
|  |  | Efficiency, |
|  |  | User-friendliness, . . . |

immediately applicable to the purchase being considered, while other parts of it are better considered **collateral knowledge** (D. E. Rose, personal communication) that simply leaves users better informed.

A very different set of assumptions from those we made about the database system are necessary to imagine the search engine working. For example, who wrote these postings? Are they a credible source of good information; what is their **authority**? Well-trained database users should ask equally skeptical questions about the data retrieved, but rarely are authority, data integrity, and the like considered part of database analysis.

But the key assumption for our IR users is that they can "listen in" on this previous "conversation" and *interpret* the text that has been left behind as containing potential answers to the current question. The search engine is charged with retrieving textual passages that are likely to answer the users' questions. Once presented with these retrievals, FOA users have more humble expectations and are willing to do more interpretive work. Because FOA searches are often even less concrete than Query 3 and are issued by users simply trying to learn <u>about</u> a topic, *semantic* issues central to the interpretation of a textual passage and its context, validity, and so on are at the heart of the FOA enterprise.

Van Rijsbergen, p. 2, table 1.1 has summarized these issues along a number of dimensions by which IR and database systems can be distinguished, and several of these are duplicated in Table 1.2. Database systems are almost always assumed to provide data items directly. Search engines provide a level of indirection, a *pointer* to textual passages that contain many facts, hopefully including some of interest. The information need of the users is quite vague when compared to that of database users. The search engine users are searching for information <u>about</u> a topic they don't completely understand. Typical database users have a fairly specific question, like Query 3, in mind. It might even be that the database is missing some data; for example, the special null value $\emptyset$ in Table 1.1 shows that the price of the third disk drive is not known. Even in this case, however, the database system "knows that it doesn't know" this information. FOA queries are rarely brought to such a sharp point; ambiguity is intrinsic to the users' expectations.

Because the queries are so general, an FOA retrieval must be described in probabilistic terms. If a particular hard disk's price is part of our database, we are certain, with probability $= 1.0$, of its value. Never would a database system reply with "This hard disk might cost about $300." As discussed in depth in Section 5.5, a search engine can use sophisticated methods for reasoning probabilistically, and available evidence might even allow it to be quite confident that retrieved items will be perceived as relevant. But never will we be entirely certain that a document is what users want; we can only have high confidence that it may be.

Finally, one of the problems in evaluating search engines is just what success criteria are to be used. We typically assume that information we get back from a database system is correct. (Try to find an ad for a database system that boasts, "Our system retrieves only right answers"!) One database system claims to be more efficient, cheaper, easier to integrate into existing code, and more user-friendly than others.

This list of ways that search engines might be distinguished from databases is far from exhaustive; Blair has proposed a more extensive analysis [Blair, 1984]. More recently, as search engine technology and WWW-inspired applications have both burgeoned, hybrids of databases and search engines have blurred the historical differences further. Some bases of database/search engine interaction are mentioned in Chapter 6.

Chapter 4 discusses the evaluation of search engines in great detail, but typically the bottom line is: Does the system help you? If you are writing a research paper, did this search engine help you find material that was useful in your research? If you are a lawyer preparing a case and you want to find every relevant judicial opinion, does the search engine offer an advantage over an equivalent amount of time combing through books in a law library? Such squishy, qualitative judgments are notoriously difficult to measure, and especially to measure consistently across broad populations of users. The next section provides a quick preview of several precise measurements that have proven useful to the IR community but would not be found persuasive within the database community.

## 1.7  How Well Are We Doing?

Suppose you and I each build an FOA search tool; how might we decide which does the better job? How might a potential customer decide on their relative values? If we use a new search engine that seems to work much better, how can we determine which of its many features are critical to this success? If we are to make a science of FOA, or even if we only wish to build consistent, reliable tools, it is vital that we establish a methodology by which the performance of search engines can be rigorously evaluated.

Just as your evaluation of a human question-answerer (professor, reference librarian, etc.) might well depend on subjective factors (how well you "communicate") and factors that go beyond the performance of the search engine (does *any* available document contain a satisfying answer?), evaluation of search engines is notoriously difficult. The field of IR has made great progress, however, by adopting a methodology for search engine evaluation that has allowed objective assessment of a task that is closely related to FOA. Here we will sketch this simplified notion of the FOA task.

The first step is to focus on a particular query. With respect to this query, we identify the set of documents *Rel* that are determined to be

Omniscient relevance

relevant to it.[†] Then a good search engine is one that can retrieve all and only the documents in *Rel*. Figure 1.10 shows both *Rel* and *Retr*, the set of documents actually retrieved in response to the query, in terms of a Venn diagram. Clearly, the number of documents that were designated both relevant and retrieved, $Retr \cap Rel$, will be a key measure of success.

But we must compare the size of the set $|Retr \cap Rel|$ to something, and several standards of comparison are possible. For example, if we are very concerned that the search engine retrieve every relevant document,

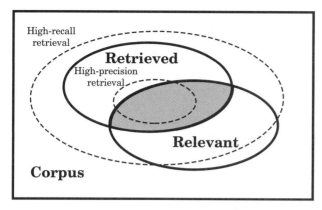

FIGURE 1.10 Comparison of Retrieved versus Relevant Documents

then it is appropriate to compare the intersection to the number of documents marked as relevant, $|Rel|$. This measure of search engine performance is known as **recall**:

$$\text{Recall} \equiv \frac{|Retr \cap Rel|}{|Rel|} \tag{1.1}$$

However, we might instead be worried about how much of what the users see is relevant, so an equally reasonable standard of comparison is what number of the documents retrieved, $|Retr|$, are in fact relevant. This measure is known as **precision**:

$$\text{Precision} \equiv \frac{|Retr \cap Rel|}{|Retr|} \tag{1.2}$$

Note that even in this simple measure of search engine performance, we have identified two legitimate criteria. In real applications, our users will often vary as to whether high precision or high recall is more important. For example, a lawyer looking for every prior ruling (i.e., judicial opinions, retrievable as separate documents) that is **on point** for his or her case will be more interested in **high-recall** behavior. The typical undergraduate, on the other hand, who is quickly searching the Web for a term paper due the next day, knows all too well that there may be many, many relevant documents somewhere out there. But the student cares much more that the first screen of **hits** be full of relevant leads.

Examples of high-recall and high-precision retrievals are also shown in Figure 1.10.

To be useful, this same analysis must be extended to consider the order in which documents are retrieved, and it must consider performance across a broad range of typical queries rather than just one. These and other issues of evaluation are taken up in Chapter 4.

## 1.8 Summary

This chapter has covered enormous ground and attempted to summarize topics that will be discussed in the rest of this text. Major points include:

- We constantly and naturally Find Out About (FOA) many, many things. Computer search engines need to support this activity, just as naturally.
- Language is central to our FOA activities. Our understanding of prior work in linguistics and the philosophy of language will inform our search engine development, and the increasing use of search engines will provide empirical evidence reflecting back to these same disciplines.
- IR is the field of computer science that traditionally deals with retrieving free-text documents in response to queries. This is done by indexing all the documents in a corpus with keyword descriptors. There are a number of techniques for automatically recommending keywords, but it also involves a great deal of art.
- Users' interests must be shaped into queries constructed from these same keywords. Retrieval is accomplished by matching the query against the documents' descriptions and returning a list of those that appear closest.
- A central component of the FOA process is the users' relevance feedback, assessing how closely the retrieved documents match what they had "in mind."
- Search engines accomplish a function related to database systems, but their natural language foundations create fundamental differences as well.

- In order to know how to shop for a good search engine, as well as to allow the science of FOA to move forward, it is important to develop an evaluation methodology by which we can fairly compare alternatives.

In this overview we've made some simplifying assumptions and raised more questions than we've answered, but that is the goal! By now, I hope you have been convinced that there are many facets to the problem of FOA, ranging from a good characterization of what users seek, to what the documents <u>mean</u>, to methods for inferring semantic clues <u>about</u> each document, to the problem of evaluating whether our search engines are performing as we intend. The rest of this book will consider each of these facets – and others – in greater detail. But like all truly great problems, issues surrounding FOA will remain long after this text is dust.

**EXERCISE 1**    How many computer science departments in the United States offer undergraduate classes in databases? In IR? How many graduate classes? How many journals or conference proceedings, associated with the ACM or IEEE, are published in each area?

## TERMS INTRODUCED IN THIS CHAPTER

| | | |
|---|---|---|
| audience | database | hyphenation |
| author | describes | indexing |
| authority | document | information need |
| automatic indexing | domain of | information |
| bigrams |    discourse |    retrieval |
| broader term | electronic artifacts | IR |
| captions | exhaustive | jargon |
| closed vocabularies | finding out about | keywords |
| collateral knowledge | genre | level of treatment |
| context | high recall | logical data model |
| controlled | hits | manual indexing |
| conventional | hypernym | marked alphabets |
| corpus | hypertext | meta-data |

morphological
narrower terms
natural language
natural
on point
open vocabularies
operators
passages
plural
precision
proxies
publication
   information
query

query language
recall
relevance feedback
relevant
retrieval method
retrieved
rhetoric
search engine
semiotics
simple queries
specific
spoken documents
success criteria
system provides

terms of art
tokens
train
transcripts
transitive
uncontrolled
user's query
users
vocabulary
vocabulary choice
vocabulary size
white space
word games
World Wide Web

# 2

# Extracting Lexical Features

## 2.1 Building Useful Tools

The promise offered by Chapter 1 is that many real-world problems can be viewed as instances of the FOA problem. The proof is to be found in concrete code – a relatively small technology base that will prove useful in a wide array of applicatons. In this chapter we will present a suite of software tools that together build a search engine for a wide variety of situations. Source code is provided so that these tools can be easily modified for applications of your own. We will work through two different examples of IR systems, in order to demonstrate how slight variations of the same basic code can handle both.

Compared to the broad generalities of Chapter 1, the technical details of this chapter will sound a very different tone. Describing a complex algorithm requires the specification of many, sometimes tedious, details. To make the software executable on machines that are likely to be available to you, the details are provided for several operating environments. But the processor speeds, internal memory, and hard disk sizes available on computers are changing dramatically each year, so many of the assumptions on which these routines are based will require constant reevaluation.

We will develop the software tools in three phases. The first phase will convert an arbitrary pile of textual objects into a well-defined corpus of documents, each containing a string of terms to be indexed. The second phase involves building efficient data structures to **invert** the *Index* relation so that, rather than seeing all the words contained in a particular document, we can find all documents containing particular keywords. All of these efforts are in anticipation of the third and final phase, which matches queries against indices to retrieve those that are most similar. These three major phases are central to building any search engine.

This chapter will be most concerned with the first two phases, which together extract lexical features. Our goal will be the extraction of a set of features worthy of subsequent analysis. As in any cognitive science, the specification of an appropriate **level of analysis** – whether it is the resolution and depth of an image, the subphonemes of continuous speech, the speech acts of language, or something else – the specification of this atomic feature set is the first important step.

This will involve a great deal of work, much of it unpleasant except to those who enjoy designing efficient algorithms and data structures (some of us actually do enjoy this!:). The promise is that we will, as a consequence of good software design, develop useful tools that allow us to spend the rest of our time exploring interesting features of language.

## 2.2 Interdocument Parsing

The first step is to break the *corpus* – an arbitrary "pile of text" – into individually retrievable *documents*. This demands that we be specific about the format of the corpus and that we decide how it is to be divided into individual documents. For all operating systems we will consider, this problem can be defined more precisely in terms of *paths, directories, files,* and *positions within files*. For any application in which the corpus can be described by the path to its root, these tools will translate directories, files, and documents-within-files into a homogeneous corpus. Of course, there are some situations (e.g., when documents are maintained within a database) that cannot be captured in these terms, but these primitives do allow a wide range of corpora to be specified.

Our model will assume that many documents may be contained within a single file and that each document occupies a contiguous region within the file.

Issues concerning structure within a single document are closely related to assumptions we may or may not be able to make about the length of the documents in question. Our assumptions about how long a typical document is will recur throughout this book. It is obvious, for example, that different document browsers are necessary if we need to browse through an entire book rather than look at a single paragraph. Less obvious is that the fundamental weighting algorithms used by our indexing techniques will depend very sensitively on the number of tokens contained in each document.

In this textbook we will focus primarily on two particular test corpora, AI theses (AIT) and email; these are discussed in more detail in Section 2.4. Each of these has natural notions of the individual document: In the case of the AIT it is the thesis's abstract, and for email it is the entire message. In both cases, more refined notions of document (the individual paragraphs within the abstract or within the email message) are possible.

With these assumptions, we can define our corpus simply with two files: one specifying full path information for each file, and a second specifying where within these files each message resides. A large portion of the task of navigating a directory full of files and visiting each of them can be accomplished using the dirent.[†] This utility allows the recursive descent through all directories from a specified root, visiting every file contained therein.

What is
dirent?

In many cases, the files we will be indexing have a great deal of syntactic structural information above and beyond the meaningful text itself. For example, our email will often contain a great deal of mail header information, as (loosely:) specified in RFC822.[†] Many text-formatting languages, for example, TeX, XML, and HTML, now produce documents with a well-defined syntax. If, for example, the documents are written in HTML, we don't want to index pseudo-words like <H1>. In many of these situations, **filters** exist that can extract just the meaningful text from surrounding header or format information; *DeTeX*[1] is an example of a useful filter for removing LaTeX and TeX markup. Use of such utilities spares us the task of parsing this elaborate structure, but it also means that more elaborate solutions for maintaining the difference between the document's index and the document's presentation must be addressed.

What is
RFC822?

---

[1] www.cs.purdue.edu/trinkle/detex/index.html

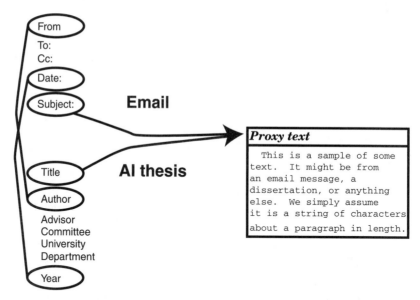

FIGURE 2.1  Parsing Email and AIT to Common Specifications

The basic data elements to be parsed from our two examples, email and AIT, are shown in Figure 2.1.

## 2.3  Intradocument Parsing

Having now focused our attention on a particular file and on the beginning and ending locations within that file associated with a particular document, we can consider this file segment simply a **stream** of characters. Reading each and every character of each and every document, deciding whether it is part of a meaningful token, and deciding whether these tokens are worth indexing will be the most computationally intensive aspect of the indexing chore; this is our "inner loop." For that reason, we will devote some real attention to making this lexical analysis as efficient as possible.

Several general criteria will shape our design. First, because we are assuming that our textual corpus is very large, we will do our best to avoid duplicating this primary text. That is, we will attempt to deal with the text in situ and not make a second copy for use by the indexing and retrieval system. Thus, we will be creating a system of pointers into locations within the corpora directories and files.

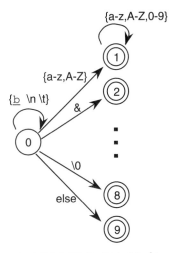

FIGURE 2.2  Finite State Machine

A wide range of alternative designs are possible even at this early stage, and so we desire as much flexibility as possible in the specification of the lexical analyzer. A **lexical analyzer generator**, such as the lex tool in Unix, allows the specification of very complicated lexical analyzers for very elaborate languages. The fundamental representation used by all such algorithms is a **finite state machine**, like that shown in Figure 2.2. This simple representation breaks the set of possible characters coming from a text stream into classes (drawn as circular states), with transitions from one state to the next on the occurrence of particular characters. By careful construction of the sets of characters (e.g., white space characters corresponding to state 0 in Figure 2.2), arbitrary text sequences can be handled very efficiently.

For our two example corpora and many other situations, the stream of characters, a straightforward analysis in terms of a simple finite state machine, will suffice. We will depend on a utility written by Christopher Fox [Fox, 1992]. This utility simultaneously achieves two critical goals. First, the lexical analyzer **tokenizes** the stream of characters into a sequence of wordlike elements. At first blush this seems straightforward: A token is anything separated by white space, where the standard definition of white space is used. But what about hyphens? Should the hyphenated phrase DATA-BASE be treated as two separate tokens or as a single one? Should a file name, like WINDOWS.EXE be treated as a single token? Which host, directory, and file elements in a full URL like www.cs.ucsd.edu/~rik are to be kept intact as individual tokens? More elaborate elements such as these can quickly demand the sophistication of a tool like lex.

The presence of digits among the alphabetic characters presents another problem. Are numbers to be allowed as tokens? Perhaps we only want to allow "special" numbers (e.g., 1776, 1984, 2001, 3.14159). Perhaps we want to use rules similar to those for programming language identifiers and require that a token begin with an alphabetic character, which may then be followed by numbers or letters.

We must also worry about the **case** of the characters at this earliest lexical analysis stage. Are we to treat capitalization as significant in distinguishing tokens from one another? An enormous reduction in vocabulary size is possible if we **fold case** so as to treat upper- and lowercase characters interchangeably. But of course then we have also precluded the possibility of many proper name analyses that may be useful for identifying **singular** people, places, or events (see Chapter 6). In some cases the semantics of the documents make decisions about case automatic. For example, if the documents are program source files, the language in question may or may not treat differences in case as significant.

## 2.3.1 Stemming and Other Morphological Processing

From the perspective of linguistics, many of the early design issues we address are considered **morphological transformations** of language, i.e., an analysis of what we can infer about language based on *structural* features. As discussed briefly in Chapter 1, the arbitrary way in which white space may or may not separate tokens whose meanings are interdependant (e.g., recall the German word GESCHWINDIGKEITS-BESCHRANKUNG and English phrase SPEED LIMIT example) will make us interested in *phrasal* units of indexing as well. In many Asian texts, the relationship between *characters* and *words* is quite radically altered. The Kanji alphabet and Unicode standards help to define the problem but bring biases of their own [Fujii and Croft, 1993].

For now we will focus on one of the most common morphological tricks, **stemming**. Stemming is a direct attempt to remove certain **surface markings** from words to reveal **root** form. Beyond deciding which characters are to be combined into tokens, Chapter 1 discussed how important it can be to use a token's root form as an index term: We can hope that our retrieval is robust even when the query contains the plural form CARS while the document contains the singular CAR. Linguists would say that the **number** feature (whether a noun is singular or plural) is morphologically **marked**. Linguists also distinguish between **inflectional** morphology like plurals, and **derivational** morphology, which can change a word's syntactic category (e.g., changing the noun PRODUCT to the verb PRODUCTIZE) and <u>meaning</u> more radically.

In stemming, suffixes are dropped. Even in the simple case of plural endings, it isn't as simple as removing s. Consider:

WOMAN/WOMEN
LEAF/LEAVES
FERRY/FERRIES
ALUMNUS/ALUMNI
DATUM/DATA

Conversely, we cannot assume that every time there is an ending s we can remove it; stemming CRISIS and CHESS to CRISI and CHES would damage their meaning.

The most common approach to this problem [Fox, 1992] is to identify more elaborate patterns over character sequences that reliably pare tokens down to their root forms. A broad range of such patterns can be defined in terms of a **context-sensitive transformation grammar**.

For example:

Rule 2.1 $(.*)SSES \rightarrow /1SS$
Rule 2.2 $(.*[AEIOU].*)ED \rightarrow /1$
Rule 2.3 $(.*[AEIOU].*)Y \rightarrow /1I$

Rule 2.1 says that strings ending in -SSES should be transformed by taking the stem (i.e., characters prior to these four) and adding only the two characters SS. Rule 2.2 says that stems containing a vowel and ending in -ED should be transformed to leave only the stem; Rule 2.3 says that stems containing a vowel and ending in -Y should be transformed to the stem with an I replacing the Y.*

---

* These rules are pseudo-code only, using grep-like syntax for regular expressions. Further, they are meant as illustrative examples. See Fox's chapter for a complete exposition of the actual rules used in Porter's stemmer [Fox, 1992].

A complete algorithm for stemming involves the specificaton of many such rules and a regime for handling conflicts when multiple rules match the same token. An early and influential algorithm due to Lovins [Lovins, 1968] specified 260 suffix patterns and used an **iterative longest match** heuristic. This means that first preference is given to the pattern (left-hand side of the grammar rule) that matches the most characters in a target token (because this prefers more specific matches over shorter, more generally applicable ones); then rules are iteratively reapplied until no other rules match.

The Porter stemmer [Porter, 1980] (included as part of the FOA software) is a simplified version of Lovin's technique that uses a reduced set of about 60 rules and organizes them into sets, with conflicts within one subset of rules resolved before going on to the next. In fact, if only the first set of rules in Porter's stemmer (focusing exclusively on plurals and the most straightforward suffixes like -ED and -ING) is used, the result has been called **weak stemming** [Walker, 1989]. A key advantage of all such rule-based grammatical representations of the stemming process (and of efficient implementations of them, such as that provided by Fox) is that modifications to the rules and to ordering among the rules can be accomplished by changing the grammar rather than by endless ad hoc hacking (ad hacking?:) in response to particular character sequences.

The use of any stemmer obviously reduces the size of the keyword vocabulary and consequently results in a compression of the index files. Such compression can vary from 10 to 50 percent, depending on the total size of the keyword vocabulary and how aggressive (e.g., how many suffix rules are used) the stemmer is.

The primary effect of stemming, however, is that two keywords that were once treated independently are considered interchangeable. Stemming is therefore an example of a *recall*-increasing operation because it will cause a keyword used in the query to match more documents.

The fundamental problem with any stemming technique, of course, is that the morphological features being stripped away may obscure differences in the words' <u>meanings</u>. For example, the token GRAVITY has two **word senses**, one describing an attractive force between any two masses and the other having to do with a serious mood. But once the word GRAVITATION has been stemmed, we have lost the information that might constrain us to the first interpretation. Krovetz

[Krovetz, 1993] considers several more sophisticated approaches to keyword morphology, including augmenting Porter's stemmer with a dictionary that is checked after each phase of stemming rules has been applied.

## 2.3.2 Noise Words

From the earliest days of IR (e.g., Luhn's seminal work [Luhn, 1957]), two related facts have been obvious: First, a relatively small number of words account for a very significant fraction of all text's bulk. Words like IT, AND, and TO can be found in virtually every sentence. Second, these noise words make very poor index terms. Users are unlikely to ask for documents about TO, and it is hard to imagine a document about BE.[†] Due then to both their frequency and their lack of indexing consequence, we will build the capability of ignoring noise words into our lexical analyzer.

But sometimes we care about noise words!

As will be discussed extensively in Chapter 3, noise words are often imagined to be the most frequently occurring words in a corpus. One problem with defining noise words in this way is that it requires a frequency analysis of the corpus prior to lexical analysis. It is possible to use frequency analyses from other corpora, assuming that the distribution of noise words is relatively constant across corpora, but such an extrapolation is not always warranted. Worse, the most frequently used words often include those that might make very good keywords. Fox notes that the words TIME, WAR, HOME, LIFE, WATER, and WORLD are among the 200 most frequently used words in general English literature [Fox, 1992, p. 113].

Instead, we will define noise words extensionally, in terms of a finite list or **negative dictionary.** The list we use, STOP.WRD, was derived by Fox from an analysis of the Brown corpus [Fox, 1990].

The relationship between these noise words and those words most critical to syntactic analysis of natural language sentences is striking. Note that the same tokens that are thrown away as noise because they have no meaning are precisely those **function words** that are most important to the *syntactic* analysis of well-formed sentences. This is the first, but not the last, suggestion of a fundamental complementarity between FOA's concern with semantics and computational linguistics' concern with syntax.

### 2.3.3 Summary

We have described the lexical analyzer in terms of the job it must do processing every document in the corpus, because this task confronts us first. But because our central task will be to *match* these documents against subsequent users' queries, it is critical that the identical lexical analysis be performed on the queries. This creates several implementation constraints (e.g., that the same code libraries are available to the indexer and to the query processing interface), but these are minor. If the query language is designed to support any special operators (e.g., Boolean combinators, proximity operators), the query's lexical analyzer may accept a superset of the tokens accepted by the document's analyzer. In any case, it is imperative if queries and documents are to be matched correctly that the same lexical analysis be applied to both streams. Using an identical code library is the easiest way to ensure this.

It may seem nonsensical to worry so much about processing each character efficiently, when we assume that some other previous process has already identified each interdocument break – doesn't such processing require the same computational effort, and, if so, doesn't this make our current efficiency worries moot?

Perhaps. A conclusive answer depends on many architecture and operating system specifics. There are two reasons we have made such assumptions. The first is that the practicalities of delivering the FOA corpora and code currently make this convenient. But the more serious reason is that the most theoretically and intellectually interesting questions involve analysis of operations downstream from the first stages of interdocument parsing: how to identify tokens, how to count them, etc. If these latter operations are made especially efficient, it means we can afford to do more experimentation, more playfully. For a text, that is the primary concern.

## 2.4  Example Corpora

In these experiments, and the rest that follow, we will consistently use two example corpora.

The first of these we will call the "Artificial Intelligence Thesis" (AIT) corpus. This is approximately 5000 Ph.D. and Master's dissertations and abstracts. Virtually every dissertation published within the last 30 years

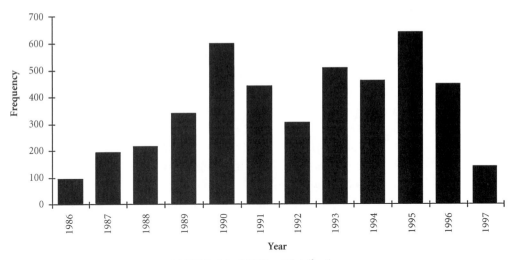

FIGURE 2.3  AIT Year Distribution

has been microfilmed by University Microfilms, Inc. (UMI).[†] The corpus is a fairly exhaustive set of theses classified as AI by UMI from the years 1987 to 1997. A histogram of the theses distribution by year is shown in Figure 2.3.

*More about AIT origins*

We will focus on a handful of characteristics of each thesis:

- Thesis number
- Title
- Author
- Year
- University
- Advisor
- Language
- Abstract
- Degree

For now, we will lump these attributes into two categories: **textual fields** and **structured attributes**. Structured attributes are ones for which we can reason more formally, using database and artificial intelligence techniques. For now, we will concentrate on only the textual fields. The abstract will be the primary textual element associated with each thesis, while its title (also a textual field) will be used as its **proxy** – a synopsis of the thesis that conveys much of its meaning in a highly abbreviated form. Proxies will prove very important surrogates for the documents (for example, when users are presented with hitlists of retrieved documents).

The second corpus we will study could not be provided on the CD because you must provide it yourself; it is all of *your* email. Email is now a fundamental form of transient, nearly immediate communication for many, but the resulting *permanent* record of these conversations can also be treated as a static, long-lived type of "literature" [Belew and Rentzepis, 1990]. We will assume that with disk storage as cheaply available as it is today, you at some point began to collect email.[†] Typically, some of this will be email others have sent you, but you may have also kept a copy of all of your "outgoing" email. Many email clients support on-the-fly segregation of email into separate folders. Minimally, this means that our procedures for indexing email must be capable of traversing elaborate directory structures. Later, we will also consider the use of this user-generated structure as a source for learning; cf. Section 7.4.

*How do I index my email?*

The directory in which you have filed an email message is one feature we may associate with each message; whether it is an incoming or outgoing message is another. But of course email also has many structured attributes associated with it, in its **header**. These include:

- From:
- To:
- Cc:
- Subject:
- Date:

In general, we will put off all consideration of structured attributes associated with documents until later. For now, simply note the many parallels between our two example corpora: Both have well-defined authors, well-defined time-stamps, and excellent and obvious candidates for proxy text.

## 2.5  Implementation

The range of potential implementations of the basic techniques discussed in this chapter and subsequent ones is quite remarkable. Each depends on features of the specific application, available hardware, and so on, such as:

- using a massively parallel supercomputer of the mid-1980s to provide current news to financial analysts [Stanfill and Kahle, 1986a];
- searching for file names as part of the MacOS Finder on a single personal computer and then extending to support file **content** searching as part of the MacOS *Sherlock*[2] utility;
- *SMART*[3] is a classic software suite designed to support experimentation into basic IR techniques (see Section 3.4.3 for more details);
- providing a generic utility for *Managing Gigabytes*[4] (MG), for example, building an index for a CD-ROM or DVD; and
- making all of the pages on a WWW server searchable via *Web Server Search Tools*[5] or *Information filtering tools*.[6]

Design decisions depend on features such as corpus size, available memory, and query response time. Two implementations have been developed to accompany this textbook, an earlier one in C and a more recent one in Java; see the *FOA Web site*[7] for details.

## 2.5.1 Basic Algorithm

We now assume that:

- prior technology has successfully broken our stream of characters, our large corpus, into a set of documents;
- within each document we have identified individual tokens; and
- noise word tokens have been identified.

Then the basic flow of what we will call the postdoc function operates as follows (see Algorithm 2.1).

---

[2] www.apple.com/sherlock/

[3] ftp://ftp.cs.cornell.edu/pub/smart/

[4] www.mds.rmit.edu.au/mg/welcome.html

[5] www.searchtools.com/tools/tools.html

[6] www.glue.umd.edu/dlrg/filter/software.html

[7] http://www.cse.ucsd.edu/~rik/FOA/

---

### Algorithm 2.1 Basic Algorithm

for every doc in corpus
  while (token = getNonNoiseToken)
   if (StemP)
   token = stem(token)
   Save Posting(token,doc) in Tree

for every token in Tree
  Accumulate ndoc(token), totfreq(token)
  Sort p ∈ Postings(token)
   descending docfreq(p) order
  write token,ndoc,totfreq,Postings

---

For every document in the corpus we will iterate through a loop until we've exhausted every token in that document. So let's call getNonNoiseToken a routine that repeatedly builds tokens from the document's stream, does whatever character assessments are required, checks it against a negative dictionary, and returns a token. If stemming is to be applied, we'll stem the word at this point. Then we will save a **posting** for that token's occurrence in that document. A posting is simply a correspondence between a particular word and a particular document, representing the occurrence of that word in that document.* That is, we have a document in front of us and it contains a set of tokens. We are now going to build a representation for each token that tells all of the documents in which ones it occurs. For each keyword we will maintain the token itself as the key used for subsequent access and the head of a linked list of all postings, each containing the document number and the number of occurrences of the keyword in that document. A sketch of these data structures is shown in Figure 2.4.

After going through every document in the corpus in this fashion, we have a large collection of postings. Here we recommend **splay trees** as an appropriate data structure for these keywords and their postings. In the C implementation shown in Algorithm 2.2, the InstallTerm() function inserts a new posting into the Terms tree.†

Implementation
details

---

\* We'll discuss other data we might also keep with the posting later; cf. Section 2.5.2.

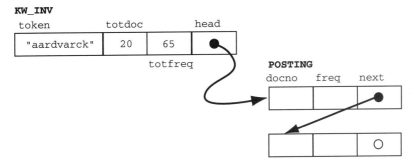

FIGURE 2.4  Basic Postings Data Structures

---

**Algorithm 2.2 `postdoc.c` Details**

void postDoc (int docno, FILE *docf, long int bpos, long int epos, char *proxy){

    ...

    GetTermString(&proxyPos, Noise, MaxTermSize,newterm);

    ...

    GetTerm(docf, Noise, MaxTermSize,newterm);

    ...

    InstallTerm(newterm, docno, Terms);

    ...

}

---

During the processing of each document, it will prove important to know how many keywords are extracted from it. This will be known as the **document's length**, denoted $length_d$; this quantity is important when *normalizing* documents of different lengths. One way to implement this computation is to maintain a small separate file `doclend.d` containing only this one number for each document.

When the set of documents has been exhausted, we need to write out this **inverted** representation to a file for subsequent processing. For every token in the splay tree (typically the traversal will be in lexicographic order), we will organize all its postings. First, we count the number of occurrences of the keyword across all the documents in the corpus; we will call this variable $totfreq_k$. A second, less obvious statistic we will maintain is how many documents contain this keyword; this variable will be called $docfreq_k$. If there is exactly one occurrence of a

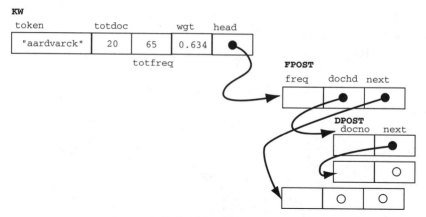

FIGURE 2.5  Refined Postings Data Structures

keyword in each document, then these two numbers will be the same. But typically there are multiple occurrences of the same keyword in a single document and $totfreq_k > docfreq_k$. Both variables will be important to us in determining appropriate weights for the *Index* relation (cf. Chapter 3).

After going through all of the documents and accumulating for each these two statistics, we must sort the postings in decreasing frequency order. The reason for this won't be apparent until we discuss the matching algorithms (cf. Section 3.5), but it turns out to be important that documents that use a keyword most often are at the beginning of the list.

Once the documents' postings have been sorted into descending order of frequency, it is likely that several of the documents in this list will have the same frequency, and we can exploit this fact to compress their representation. Figure 2.5 shows the POSTING list broken into a list of FPOST sublists, one for unique frequency count.

## 2.5.2  Fine Points

### Changing Indices for Dynamic Corpora

One reason to keep raw frequency counts in the inverted keyword file used by our experimental implementation is that this provides maximum flexibility as we consider various keyword weighting schemes. But there is another reason these raw statistics are useful in real applications.

It is often important to be able to *update* a corpus's index as documents are added to or deleted from it. Retention of raw keyword frequency information allows these statistics to be updated as our corpus changes. Adding a new document simply requires that it be analyzed (as outlined earlier), simply incrementing existing counters for each keyword.[†] Similarly, deletion of documents from an index exploits the full text of the document itself to identify all keywords it contains. For each keyword then, posting counts are simply decremented.[*]

*Implementation details*

## Posting Resolution

Typically we need only keep track of *which* document contains the posting. But an important element of many query languages is **proximity** operators, which allow users to specify how close two keywords must be (adjacent words, within the same sentence, within the same paragraph, within a *k*-word window of one another, etc.). To support such queries, we may also be concerned with recording higher **resolution** posting information than which document it is in. For example, many systems retain the exact *character* position of the (beginning of the) keyword. Figure 2.6 shows the elaborate data structure used by the STAIRS IR system.[†] In addition to very high-resolution postings, this representation supports other query attributes (e.g., security).[†]

*More about STAIRS*

*Proximity searching with low-resolution posting information*

## Emphasizing Proxy Text

The fact that keyword tokens occur in both the proxy text and the main text of the document gives us the opportunity to treat them differently. For example, we can *emphasize* the importance of words used in the proxy over those occurring in the raw text. This would be sensible if we believed that those occurrences in, for example, the subject of a message or the title of a dissertation, are better characterizations of a document than words picked from the text of the abstract or the text of the email message. In our code, this emphasis will be controlled by an integer variable `EmphProxy`, which notes occurrences of keywords in the proxy by doubling (`EmphProxy = 2`) or tripling (`EmphProxy = 3`) the keyword counters for proxy text.

---

[*] The optimized `fpost` data structure makes this update awkward as well.

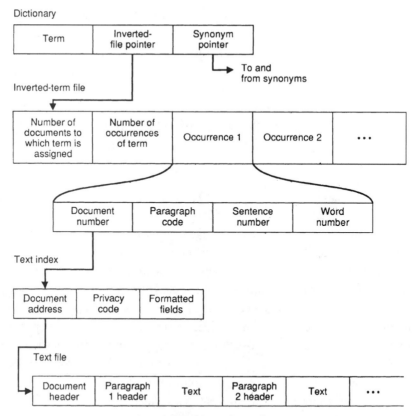

FIGURE 2.6 STAIRS Posting Information
Reproduced with permission from Salton and McGill [Salton and McGill, 1983, figure 8.5, p. 244]

## Document Number

Because we have made the first stage of our processing flexible with respect to how a corpus extends across multiple files in general, *two* numbers will uniquely identify each of your documents: its file number and the document number within that file. For that reason, and because each posting must retain a unique identifier for each document, it becomes important to construct a single number that folds them together. Maintaining a single integer, instead of two integers, therefore becomes a worthwhile space-saver.

One simple way to accomplish this is to multiply the document's file number by some number larger than the maximum number of documents within any file, and then add its document number. Just

```
Subject:        Re: IDE or SCSI?
From:           helpful@urban.or.jp (me @ my humble abode)
Date:           1997/08/29
Message-Id:     <3406f93a.50446926@nnrp.gol.com>
Newsgroups:     comp.os.ms-windows.nt.setup.hardware,comp.windows.nt.misc
[More Headers]

On Thu, 28 Aug 1997 23:10:03 GMT, Michael Query <query@dpi.qld.gov.au> wrote:

>My question is, should I get another 2 Gb SCSI disk for putting the
>OS (NT 4.0 WS), software, etc on, or should I get an IDE disk for this?

Having played around with different configs for a while, I'd say go SCSI. I'd
do that even if I had to get a second SCSI controller.

(You'll "hear" a lot of people arguing that IDE is good enough, but if you are
after overall improved performance SCSI is best.)

my 2Y.
```

FIGURE 2.7  Quoted Lines in an Email Message

how large a number this must be and whether your machine/compiler efficiently supports integers this large (or whether you are better off keeping the two numbers separate) will vary considerably. For this reason it makes good sense to isolate these issues in a separate routine.

## Dependencies on Document Type

The process of indexing has been idealized as having a first stage, where we worry about what kind of document it is (e.g., whether it's a thesis or an email message), and then assuming that subsequent processing is completely independent of document type. Like all software designs, this idealization breaks down in the face of real data.

Consider email messages. One common element of these documents is *quoted* text from another email message. Often this is marked by a > prefix, as shown in Figure 2.7. The role of interdocument citations like this is considered in depth in Section 6.1, but for now, a reasonable design decision is that all text should be indexed only once. This is especially appropriate if we have both the original email message and the quoted version of it; we might want to elide (ignore) quoted lines.

Other software designs are possible, but the easiest way to implement this is to check for quoted lines within the postdoc routine; if the first character of a line is a greater-than symbol, don't do any of the subsequent processing. Don't check it against noise words, don't stem, don't index, and don't install it in the term tree. Unfortunately, this creates precisely the kind of email-specific processing that should be avoided by well-engineered software.

## 2.5.3 Software Libraries

As much as possible, we will depend on standard libraries for some of our basic utilities. In particular, it is recommended that you use:

- gethash – This is the standard hashtable routine, part of most Unix distributions.
- stopper – Chris Fox's lexical analyzer, also incorporating stopword removal. This code accompanies Fox's chapter, "Lexical Analysis and Stoplists" [Fox, 1992].
- splay – Splay trees provided many of the benefits of balanced binary trees without many of the hassles of perfectly balanced (e.g., AVL) trees [Sleator and Tarjan, 1985]. This implementation was written by David Brower [Brower, 1994, chapter 10].
- stem – This is the "Porter" stemmer, a pattern-matching affix-removal stemmer [Porter, 1980].

**EXERCISE 1**  Extend the software to allow a document to comprise multiple noncontiguous textual fields.

**EXERCISE 2**  Take a large LaTeX document and run it repeatedly through LaTeX2HTML, systematically varying the logical unit of document structure at which individual HTML pages are constructed. Discuss the impact of these "arbitrary" decisions on the weight of the keywords.

## TERMS INTRODUCED IN THIS CHAPTER

| | | |
|---|---|---|
| **case** | **derivational** | **fold case** |
| **content** | **document's length** | **function words** |
| **context-sensitive transformation grammar** | **filters** | **header** |
| | **finite state machine** | **inflectional** |
| | | **invert** |

inverted

iterative longest
   match

level of analysis

lexical analyzer
   generator

marked

morphological
   transformations

negative dictionary

number

posting

proximity

proxy

resolution

root

singular

splay trees

stemming

stream

structured
   attributes

surface markings

textual fields

tokenizes

weak stemming

word senses

# 3

# Weighting and Matching against Indices

*The Bible Code as Ouija Board*: The fascination with the subliminal, the camouflaged, and the encrypted is ancient. Getting a computer to munch away at long strings of letters from the Old Testament is not that different from killing animals and interpreting the entrails, or pouring out tea and reading the leaves. It does add the modern impersonal touch – a computer found it, not a person, so it must be "really there." But computers find what people tell them to find. As the programmers like to say, "prophesy in, prophesy out." [Menaud, 1996]

## 3.1 Microscopic Semantics and the Statistics of Communication

In the last chapter, we described the FOA process linguistically, in terms of words that occur in documents, morphological features of these words, structures organizing the sentences of documents, etc. We now want to treat all of these words – which have <u>meaning</u> to their authors and to us reading them – as a <u>meaning</u>less stream of data: word after word after word. (Imagine it coming from some SETI radio telescope, eavesdropping on the communication of some other planet!) We will now seek patterns and trends common to this data, using the same sorts of statistical tricks that physicists typically use on their data streams. What

TABLE 3.1 English Letter Frequencies

| Letter | Frequency | Letter | Frequency |
|--------|-----------|--------|-----------|
| E | .120 | F | .024 |
| T | .085 | M | .024 |
| A | .077 | W | .022 |
| I | .076 | Y | .022 |
| N | .067 | P | .020 |
| O | .067 | B | .017 |
| S | .067 | G | .017 |
| R | .059 | V | .012 |
| H | .050 | K | .007 |
| D | .042 | Q | .005 |
| L | .042 | J | .004 |
| U | .037 | X | .004 |
| C | .032 | Z | .002 |

can we learn from looking at the statistics of our data stream, treating text as <u>meaning</u>less and attempting to infer a new notion of <u>meaning</u> from those statistics?

But now let's narrow our focus, all the way down to the bits and characters used to represent the corpus as, for example, a file on a physical device, like a hard disk. Imagine that you are an archaeologist trying to study some civilization that left this evidence behind. How might you interpret this modern Rosetta Stone?

Let's ignore those issues relating to basic ASCII encoding. That is, suppose we have special knowledge of a character set. Then the frequency of these characters' occurrences would already give us a great deal of information. Anyone who has studied simple cipher techniques (or played Scrabble) knows that a table of most frequently used letters (cf. Table 3.1 [Welsh, 1988]) can be used to break simple codes.

In this chapter we will move another level above characters. We will consider morphological transformations we can perform on character sequences that help us to identify root words. We will briefly mention phrases by which multiple words can be joined into simple phrasal units.

At each level we will ask very similar questions: What is our unit of analysis; i.e., what are we counting? Then, what does the distribution of frequency occurrences across this level of features tell us about the pattern of their use? What can we tell about the <u>meaning</u> of these features, based on such statistics [Francis and Kucera, 1982]?

In fact, many influential thinkers have looked at such patterns among symbols. Going back to some of the most ancient writings suggests that statistical analyses of the original Hebrew characters and their positions within the two-dimensional array of the page reveals new "codes" [Witztum et al., 1994; Drosnin, 1997].

Donald Knuth, one of computer science's most renowned theoreticians, has analyzed an apparently random verse (Chapter 3, verse 16) from 59 of the Bible's books and used these verses as the basis of **stratified sampling** of the approximately 30,000 Biblical verses [Knuth, 1990]. He found, for example, that the 3:16 verses were particularly rich in occurrences of YHWH, the ancient Hebrew name for God. Personally, Knuth considered this analysis the source for "historical and spiritual insights," as part of a Bible study class he led. But speaking *scientifically*, how can we find <u>meaning</u> in text, and how are such attempts to be distinguished from the kinds of "Ouija board" numerology criticized by Menaud in the quotation opening this chapter?

## 3.2 Remember Zipf

Looking at our corpus as a very long string of characters, something that even a monkey could generate, provides a useful baseline against which we can evaluate larger constructs.

Associate with each word $w$ its frequency $F(w)$, the number of times it occurs anywhere in the corpus. Now imagine that we've sorted the vocabulary according to frequency so that the most frequently occurring word will have rank $r = 1$, the next most frequently used word will have $r = 2$, and so on.

George Kingsley Zipf (1902–50) has become famous for noticing that the distribution we find true of our corpus is in fact very reliably true of any large sample of natural language we might consider. Zipf [Zipf, 1949] observed that the words' rank-frequency distribution can be fit very closely by the relation:

$$F(r) = \frac{C}{r^\alpha}, \quad \alpha \approx 1, \quad C \approx 0.1 \tag{3.1}$$

This empirical rule is now known as Zipf's law.

But why should this pattern of word usage, something we can reasonably expect to vary with author or type of publication, be so

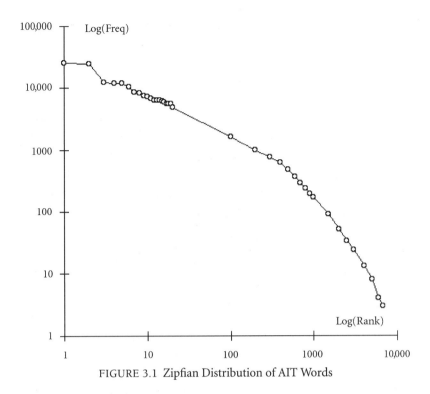

FIGURE 3.1 Zipfian Distribution of AIT Words

universal? What's more, the notion of "word" used in this formula has varied radically: in tabulations of word frequencies by Yule and Thorndike, words were stemmed to their root form; Yule counted only nouns [Yule, 1924; Thorndike, 1937]. Dewey [Dewey, 1929] and Thorndike collected statistics from multiple sources; others were collected from a single work (for example, James Joyce's *Ulysses*). The frequency distribution for a small subset of (nonnoise words in) our AIT corpus is shown in Figure 3.1. Note the nearly *linear*, negatively sloped relation when frequency is plotted as a function of rank, and both are plotted on log scales.

## 3.2.1  Looking for Meaning in All the Wrong Places (At the Character Level)

The ubiquity of data obeying Zipf's law has made it a lightning rod, attracting a number of "explanations." These explanations come from an extremely impressive set of original thinkers, in widely ranging disciplines:

- Noam Chomsky, the most influential linguist of the past 30 years, together with George Miller, the mathematical psychologist famous for such insights as the "$7 \pm 2$ chunks" of memory limitation [Miller, 1957];
- Herbert Simon, the Nobel Prize–winning economist and one of the fathers of artificial intelligence [Simon, 1955]; and
- Benoit Mandelbrot, the mathematician and physicist most famous for his work on fractals [Mandelbrot, 1953].

Herbert Simon, a keen observer of much cognitive activity, suggests that the ubiquity of Zipf's law across heterogeneous collections should make us somewhat suspicious of its ability to address the "fine structure" of linguistics:

> No one supposes that there is any connection between horse kicks suffered by soldiers in the German army and blood clots on a microscope slide other than that the same urn scheme provides a satisfactory abstract model of both phenomena. It is in the same direction that we shall look for an explanation of the observed close similarities among the five classes of distributions. . . . [Simon, 1955]

(With "urn," Simon is referring to mathematical models, e.g., related to Poisson processes. See Section 3.3.2 for more on the "five classes" of Simon's models.)

We therefore begin this section by reviewing a number of early attempts to explain the phenomena underlying Zipf's law; its mathematical derivation is reserved for Chapter 5.

## 3.2.2 Zipf's Own Explanation

To explain his empirical observations, Zipf himself proposed a theoretical model that described the ultimate purpose of communication between authors and readers.

Zipf's theory was extraordinarily broad, addressing not only (!) patterns in text but also patterns across all human activities. According to Zipf's fundamental **Principle of Least Effort** all activities can be viewed as interactions between *jobs* needing to be done and *tools* developed to accomplish the jobs. In a mature society in which a variety of jobs and tools have existed for some time, a "reciprocal economy" forms. That is, there is a set of tools appropriate for doing certain jobs, and there is a set of jobs requiring certain tools. The Principle of Least Effort asserts that a person attempting to apply a tool to a job does so in order to minimize the probable effort in using that tool for that particular job.

In applying this principle to texts, Zipf makes an important correspondence – words work as tools, accomplishing jobs we need done. To simplify the situation greatly, imagine that the job an author is attempting to accomplish is simply to "point" to some **referent**, something in the world.[†] Authors would find it most convenient to simply use one word all the time for all the jobs they are trying to accomplish. It makes their task much easier; picking the right word is effortless. The author has a pressure toward **unification** of the vocabulary.

Pointing

From the reader's point of view, it would be least ambiguous if a unique term were used for every possible function, every possible interpretation, every meaning. Readers therefore have a pressure toward **diversification** of the vocabulary. This leads to the **vocabulary balance** we observe in Zipf's rule. Zipf hypothesized that interplay between the forces of diversification and unification results in the use of existing words, which does not extend the vocabulary in most situations, together with the inclusion of new words in those novel situations that demand them. The trick is to find an **economy of language** that best satisfies both writer and reader. Note, however, that the maintenance of the balance requires that authors receive *feedback* from their readers, confirming that they are both "pointing" to the same referent.

Blair has extended Zipf's analysis, considering Zipf's tool/job setting as it's applied to our FOA task [Blair, 1990; Blair, 1992]. He argues that one of the primary reasons FOA systems fail is that the vocabulary balance is upset. The system of descriptors indexing the authors' works (for example, the library or the Web), standing between the authors who are writing the books and the searchers attempting to find them, *breaks the feedback channel* that keeps the shared vocabulary in balance when author and reader are in direct contact.

### 3.2.3 Benoit Mandelbrot's Explanation

The early days of cybernetics were heady, and Zipf was not alone in seeking a grand, unifying theory to explain the phenomena of communication on computational grounds like those proving so successful in physics. Benoit Mandelbrot was equally ambitious.

Mandelbrot's background as a physicist is clear when he considers the message decoder as a physical piece of apparatus, ". . . cutting a continuous incoming string of signs into groups, and recoding each group separately" [Mandelbrot, 1953]. This "differentiator" complements an "integrator," which reconstitutes new messages from individual words. Within this model communication can be considered "fully analogous to the perfect gas of thermodynamics." Minimizing the cost of transmission corresponds to minimization of free energy in thermodynamics.

Mandelbrot was also interested in how the critical parameter $\alpha$ varied from one vocabulary to another. Extending the physical analogy of thermodynamic energy, the **informational temperature** or **temperature of discourse** is proportional to $1/\alpha$, which Mandelbrot argues provides a much better measure of the richness of a vocabulary than simply counting the number of words it contains.

The value $1/\alpha$ can also be used to relate our analysis of Zipf's law to Mandelbrot's fractals. If the letters of our alphabet are imagined to be digits of numbers base $n + 1$ and a leading decimal point is placed before each word, then each word corresponds to a number between 0 and 1.

> The construction amounts in effect to cutting out of $[0, 1]$ all the numbers that include the digit 0 otherwise than at the end. One finds that the remainder is a Cantor dust, the fractal dimension of which is precisely $1/\alpha$. [Mandelbrot, 1982, p. 346]

Mandelbrot proposed a more general form of Zipf's law:

$$F(r) = \frac{C}{(r + b)^{\alpha}} \qquad (3.2)$$

which has proved important in analysis of the relationship between word frequencies and their rank (cf. Section 5.1).

Mandelbrot also suggested this as a potential model of cognition:

> Whatever the detailed structure of the brain it recodes information many times. The public representation through phonemes

is immediately replaced by a private one through a string of nerve impulses.... This recorded message presumably uses fewer signs than the incoming one; therefore when a given message reaches a higher level it will have been reduced to a choice between a few possibilities only without the extreme redundancy of the sounds. The last stages are "idea" stages, where not only the public representation has been lost, but also the public elements of information. [Mandelbrot, 1953, pp. 488–9]

Mandelbrot makes other provocative suggestions, for example, that schizophrenics provide the best test of his theory because these individuals impose the fewest "semantic constraints" on the random process (generating language) of interest?!

Although he was unsuccessful at his more ambitious goal of wedding a physical model of communcation to models of semantics such as Saussure's, Mandelbrot was probably the first to characterize the real truth underlying Zipfian distributions. This derivation is put off until Chapter 5. We conclude here with one more historical perspective, due to Herbert Simon, and a couple of more modern rediscoveries of Zipfian phenomena.

## 3.2.4 Herbert Simon's Explanation

Simon considered a very different model, focused on the author's activity of constructing a text. Simon's model is based on two assumptions. First, that new words – **neologisms** – introduced by the author and not previously used are introduced at some constant probability. Second, that the probability of a word having occurred exactly $i$ times is proportional to the total number of occurrences of all words that have appeared exactly $i$ times. These assumptions allow Simon to use the basic mathematics of "pure birth processes" to account for word frequency rankings.*

Simon was interested in models for the "associative" processes underlying authors' cognition, "... sampling earlier segments of the word sequence" [Simon, 1955, p. 434] as they compose. He acknowledged

---

* In the same paper, "On a class of skew distributions" [Simon, 1955], Simon gives similar accounts for the numbers of papers published by scientists, city populations, and distributions of biological taxa.

that authors also use processes of "imitation: sampling segments of word sequences from other works of other authors, and, of course, from sequences he has heard." Simon imagined this model as potentially applying to three different distributions:

- the distribution of word frequencies in the whole historical sequence of words that constitute a language;
- the distribution of word frequencies in a continuous piece of prose; and
- the distribution of word frequencies in a sample of prose assembled from compositive sources.

He seems most engaged by the second of these alternatives, considering the activity of a particular author. (He uses James Joyce's *Ulysses* as an example.)

Obviously this word-based model provides a very different explanation of Zipf's law from Mandelbrot's and Miller's character-based ones. Simon was familiar with such models but argued [Simon, 1955, p. 435] that his own "averaging rather than [Miller's] maximizing assumptions" are more desirable. But as Miller notes, "The assumption of maximization can be replaced by the assumption of random spacing" [Miller, 1957, p. 313]. Worse, in terms of the empirical bottom line, Simon's equation does not fit available data as well.

## 3.2.5 More Recent Zipfian Sightings

The debate concerning these models dates back almost 40 years, but Zipfian distributions and attempts to explain them continue to arise. For example, many have been struck by language-like properties exhibited by the long sequences of *genetic* codes found in the DNA of all living species. That is, a simple "alphabet" of four nucleic acid **base-pairs** (BPs) (A, C, G, T in DNA) grouped into three-letter **codons** that <u>mean</u> one of twenty possible "words" corresponding to amino acids has led many to wonder what we might learn by viewing the genome as a linguistic object [Sereno, 1991].

Mantegna et al. [Mantegna et al., 1994] was led to consider the "word" frequency distributions of such words in the DNA "corpus." They considered differences in the distributions across coding regions of the genome as well as noncoding regions that are never expressed. Their first result is that this sequence data does indeed contain "linguistic features," especially in the noncoding regions. By analyzing various genetic corpora (e.g., approximately a million BPs taken from 14 mammalian sequences), they found that, in contrast to what we might expect of completely random sequences, the rank-frequency distribution of six-BP words could be well fit by a (log–log linear) Zipf exponent equal to −0.28. They conclude:

> These results are consistent with the possible existence of one (or more than one) *structured biological languages* present in noncoding DNA sequences. [Mantegna et al., 1994, italic not in original]

Subsequent analysis, however, makes it quite clear that any such interpretations are ill-founded [Bonhoeffer et al., 1996]. Deviations from fully random sequence behavior can be attributed to two simple characteristics of biological sequence data. First, define $H(n)$ to be the entropy of the distribution of $n$-length nucleotide sequences. Then the redundancy $R(n)$ of length $n$ words is:

$$R(n) = 1 - \frac{H(n)}{2n} \qquad (3.3)$$

so the nonrandom $R(1)$ reflects a simple increase with the *variance* of the four base-pairs, a well-known biological fact. Further, very short range correlations between nucleic acids (easy to imagine given the basic three-letter genetic code) means that in DNA the most common words are simply combinations of the most probable letters, especially in regions of short repeats. There are still interesting questions (e.g., why coding and noncoding regions differ in their nucleic acid frequencies), but none that suggest any large-scale language-like properties within the DNA sequence.

A final recent example of how Zipf-like distributions arise is offered by analyses of **WWW surfing** behaviors [Huberman et al., 1998] and makes this same point (but cf. Section 8.1 for more recent, apparently contradictory data generated from massive Alta Vista logs). Consider each page click by a browsing user to be a "character" and the amount of time spent by the same user on a host to be the length of a "word." Then (surprise!), empirical data capturing the rank-frequency

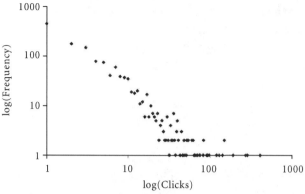

FIGURE 3.2  Rank/Frequency Distribution of Click-Paths
From [Huberman, 1998]. Reprinted with permission of *Science*

distribution of each WWW surfing "ride" again show a (log–log linear) Zipfian relationship with slope equal to −1.5, as shown in Figure 3.2.

Huberman et al. also propose a model explaining this empirical data. Assume that the "value" (what we might think of as perceived relevance) $V(L)$ of each page in a browsing sequence of length $L$ goes up or down according to identical, independently distributed (iid) Gaussian random variables $\epsilon_L$:

$$V(L) = V(L-1) + \epsilon_L \tag{3.4}$$

Using economic reasoning, Huberman et al. then hypothesize:

> ... an individual will continue to surf until the expected cost of continuing is perceived to be larger than the discounted expected value of the information to be found in the future. ... Even if the value of the current page is negative, it may be worthwhile to proceed, because a collection of high value pages may still be found. If the value is sufficiently negative, however, then it is no longer worth the risk to continue. [Huberman et al., 1998]

If users' browsing behaviors follow a random walk governed by these considerations, Huberman et al. show that the passage times to this cutoff threshold are given by the inverse Gaussian distribution:

$$\Pr(L) = \sqrt{\frac{\lambda}{2\pi L^3}} \exp\left[\frac{-\lambda(L-\mu)^2}{2\mu^2 L}\right] \tag{3.5}$$

where $\mu$ is the mean of the random walk length variable $L$, $\mu^3/\lambda$ is its variance, and $\lambda$ is a scaling parameter.

### 3.2.6 Summary

I have provided this historical background because these eminent scientists' stories remain compelling. The plausibility of the proposed theories, coupled with our retrospective knowledge of their incorrectness, also provides a sobering background as we attempt to infer semantic properties from the statistics arising in FOA. As we shall discuss in Chapter 5 (cf. Section 5.1), the real basis of Zipf's law can be traced to much simpler mechanisms, relating only to patterns of characters rather than any underlying semantics or purposes. Benoit Mandelbrot, George Miller, and Noam Chomsky have shown that the underlying phenomena relating a word's frequency to its rank order is obeyed as much by *random text* – generated by monkeys at typewriters, for example – as by samples of text (the Bible, James Joyce's *Ulysses*, etc.) we seem to find more literate.

The fact that the simple, four-character sequence ZIPF should bring together such a rich combination of mathematical and semantic issues is ironic, to say the least. There is obviously a great deal we can predict about our language by assuming nothing more than we would about monkeys at keyboards. At the same time, the fact that we can change the <u>meaning</u> of a simple sequence of characters, for example, the title of this section REMEMBER ZIPF, dramatically by adding a single additional character to form either REMEMBER ZIPF! or REMEMBER ZIPF? should make it clear how much more there still is to say.

## 3.3  A Statistical Basis for Keyword Meaning

### 3.3.1  Lexical Consequences, Internal/External Perspectives

The plot in Figure 3.2 is based on word-frequency statistics like those shown in Table 3.2. Note that on the log-log plot in Figure 3.2, frequency is a nearly linear inverse function of rank.

One way to make the various lexical decisions considered in the last chapter is to consider the effects of various decisions in terms of statistics such as these. Table 3.3 shows the statistics for stemmed, nonnoise

TABLE 3.2 AIT Keywords Frequency/Rank Distribution.

| Rank | Frequency | Keyword | Rank | Frequency | Keyword |
|------|-----------|---------|------|-----------|---------|
| 1 | 25,438 | system | 20 | 4836 | algorithm |
| 2 | 24,745 | univers | 100 | 1646 | dissert |
| 3 | 12,107 | base | 200 | 971 | util |
| 4 | 11,938 | network | 300 | 767 | zurich |
| 5 | 11,930 | model | 400 | 624 | genet |
| 6 | 10,303 | de | 500 | 474 | event |
| 7 | 8568 | knowledg | 600 | 363 | definit |
| 8 | 8320 | neural | 700 | 289 | underli |
| 9 | 7465 | process | 800 | 234 | explicit |
| 10 | 7293 | design | 900 | 196 | teach |
| 11 | 6758 | control | 1000 | 171 | lisp |
| 12 | 6308 | intellig | 1500 | 89 | advis |
| 13 | 6308 | develop | 2000 | 51 | compound |
| 14 | 6243 | use | 2500 | 33 | praisal |
| 15 | 6074 | learn | 3000 | 24 | af |
| 16 | 5837 | applic | 4000 | 13 | meshe |
| 17 | 5617 | expert | 5000 | 8 | hermeneut |
| 18 | 5558 | approach | 6000 | 4 | html |
| 19 | 5464 | comput | 6660 | 3 | replai |

word tokens (shown in `monospaced font`, e.g., `SYSTEM`), together with noise words (shown in *italics*, e.g., *the*). As expected, the noise words occur very frequently. But it is interesting to contrast those very frequent words defined a priori in the negative dictionary with those that occur especially frequently in this particular corpus. In many ways these are excellent candidates for **external keywords**: characterizations of this corpus's content, from the "external" perspective of general language use. That is, these are exactly the words (cf. `NEURAL NETWORK`, `BASE`, `LEARN`, `WORLD`, `KNOWLEDGE`) that could suggest to a WWW browser that the AIT corpus might be worth visiting. Once "inside" the topical domain of AI, however, these same words (cf. `SYSTEM`, `MODEL`, `PROCESS`, `DESIGN`) become as ineffective as other noise words, as **internal keywords**, discriminating the contents of one AIT dissertation from the next.

Table 3.3 also shows statistics both with and without stemming. For example, the token `SYSTEM` itself appeared only 8632 times; variations like `SYSTEMS` and `SYSTEMATIC` must account for the other 12,856. This simple example also demonstrates how issues of phrase recognition

TABLE 3.3  Consequences of Lexical Decisions on Word Frequencies

| Token | Frequency | Unstemmed Frequency | Token | Frequency | Unstemmed Frequency |
|-------|-----------|---------------------|-------|-----------|---------------------|
| the | 78,428 | | that | 9820 | |
| of | 50,026 | | are | 9792 | |
| and | 33,834 | | LEARN | 9293 | |
| a | 31,347 | | WORLD | 8103 | |
| to | 28,666 | | la? | 7678 | |
| in | 21,512 | | an | 7593 | |
| SYSTEM | 21,488 | 8,632 | KNOWLEDG | 7410 | 5,496 |
| is | 18,781 | | NEURAL | 7220 | 3,912 |
| MODEL | 14,772 | 4,796 | with | 7197 | |
| for | 14,640 | | as | 6964 | |
| de? | 11,923 | | on | 6920 | |
| NETWORK | 10,306 | 3,965 | by | 6886 | |
| this | 10,095 | | PROCESS | 6569 | 2,900 |
| BASE | 9838 | | DESIGN | 6362 | 3,308 |

(cf. NEURAL NETWORK) and other messy issues (e.g., the presence of *French* noise words in some of the dissertation abstracts but not in our English negative dictionary) can arise in even the simplest, "cleanest" corpora.

## 3.3.2  Word Occurrence as a Poisson Process

When the words contained in a corpus are ranked and shown to be distributed according to a Zipfian distribution, an obvious but important observation can be made: The most frequently occurring words are not really <u>about</u> anything. Words like NOT, OF, THE, OR, TO, BUT, and BE obviously play an important *functional* role, as part of the syntactic structure of sentences, but it is hard to imagine users asking for documents <u>about</u> OF or <u>about</u> BUT. Define **function words** to be those that have only (!) a syntactic function, for example, OF, THE, BUT, and distinguish them from **content words**, which are descriptive in the sense that we're interested in them for the indexing task. This is one of the first – but most certainly not the last – examples FOA makes using a priori determinations of a word's *semantic* utility based on its *statistical* properties.

For example, we might hope that function words occur *randomly* throughout arbitrary text, while content words do not. One ubiquitous model of randomness is as a **Poisson process**, used in the past to model things like:

- raisins' distribution across slices of bread; or
- misprints' distribution across printed pages; or
- the distribution of people's birthdays across days of the year.

In the case of our documents, we'll start with a slightly simpler **Bernoulli** model wherein we imagine an author making *binary* decisions, picking a keyword $k$ with probability $p_k$. Then in a document of length $L$ the probability that a keyword was selected exactly $n$ times in document $d$ is:

$$\Pr(f_{kd} = n) = \binom{L}{n} (p_k)^n (1 - p_k)^{L-n} \tag{3.6}$$

In other words, we'd expect it to occur an average of $p_k \cdot L$ times in a document of length $L$.

As $L \to \infty$ and $p \to 0$ (and the mean value $\lambda \equiv p \cdot L \to 1$), the Poisson distribution:

$$\Pr(f_{kd} = n) = \frac{e^{-\lambda}(\lambda)^n}{n!} \tag{3.7}$$

converges to this same distribution. We will generally be interested in a large set of parameters $\lambda_k$, each corresponding to a particular keyword $k$. If we imagine a Bernoulli-like experiment, where individual function words are placed with low probability and observed across the many "experiments" of words occurring in documents, we can expect that a particular word $k$ will occur $n$ times in a randomly selected document according to a Poisson distribution. (Because documents are of different lengths, we must also take care to normalize them all to the same number of experiments.)

As an example of how a Poisson model might be applied to good use, work pioneered by Bookstein and Swanson in the mid-1970s proposed that function words are distributed according to a relatively constant Poisson distribution, while content words are not [Bookstein and Swanson, 1974; Bookstein and Kraft, 1977, Croft and Harper, 1979]. That is, when a keyword is found in a document, it is for one of two possible reasons: Either it just happens (randomly) to be there, or it really

<u>means</u> something. Robertson and Walker [Robertson and Walker, 1994] distinguish the latter **elite** occurrences of a keyword:

> We hypothesize that occurrences of a term in a document have a random or stochastic element, which nevertheless reflects a real but hidden distinction between those ... "elite" documents which are <u>about</u> the concept represented by the term and those which are not. We may draw an inference about eliteness from the term frequency, but this inference will of course be probabilistic. Furthermore, relevance (to a query which may of course contain many concepts) is related to eliteness rather than directly to term frequency, which is assumed to depend *only* on eliteness. [Robertson and Walker, 1994, p. 233, underline not in original]

?1, 2

In addition to discriminating function from content words, the Poisson model has been used to measure the *degree* to which a content word is effective as a keyword for a document [Robertson and Walker, 1994]. If we assume that a potential keyword effectively describes some documents in a corpus but occurs at the level of chance throughout the rest of the corpus, the distribution of this keyword across the corpus can be described as the mixture of a Poisson process with some other distribution.

The so-called **two-Poisson model** models both distributions (i.e., one over the *Rel* documents that could accurately be characterized as <u>about</u> this keyword and a second over the rest of the $\overline{Rel}$ documents, which are not) as Poisson, but with distinct means $\lambda_w^1$ and $\lambda_w^2$, with the superscripts 1 and 2 referring to the *Rel* and $\overline{Rel}$ distributions, respectively. One advantage of assuming that both distributions are Poisson and that we only need to discriminate between two classes (relevant versus nonrelevant) is that a single-parameter $p_{rel} \equiv \Pr(Relevance)$ controls the probability that the word $w$ is relevant:

$$\Pr(d \text{ \underline{about} } w \mid k \text{ occurrences of } w$$

$$= \frac{p_{rel}e^{-\lambda_k^1}(\lambda_k^1)^n}{p_{rel}e^{-\lambda_k^1}(\lambda_k^1)^n + (1 - p_{rel})e^{-\lambda_k^2}(\lambda_k^2)^n} \qquad (3.8)$$

This probability can then be used as part of a decision theoretic model related to the costs of indexing too many or too few documents with a keyword $w$ (cf. Section 5.5.6).

### 3.3.3 Resolving Power

Zipf observed that the frequency of words' occurrence varies dramatically, and Poisson models explore deviations of these occurrence patterns from purely random processes. We now make the first important move toward a theory of *why* some words occur more frequently and how such statistics can be exploited when building an index automatically.

Luhn, as far back as 1957, said clearly:

> It is hereby proposed that the frequency of word occurrence in an article furnishes a useful measurement of word significance. [Luhn, 1957]

That is, if a word occurs frequently, more frequently than we would expect it to occur within a corpus, then it is reflecting *emphasis* on the part of the author <u>about</u> that topic. But the raw frequency of occurrence in a document is only one of two critical statistics recommending good keywords.

Consider a document taken from our AIT corpus, and imagine using the keyword ARTIFICIAL INTELLIGENCE with it. By construction, virtually every document in the AIT is <u>about</u> ARTIFICIAL INTELLIGENCE!? Assigning the keyword ARTIFICIAL INTELLIGENCE to every document in AIT would be a mistake, not because this document isn't <u>about</u> ARTIFICIAL INTELLIGENCE, but because this term cannot help us *discriminate* one subset of our corpus as relevant to any query. If we change our search task to looking not only in our AIT corpus but through a much larger collection (for example, all computer industry newsletters), then associating ARTIFICIAL INTELLIGENCE with those articles in our AIT subcorpus becomes a good idea. This term helps to distinguish AI documents from others.

The second critical characteristic of good indices now becomes clear: A good index term not only characterizes a document *absolutely*, as a feature of a document in isolation, but also allows us to discriminate it *relative* to other documents in the corpus. Hence keywords are not strictly properties of any single document, but they reflect a relationship between an individual document and the collection from which it might be selected.

These two countervailing considerations suggest that the best keywords will not be the most ubiquitous, frequently occurring terms, nor

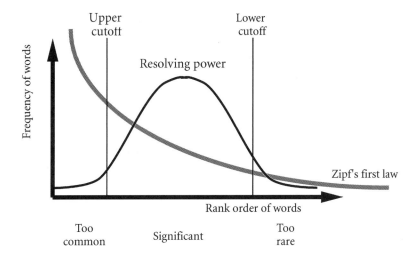

FIGURE 3.3  Resolving Power

those that occur only once or twice, but rather those occurring a moderate number of times. Using Zipf's rank ordering of words as a baseline, Luhn hypothesized a modal function of a word's rank he called **resolving power**, centered exactly at the middle of this rank ordering. If resolving power is defined as a word's ability to *discriminate* content, Luhn assumed that this quantity is maximal at the middle and falls off at either very high or very low frequency extremes, as shown in Figure 3.3.* The next step is then to establish maximal and minimal occurrence *thresholds* defining useful, midfrequency index terms. Unfortunately, Luhn's view does not provide theoretical grounds for selecting these bounds, so we are reduced to the engineering task of tuning them for optimal performance.

We'll begin with the maximal-frequency threshold, which is used to exclude words that occur too frequently. For any particular corpus, it is interesting to contrast this set of most-common words with the negative dictionary of noise words, defined in Section 2.3.2. While there is often great overlap, the negative dictionary list has proven itself to be useful across many different corpora, while the most frequent tokens in a particular corpus may be quite specific to it.

Establishing the low-frequency threshold is less intuitive. Assuming that our index is to be of limited size, including a certain keyword means we must exclude some other. This suggests that a word that occurs in

* After [van Rijsbergen, p. 16, figure 2.1].

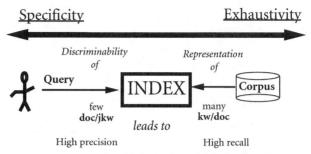

FIGURE 3.4 Specificity/Exhaustivity Trade-Offs

exactly one document can't possibly be used to help discriminate that document from others regularly. For example, imagine a word – suppose it is DERIVATIVE – that occurs exactly once, in a single document. If we took out that word DERIVATIVE and put in any other word, for example, FOOBAR, in terms of the word frequency co-occurrence statistics that are the basis of all our indexing techniques, the relationship between that document and all the other documents in the collection will remain unchanged. In terms of overlap between what the word DERIVATIVE means, in the FOA sense of what this and other documents are about, a single word occurrence has no meaning!

The most useful words will be those that are not used so often as to be roughly common to all of the documents, and not so rarely as to be (nearly) unique to any one (or a small set of) document. We seek those keywords whose *combinatorial* properties, when used in concert with one another as part of queries, help to compare and contrast topical areas of interest against one another.

### 3.3.4 Language Distribution

We next move beyond characteristics of single keywords to an analysis of the *distribution* of the entire set of index terms. Any index, whether constructed manually or automatically based on word frequency patterns, is defined by a tension between **exhaustivity** on the one hand and **specificity** on the other. An index is exhaustive if it includes many topics. It is specific if users can precisely identify their information needs.

Unfortunately, these two intuitively reasonable *desiderata* are in some sense at odds with one another, as suggested by Figure 3.4. The best explanation of this trade-off is in terms of precision and recall (cf. Section 4.3.4): High recall is easiest when an index is exhaustive but is not very specific; high precision is best accomplished when the index is not very exhaustive but is highly specific. If we assume that the same index must serve many users, each with varying expectations regarding the precision and recall of their retrieval, the best index will be at some balance point between these goals.

If we index a document with many keywords, it will be retrieved more often; hence we can expect higher recall, but precision may suffer. Van Rijsbergen has talked about this extreme as a "document" orientation, or **representation bias** [van Rijsbergen, pp. 24, 29]. A document-oriented approach to index-building focuses the system builder's attention on a careful representation of each document, based on an analysis of what it is <u>about</u>.

However, an index's fundamental purpose is to reconcile a corpus's many document descriptions with the many anticipated users' queries. We could equally well analyze the problem from a **query-oriented** perspective – How well do the query terms *discriminate* one document from another?

From the users' perspective, we'd like to have these queries match meaningfully onto the vocabulary of our index. From the perspective of the corpus, we'd like to be able to discriminate one document from another. These are very different perspectives on an index, and they reflect a fundamental **vocabulary mismatch** [Furnas et al., 1987] between the way users describe their interests and the way documents have been described.

If an indexing vocabulary is specific, then a user should expect that just the right keyword in a **magic bullet query** will elicit all and only relevant documents. The average number of documents assigned to specific keywords should be low. In an exhaustive indexing, the many aspects of a document will each be reflected by expressive keywords; on average many keywords will be assigned to a document:

$$Exhaustivity \; \propto \; \left\langle \frac{kw}{doc} \right\rangle$$

$$Specificity \propto^{-1} \left\langle \frac{doc}{kw} \right\rangle \propto \left\langle \frac{kw}{doc} \right\rangle \tag{3.9}$$

The important observation is that these two averages must be taken across different distributions. We already know from Zipf's law that the

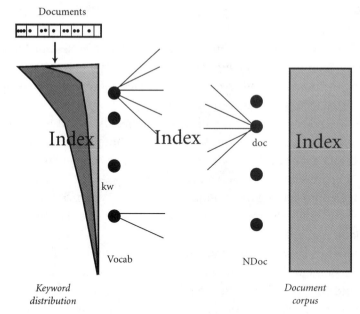

FIGURE 3.5  Indexing Graph

number of occurrences varies dramatically from one keyword to another. Once we make an assumption about how keywords occur within separate documents, we can derive the distribution of keywords across documents. However, the distribution of keywords assigned to documents can be expected to be much more uniform; documents are <u>about</u> a nearly uniform or constant number of topics. Figure 3.5 represents the index as a graph, where edges connect keyword nodes on the left with document nodes on the right. The *Index* graph is a bipartite graph, with its nodes divided into two subsets (keywords and documents) and nodes in one set having connections only with those in the other. If we assume that the total number of edges must remain constant, we can assume that the total area under both distributions is the same. The quantity capturing the exhaustivity/specificity trade-off is therefore the ratio of *Vocab* to corpus size *NDoc*.

Although this analysis is crude, it does highlight two important features of every index. First, in most applications *NDoc* is fixed and *Vocab* is a matter of discretion, a free variable that can be tuned to increase or decrease specificity and exhaustivity. Second, certainly in most modern applications (i.e., with the huge disk volumes now common), *NDoc* ≫ *Vocab*. This is one of the most important ways in which experimental collections (including AIT) differ from real corpora. A useful indexing vocabulary can be expected to be of a relatively constant size, *Vocab* ≈ $10^3$ to $10^5$, while corpora sizes are likely to vary dramatically, *NDoc* ≈ $10^4$ to $10^9$.

Along similar lines, it is always useful to think about what this means in the context of the WWW, where the notion of a *closed* corpus disappears. The WWW is an organic, constantly growing set of documents; our vocabulary for describing it is more constrained.

Several other basic features of an index are shown in Figure 3.5. The flipped histogram along the left side is meant to reflect the Zipfian distribution of keywords, with the most frequent keywords beginning at the top. Recall that this distribution captures the *total* number of word occurrences, regardless of how these occurrences are distributed across interdocument boundaries. A second distribution is also sketched, suggesting how the *number of documents* versus word occurrences might be distributed; we can expect these two quantities to be at least loosely correlated. The distinction between intra- and interdocument word frequencies is a topic we'll return to in Section 3.3.7.

## 3.3.5 Weighting the *Index* Relation

The simplest notion of an index is binary – either a keyword is associated with a document or it is not. But it is natural to imagine *degrees* of about-ness. We will capture this strength of association with a single real number, a **weight**, capturing the strength of the relationship between keyword and document. This weight can be used in two different ways. The first is to reduce the number of links to only the most significant relationships, those with the highest weights. In this respect a weighted indexing system is a more general formulation than a binary formulation; we can always go to a binary relation from the weighted one. This might make weights useful even if our retrieval method is Boolean (as it often was in early information retrieval (IR) systems). But a second and today more common reason for using a weighted indexing relation is that the retrieval method can exploit these weights directly.

One way to describe what this number <u>means</u> is probabilistic: We seek a measure of a document's relevance, conditionalized on the belief that a keyword is relevant:

$$w_{kd} \propto \Pr(d \text{ relevant} \mid k \text{ relevant}) \tag{3.10}$$

Note that this is a *directed* relation; we may or may not believe that the symmetric relation

$$w_{dk} \propto \Pr(k \text{ relevant} \mid d \text{ relevant}) \tag{3.11}$$

should be the same. Unless otherwise specified, when we refer to a weight $w$ we will intend it to mean $w_{kd}$.

In order to compute statistical estimates for such probabilities we define several important quantities:

$f_{kd} \equiv$ number of occurrences of keyword $k$ in document $d$

$f_k \equiv$ total number of occurrences of keyword $k$ across entire corpus

$D_k \equiv$ number of documents containing keyword $k$ $\tag{3.12}$

We will make two demands on the weight reflecting the degree to which a document is <u>about</u> a particular keyword or topic. The first one goes back to Luhn's central observation [Luhn, 1961]: *Repetition is an indication of emphasis.* If an author uses a word frequently, it is because he or she thinks it's important. Define $f_{kd}$ to be the number of occurrences of keyword $k$ in a document $d$.

Our second concern is that a keyword be a useful *discriminator* within the context of the corpus. Capturing this notion of corpus-context statistically proves much more difficult; for now, we simply give it the name $discrim_k$.

Because we care about both, we will devise our weight to be the *product* of the two factors, corresponding to their conjunction:

$$w_{kd} \propto f_{kd} \cdot discrim_k \tag{3.13}$$

We will now consider several different index weighting schemes that have been suggested over the years. These all share the same reliance on $f_{kd}$ as a measure of keyword importance within the document and the same product form as Equation 3.13. What they do not share is how best to quantify the discrimination power *discrim_k* of the keyword.

## 3.3.6 Informative Signals versus Noise Words

We begin with a weighting algorithm derived from information theory. Information theory has proven itself to be an extraordinarily useful model of many different situations in which some *message* must be communicated across a noisy *channel* and our goal is to devise an *encoding* for messages that is most robust in the face of this noise.

In our case, we must imagine that the "messages" describe the content of documents in our corpus. On this account, the amount of information we get <u>about</u> this content from a word is inversely proportional to its probability of occurrence. In other words, the least *informative* word in our corpus is the one that occurs approximately uniformly across the corpus. For example, the word THE occurs at about the same frequency across every document in the collection; its probability of occurrence in any one document is almost uniform. We gain the least information about the document's contents from observing it.[†]

Salton and McGill [Salton and McGill, 1983], following Dennis [Dennis, 1967], use Shannon's classic binary logarithm to measure the amount of information conveyed by each word's occurrence in bits and **noise** to be the absence of information:

What is "information"?

$$p_k = \Pr(\text{keyword } k \text{ occurs}) \qquad (3.14)$$

$$Info_k \equiv -\log\, p_k \qquad (3.15)$$

$$Noise_k \equiv -\log\,(1/p_k) \qquad (3.16)$$

Note that our evidence about the *probability* of a keyword occurring comes from *statistics* of how frequently it occurs. We must compare how frequently a keyword occurs in a particular document, relative to how frequently it occurs throughout the entire collection. We can calculate the expected noise associated with a keyword across the corpus, and from this we can infer its remaining **signal**. Signal then becomes another measure we can use to weight the frequency of occurrence of the keyword

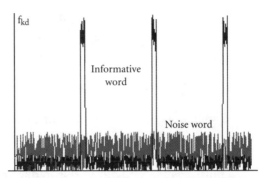

FIGURE 3.6  Hypothetical Word Distributions

document:

$$\langle Noise_k \rangle = \langle p_k \log(1/p_k) \rangle = \sum_d \frac{f_{kd}}{f_k} \log \frac{f_k}{f_{kd}} \qquad (3.17)$$

$$Signal_k = \log f_k - Noise_k \qquad (3.18)$$

$$w_{kd} = f_{kd} * Signal_k \qquad (3.19)$$

Two hypothetical distributions, for a noise word and a useful index term, are shown in Figure 3.6. A noise word is equally likely to occur anywhere; its distribution is nearly uniform. On the other hand, if all of the occurrences of a keyword are localized in a few documents (conveniently clustered together in the cartoon of Figure 3.6) and mostly zero everywhere else, this is an informative word. You've learned something <u>about</u> the document's content when you see it.

### 3.3.7  Inverse Document Frequency

Up to this point, we've been concerned only with the total number of times a word occurs across the entire corpus. Karen Sparck Jones has observed that, from a discrimination point of view, what we'd really like to know is the *number of documents* containing a keyword. This thinking underlies the **inverse document frequency** (IDF) weighting:

> The basis for IDF weighting is the observation that people tend to express their information needs using rather broadly defined, frequently occurring terms, whereas it is the more specific, i.e.,

low-frequency terms that are likely to be of particular importance in identifying relevant material. This is because the number of documents relevant to a query is generally small, and
thus any frequently occurring terms must necessarily occur in
many irrelevant documents; infrequently occurring terms have
a greater probability of occurring in relevant documents – and
should thus be considered as being of greater potential when
searching a database. [Sparck Jones and Willett, 1997, p. 307]

Rather than looking at the raw occurrence frequencies, we will aggregate occurrences within any document and consider only the *number
of documents* in which a keyword occurs. IDF proposes, again using a
"statistical interpretation of term specificity" [Sparck Jones, 1972], that
the value of a keyword varies inversely with the log of the number of
documents in which it occurs:

$$w_{kd} = f_{kd} * \left( \log \frac{Norm}{D_k} + 1 \right) \tag{3.20}$$

where $D_k$ is as defined in Equation 3.12.

The formula in Equation 3.20 is still not fully specified in that the
count $D_k$ must be normalized with respect to a constant *Norm*. We could
normalize with respect to the total number of documents in the corpus
[Sparck Jones, 1972; Croft and Harper, 1979]; another possibility is to
normalize against the maximum document frequency (i.e., the most
documents any keyword appears in) [Sparck Jones 1979a; Sparck Jones,
1979b]:

$$Norm = \begin{cases} NDoc & \text{or} \\ argmax_k D_k \end{cases} \tag{3.21}$$

Today the most common form of IDF weighting is that used by
Robertson and Sparck Jones [Robertson and Sparck Jones, 1976], which
normalizes with respect to the number of documents not containing a
keyword ($NDoc - D_k$) and adds a constant of 0.5 to both numerator
and denominator to moderate extreme values:

$$w_{kd} = f_{kd} * \left( \log \frac{(NDoc - D_k) + 0.5}{D_k + 0.5} \right) \tag{3.22}$$

## 3.4 Vector Space

One of life's most satisfying pleasures is going to a good library and browsing in an area of interest. After negotiating the library's organization and finding which floor and shelves are associated with the **call numbers** of your topic, you are *physically* surrounded by books and books, all of interest to you. Some are reassuring old friends, already known to you; others are new books by familiar authors, and (best of all!) some are brand-new titles by unknowns.

This system works because human catalogers have proven themselves able to reliably and consistently identify the (primary!) topic of a book according to conventional systems of subject headings like the Library of Congress Subject Headings or the Dewey Decimal system.

Our goal is to abstract away from this very friendly notion of *physical* space in the library to a similar but generalized notion of **semantic** space in which documents <u>about</u> the same topic remain close together. But rather than allowing ourselves to be restricted by the physical realities of three-dimensional space and the fact that books can only be shelved in a single place in a library, we will consider abstract spaces of thousands of dimensions.[†]

*Virtual spaces*

We can make concrete progress toward these lofty goals beginning with the *Index* **matrix** relating each document in a corpus to all of its keywords. A very natural and influential interpretation of this matrix (due to Gerry Salton [Salton et al., 1975; Salton and McGill, 1983]) is to imagine each and every keyword of the vocabulary as a separate dimension of a **vector space**. In other words, the **dimensionality** of the vector space is the size of our vocabulary. Each document can be represented as a vector within such a space. Figure 3.7 shows a very simplified (binary) *Index* matrix, and a cartoon of its corresponding vector representation.

Estimates of the vocabulary size of a native speaker of a language approach 50,000 words; if you are articulate, your speaking and reading vocabularies might be 100,000 or more words. Assuming that we have a modest $10^6$ document corpus, this matrix is something like $10^6 \times 10^5$.

*Sparse vector spaces*

That's a big matrix, even by modern supercomputing standards.[†]

In addition to the vectors representing all documents, another vector corresponds to a query. Because documents and queries exist within a common vector space, we naturally characterize how we'd like our

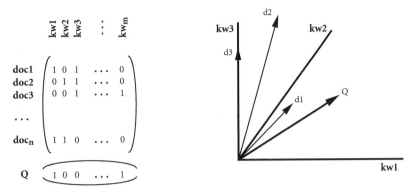

FIGURE 3.7  Vector Space

retrieval system to work – just as we go to a physical location in the library to be *near* books <u>about</u> a topic, we seek those documents that are *close to* our query vector. This is a useful characterization of what we'd like our retrieval system to accomplish, but it is still far from a specification of an algorithm for accomplishing it. For example, it seems to require that the query vector be compared against each and every document, something we hope to avoid.[†]

An even more important issue to be resolved before the vector space model can be useful is being specific about just what it means for a document and query to be close to one another. As will be discussed in Section 5.2.2, there are many plausible measures of proximity within a vector space. For the time being, we will assume the use of the **inner product** of query and document vectors as our metric:

$$Sim(\mathbf{q}, \mathbf{d}) = \mathbf{q} \cdot \mathbf{d} \qquad (3.23)$$

People have difficulty imagining spaces with more than the three physical dimensions of experience, so it is no wonder that abstract spaces of $10^5$ dimensions are difficult to conceptualize. Sketches like Figure 3.7 do the best they can to convey ideas in the three dimensions we appreciate, but it is critically important that we not let intuitions based on such small-dimensional experiences bias our understanding of the large-dimensional spaces actually being represented and searched.

Implementation hack

### 3.4.1 Keyword Discrimination

We can immediately use this vector space for something useful, as the source of yet another approach to the question of appropriate keyword weightings. Recall that in Figure 3.7 our initial assumption was that each and every keyword was to be used as a dimension of the vector space. Now we ask: What would happen if we removed one of these keywords?

The first step is to extend the measure $Sim(\mathbf{q}, \mathbf{d})$ of document-query similarity to measure *interdocument* similarities $Sim(\mathbf{d}_i, \mathbf{d}_j)$ as well. Then, for an arbitrary measure of document-document similarity (e.g., the inner product measure mentioned earlier), we consider all pairs of documents and then the **average similarity** across all of them.[†]

There's a quicker way to compute average similarity

$$Sim(d_i, d_j) \equiv \text{Similarity among documents} \qquad (3.24)$$

$$D^* \equiv \text{Centroid; average document} \qquad (3.25)$$

$$\overline{Sim_k} \equiv \frac{1}{NDoc^2} \sum_{i,j} Sim(d_i, d_j) \qquad (3.26)$$

Recall that our goal is to devise a representation of documents that makes it easy for queries to discriminate among them. Because each keyword corresponds to a dimension, *removing* one results in a *compression* of the space into $K - 1$ dimensions, and we can expect that the representation of each document will change at least slightly. For example, removing a dimension along which the documents varied significantly means that vectors that were far apart in the $K$-dimensional space are now much closer together.

This observation can be used to ask how useful each potential keyword is. If it is discriminating, removing it will result in a significant compression of the documents' vectors; if removing it changes very little, the keyword is less helpful. Using the average similarity as our measure of how close together the documents are, and asking this question for each and every keyword, we arrive at yet another measure of keyword discrimination:

$$\overline{Sim_k} \equiv \overline{Sim} \text{ when } term_k \text{ removed} \qquad (3.27)$$

$$\text{Disc}_k \equiv \overline{Sim_k} - \overline{Sim} \qquad (3.28)$$

$$w_{kd} = f_{kd} * \text{Disc}_k \qquad (3.29)$$

## 3.4.2  Vector Length Normalization

One good example involves the *length* of document and query vectors. So far, we have placed no constraint on the number of keywords associated with a document. This means that long documents, which, *caeteris paribus*, can be expected to give rise to more keyword indices, can be expected to match (more precisely, have nonzero inner product with) more queries and be retrieved more often. Somehow (as discussed in Section 1.4) this doesn't seem fair: The author of a very short document who worked hard to compress the <u>meaning</u> into a pithy few paragraphs is less likely to have his or her document retrieved, relative to a wordy writer who says everything six times in six different ways!

These possibilities have been captured by Robertson and Walker in a pair of hypotheses regarding a document's **scope** versus its **verbosity**:

> Some documents may simply cover more material than others . . . (the "Scope hypothesis"). An opposite view would have long documents like short documents but longer: in other words, a long document covers a similar scope to a short document, but simply uses more words (the "Verbosity hypothesis"). [Robertson and Walker, 1994, p. 235]

Once we have decided that *about*-*ness is conserved* across documents, all documents' vectors will have constant length. If we make the same assumption about the query vector, then all of the vectors will lie on the surface of a sphere, as shown in Figure 3.8. Without loss of generality, we will assume that the radius of the sphere is unity.

### Making Weights Sensitive to Document Length

Unfortunately, this very simple normalization is often inadequate, as can be shown in terms of the inverse document frequency (IDF) weights discussed in Section 3.3.7. IDF weighting highlights the distinction between *inter-* and *intradocument* keyword occurrences. Because its primary focus is on discrimination among documents, intradocument occurrences of the same keyword become insignificant. This makes IDF very sensitive to the definition of how document boundaries are defined (cf. Section 2.2), as suggested by Figure 3.9.

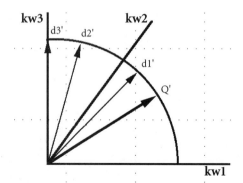

FIGURE 3.8 Length Normalization of Vector Space

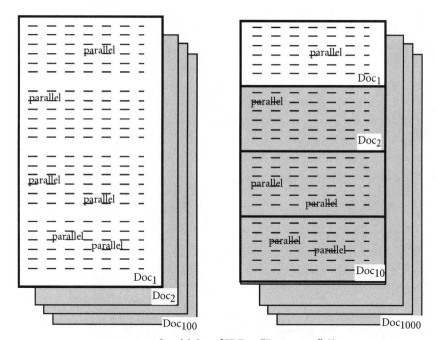

FIGURE 3.9 Sensitivity of IDF to "Document" Size

The IDF weight that results from encapsulating more text within the same "document" is, in a sense, the converse of normalizing the number of keywords assigned to every document. In either case, the advantage of using the paragraph as our canonical document (cf. Section 1.4), and/or relying on all documents in the corpus to be of nearly uniform size (as in the AIT dissertation abstracts) is apparent.

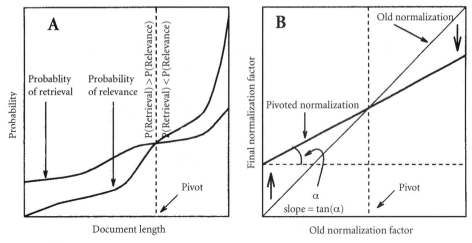

FIGURE 3.10 Pivot-Based Document Length Normalization. From [Singhal et al., 1996]. Reproduced with permission of the Association of Computing Machinery.

The OKAPI retrieval system of Robertson et al. [Robertson and Walker, 1994] has proven itself successful (in retrieval competitions like TREC; cf. Section 4.3.3) by combining IDF weightings with corpus-specific sensitivities to the lengths of the documents retrieved. They propose that the average length of all documents in a corpus, $\overline{DLen}$, provides a "natural" reference point against which other documents' lengths can be compared.

Define $Len(d)$ to be the number of keywords associated with the document. OKAPI then normalizes the first component of our weighting formula, keyword frequency, by a term that is sensitive to each document's deviation from this corpuswide average:

$$w_{kd} = \frac{f_{kd}}{(k \cdot Len(d)/\overline{DLen}) + f_{kd}} \cdot \left( \log \frac{(NDoc - D_k) + 0.5}{D_k + 0.5} \right) \quad (3.30)$$

Robertson and Walker report that $k \approx 1.0 - 2.0 \, |Q|$ seems to work best, where $|Q|$ is the number of query terms.

Singhal et al. [Singhal et al., 1996] approach the problem of length normalization by doing a post hoc analysis of the distributions of retrieved versus relevant documents (in the TREC corpus) as a function of their length. A sketch of typical curves is shown in Figure 3.10.A. The fact that these two distributions cross suggests a corpus-specific **length normalization pivot** value, $p$, below which match scores are reduced and above which they are increased. The amount of this linear increase or decrease, shown as the **length normalization slope** $m$ of the length normalization function in Figure 3.10.B, is the second corpus-specific parameter of Singhal et al.'s model. Returning to the "generic" form of the weighting function originally given in Equation 3.13, the pivot-based length normalization is:

$$w_{kd} = \frac{f_{kd}}{(1-m) \cdot p + m \cdot norm} \cdot discrim_k \qquad (3.31)$$

where *norm* is whatever other normalization factor (e.g., cosine) is already in use; several possible values are given in the next section.

Both OKAPI and pivot-based document length normalizations rely on the specification of additional corpus-specific parameters ($k_1$ and $p, m$, respectively). Although the addition of yet more "knobs to twiddle" is generally to be avoided in a retrieval system, recent experience with machine learning techniques suggests the possibility of *training* such parameters to best match each corpus. This approach is sometimes called a **regression** technique and is discussed more fully in Chapter 7.

### 3.4.3 Summary: SMART Weighting Specification

Although the variety of potential keyword weighting schemes (signal/noise, IDF, keyword discrimination, etc.) may seem large, there is in fact a systematicity to this variation.

SMART is an extremely influential and widely used software system for investigating IR techniques [Salton, 1971; Buckley, 1985]. One secret of its success is that SMART provides a simple parameter-driven mechanism for easily changing from one form of index weighting to another.

In SMART, the weight is decomposed into three factors:

$$w_{kd} = \frac{freq_{kd} * discrim_k}{norm} \qquad (3.32)$$

Each of these components can then be specified independently:

$$
freq_{kd} = \begin{cases} \{0, 1\} & \text{binary} \\[2ex] \dfrac{f_{kd}}{\max\limits_{k}(f_{kd})} & \text{maxNorm} \\[3ex] \dfrac{1}{2} + \dfrac{1}{2}\dfrac{f_{kd}}{\max\limits_{k}(f_{kd})} & \text{augmented} \\[3ex] \ln\left(f_{kd}\right) + 1 & \text{log} \end{cases} \tag{3.33}
$$

$$
discrim_{k} = \begin{cases} \log\dfrac{NDoc}{D_k} & \text{inverse} \\[3ex] \left(\log\dfrac{NDoc}{D_k}\right)^2 & \text{squared} \\[3ex] \log\dfrac{NDoc - D_k}{D_k} & \text{probabilistic} \\[3ex] \dfrac{1}{D_k} & \text{frequency} \end{cases} \tag{3.34}
$$

$$
norm = \begin{cases} \sum\limits_{vector} w_i & \text{sum} \\[3ex] \sqrt{\sum\limits_{vector} w_i^2} & \text{cosine} \\[3ex] \sum\limits_{vector} w_i^4 & \text{fourth} \\[3ex] \max\limits_{vector}(w_i) & \text{max} \end{cases} \tag{3.35}
$$

## 3.5  Matching Queries against Documents

In Chapter 2 we first identified documents, then lexical features to be associated with each. Then we built an inverted keyword list to make going from keywords to documents about those keywords as easy as possible. Now we'll become specific about how we measure the similarity between a document and a query.

The discussion of matching queries and documents is simplified if we adopt the vector space perspective of Section 3.4 and imagine both the query $q$ and all documents $d$ to be vectors in a space of dimensionality equal to $NKw$, the keyword vocabulary size.

In this space, the answer to the question of which documents are the best match for a query seems straightforward – those documents that are most *similar,* relative to some particular **metric** *Sim* measuring distance between points in the space. Students of algebra and abstract vector spaces know that many different choices are possible; see Section 5.2.2.

### 3.5.1 Measures of Association

Given a vocabulary of lexical indexing features, our central concern will be how to moderate the raw frequency counts of these features in documents (and, to a lesser extent, queries) based on *distributional* characteristics of that feature across the corpus. We will be led to use real-valued weights to capture these relations, but we begin with cruder methods: simply counting shared keywords.

The most direct way to say that a query and a document are similar is to measure the *intersection* of their respective feature sets. Let $K_q$ be the set of keyword features used in a query and $K_d$ be the analogous set found in a document. The **coordination level** is exactly how many terms in the query overlap with terms in the document:

$$CoordLevel(\mathbf{q}, \mathbf{d}) = \left| \left( K_{\mathbf{q}} \cap K_{\mathbf{d}} \right) \right| \qquad (3.36)$$

If we have many, many features and our query and documents are highly variable, then the presence of any significant overlap may be enough to identify the set of documents of interest. On the other hand, if there is a great deal of overlap between our query and many of the documents, then simply counting how big this intersection is will look like a gross measure. This fine line between one or two documents matching a query and an avalanche of thousands occurs regularly as part of FOA.

One part of the problem is **normalization** – the coordination level of intersecting features shared by both query and document seems a good measure of their similarity, but compared to what? It's easy to show that this normalization matters. Consider the case where $CoordLevel(q, d) = 1$, and imagine first that $K_q = K_d = 1$ also; i.e., a single-word query and a one-word document. In this case the two match on the one feature they each have. Intuitively, this is a perfect match; you couldn't do any better. But now imagine that the query includes 10 keywords, the document contains 1000 words, but still $CoordLevel(q, d) = 1$. The same intuition suggests that this should be judged a much poorer match, but our measure does not reveal this. Unless we normalize by something that reflects how many other features we might have matched, we can't have a useful measure of association.

One natural normalizer is to take the *average* of the number of terms in the query and in the document and compare the size of the intersection to it. This gives us the Dice coefficient:

$$Sim_{Dice}(\mathbf{q}, \mathbf{d}) = 2\frac{\left|\left(K_{\mathbf{q}} \cap K_{\mathbf{d}}\right)\right|}{|K_{\mathbf{q}}| + |K_{\mathbf{d}}|} \tag{3.37}$$

The average number of features may or may not be appropriate, again depending on what a typical query and typical document are. Often a document has many, many keywords associated with it, and queries have only one or two. This average is not a very good characterization of either.

Another perspective on similarity says that missing features are as significant as shared ones. The **simple matching coefficient** gives equal weight to those features *included* in both query and document and those *excluded* from both and normalizes by the total number of keyword features $NKw$:

$$Sim_{simple}(\mathbf{q}, \mathbf{d}) = \frac{\left|\left(K_{\mathbf{q}} \cap K_{\mathbf{d}}\right)\right| + \left|\left(\left(NKw - K_{\mathbf{q}}\right) \cap \left(NKw - K_{\mathbf{d}}\right)\right)\right|}{|NKw|}$$
$$\tag{3.38}$$

## 3.5.2 Cosine Similarity

We will focus here on the **cosine** measure of similarity. Not only does this respect the useful mathematical properties mentioned at the beginning of this section, but it is consistent with a geometric interpretation of the vector space that many find insightful:

$$Sim(\mathbf{q}, \mathbf{d}) = \cos(\mathbf{q} \angle \mathbf{d})$$

$$= \frac{\mathbf{q} \cdot \mathbf{d}}{\|\mathbf{d}\| \, \|\mathbf{q}\|}$$

$$= \frac{\displaystyle\sum_{k \in (q \cap d)} w_{kd} \cdot w_{kq}}{\|\mathbf{d}\| \, \|\mathbf{q}\|}$$

$$= \frac{\displaystyle\sum_{k \in (q \cap d)} w_{kd} \cdot w_{kq}}{\sqrt{\displaystyle\sum_{k \in d} (w_{kd})^2} \sqrt{\displaystyle\sum_{k \in q} (w_{kq})^2}} \tag{3.39}$$

## 3.6  Calculating TF-IDF Weighting

Following the careful empirical investigation of Salton and Buckley [Salton and Buckley, 1988d; Salton and Buckley, 1990] and many others since [Harman, 1992a], we will concentrate on the **TF-IDF** weighting, which multiplies the raw **term frequency** (TF) of a term in a document by the term's inverse document frequency (IDF) weight:

$$idf_k = \log\left(\frac{NDoc}{D_k}\right) \tag{3.40}$$

$$w_{kd} = f_{kd} \cdot idf_k \tag{3.41}$$

where $f_{kd}$ is the frequency with which keyword $k$ occurs in document $d$, $NDoc$ is the total number of documents in the corpus, and $D_k$ is the number of documents containing keyword $k$.

Due to the wide variety observed in users' query patterns, methods for weighting queries vary more, primarily depending on the *length* of the query. We will consider two weighting methods, especially designed for "short" and "long" queries. *Short* queries (of as few as one or two terms; cf. [Silverstein et al., 1999]) seem typical of those issued by Web search engine users. For these, we can assume multiple occurrences of the same keyword will be rare, and we ignore length normalization. This leaves us with simply the term's inverse frequency weight:

$$w_{kq\,\text{short}} = idf_k \qquad (3.42)$$

*Long* queries are often generated indirectly, as the result of *RelFbk* from the users in response to prior retrievals. The long query corresponds to a particular *document* that the users like; searching for others like a known target is called **query-by-example**. By symmetry, it makes sense to use the same weighting of terms in this query-cum-document as we used for documents (Equation 3.40):

$$w_{kq\,\text{long}} = f_{kq}\,idf_k \qquad (3.43)$$

Notice that once the lengths of the **q** and **d** vectors in the denominator of Equation 3.39 are known, the computation of *Sim* requires a simple sum of products over all terms shared by query and document. Because both these lengths can be computed independently, it makes sense to compute them first.[†]

In fact, the document length *Len*(**d**) can be computed before any query activity takes place:

*Implementation: Storing document lengths*

$$Len(\mathbf{d}) = \sqrt{\sum_{k\in d} w_{kd}^2} = \sqrt{\sum_{k\in d} \left(f_{kd}\,idf_k\right)^2} \qquad (3.44)$$

With these definitions in place, we can begin to design an algorithm for computing similarity.

## 3.7  Computing Partial Match Scores

With length normalization to the side, we can concentrate on the main calculation of matching, summing the weight products of terms shared by query $q$ and document $d$:

$$\sum_{k\in(q\cap d)} w_{kd} \cdot w_{kq} \qquad (3.45)$$

This mathematical characterization hides a number of messy details associated with actually computing it. We will need to make efficient use of two data structures in particular. The first is the inverted index (recall

Figure 3.5). The critical feature of this organization is that we can, for each term in the query, find the set of all document postings associated with it. In particular, the freq statistic maintained with each posting allows us to compute the weight $w_{kd}$ we need for each. Even with these efficiencies, however, the need to consider every document posting for every query term can create a serious processing demand, and one that must be satisfied immediately – the users are waiting!

Because the elements of the sum can be reordered arbitrarily, we will consider a **partial ranking** (a.k.a. filtering, or pruning) algorithm that attempts to include the dominant elements of the sum but ignore small, inconsequential ones [Salton, 1989; Buckley and Lewit, 1985; Harman and Candela, 1990].

The fact that $w_{kq}$ and $w_{kd}$ vary considerably suggests that, by ordering the inclusion of products into the sum, we may be able to truncate this process when they become smaller than we care to consider.

We therefore begin by sorting the terms in decreasing order of query weights $w_{kq}$. Considering terms in this order means we can expect to accumulate the match score beginning with its largest terms. Then the fact that our list of postings was similarly (and not coincidentally) ordered by decreasing frequency means that:

$$(\forall\, j > i)\ w_{kd_i} > w_{kd_j} \tag{3.46}$$

Once these weights diminish below some threshold $\tau_{add}$, we can stop going down the postings list. (In fact, it may be that the weight associated with the very first posting is too small and we can ignore all weights associated with this term.)

The second important data structure is an **accumulator** queue in which each document's match score is maintained. Because each query term may add an additional term to the match score for a particular document, these accumulators will keep a running total for each document. For moderate corpus sizes, it may not be unreasonable to allocate an accumulator for each document, but this can demand too much memory for very large corpora. Define *NAccum* to be the number of accumulators we are willing to allocate. Then one obvious way to restrict this set is to only allocate an accumulator when a document's score becomes significant, again in comparison to some threshold $\tau_{insert}$. Because we will be processing query terms in decreasing $w_{kq}$ order and heuristically value the space associated with new accumulators more than the slightly longer time to run down posting lists a bit further, we can assume that $\tau_{insert} > \tau_{add}$.

Picking appropriate values for these two thresholds is something of a black art, but Persin [Persin, 1994] reports one especially careful experiment in which both are made proportional to the most highly matched document's accumulator $A^*$ (i.e., $A^*$ is the maximum match score in any document's accumulator):

$$\tau_{insert} = \eta_{insert} \cdot A^* \qquad (3.47)$$

$$\tau_{add} = \eta_{add} \cdot A^* \qquad (3.48)$$

Persin's experiments suggest that values of $\eta_{insert} = 0.07$, $\eta_{add} = 0.001$ give retrieval effectiveness near that of full matches (i.e., considering all query-document term products) while minimizing *NAccum*.[†]

These two thresholds divide the range of possible query-document term products into three conditions:

$$w_{kd} \cdot w_{kq} > \tau_{insert} \qquad \text{Always add; create new accumulator } A_d \text{ if necessary}$$

$$\tau_{add} < w_{kd} \cdot w_{kq} \leq \tau_{insert} \qquad \text{Add only if accumulator } A_d \text{ already exists}$$

$$w_{kd} \cdot w_{kq} \leq \tau_{add} \qquad \text{Ignore; move on to the next query term}$$

We want to remain flexible with respect to both long and short queries, so we will assume that the query weights $w_{kq}$ are precomputed and passed to our ranking procedure.[*] Using our definition for $w_{kd}$ and focusing first on the $\tau_{insert}$ threshold:

$$w_{kd} \cdot w_{kq} > \tau_{insert}$$
$$\iff (f_{kd} \cdot idf_k) \cdot w_{kq} > \tau_{insert}$$
$$\iff f_{kd} > \frac{\tau_{insert}}{idf_k w_{kq}} \qquad (3.49)$$
$$\iff f_{kd} > \frac{\eta_{insert} A^*}{idf_k w_{kq}}$$

> Partial matching isn't just more efficient; it works better too!

---

[*] However, it is generally more efficient to retain "raw" frequency counts in the postings (as integers) rather than length-normalized weights $w_{kd}$ (as floats). This means that length normalization of documents is performed *after* the partial ranking match has been completed.

---

**Algorithm 3.1 Partial Ranking**

prank(qry[], A) {
// qry = vector of $< keyword, weight >$ pairs
// A = queue of $< docid, score >$ accumulators
// initially empty and returned with most highly ranked
    Sort(qry, & descending WgtCmp);
    for ($q \in$ query ) {
        $\tau_{insert} = (\eta_{insert} \cdot A^*)/(q.wgt \cdot idf_q)$;
        $\tau_{add} = (\eta_{add} \cdot A^*)/(q.wgt \cdot idf_q)$;
        for ($fp \in$ fpost($q$)) {
            if ($fp.freq <= \tau_{add}$)
                break;
            newscore = $fp.freq \cdot idf_q \cdot q.wgt$;
            for ($dp \in$ dpost($fp$)){
                fnd = hashfind(docTbl, docno);
                if(fnd OR dwgt $> \tau_{insert}$) {
                    if (fnd)
                        fnd.score $+=$ newscore;
                    else {
                        hashadd(docTbl, docno);
                        if(length(A) $> NAccum$)
                            pop(A);
                        insertQ(newscore, docno, A);
                    }
                  $A^* = $ max($A^*$,fnd.score,newscore);
                }
            }
        }}//eo-posting loops
    }//eo-qry loop
}

---

This finally becomes an operational question we can apply with respect to each posting's frequency $f_{kd}$. Note that this threshold must be updated every time we move to a new term of the query. Of course, the computation of $\tau_{add}$ proceeds similarly.

All the basic features of a partial ranking algorithm are now in place, and a pseudo-code sketch is shown in Algorithm 3.1. It also includes a few minor complications. First, a hashtable is required to find accumulators associated with a particular docno. Second, the set of accumulators $A_d$ is described as a queue, but it must be slightly trickier than most: It must maintain them in order so that only the top *NAccum* are maintained, and it must support length() queries and a pop() function when it is full. Nondeterministic skip lists [Pugh, 1990] are recommended for this purpose [Cutting and Pedersen, 1997].

?5, 6, 7, 8, 9

## 3.8 Summary

We've covered enormous ground in this chapter. We began by wondering just what it might <u>mean</u> to try to understand communicative acts, like the publication of a document or the posing of a question or query. We looked in some detail at one of the most fundamental characteristics of texts, Zipf's law, and found it to be, in fact, quite <u>meaning</u>less! But the next level of features, tokens like those produced by the machinery of Chapter 2, supported a rich analysis of the index, as a balance between the vocabularies of the documents' authors and searchers' subsequent queries. The vector space provides a concrete model of potential keyword vocabularies and what it might mean to match within this space. Finally, we considered an efficient implementation of nearly complete matching. In the next chapter we will consider the problem of evaluating how well all these techniques work in practice.

However, there are gaps in this story that are so obvious we don't even need to measure them. Some of the gaps involve implementation issues that can be critical, especially when faced with very large corpora [Harper and Walker, 1992]. Parallel implementation techniques, for example, those pioneered on "massively parallel" SIMD (single instruction/multiple data) Connection Machines, become important in this respect [Salton and Buckley, 1988c; Stanfill and Kahle, 1986a; Stone, 1987]. In the modern age of multiple search engines each indexing (only partially overlapping versions [Lawrence and Giles, 1998]) of the WWW techniques for **fusing** multiple hitlists into a single list for the same user suggests another level of parallelism in the FOA task [Voorhees et al., 1995].

However, linguists, in particular, must have more serious, implementation-independent concerns. Imagine that you are someone who has studied the range of human languages and who appreciates both their wide variety and equally remarkable commonalities. You would be appalled at the violence we have done to the *syntactic structure* of language. For linguists, Finding Out About documents by counting their words must seem like trying to understand Beijing by listening to a single microphone poised high over the city: You can pick up on a few basic trends (like when most people are awake), but most of the texture is missing!

DOG BITES MAN and MAN BITES DOG clearly <u>mean</u> two different things. Word order obviously conveys <u>meaning</u> beyond that brought by the three words. And the problem doesn't end with word order. Look how different the <u>meaning</u> of these phrases are:

- NEUTRALIZATION OF THE PRESENT
- REPRESENTING NEUTRONS
- REPRESENTATIONS, NOT NEUTRONS

despite the fact that all of them (conceivably) reduce to the same set of indexable tokens! Note especially how critical the same "noise" words thrown away on statistical grounds (in Chapter 2) are when analyzing a sentence's syntactic structure.

The attempt to understand the phenomena of <u>meaning</u> by looking for patterns in word frequency statistics alone is reminiscent of the tea leaves and entrails of this chapter's opening quote. Still, the success of many WWW search engines that use very little beyond this kind of gross analysis suggests that there is much more information in the statistics than traditional, syntactically focused linguists might have believed.

---

**EXERCISE 1**  Find the average word frequency statistic $\lambda_k$ for words in our noise word negative dictionary. Also compute it for an equal number of the most frequently occurring words used as index terms for the AIT corpus. How well can varying $\lambda_k$ be used to discriminate functional from content-descriptive terms?

**EXERCISE 2**  Derive a statistical test for goodness of fit with a Poisson distribution.

**EXERCISE 3**  Collect word frequency statistics for all (unstemmed) tokens in the AIT corpus, and identify the 100 most frequently occurring words. Then contrast this set with the words in STOP.WRD. Which words are common to both sets? Which words are very common in AIT but not already part of the negative dictionary? Which words are part of the negative dictionary but do not occur frequently in AIT?

**EXERCISE 4**  Pick $k$ keywords randomly. Plot the distribution of coordination levels for all documents matching at least one of these. Now repeat this experiment 10 times and plot the mean with standard deviation bars. Iterate this exercise for $1 \le k \le 10$.

**EXERCISE 5**  What fraction of all total postings are pruned by prank?

**EXERCISE 6**  For one long and one short query, vary *NAccum* from 10 to 100 percent of *NDoc* (in increments of 10 percent) and analyze the resulting retrieval performance.

**EXERCISE 7**  As presented, the thresholds pruning postings from consideration in the prank() algorithm are very sensitive to $A^*$, the best matching document's score. Replace this dependence with one on the *average* of the top $k$ documents' scores.

**EXERCISE 8**  As presented, the $\tau_{insert}$ threshold (used to determine when new accumulators are added) ignores how full the queue already is. So, for example, postings might not initially be added even when the queue is entirely empty. (There is also a near-bug in the code, arising when the smallest element of the queue is popped even though it may be larger than the *newscore* being added.) Propose, implement, and test a new decision rule that is sensitive to both the fullness of the queue and $A^\circ$, its smallest element's score.

**EXERCISE 9**  Describe sensitivities of the prank algorithm to document length normalization. That is, under which conditions might the document ordering performed under unnormalized posting frequencies be invalid?

TERMS INTRODUCED IN THIS CHAPTER

accumulator
average similarity
base-pairs
Bernoulli
call numbers
codons
content words
coordination level
cosine
dimensionality
diversification
economy of language
elite
exhaustivity
external keywords
function words
fusing
inner product
internal keywords
inverse document
   frequency

informational
  temperature
length normalization
  pivot
length normalization
  slope
magic bullet query
matrix
neologisms
noise
normalization
partial ranking
poisson process
principle of least
  effort
query-by-example
query-oriented
referent
regression
representation bias
resolving power

scope
semantic
signal
simple matching
  coefficient
specificity
stratified sampling
temperature of
  discourse
term frequency
TF-IDF
two-Poisson
  model
vector space
verbosity
vocabulary balance
vocabulary
  mismatch
unification
weight
WWW surfing

# 4

# Assessing the Retrieval

We've come a long way since Chapter 1, where we first sketched the full range of activities we might consider FOA. As Chapter 2 considered the various ways of breaking text into indexable features, and Chapter 3 explained the various ways of weighting combinations of these features to identify the best matches to a query, I hope you have been aware of how many *alternatives* have been mentioned! That is, rarely has there been a single method that can be proven to be better than all others. IR has traditionally been driven by empirical demonstrations, and the range of commercial competitors now trying to provide the "best" search of the WWW makes it likely this performance orientation will continue. But whether we are search engineers, scientists objectively assessing one particular technique, or consumers of WWW search engine technology interested in buying and using the best, a solid basis of performance *assessment* is critical.

Several perspectives on assessment are possible. In the first chapter FOA was viewed as a *personal* activity, adopting the users' points of view. Section 4.1 will continue in this theme, considering how users assess the results of their retrievals and how they can express their opinions using relevance feedback (*RelFbk*). Oddy is credited with first identifying this important stream of data, naturally provided by users as a part of their FOA browsing [Oddy, 1977; Belkin et al., 1982].

But in this book we are also concerned with FOA from the IR *system builder's* point of view. Ideally, we would like to construct a search engine that robustly finds the "right" documents for each query and for each user. The second section of this chapter discusses performance measures of *statistical* properties that are reliable across large numbers of users and their highly variable queries. The key to these measures is having some insight into which documents *should* have been retrieved, typically because some idealized **omniscient expert** has determined (within a specially constructed experimental situation) that certain documents "should" have been retrieved. Alternatively the *RelFbk* of many users can be combined to form a **consensual** opinion of relevance, as described in Section 4.4.

A concrete notion of **relevance** would seem a fundamental precondition for understanding either an individual's *RelFbk* or how this can be used to assess a search engine. But in this respect, information retrieval generally, and *RelFbk* in particular, is like many other academic areas of study (including artificial intelligence and genetics) in that the lack of a fully satisfactory definition of the core concept (information, intelligence, genes, and so on) has not entirely stopped progress. That is, a great deal can be done by **operationalizing** *RelFbk* to be simply those **relevance assessment** behaviors produced as part of an FOA dialog. This operational simplification will hold us until fundamental issues of language and communication are again addressed in Section 8.2.1.

## 4.1  Personal Assessment of Relevance*

### 4.1.1  Cognitive Assumptions

"Garbage in, garbage out" is one of the first insights every software developer learns, and FOA is no exception. The primary source of data considered by traditional IR methods, and the focus of Chapters 2 and 3 of this text, are the documents of the corpus, particularly the keywords they contain. (Chapter 6 will consider the use of other document attributes.) A fundamental feature of the broader FOA view is that *browsing users provide an equally important source of data* concerning

---

* Portions previously published with John Hatton [Belew and Hatton, 1996].

what keywords <u>mean</u> and what documents are <u>about</u>. It is therefore appropriate to begin by characterizing who these users we will be watching are.

We begin with one important cognitive assumption we must make about our users: How *thorough* an FOA search do they wish to perform? Is this an important search to which the users are willing to dedicate a great deal of time and attention, or will a quick, cursory answer suffice? For example, Chapter 1 mentioned how much less thorough the typical undergraduate (doing some quick research before submitting a term paper) is than the Ph.D. candidate (who wants to ensure his or her proposed dissertation topic is new). The typical WWW searcher seems satisfied with only a few useful leads, but the professional searcher (a lawyer looking for any case that might help, a doctor looking for any science that might heal a patient) will search diligently if there is even a small chance of finding another relevant document. This kind of variability can be observed not only across different classes of users but even across the same user at different times.[†]

In for a fact,
stay for a lesson

## Prototypic Retrievals

From the perspective of cognitive psychology, the task facing users who are asked to produce relevance feedback (*RelFbk*) can best be described as one of **object recognition**, in the tradition of Rosch and others [Rosch and Mervis, 1975; Rosch, 1977]. The object to be recognized is an internally represented *prototypic* document satisfying the users' information need. In this case, the prototype corresponds to the model the subjects maintain of ideally relevant documents. As users consider an actual retrieved document's relevance, they evaluate how well it *matches* the prototype. Barry and others have suggested the many and varied features over which prototypes can be defined [Barry, 1994]. Only a small number of these may be revealed by any one of the users' queries, of course.

Here we will simply assume that users are capable of grading the *quality* of this match. Users might be asked to score the quality of relevance match according to a five-point scale like that shown in Figure 4.1. Users can qualify the middle Relevant response either by weakening it (Possibly Relevant) or strengthening it (Critically Relevant). Such distinctions are often made in experimental settings (e.g., in the use of the STAIRS

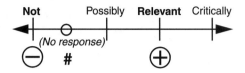

FIGURE 4.1 Relevance Scale

retrieval system by lawyers [Blair and Maron, 1985]) and relate to the different purposes for FOA that different users may have. To make these distinctions concrete, we might imagine "Critically Relevant" to apply only to those documents that must be read even for an undergrad term paper, while "Possibly Relevant" would be much more broadly applied to those a Ph.D. student needs as part of his or her literature review.

For now, however, we will simplify the types of *RelFbk* to allow users to reply with only a single grade of "Relevant" ($\oplus$) or "Not Relevant" ($\ominus$). These two assessments require overt action on the part of subjects; "No response" (#) is the default *RelFbk* assessment for documents not receiving any other responses. Again, this frees users from the much more cognitively demanding task of exhaustively assessing every retrieved document. Those documents that "jump out" at users as particularly good – or especially bad – examples of the prototype they seek provide the most informative *RelFbk*. Figure 4.1 also introduces a color-code convention in the electronic version: $\oplus$ will be used to indicate positive *RelFbk* and $\ominus$ to indicate negative *RelFbk*.

### *RelFbk* is Nonmetric

As we move from a cognitive understanding of the users' tasks to statistical analyses of their behaviors, we must understand one important feature of the *RelFbk* data stream: *RelFbk* is **nonmetric** data. That is, while users find it easy and natural to critique retrieved documents with $\oplus$, $\ominus$, and #, they would find it much more difficult to reliably assign *numeric* quantities reflecting something like the relative applicability of each retrieval.

Think for a moment just why this is hard, by imagining your reactions to a typical retrieval. Is the first document to be rated 10 or 6743? If you rate the first document as 10, the second as 6, and the third as 2, then you must ensure that the third document is exactly as much less relevant

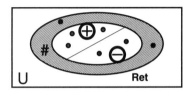

FIGURE 4.2 *RelFbk* Labeling of the *Retr* Set

than the second as the second is from the first. Trying to keep all $Rel(d_i)$ assessments consistent in the metric sense, for many retrieved documents or any other set, makes people crazy.

This is not only a property of relevance assessments. A large literature on psychological assessment [Kruskal, 1977a; Kruskal, 1977b; Shepard et al., 1972] has demonstrated that human subjects can quite easily and reliably sort objects into "piles," and that they like one pile *better than another*. Yet the same people find it more difficult to quantify how much they like each object, let alone make these quantitative assessments consistent with one another. Reliable estimates of both cognitive qualities would be necessary if we are to have a true preference *metric*.*

Rather than assuming that users can provide a separate score for each retrieved document, we will treat this as an ordered nonmetric scale of increasing **preference**:

$$\ominus \prec \# \prec \oplus \tag{4.1}$$

Each of these assumptions about what "relevance" is and how it can be measured is a matter of considerable debate [Wilson, 1973; Froehlich, 1994] and is likely to be the topic of much future work. It is also interesting to note that in our later attempts at a comprehensive model of how and why humans use language, "relevance" again plays a central role (cf. Section 8.2.2).

## 4.2 Extending the Dialog with *RelFbk*

Figure 4.2 focuses on a single instance of *RelFbk*, shown as a labeling over the set of *Retr* documents. But beyond any one reaction to a single

---

* The fact that *RelFbk* is fundamentally nonmetric will have real consequence, for example, in the learning mechanisms that use it; cf. Chapter 7.

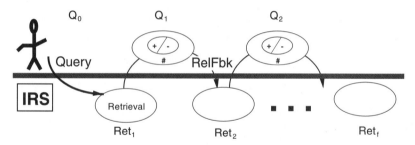

FIGURE 4.3  Query Session, Linked by *RelFbk*

retrieved set *product*, a central premise of the FOA *process* is that users' reactions to just-retrieved documents provide the pivotal linkage between assessments, to form the FOA search dialog. This is perhaps more clear in Figure 4.3, where *RelFbk* is used to link a series of reactions into a **query session**.

Attempts to support this searching process, and then attempts to rigorously evaluate how well software systems support browsing users as they FOA, is one of the most vexing issues within IR evaluation [Daniels et al., 1985; Saracevic et al., 1988; Larson, 1996; Oddy et al., 1992; O'Day and Jeffries, 1993; Cawsey et al., 1992; Russel et al., 1993; Koenemann and Belkin, 1996]. Part of the problem is the misconception that if a search engine works perfectly and the user issues the perfect magic bullet query, out will spill all and only relevant documents! Such simplistic definitions of optimality come naturally to computer scientists; library scientists, who are used to the naturalistic behaviors of real patrons in their libraries, know that a much more extended and nebulous form of support is required.

Marcia Bates's famous **berrypicking** metaphor [Bates, 1986; Bates, 1989] is useful here:

> [A] query is not satisfied by a single final retrieved set, but by a series of selections of individiual references and bits of information at each stage of the ever-modifying search. A bit-at-a-time retrieval of this sort is here called berrypicking. This term is used by analogy to picking huckleberries or blueberries in the forest. The berries are scattered on the bushes; they do not come in bunches. One must pick them one at a time. One could

do berrypicking of information without the search need itself changing (evolving) but ... [we] consider searches that combine both of these characteristics. [Bates, 1989, p. 410]

In addition to highlighting the same iterative browsing behavior central to FOA's characterization of the dialog, the "evolving" character of the information need in Bates's metaphor is also important. Imagine that you are in the forest on an idyllic day with only one purpose: to fill your bucket with the best blueberries you can find. Early in the day, with your whole afternoon in front of you, you are likely to be very choosy. At this juncture, you could bump into a bush full of blueberries that were not as ripe or as large as you *imagine must exist* somewhere else in the forest, and not drop a single one into your basket. But late in the afternoon, if you have had poor luck and little to show for your efforts, you could come across an even worse bush and grab every single berry, even the shriveled ones!

Applying this metaphor to FOA is provocative in many respects. For example, it suggests that maintaining an explicit representation of the retrieved document "basket" might be a useful addition to any search engine interface. It predicts a time course to the distribution of users' *RelFbk* assessments. For now, we simply observe that it seems quite likely that an assessment of one document's relevance will depend greatly on the "basket" of other documents we have already seen. The general idea of thinking of an "evolutionary ecology of information foraging" [Pirolli and Card, 1997] has become less metaphoric and more concrete as information search agents (like the InfoSpiders described in Section 7.6) explore the "environment" of the WWW.

## 4.2.1  Using *RelFbk* for Query Refinement

While Figure 4.2 showed the retrieved set of documents as a simple set, it is interesting to impose the *RelFbk* labeling on the retrieved documents viewed in vector space. Figure 4.4 shows a query vector and a number of retrieved documents, together with a plausible distribution of *RelFbk* over them. That is, we can expect that there is some localized region in vector space where $\oplus$ relevant documents are most likely to occur. If we believe that these positively labeled retrieved documents are in fact clustered, it becomes appropriate to consider a hypothetical **centroid**

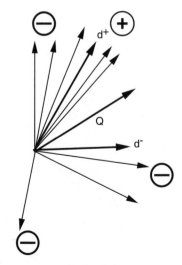

FIGURE 4.4  *RelFbk* Labels in Vector Space

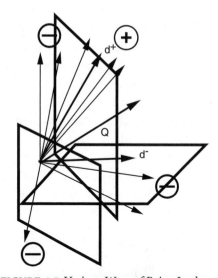

FIGURE 4.5  Various Ways of Being Irrelevant

(average) document $d^+$, which is at the center of all those documents that users have identified as relevant.

It is less reasonable, however, to imagine that the *negatively* labeled ⊖ documents are similarly clustered. Documents that were inappropriately retrieved failed to be relevant for one reason or another; there may be several such reasons. These are shown as discriminating planes in Figure 4.5.

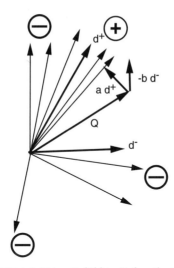

FIGURE 4.6  Using *RelFbk* to Refine the Query

The vector space view also lets us easily portray two very different uses to which *RelFbk* information might be applied. Most typically, *RelFbk* is used to refine the user's query. Figure 4.6 represents this refinement in terms of two changes we can make to the initial query vector. The first is to "take a step toward" the centroid of the positive *RelFbk* cluster. The size of this step[†] reflects how confident we are that the positive cluster centroid is a better characterization of the user's interests than the original query. *Neural-net style learning*

There is one important difference between the query and even a slight perturbation of it toward a cluster's centroid: While the original query vector is often very sparse and results from just those few words used in the user's original query, any movement toward the centroid will include (linear combinations of) all those keywords used in any of the positively labeled documents. The additional difficulty in implementing this more densely filled feature vector becomes a serious obstacle in many system implementations. The fact that *RelFbk*-refined queries involve many more nonzero keyword entries also means that query weighting and matching techniques may be sensitive to this difference.

Seminal work on the use of *RelFbk* was done by Salton, especially with students Rocchio, Brauen, and Ide in the late 1960s and early 1970s [Rocchio, 1966; Brauen, 1969; Salton, 1972]. More recent students have extended the theory of query refinement and related it to topics in machine learning [Buckley et al., 1994; Buckley and Salton, 1995; Allan, 1996].

Some of these experiments explored a second modification to the query vector. In addition to moving *toward* the $d^+$ center of $\oplus$, it is also plausible to move *away from* the irrelevant retrieved documents $\ominus$. As noted earlier, however, it is much less likely that these irrelevant documents are as conveniently clustered. As Salton [Salton and McGill, 1983] reported:

> ... retrieval operation is most effective when the relevant documents as well as the non-relevant documents are tightly clustered and the difference between the two groups is as large as possible.... The *RelFbk* operation is less favorable in the more realistic case where the set of non-relevant documents covers a wider area of the space. [p. 145]

One possible strategy is to take a single element $d^-$ of the irrelevant retrieved documents (for example, the most highly ranked irrelevant retrieval) and define the direction of movement with respect to it alone.

As we have discussed in connection with Figure 4.2, *RelFbk* helps to link individual queries into a browsing sequence. And so, although we have focused here on the simplest form of query refinement, with respect to the users' initial queries, *RelFbk* can be given again and again. An initial query vector is moved toward the centroid of documents identified as relevant (and perhaps away from an especially bad one); this modified query instigates a new retrieval, which is again refined. In practice, it appears that such adjustments result in diminishing returns after only a few iterations of query refinement [Salton and McGill, 1983; Stanfill and Kahle, 1986b].

However, Section 7.3 will discuss a type of FOA in which a document corpus is constantly changing and the user's interest in a topic is long-lived. In this case, we can imagine the query as a **filter** against which a constant stream (e.g., of newly published Web documents) is applied. *RelFbk* has also been used in this setting, to make ongoing changes to the query/filter that continue to improve its effectiveness [Allan, 1996].

Using *RelFbk* for query refinement produces results that are immediately satisfying to the users. First, it automatically generates a new query with which they can continue their browsing process. Second, the statistical analysis of positively labeled retrieved documents can provide other forms of useful information to the users as well. For example, rather than

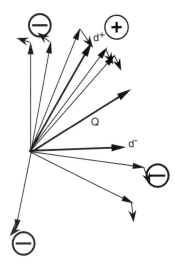

FIGURE 4.7  Document Modifications due to *RelFbk*

simply retrieving a new set of documents, new *keywords* that are not in the users' original queries but are present in positively labeled documents at statistically significantly levels can be suggested to the users as new vocabulary. Conversely, words that were in the original query but are *negatively* correlated with $d^+$ (and/or positively correlated with $d^-$) can also be identified.

## 4.2.2  Using *RelFbk* to Adapt Documents' Indices

An alternative use of *RelFbk* is to make changes to the documents rather than to the query. Previously, the argument was that it is sensible to make the query look more like those documents the users liked; now the argument is the converse: Documents found relevant to a query should be described more like the query used to identify them. Changes made to document vectors according to this heuristic are known as **document modifications** and are shown in Figure 4.7.

Note that unlike query modification, adaptive document modifications made in response to *RelFbk* are not expected to be of (immediate) use to the users who provide it. Instead, the hope is that these changed document representations will be available later, to others who might be searching. As Salton [Salton and McGill, 1983] described the goal:

Following a large number of such interactions documents which are wanted by the users will have been moved slowly into the active portion of the document space – that part in which large numbers of users' queries are concentrated, while items which are normally rejected will be located on the periphery of the space. [p. 145]

This provocative proposal, *allowing a search engine to learn from its users*, is considered in much greater detail in Chapter 7.

### 4.2.3 Summary

We have been discussing *RelFbk* from the individual user's point of view. We've focused on how this information might be collected and how it might be used, both in the short term to modify users' retrievals and in a longer-term way to change the documents' indices. Now we want to consider a third use for *RelFbk* information. When we have more than one system to use for retrieval and would like to evaluate which is doing the better job, users' assessments of retrieved documents' relevance can be used as "grades." If one system can consistently, across a range of typical queries, more frequently retrieve documents that the users mark as relevant and fewer that they mark as irrelevant, then that system is doing a better job.

## 4.3  Aggregated Assessment: Search Engine Performance

The last section considered the assessment problem from the perspective of a single individual, the browsing user. Now we would like to generalize on this individual performance to attempt to obtain statistically significant observations.

### 4.3.1 Underlying Assumptions

As with all scientific models, our attempts to evaluate the performance of a search engine rests on a number of assumptions. Many of these involve the user and simplifying assumptions about how users assess the relevance of documents.

1. **Real FOA versus Laboratory Retrieval.** From the FOA perspective, users retrieve documents as part of an extended search process. They do this often, and because they need the information for something important to them. If we are to collect useful statistics about FOA, we must either capture large numbers of such users "in the act" (i.e., in the process of a real, information-seeking activity) or attempt to create an artificial laboratory setting. The former is much more desirable but makes strong requirements concerning a desirable corpus, a population of users, and access to their retrieval data. So, typically, we must work in a lab. The first big assumption, then, is that our lab setting is similar to real life; i.e., "guinea pig" users will have reactions that mirror real ones.[†]

2. **Intersubject Reliability.** Even if we assume we have a typical user and that this user is engaged in an activity that at least mirrors the natural FOA process, we have to believe that this user will assess relevance the same as everyone else! But clearly, the educational background of each user, the amount of time he or she has to devote to the FOA process relative to the rest of the task, and similar factors will make one user's reaction differ from another's. For example, there is some evidence that stylistic variations also impact perceived relevance [Karlgren, 1996]. The *consensual* relevance statistic (cf. Section 4.3.2) is one mechanism for aggregating across multiple users.

"With Web search engines don't we have access to enormous numbers of users searching the same corpus?" [SG]

This becomes a concern with **intersubject reliability**. If we intend to make changes to document representations based on one user's *RelFbk* opinions, we would like to believe that there is at least some consistency between this user's opinion and those of others. This is a critical area for further research, but some encouraging, preliminary results are available. For example, users of a multilingual retrieval system that presents some documents in their first language ("mother tongue") and others in foreign languages they read less well, seem to be able to provide consistent *RelFbk* data even for documents in their second, weaker language [Sheridan and Ballerini, 1996].

3. **Independence of Interdocument Relevance Assessments.** Finally, notice that the atomic element of data collection for relevance assessments is typically a $(query_i, document_j)$ pair: $document_j$ is relevant to $query_i$. Implicitly, this assumes that the relevance of a document can be assessed *independently* of assessments of other documents. Again, this is a very questionable assumption.

Recall also that often the *proxy* on which the user's relevance assessment depends is distinct from the document itself. The user sees only the proxy, a small sample of the document in question, for example, its title, first paragraph, or bibliographic citation. While we must typically take user reaction to the proxy as an opinion about the whole document, this inference depends critically on how informative the proxy is. Cryptic titles and very condensed citation formats can make these judgments suspect. And of course the user's ultimate assessment of whether a document is relevant, after having read it, remains a paradox.

## 4.3.2 Consensual Relevance

In most search engine evaluation, the assumption has been that a single expert can be trusted to provide reliable relevance assessments. Whether any one, "omniscient" individual is capable of providing reliable data about the appropriate set of documents to be retrieved remains a foundational issue within IR. For example, a number of papers in a recent special issue of the *Journal of the American Society for Information Systems* devoted to relevance advocated a move toward a more "user-centered, situational" view of relevance [Froehlich, 1994].

Our attention to the opinions of individual users suggests the possibility of *combining* evidence from *multiple* human judges. Rather than having relevance be a Boolean determination made by a single expert, we will consider "relevance" to be a *consensual, central tendency of the searching users' opinions*. The relevance assessments of individual users and the resulting central tendency of relevance is suggested by Figure 4.8. Two features of this definition are significant. First, consensual relevance posits a "consumers'" perspective on what will count as IR system success. A document's relevance to a query is not going to be determined by an expert in the topical area, but by the users who are doing the searching. If they find it relevant, it's relevant, whether or not some domain expert thinks the document "should" have been retrieved.

Second, consensual relevance becomes a statistical, aggregate property of multiple users' reactions rather than a discrete feature elicited from any one individual. By making relevance a *statistical* measure, our confidence in the relevance of a document (with respect to a query)

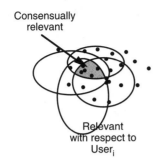

Consensually
relevant

Relevant
with respect to
User$_i$

FIGURE 4.8  Consensual Relevance

increases as more relevance assessment data are collected. This reliance on statistical stability creates a strong link between IR and machine learning (cf. Chapter 7). Allen's investigation into idiosyncratic cognitive styles of browsing users [Allen, 1992] and Wilbur's assessment of the reliability of *RelFbk* across users [Wilbur, 1998] provide a more textured view of how multiple relevance assessments can be compared and combined.

It seems, however, that our move from omniscient to consensual relevance has only made the problem of evaluation that much more difficult. Test corpora must be large enough to provide robust tests for retrieval methods, and multiple queries are necessary to evaluate the overall performance of a search engine. Getting even a single person's opinion about the relevance of a document to a particular query is hard, and we are now interested in getting many! However, software like RAVE (cf. Section 4.4) allows an IR experimenter to effectively collect large numbers of relevance assessments for an arbitrary document corpus.

## 4.3.3  Traditional Evaluation Methodologies

Before surveying all of the ways in which evaluation *might* be performed, it is worthwhile to sketch how it has typically been done in the past [Cleverdon and Mills, 1963]. In the beginning, computers were slow and had very limited disk space and even more limited memories; initial test corpora needed to be small, too. One benefit of these small corpora was that it allowed at least the possibility of having a set of test queries compared *exhaustively* against every document in the corpus.

The source of these test queries, and the assessment of their relevance, varied in early experiments. For example, in the Cranfield experiments [Lancaster, 1968], 1400 documents in metallurgy were searched according to 221 queries generated by some of the documents' authors. In Salton's experiments with the ADI corpus, 82 papers presented at a 1963 American Documentation Institute meeting were searched against 35 queries and evaluated by students and "staff experts" associated with Salton's lab [Salton and Lesk, 1968]. Lancaster's construction of the MEDLARS collection was similar [Lancaster, 1969].

As computers have increased in capacity, reasonable evaluation has required much larger corpora. The Text Retrieval Conference (TREC), begun in 1992 and still held annually, has set a new standard for search engine evaluation [Harman, 1995]. The TREC methodology is notable in several respects. First, it avoids exhaustive assessment of all documents by using the **pooling** method, a proposal for the construction of "ideal" test collections that predates TREC by decades [Sparck Jones and van Rijsbergen, 1976]. The basic idea is to use each search engine independently and then "pool" their results to form a set of those documents that have at least this recommendation of potential relevance. All search engines retrieve ranked lists of $k$ potentially relevant documents, and the *union* of these retrieved sets is presented to human judges for relevance assessment.

In the case of TREC, $k = 100$ and the human assessors were retired security analysts, like those that work at the National Security Agency (NSA) watching the world's communications. Because only documents retrieved by one of the systems being tested are evaluated there remains the possibility that relevant documents remain undiscovered, and we might worry that our evaluations will change as new systems retrieve new documents and these are evaluated. Recent analysis seems to suggest that, at least in the case of the TREC corpus, evaluations are in fact quite stable [Voorhees, 1998].

An important consequence of this methodological convenience is that *unassessed documents are assumed to be irrelevant.* This creates an unfortunate dependence on the retrieval methods used to nominate documents, which we can expect to be most pronounced when the methods are similar to one another. For example, if the alternative retrieved sets are the result of manipulating single parameters of the same basic retrieval procedure, the resulting assessments may have overlap with, and hence be useless for comparison of, methods producing significantly different retrieval sets. For the TREC collection, this problem was handled by drawing the top 200 documents from a wide range of 25 methods, which had little overlap [Harman, 1995]. Vogt [Vogt and Cottrell, 1998] has explored how similarities and differences between retrieval methods can be similarly exploited as part of combined, hybrid retrieval systems (cf. Section 7.5.4).

It is also possible to *sample* a small subset of a corpus, submit the entire sample to review by the human expert, and *extrapolate* from the number of relevant documents found to an expected number across the entire corpus. One famous example of this methodology is Blair and Maron's assessment of IBM's STAIRS retrieval system [Blair and Maron, 1985] of the early 1980s. This evaluation studied the real-world use of STAIRS by a legal firm as part of a **litigation support** task: 40,000 memos, design documents, etc. were to be searched with respect to 51 different queries. The lawyers themselves then agreed to evaluate the documents' relevance. As they reported:

> To find the unretrieved relevant documents we developed sample frames consisting of subsets of *unretrieved* databases that we believed to be rich in relevant documents. . . . Random samples were taken from these subsets, and the samples were examined by the lawyers in a blind evaluation; the lawyers were not aware they were evaluating sample sets rather than retrieved sets they had personally generated. The total number of relevant documents that existed in these subsets could then be estimated. We sampled from subsets of the database rather than the entire database because, for most queries, the percentage of relevant documents in the database was less than 2%, making it almost impossible to have both manageable sample sizes and a high level of confidence in the resulting Recall estimates. Of course, no extrapolation to the entire database could be made from these Recall calculations. Nonetheless, the estimation of the number of relevant unretrieved documents in the subsets did give us a maximum value for Recall for each request. [Blair and Maron, 1985, pp. 291–293]

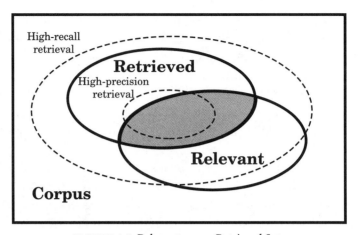

FIGURE 4.9  Relevant versus Retrieved Sets

Killing the
messenger

This is a difficult methodology, but it allows some of the best estimates of Recall available. And the news was not good: On average, retrievals captured only 20 percent of relevant documents![†]

In short, methodologies for valid search engine evaluations require much more sophistication and care than is generally appreciated. Careful experimental design [Tague-Sutcliffe, 1992], statistical analysis [Hull, 1993], and presentation [Keen, 1992] are all critical.

### 4.3.4  Basic Measures

Figure 4.9 shows the relationship between relevant (*Rel*) and retrieved (*Retr*) sets as a Venn diagram, against the backdrop of the universe $U$ of the rest of the documents of the corpus. Obviously, our focus should be on those documents that are in the *intersection* of *Rel* and *Retr* and on making this intersection as large as possible. Informally, we will be most happy with a *Rel* set when it best overlaps with the *Retr* set, and therefore we seek evaluation measures that reflect this. The basic relations between the *sizes* of these sets can also be captured in the **contingency table** of Table 4.1.

We know we want the intersection of the *Rel* and *Retr* sets to be large, but large relative to what?! As mentioned in Chapter 1, if we are most focused on the *Rel* set and use it as our standard of comparison,

TABLE 4.1  Contingency Table

|  | Relevant | Not Relevant |  |
|---|---|---|---|
| Retrieved | $Ret \wedge Rel$ | $Ret \leftrightarrow \overline{Rel}$ | $NRet^a$ |
| Not retrieved | $\overline{Ret} \leftrightarrow Rel$ | $\overline{Ret} \leftrightarrow \overline{Rel}$ | $NNRet^b$ |
|  | $NRel^c$ | $NNRel^d$ | $NDoc^e$ |

[a] $NRet$ is the number of retrieved documents.
[b] $NNRet$ is the number of documents not retrieved.
[c] $NRel$ is the number of relevant documents.
[d] $NNRel$ is the number of irrelevant documents.
[e] $NDoc$ is the total number of documents.

we'd like to know what fraction of these we've retrieved. This ratio is called **recall**:

$$Recall \equiv \frac{|Ret \cap Rel|}{|Rel|} \tag{4.2}$$

Anticipating the probabilistic analysis of Section 5.5, we can think of *Recall* as (an estimate of) the *conditional probability* that a document will be retrieved, given that it is relevant: $Pr(Ret|Rel)$.

Conversely, if we instead focus on the *Ret* set, we are most interested in what fraction of these are relevant; this ratio is called precision:

$$Precision \equiv \frac{|Ret \cap Rel|}{|Ret|} \tag{4.3}$$

Similarly, this is the probability that a document will be relevant, given that it is retrieved: $Pr(Rel|Ret)$. A closely related but less common measure is called **fallout**, where we (perversely!) focus on the irrelevant documents and the fraction of them retrieved:

$$Fallout \equiv \frac{|\overline{Ret} \cap Rel|}{|\overline{Ret}|} \tag{4.4}$$

The close relationship between these three measures can be defined precisely, if the generality $G$ of the query (cf. Section 4.3.7) is known:

$$Precision = \frac{Recall \cdot G}{Recall \cdot G + Fallout \cdot (1 - G)} \tag{4.5}$$

This is $Pr(Ret|\overline{Rel})$. These two measures, *Recall* and *Precision,* have remained the bedrock of search engine evaluation since they were first introduced by Kent in 1955 [Kent et al., 1955; Saracevic, 1975]. By far the most common measures of search engine performance are just the pair of measures, *Precision* and *Recall.*

Ideally, of course, we'd like a system that has *both* high precision and high recall: only relevant documents and all of them. But real-world, practical systems must select documents based on features that are only statistically useful indicators of relevance; we can never be sure. In this case efforts made to improve recall must retrieve more documents, and it is likely that precision will suffer as a consequence. The best we can hope for is some balance.

In some applications it is nevertheless desirable to evaluate IR system performance according to a single measure rather than the two-dimensional *Recall/Precision* criteria.[†] We will return to this topic in Section 4.3.8.

*Single dimensions for simple minds*

### 4.3.5 Ordering the *Retr* Set

> Do not worry about large numbers of results: the best ones come first! (www.AltaVista.com, 1998)

The next step is to move beyond thinking of *Retr* as simply a set. We will suppose that retrieved documents are returned *in some order* by the search engine, reflecting its assessment of how well each document matches the query. Following current Web vernacular, we will call this ordering of the *Retr* set a **hitlist** and a retrieved document's position its **hitlist rank** $Rank(d_i)$. This is a positive integer assigned to each document in the *Retr* set, in descending order of similarity with respect to the matching function $Match(q, d)$:

$$Match(q, d) \in \Re$$

$$Rank(d) \in \mathcal{N}^+$$

$$Rank(d_i) < Rank(d_j) \Leftrightarrow Match(q, d_i) > Match(q, d_j) \quad (4.6)$$

Sparck Jones [Sparck Jones, 1972] and others have historically referred to a document's rank in *Retr* as its "coordination level" (cf. Eq. 3.36). Strictly speaking, coordination level refers to the number of keywords shared by document and query. In Boolean retrieval systems, sensitive only to the presence or absence of keywords, ranking by co-ordination level may be the only available measure on document/query similarity.

For long queries, hitlist rank and coordination level are likely to be similar, because it is unlikely that different documents will match exactly the same number of words from the query. But for short queries, it is likely that coordination level will only *partially order* the *Retr* set. This is why van Rijsbergen, p. 161, speaking of the Boolean systems typical at that time, said, "Unfortunately, the ranking generated by a matching function is rarely a simple ordering, but more commonly a weak ordering." Most modern search engines, however, exploit keyword *weightings* and can provide much more refined measures, thereby providing a **total ordering** of the hitlist.

According to the Probability Ranking Principle (cf. Section 5.5.1), a retrieval system is performing optimally if it retrieves documents in order of decreasing *probability of relevance*. For now we simply assume that there is a total ordering imposed over *Retr*. We will use the hitlist ranking to effectively define a series of retrievals. Setting a very high threshold on this ordering would mean retrieving a very small set, while setting a lower threshold will retrieve a much larger one.

Now consider a particular query $q$ and the set $Rel_q$ of relevant documents associated with it. Assuming that *Retr* is totally ordered makes it possible for us to define the fundamental analytic tool for search engine performance: the **Recall/Precision curve** (Re/Pre curve). The basic procedure is to consider each retrieved document in hitlist rank order and to ask for the precision and recall of the retrieval of all documents up to and including this one.

Consider the first of the two hypothetical retrievals shown in Table 4.2.

With respect to this query, we will assume there are exactly five relevant documents out of a total of 25 in the corpus. The very first one retrieved is deemed relevant; if we stopped retrieval at this point, our recall would be 0.2 (because we would have retrieved one of five relevant documents), and our precision is perfect (the one retrieved document is relevant). Our good luck continues as we consider the next document, which is also relevant; this generates a second Re/Pre data point of (0.4,1.0). We are not so lucky with the third document retrieved; precision drops to 0.67 and recall remains at 0.4. Proceeding down the

TABLE 4.2 Two Hypothetical Retrievals

| | Query 1 | | | | Query 2 | | | |
| --- | --- | --- | --- | --- | --- | --- | --- | --- |
| | Relevant? | NRel | Recall | Precision | Relevant? | NRel | Recall | Precision |
| 1 | 1 | 1 | 0.20 | 1.00 | 0 | 0 | 0.00 | 0.00 |
| 2 | 1 | 2 | 0.40 | 1.00 | 0 | 0 | 0.00 | 0.00 |
| 3 | 0 | 2 | 0.40 | 0.67 | 0 | 0 | 0.00 | 0.00 |
| 4 | 1 | 3 | 0.60 | 0.75 | 1 | 1 | 0.50 | 0.25 |
| 5 | 0 | 3 | 0.60 | 0.60 | 0 | 1 | 0.50 | 0.20 |
| 6 | 0 | 3 | 0.60 | 0.50 | 0 | 1 | 0.50 | 0.17 |
| 7 | 0 | 3 | 0.60 | 0.43 | 0 | 1 | 0.50 | 0.14 |
| 8 | 0 | 3 | 0.60 | 0.38 | 0 | 1 | 0.50 | 0.13 |
| 9 | 0 | 3 | 0.60 | 0.33 | 0 | 1 | 0.50 | 0.11 |
| 10 | 0 | 3 | 0.60 | 0.30 | 0 | 1 | 0.50 | 0.10 |
| 11 | 0 | 3 | 0.60 | 0.27 | 0 | 1 | 0.50 | 0.09 |
| 12 | 0 | 3 | 0.60 | 0.25 | 0 | 1 | 0.50 | 0.08 |
| 13 | 0 | 3 | 0.60 | 0.23 | 0 | 1 | 0.50 | 0.08 |
| 14 | 0 | 3 | 0.60 | 0.21 | 0 | 1 | 0.50 | 0.07 |
| 15 | 1 | 4 | 0.80 | 0.27 | 1 | 2 | 1.00 | 0.13 |
| 16 | 0 | 4 | 0.80 | 0.25 | 0 | 2 | 1.00 | 0.13 |
| 17 | 0 | 4 | 0.80 | 0.24 | 0 | 2 | 1.00 | 0.12 |
| 18 | 0 | 4 | 0.80 | 0.22 | 0 | 2 | 1.00 | 0.11 |
| 19 | 0 | 4 | 0.80 | 0.21 | 0 | 2 | 1.00 | 0.11 |
| 20 | 0 | 4 | 0.80 | 0.20 | 0 | 2 | 1.00 | 0.10 |
| 21 | 0 | 4 | 0.80 | 0.19 | 0 | 2 | 1.00 | 0.10 |
| 22 | 0 | 4 | 0.80 | 0.18 | 0 | 2 | 1.00 | 0.09 |
| 23 | 0 | 4 | 0.80 | 0.17 | 0 | 2 | 1.00 | 0.09 |
| 24 | 0 | 4 | 0.80 | 0.17 | 0 | 2 | 1.00 | 0.08 |
| 25 | 1 | 5 | 1.00 | 0.20 | 0 | 2 | 1.00 | 0.08 |

retrieval in rank order, and plotting each point in this fashion gives the Re/Pre curve shown in Figure 4.10.

At this point we can already make several observations. Asymptotically, we know that the final recall must go to one; once we have retrieved every document we've also retrieved every relevant document. The precision will be the ratio of the number of relevant documents to the total corpus size. Ordinarily, unless we are interested in very general queries or very small sets of documents, this ratio will be very close to zero.

The other end of the curve, however, turns out to be much less stable. We would hope that a retrieval system's very first candidate for retrieval, the document with hitlist rank = 1, will be relevant, but it may not be.

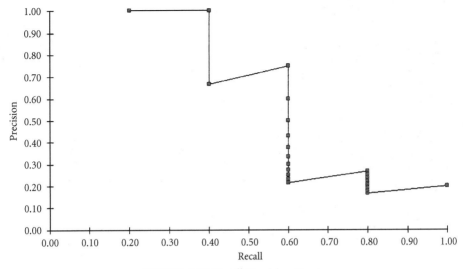

FIGURE 4.10  Recall/Precision Curve

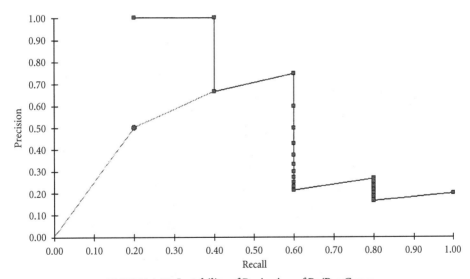

FIGURE 4.11  Instability of Beginning of Re/Pre Curve

Figure 4.11 shows a second pair of hypothetical data points (dashed line), corresponding to the case that a *single* irrelevant document is ranked higher than the relevant ones. This relatively small change in assessment creates a fairly dramatic effect on the curve, with real consequence once

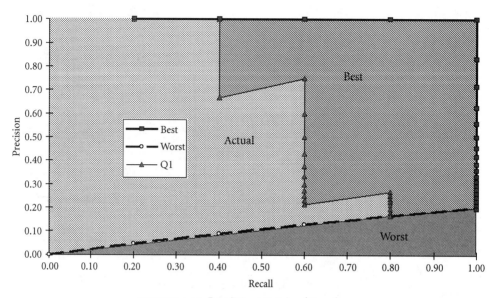

FIGURE 4.12  Best/Worst Retrieval Envelope

we need to juxtapose multiple queries' curves (see Section 4.3.7). Such instability is an inevitable consequence of the definitions of *Precision* and *Recall*: If the first retrieved document happens to be relevant, its Re/Pre coordinates will be less than 1, and $\frac{1}{NRel}$ greater than 1; otherwise it will be $< 0, 0 >$.

Figure 4.12 puts this particular retrieval in the context of the best and worst retrievals we might imagine. The best possible retrieval (hashed) would be to retrieve the five relevant documents first, and then all other documents. This would produce the upper, square Re/Pre curve. Alternatively, the worst possible retrieval (shaded) would retrieve all but the relevant documents before returning these; this produces the lower line.

## 4.3.6  Normalized Recall and Precision

The best/worst "envelope" surrounding an actual Re/Pre curve is related to a similar comparison known as **normalized recall** [Rocchio, 1966]. Imagine plotting the *fraction* of relevant documents retrieved as a function of the fraction of the total number of documents retrieved. Such a function is plotted in Figure 4.13. Comparing the area between the actual retrieval and the worst case (shaded) to the total area between the

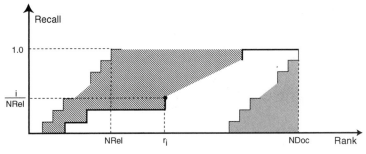

FIGURE 4.13 Normalized Recall

best (hashed) and worst cases (that above the region) is very much like the best/worst-case envelope of Figure 4.12.

We can derive expressions for this area. Let $r_i$ be the hitlist rank of the $i$th relevant document. Then the area under the curve corresponding to any actual query is (if we define $r_0 = 0$):

$$Actual = \sum_{i=1}^{NRel}(r_i - r_{i-1})\frac{i}{NRel} \tag{4.7}$$

In the best case $r_i = i$:

$$Best = \sum_{i=1}^{NRel}\frac{(i - (i - 1)) \cdot i}{NRel} = \frac{1}{NRel}\sum_{i=1}^{NRel}i = \frac{NRel + 1}{2} \tag{4.8}$$

when $NRel \rightarrow \infty$. In the worst case $r_i = NDoc - NRel + i$:

$$Worst = \sum_{i=1}^{NRel}\frac{((NDoc - NRel + i) - (NDoc - NRel + i - 1)) \cdot i}{NRel}$$

$$= NDoc - NRel \tag{4.9}$$

## 4.3.7 Multiple Retrievals across Varying Queries

It should come as no surprise, given the wide range of activities in which FOA is a crucial component, that there is enormous variability among the kinds of queries produced by users. The next step of our construction is therefore to go beyond a single query to consider the performance of a system across a set of queries.

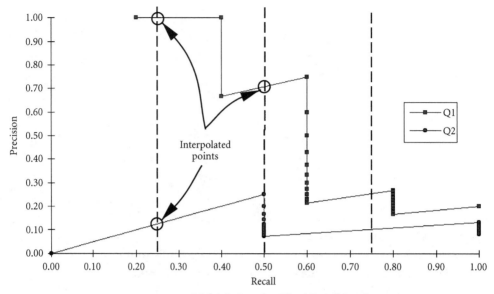

FIGURE 4.14  Multiple Queries, Fixed Recall Levels

One obvious dimension to this variability concerns the "breadth" of the query: How general is it? If the *Rel* set for a query is known, this can be quantified by **generality**, comparing the size of *Rel* to the total number of documents in the corpus:

$$Generality_q \equiv \frac{|Rel_q|}{NDoc} \qquad (4.10)$$

There are many other ways in which queries can vary, and the fact that different retrieval techniques seem to be much more effective on some types of queries than others makes this a critical issue for further research. For now, however, we will treat all queries interchangeably but consider average performance across a set of them.

Figure 4.14 juxtaposes two Re/Pre curves corresponding to two queries. Query 1 is as before, and Query 2 is a more specific query, as evidenced by its lower asymptote. Even with these two queries, we can see that, in general, there is no guarantee that we will have Re/Pre data points at any particular recall level. This necessitates **interpolation** of data points at desired recall levels. The typical interpolation is done at prespecified recall levels, for example, 0, 0.25, 0.5, 0.75, and 1.0. As van Rijsbergen, p. 152 discusses, a number of interpolation techniques

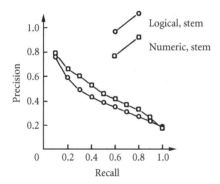

FIGURE 4.15  11-Point Average Re/Pre Curves.
From [Salton and Lesk, 1968]. Reproduced with permission of Prentice-Hall

are available, each with its own biases. Because each new relevant document added to our retrieved set will produce an increase in precision (causing the saw-tooth pattern observed in the graph), simply using the next available data point above a desired recall level will produce an overestimate, while using the prior data point will produce an underestimate.

With preestablished recall levels, we can now juxtapose an arbitrary number of queries and average over them at these levels. For 30 years the most typical presentation of results within the IR community was the **11-point average** curves, like those shown in Figure 4.15 [Salton and Lesk, 1971; Salton and Lesk, 1968]. (These data happen to show performance on the ADI corpus of Boolean versus weighted retrieval methods; they include only the last 10 data points.)

It is not uncommon to see research data reduced even further. If queries are *averaged* at fixed recall levels and then all of these recall levels are *averaged* together, we can produce a single number that measures retrieval system performance. Note the serious bias this last averaging across recall levels produces, however. It says that we are as interested in how well the system did at the 90 percent recall level as at 10 percent!? Virtually all users care more about the first screenful of hits they retrieve than the last.

This motivates another way to use the same basic recall/precision data. Rather than measuring at fixed recall levels, statistics are collected at the 10-, 25-, and 50-document retrieval levels. Precision within the first 10 or 15 documents is arguably a much closer measure of standard browser effectiveness than any other single number.

All such atempts to reduce the Re/Pre plot to a single number are bound to introduce artifacts of their own. In most cases the full Re/Pre curve picture is certainly worth a thousand words. Plotting the entire curve is straightforward and immediately interpretable, and it lets viewers draw more of their own conclusions.

We must guard against taking our intuitions based on this tiny example (with only 25 documents in the entire corpus) too seriously when considering results from standard corpora and queries. For example, our first query had fully 20 percent of the corpus as relevant; even our second query had 8 percent. In a corpus of a million documents, this would mean 80,000 of them were relevant!? Much more typical are queries with a tiny fraction, perhaps 0.001 percent, relevant. This will mean that the precision asymptote is very nearly zero. Also, we are likely to have many more relevant documents, resulting in a much smoother curve.

### 4.3.8 One-Parameter Criteria

This section began with recall and precision, the two most typical measures of search engine performance. From that beginning, richer, more elaborate characterizations of how well the system is performing have been considered. But even having the *two* measures of recall and precision, it is not a simple matter to decide whether one system is better or worse than another. What are we to think of a system that has good recall but poor precision, relative to another with the opposite feature?

For example, if we wish to optimize a search engine with respect to one or more design parameters (e.g., the exact form of the query/document matching function, cf. Section 5.3.1), effective optimization becomes much more difficult in **multicriterial** cases. Such thinking has generated **composite** measures based on the basic components of recall and precision.

For example, Jardine and van Rijsbergen [Jardine and van Rijsbergen, 1971; van Rijsbergen, 1973] originally proposed the **F-measure** for this purpose:

$$F_\beta \equiv \frac{(\beta^2 + 1) \cdot Precision \cdot Recall}{\beta^2 Precision + Recall} \qquad (4.11)$$

van Rijsbergen, p. 174 * has since defined the closely related **effectiveness**

---

* Van Rijsbergen's original paper used the function symbol $E$ rather than the $F$ we use here. The substitution is made to maintain the $E \rightarrow$ "effectiveness" mnemonic.

of measure $E$, which uses $\alpha$ to smoothly vary the emphasis given to precision versus recall:

$$E_\alpha \equiv 1 - \left( \frac{\alpha}{Precision} + \frac{1 - \alpha}{Recall} \right)^{-1} \qquad (4.12)$$

The transform $\alpha = \frac{1}{\beta^2 + 1}$ converts easily between the two formulations, with $E = 1 - F$. Van Rijsbergen, p. 174 also presents an argument that a perfectly even-handed balance of precision against recall at $\alpha = 0.5$ is most appropriate. Setting $\alpha = 0.5$, $\beta = 1$ also has the pleasing consequence that the $F$, statistic corresponds to the **harmonic mean** of *Precision* and *Recall.*

As discussed at some length in Section 7.4, it is possible to view retrieval as a type of classification task: Given a set of features for each document (e.g., the keywords it contains), classifiy it as either *Rel* or $\overline{Rel}$ with respect to some query. Lewis and Gale [Lewis and Gale, 1994] used the $F_\beta$ measure in the context of text classification tasks, and they recommend a focus on the same $\beta = 1.0$ balance. **Classification accuracy** measures how often the classification is correct. If we associate the choice to retrieve a document with classifying it as *Rel*, we can use the variables defined in the contingency table of (Table 4.1):

$$Accuracy \equiv \frac{|\ Retr \cap Rel\ | + |\ \overline{Retr} \cap \overline{Rel}\ |}{NDoc} \qquad (4.13)$$

## Sliding Ratio

The fact that the *Retr* set is ordered makes it useful to compare two rank orderings directly. If the "correct," idealized ranking is known (for example, one corresponding to perfectly decreasing probability of relevance), then an actual search engine's hitlist ranking can be compared against this standard. More typically, the rankings of two retrieval systems are compared to one another.

Given two rankings, we will prefer the one that ranks relevant documents ahead of irrelevant ones. If our relevance assessments are binary, with each document simply marked as relevant or irrelevant,* the normalized recall measure considered in Section 4.3.6 (or the

---

* As always, these assessments of relevance are with respect to some particular query.

expected search length measure to be described in Section 4.3.10) is the best we can do in distinguishing the two rankings.

But if we assume instead that it is possible to impose a more refined measure $Rel(d_i)$ than simply $Rel/\overline{Rel}$ (e.g., recall the richer preference scale of Figure 4.1), more sophisticated measures are possible. In this case, we prefer a ranking that ranks $d_i$ ahead of $d_j$ just in case $Rel(d_i) > Rel(d_j)$. One way to quantify this preference is to sum the $Rel(d_i)$ for the $NRet$ most highly ranked documents:

$$\sum_{i=1}^{NRet} Rel(d_i) \tag{4.14}$$

The ratio of this measure, computed for each of the two systems' rankings, is called the **sliding ratio** score [Pollack, 1968]:

$$\frac{\sum_{i=1}^{Rank_1(d_i) \leq NRet} Rel(d_i)}{\sum_{i=1}^{Rank_2(d_i) \leq NRet} Rel(d_i)} \tag{4.15}$$

As $NRet$ increases, this ratio comes closer to unity:

$$\lim_{NRet \to NDoc} \frac{\sum_{i=1}^{Rank_1(d_i) \leq NRet} Rel(d_i)}{\sum_{i=1}^{Rank_2(d_i) \leq NRet} Rel(d_i)} = 1 \tag{4.16}$$

and so it is most useful for distinguishing between two rankings when only a small $NRet$ is considered.

## Point Alienation

The sliding ratio measure provides a more discriminating measure but depends entirely on the availability of *metric $Rel(d_i)$* measures for retrieved documents. As discussed in Section 4.1.1, it is much easier to derive nonmetric assessments directly from *RelFbk* data given naturally as part of users' browsing:

$$\ominus \prec \# \prec \oplus \tag{4.17}$$

In an effort to exploit the nonmetric preferences often provided by human subjects, Guttman [Guttman, 1978] defined a measure known as **point alienation**. Bartell has pioneered a variation of it for use with document rankings rated by *RelFbk* [Bartell et al., 1994a]. The basic idea is deceptively simple: Compare the difference in rank between two differentially preferred documents to the *absolute difference* of these ranks:

$$J \equiv \sum_{d \succ d'} \frac{Rank(d) - Rank(d')}{|Rank(d) - Rank(d')|} \qquad (4.18)$$

If $d$ is really preferred over $d' - (d \succ d') -$ (e.g., if some user has marked $d$ as *Rel* but said nothing about $d'$), we can hope that $Rank(d) < Rank(d')$,* and so the numerator $(Rank(d) - Rank(d'))$ will be negative; if, on the other hand, the two documents are incorrectly ordered by the ranking, the numerator will be positive. Comparing this arithmetic difference to its absolute value, and then summing over the rankings for all pairs of documents $(d, d')$ that are differentially preferred $(d \succ d')$ gives Equation 4.18.

## 4.3.9  Test Corpora

By **test corpora** we refer to collections of documents that have associated with them a series of queries for which relevance assesments are available. One of the earliest such test sets was a collection of 1400 research papers on aerodynamics developed by C. Cleverdon in the mid-1960s, known as the Cranfield corpus [Cleverdon and Mills, 1963]. For most of the 1980s, a set of corpora known as CACM, CISI, INSPEC, MED, and NPL (sometimes referred to as the **Cornell corpora**) were developed, maintained, and distributed by Gerald Salton and his students at Cornell; it became the de facto standard for testing within the IR community. For some time, the most influential test corpora have been the ***TREC corpora***[1] associated with the Text Retrieval Evaluation Conference meetings [Harman, 1995].

Table 4.3 gives a sample of statistics for a number of the most widely used corpora. One obvious trend is the increasing size of these collections over time. The ***Reuters corpus***[2] classification labels are invaluable for

---

* Note that my notation deviates from Bartell's somewhat. In particular, we assume here that *Rank*() increases from most- to least-highly ranked document, so that the first element of the hitlist has *Rank* = 1.

[1]  potomac.ncsl.nist.gov/trec/

[2]  www.research.att.com/ lewis/reuters21578.html

TABLE 4.3  Common Test Corpora

| Collection | NDocs | NQrys | Size (MB) | Term/Doc | Q-D RelAss |
|---|---|---|---|---|---|
| ADI | 82 | 35 | | | |
| AIT | 2109 | 14 | 2 | 400 | >10,000 |
| CACM | 3204 | 64 | 2 | 24.5 | |
| CISI | 1460 | 112 | 2 | 46.5 | |
| Cranfield | 1400 | 225 | 2 | 53.1 | |
| LISA | 5872 | 35 | 3 | | |
| Medline | 1033 | 30 | 1 | | |
| NPL | 11,429 | 93 | 3 | | |
| OSHMED | 34,8566 | 106 | 400 | 250 | 16,140 |
| Reuters | 21,578 | 672 | 28 | 131 | |
| TREC | 740,000 | 200 | 2000 | 89-3543 | $\approx 100,000$ |

training classifiers (cf. Section 7.4). With our AIT corpus, the OSHMED [Hersh, 1994] is one of the few to provide multiple relevance assessments of the same $\langle q, d \rangle$ pair.

Figure 4.16 shows a sample query from the TREC experiments. For this query, and hundreds like it, considerable manual effort has gone into assessing whether documents in the TREC corpus should be considered "relevant." Note the way the "basic" query (Line 2) has been embellished with general and specific topical orientation (Lines 1 and 3), important terms and abbreviations have been explicated, etc. This is much more

```
1 >     Science and Technology
2 >     AIDS treatments
3 >     Document will mention a specific AIDS or ARC treatment.
4 >     To be r, a document must include a reference to at least one specific potential Acquired
        Immune Deficiency Syndrome (AIDS or AIDS Related Complex treatment.
5 >     1. Acquired Immune Deficiency Syndrome (AIDS, AIDS Related Complex (ARC
6 >     2. treatment, drug, pharmaceutical
7 >     3. test, trials, study
8 >     4. AZT, TPA
9 >     5. Genentech, Burroughs-Wellcome
10 >    ARC - AIDS Related Complex
11 >    . A set of symptoms similar to AIDS.
12 >    AZT - Azidothymidine, a drug for the treatment of Acquired Immune Deficiency
        Syndrome, its related pneumonia, and for severe AIDS Related Complex.
13 >    TPA - Tissue Plasminogen Activator - a blood clot-dissolving drug.
14 >    treatment - any drug or procedure used to reduce the debilitating effects of AIDS or
        ARC.
```

FIGURE 4.16  TREC Query

information than most users typically provide, but it also allows much more refined assessment of systems' performance.

As the testing procedures of the TREC participants have developed over the years, multiple "tracks" have formed, corresponding to typical search engine usage patterns. The task on which we have focused throughout this section is termed **ad hoc retrieval**, in the sense that a constant corpus is repeatedly searched with respect to a series of ad hoc queries. This is distinguished from the **routing** task, which assumes a relatively constant standing set of queries (for example, corresponding to the interests of various employees of the same corporation). Then, an ongoing stream of documents is compared, with relevant documents routed to appropriate recipients.

More recently, a special type of routing termed **filtering** has also been considered. In the filtering task, the standing query is allowed to adapt to the stream of *RelFbk* generated by the users as they receive and evaluate routed documents (cf. Section 7.3).

## 4.3.10 Other Measures

The performance measures already listed are by far the most common ways in which search engines are evaluated in the literature. Several others, however, have been important in the past and may again prove useful in some situations.

### Expected Search Length

The ordered list of relevance assessments described in Section 4.3.5 also recommends another, holistic evaluation of the entire retrieval's behavior; this method is known as **expected search length** (ESL). ESL considers the length of a "path" as users walk down the ordered hitlist, measuring how many irrelevant documents were seen on this path before each relevant document; "expected" refers to the average length of each path ending in a relevant document. Cooper initially proposed this model to measure the work a search engine saves, in comparison to searching the entire collection at random [Cooper, 1968].

Given that a search engine retrieves documents in hitlist order, ESL also requires a criterion by which the users' wandering paths are stopped. Van Rijsbergen, p. 160 discusses a number of predicates that might be used to terminate the search: some fixed number of relevant documents, some fraction of all relevant documents, etc. Because the generality of queries can vary considerably, it is desirable to terminate the ESL after some *fixed* fraction $E$ of relevant documents has been retrieved.

For this same reason, it makes sense to normalize ESL with respect to the number of relevant documents we might expect to retrieve if we were retrieving at random. If we use *NRet* for the number of retrieved documents (i.e., those satisfying the predicate mentioned earlier), we can estimate the expected random search length *RandSL* as:

$$RandSL \equiv \frac{NRet \cdot (NDoc - Rel)}{Rel + 1} \qquad (4.19)$$

Then the **expected search length reduction factor**

$$ESLRF \equiv \frac{RandSL - ESL}{RandSL} \qquad (4.20)$$

captures the amount a real search method improves over the random case.

?2

### Operating Characteristic Curves

Swets [Swets, 1963] enumerated a number of abstract desiderata (quoted by van Rijsbergen, p. 155 ) that we might wish for any assessment measure. According to these, IR's standard Re/Pre plot leaves much to be desired, in particular because this two-dimensional assessment makes direct comparison impossible. Swets therefore recommended an analysis from the perspective of signal detection, based on several key assumptions:

**ASSUMPTION 1**   *There is a "relevant" signal we wish to distinguish from background noise. We can consider the worst case to be comparison against an "irrelevant" signal, with both signals imposed over the data collection. We can imagine that this signal is generated by the presence or absence of some keywords.*

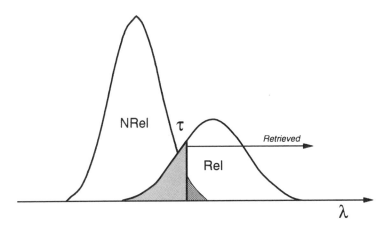

FIGURE 4.17 Distinguishing between Overlapping Distributions

**ASSUMPTION 2**  *These two signals are to be discriminated according to only a single dimension.*

**ASSUMPTION 3**  *These signals are both distributed* normally *across the corpus.*

In this idealized case, we get a picture similar to Figure 4.17. Then, because our corpus has been ordered by the ranking, the goal becomes to select a value $Rank_\tau$ that best separates these two modal distributions.

Using a simple retrieval rule that retrieves a document if its value is above the threshold $Rank_\tau$, wherever we place this threshold we are bound to make two types of errors. There will be some *Rel* documents that fall below our threshold (shaded in Figure 4.17) and some irrelevant documents that fall above it (cross-hatched). Following signal detection theory we can call the first set "FALSE− " errors and the second "FALSE+" errors. (These are often called Type 1 and Type 2 errors, respectively.) Note that the ratio of the right tail of the *Rel* curve (the area *not* cross-hatched in in Figure 4.17) to the total area under the *Rel* curve corresponds exactly to the *Recall* measure defined earlier (Equation 4.2), while the ratio of the right tail of the *NRel* curve (cross-hatched in Figure 4.17) to the total area under the *NRel* curve corresponds exactly to *Fallout* (Equation 4.4).

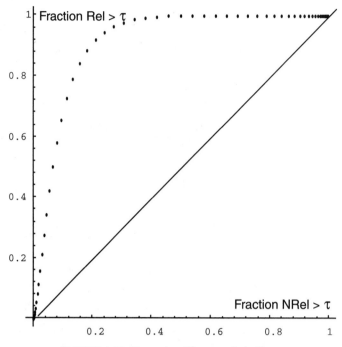

FIGURE 4.18  Operating Characteristic Curve

The parametric curve defined by the percentage of *Rel* versus $\overline{NRel}$ documents retrieved as $\tau$ is varied is called the **operating characteristic curve**. Obviously, if these two distributions are identical, this curve will be exactly a diagonal line, from (0,0) to (1,1). If the mean value of the *Rel* distribution is greater than that of the $\overline{NRel}$, the operating characteristic curve is moved closer to the upper-left corner, as shown in Figure 4.18.

While Swets (and subsequently others [Robertson, 1969; Bookstein and Kraft, 1977]) then considered fairly elaborate tests to discriminate the relative performance of retrieval systems with respect to such curves, it is fair to say that the 1979 assessment of van Rijsbergen, p. 154 still stands:

> . . . although the Swets model is theoretically attractive and links IR measurements to ready-made and well-developed statistical theory, it has not found general acceptance amongst workers in the field.

Optimal selection of $Rank_\tau$ depends on specification of the **costs** (losses) of making FALSE+ or FALSE− errors. For example, if you are an overworked and underpaid law clerk and you read an irrelevant document (FALSE+), you've wasted precision attention, but that's all; if you miss a reference you should have found (FALSE−) the cost might be huge. But if you're a partying undergraduate with one more term paper between you and summer vacation, your assessments might be quite different. Section 5.5.6 gives an example of how explicit models of these various costs can be incorporated within a Bayesian decision-making framework.

## 4.4  RAVE: A Relevance Assessment VEhicle

Section 4.3.2 argued that the opinions of many users concerning the relevance of a document to a query provides a more robust characterization than any single expert. It seems, however, that our move from omniscient to consensual relevance has only made the problem of evaluation that much more difficult: Test corpora must be large enough to provide robust tests for retrieval methods, and multiple queries are necessary to evaluate the overall performance of an IR system. Getting even a single person's opinion about the relevance of a document to a particular query is hard, and we are now interested in getting many!

This section describes RAVE, a relevance assessment vehicle that demonstrates that it is possible to operationally define relevance in the manner we suggest. RAVE is a suite of software routines that allow an IR experimenter to effectively collect large numbers of relevance assessments for an arbitrary document corpus. It has been used with a number of different classes of students to collect the relevance assessments used for evaluation with respect to the AIT corpus; your teacher may have you participate in a similar experiment. It can also be used to collect assessments for other document corpora and query sets.

### 4.4.1  RAVeUnion

It would be most useful if, for every query, the relevance of every document could be assessed. However, the collection of this many assessments, for a corpus large enough to provide a real retrieval test, quickly becomes much too expensive. But if the evaluation goal is relaxed to being the *relative* comparison of one retrieval system to one or more alternative systems, assessments can be constrained to only those documents retrieved by one of the systems.

We therefore follow the pooling procedure used by many other evaluators, viz., using the proposed retrieval methods themselves as procedures for identifying which documents are worth assessing.

The first step in constructing a RAVE experiment is to combine the ranked retrieval lists of the two or more retrieval methods, creating a single list of documents ordered according to how interested we are in having them assessed by a subject.

More elaborate ways of merging ranked lists

RAVeUnion produces the most straightforward "zipper" merge of the lists, beginning with the most highly ranked and alternating one.[†] The output of RAVeUnion is a file of (query, document) pairs along with a field that indicates if the pair was uniquely suggested by only one of the methods. This last information can be used to compare the average relevance scores of documents suggested by one method alone to those retrieved by more than one.

## 4.4.2 RAVePlan

A second challenge is to find the desired density or redundancy of sample points. That is, for each document that we believe may be relevant to a query, how many subjects should evaluate it? The answer will vary depending on such factors as the number of participants, their expertise, their motivation to produce quality judgments, how long each will spend rating documents, etc. A higher density means that fewer documents will be evaluated, but also that the intersubject cumulative assessment is likely to be more statistically stable. This can be especially important when *RelFbk* is to be used to train the system.

The trade-off between the most important of these factors is captured in the following formula:

$$x = \frac{NR}{STQ} \tag{4.21}$$

where

$x =$ number of documents to be evaluated for each query

$N =$ number of subjects

$R =$ expected subject efficiency (votes/user/time)

$S =$ desired density (votes/document)

$T =$ time spent by subjects

$Q =$ number of queries to be evaluated

Note that this formula ignores the overlap between queries that occurs when users see a document that may be relevant to two or more of the queries in their list. Care must be taken, therefore, to minimize expected overlap between the topical areas of the queries. We have also found that the assessment densities constructed using this formula are unfortunately uneven. The main source of these is variability in $R$, the rate at which subjects are able to produce relevance assessments.

RAVePlan takes as input a list of $Q$ query specifications, a list of $N$ subject logins, the desired density $S$, and the number of documents $R*T$ that should be allocated to each subject. The query specifications indicate which queries can go in which fields and which queries should not be shown together. This allows us to limit possible interactions between queries about similar topics.[†]

RAVePlan outputs two files. The plan file, which is an input to the RAVE interactive application, lists each subject ID along with the queries and document numbers that have been selected for that subject. The assignments file is a list of document-query pairs, which tells us which query we expect the document to be relevant to. RAVeCompile uses this file after data collection is complete to generate true and false-positive measures.

A better
RAVePlan

## 4.4.3  Interactive RAVE

The interactive portion of RAVE is an HTML document, as shown in Figure 4.19. The top of RAVE's window displays the three queries against which the subject is to judge each document. Two queries are short sentences or phrases, in this case REASONING ABOUT UNCERTAINTY

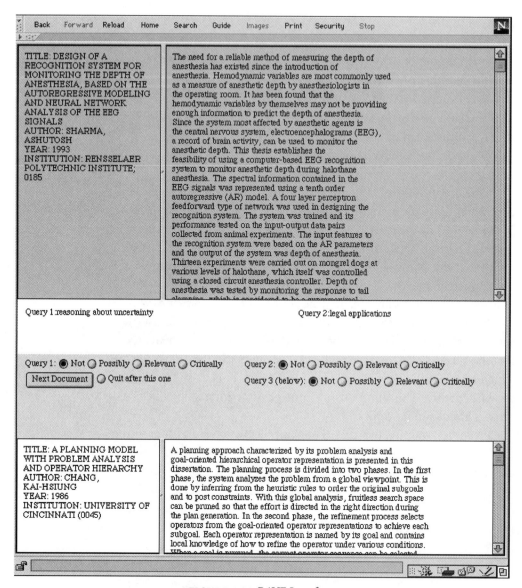

FIGURE 4.19 RAVE Interface

and LEGAL APPLICATIONS, and the third is a scrolling pane containing the text of the long, *RelFbk*-defined document (in this example, the thesis A PLANNING MODEL WITH PROBLEM ANALYSIS...). While the subject is asked to judge the documents shown to him or her as being <u>about</u> the two short queries, the task associated with the *RelFbk-*document query is to find "documents like this."

Beneath each query the RAVE window contains four radio buttons labeled "Not" (relevant), "Possibly" (relevant), "Relevant," and "Critically" (relevant). Because we asked our subjects to spend two hours each but could not assume their participation would be continuous, there is a "Quit" button that allows the subject to suspend the session; when the subject launches RAVE again, the session is resumed where he or she left off. Finally, the "Next" button is pressed after the subject has read and recorded his or her relevance assessments for a document.

### 4.4.4 RAVeCompile

RAVeCompile processes the votes recorded by interactive RAVE, creating a relevance assessment file and some statistics about each query and subject. The first step is to map the four-valued relevance assessments into the Boolean relevant/nonrelevant discriminations typically used by standard IR evaluation techniques. RAVeCompile lets the experimenter configure a simple predicate of the following form:

$$s = a \cdot NPoss + b \cdot NRel + c \cdot NCrit$$

$$NVote = NPoss + NRel + NCrit$$

$$RelP = (NVote \geq Quorum) \land (s \cdot NVote \geq MinAvg)$$

where

$$
\begin{aligned}
s &= \text{weighted aggregate score across relevance levels} \\
a &= \text{weight assigned to votes of "possibly relevant"} \\
b &= \text{weight assigned to votes of "relevant"} \\
c &= \text{weight assigned to votes of "critically relevant"} \\
NVote &= \text{total number of active votes collected for } (q, d) \text{ pair} \\
Quorum &= \text{minimum number of votes required for } (q, d) \text{ to be} \\
&\quad \text{considered relevant} \\
MinAvg &= \text{minimum weighted sum required for } (q, d) \text{ to be} \\
&\quad \text{considered relevant}
\end{aligned}
$$

In one set of experiments [Belew and Hatton, 1996], the data used two predicates constructed in this fashion. These are:

- **permissive:** if (two or more POSSIBLE votes) or (at least one RELEVANT vote)
- **stringent:** if (two or more RELEVANT votes) or (at least one CRITICAL vote)

## 4.5  Summary

In this chapter we began by making some assumptions about users of a search engine in order to figure out how well the system is satisfying users' information needs. We focused on two separate notions of assessment: first, assessing the relevance of documents retrieved by the system in response to a particular query, and second, assessing the search engine's overall utility through aggregating relevance judgments provided by many users performing many queries.

Section 4.1 discussed both metric and nonmetric relevance feedback and the difficulties in getting users to provide relevance judgments for documents in the retrieved set. We saw, however, that relevance feedback could be used to either suggest query refinements to the users or to modify the underlying document representations to improve future system performance.

The concept of consensual relevance introduced in Section 4.2 addresses an issue raised in Chapter 1, where we asked what success criteria can be used in evaluating a search engine. Consensual relevance tells us that relevant documents are those documents that many users find to be useful. We can ask how useful a particular search engine is, or compare one search engine with another, by posing the question: How useful (relevant) do users find the documents retrieved in response to queries?

To answer that question we quantified several measures of system performance. The generality of a query is a measure of what fraction of documents in the corpus is relevant to the query. Fallout measures the fraction of irrelevant documents found in the retrieved set of a given query. The key notions of recall, the fraction of relevant documents in the retrieved set, and precision, the fraction of retrieved documents that are relevant, allow us to make direct comparisons between two search engines' performances on any query. Other methods of comparison include sliding ratio, point alienation, expected search length, and operating characteristic curves.

**EXERCISE 1**    Issue a query of your choosing to any Web search engine that will retrieve 10 or more hits. Using the order of retrieval as an index, go to *odd* retrieval documents (i.e., hits 1, 3, 5, etc.) and assign to each a score in the range $[-10, +10]$ indicating how relevant you found it. Now repeat the exercise for the *even* documents. Finally, analyze your assessments for each of the triplets of documents: 1, 4, 7; 2, 5, 8; and 3, 6, 9. How well do they satisfy the required properties of a metric (cf. Section 5.2.2)?

**EXERCISE 2**    Compute the ESL of a random retrieval using each of the following two predicates:

1. $N$ relevant documents; and

2. $P$ percent of relevant documents.

Discuss the effect of the measures relative to query generality.

## TERMS INTRODUCED IN THIS CHAPTER

11-point average
ad hoc retrieval
berrypicking
centroid
classification
   accuracy
composite
consensual
contingency
   table
Cornell corpora
costs
document
   modifications
effectiveness

expected search
   length
expected search
   length reduction
   factor
F-measure
fallout
filter
filtering
generality
harmonic mean
hitlist
hitlist rank
intersubject
   reliability

interpolation
litigation
   support
multicriterial
nonmetric
normalized recall
object recognition
omniscient
   expert
operating
   characteristic
   curve
operationalizing
permissive
point alienation

# 5

# Mathematical Foundations

No inquiry can go very far without a rigorous notion of where it's been. Mathematics continues to provide our most reliable representation for the construction of new hypotheses and their testing. This chapter pulls together a wide range of mathematical issues arising in the FOA context.

## 5.1 Derivation of Zipf's Law for Random Texts

As before, we begin by defining a word to be any sequence of characters separated by spaces. Let us therefore consider an alphabet of $M$ characters, interspersed with a specially designated space character $\emptyset$. We will consider an especially simple model (similar to that used by many others [Li, 1992; Miller, 1957; Hill, 1970; Hill, 1974]) in which a random monkey generates words by hitting all keys – space and letters – with equal probability $p$:

$$p = Pr(\emptyset) = Pr(\text{A}) = \cdots = Pr(\text{Z}) = \frac{1}{M+1} \qquad (5.1)$$

We can use **lexicographic trees** to conveniently organize words of length $k$, say, by the order in which the $k$ characters occur prior to the terminating space, as shown in Figure 5.1 This shows a set of $M + 1$ trees, each rooted in the words' starting character. Leaf nodes at level $k$

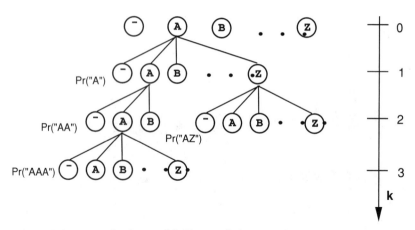

FIGURE 5.1 Lexicographic Tree Underlying Zipfian Distribution

are all labeled with the probability of the sequence of $k-1$ characters prior to the space occurring at level $k$.

One immediate observation is that $N_k$, the number of words $w_i$ of length $k$ or less, is:

$$N_k \equiv Number(w_i \mid i \leq k) = \sum_{i=1}^{k} M^i = \frac{M(1 - M^k)}{1 - M} \qquad (5.2)$$

In an infinitely long sequence of characters generated according to Equation 5.1, we will expect to find a "word" $w_k$ terminating at level $k$ (i.e., a string of $k$ unbroken nonspace characters bracketed by two spaces) with probability defined in terms of the independent character probabilities $p$:

$$p_k \equiv \Pr(w_k) = p^{k+2} = \frac{c}{(M + 1)^{k+2}} \qquad (5.3)$$

We can compute $c$, the constant of proportionality, by including all the $M^k$ words of length $k$ and summing these probabilities over all possible

Double-counting spaces?!

words (including unrealistic, infinitely long ones!):[†]

$$\sum_{k=1}^{\infty} c \cdot M^k p_k = 1 \Rightarrow c = \frac{(M + 1)^2}{M}$$

$$\therefore p_k = \frac{1}{M(M + 1)^k} \qquad (5.4)$$

Next consider the rank of these words. Because the probability of a word's occurrence is an exponentially decreasing function of its length, we know that the $M$ highest ranked words are the one-character words; next come the $M^2$ two-letter words; and so on. Using Equation 5.2 we therefore know how the rank $r_k$ of all words $w_k$ terminating on level $k$ must be bounded above and below:

$$N_{k-1} < r_k \leq N_k$$

$$\tilde{r}_k = \frac{N_{k-1} + 1 + N_k}{2} = (M^k - 1)\frac{M+1}{2(M-1)} \qquad (5.5)$$

where $\tilde{r}_k$ denotes a compromise "average" rank for all the $M^k$ equiprobable words.*

Note that Equations 5.4 and 5.5 define the words' probability and rank, respectively, in terms of the common metric $k$. As Li [Li, 1992] notes, Zipf's law is fundamentally about this transformation, from an exponential distribution onto a rank variable.

Solving both equations for $k$:

$$k = -\frac{\ln(M \cdot p_k)}{\ln(M+1)}$$

$$k = \frac{\ln\left(\frac{2(M-1)\tilde{r}_k}{M+1} + 1\right)}{\ln M} \qquad (5.6)$$

we can now set them equal and derive an expression for a word's probability in terms of its rank:

$$\frac{\ln(M \cdot p_k)}{\ln(M+1)} = -\frac{\ln\left(\frac{2(M-1)\tilde{r}_k}{M+1} + 1\right)}{\ln M}$$

$$p_k = \frac{1}{M}\left(\frac{2(M-1)\tilde{r}_k}{M+1} + 1\right)^{\frac{-\ln(M+1)}{\ln M}} \qquad (5.7)$$

This has the functional form required by Mandelbrot's generalized Zipf's law (cf. Equation 3.2):

$$p_k = \frac{C}{(\tilde{r}_k + B)^\alpha}$$

where

$$C = \frac{1}{M}\left(\frac{M+1}{2(M-1)}\right)^\alpha, \quad B = \frac{M+1}{2(M-1)}, \quad \alpha = \frac{\ln(M+1)}{\ln M} \qquad (5.8)$$

---

* The model can be extended by replacing this simple average with distributional information, for example, incorporating realistic character frequency information.

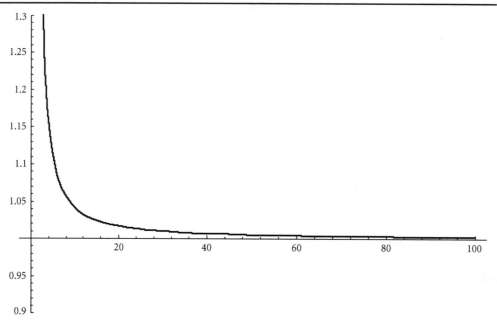

FIGURE 5.2 $\alpha$ as Function of $M$, Number of Distinct Characters

## 5.1.1 Discussion

Obviously these formulas all depend on the alphabet size selected, and this will certainly not be fixed across the systems considered. For example, it is not unusual for an IR system to "fold case," i.e., to treat upper- and lowercase letters interchangeably, but many also preserve this case information. The capitalization of proper names will sometimes provide critical clues for appropriate index terms. Similarly, our choice of which characters we use to break the stream into wordlike tokens has consequence.

Fortunately for the robustness of Zipf's law, the alphabets typically considered in these analyses are generally large enough that differences between only uppercase or upper- and lowercase alphabets are inconsequential. Figure 5.2, showing how quickly $\alpha$ becomes nearly unity as the size of the character set grows, also makes it clear why Zipf's simpler hyperbolic form is an adequate approximation.

It is also interesting to note a potential connection between Zipf's law and information theory. Mandelbrot [Mandelbrot, 1953; Mandelbrot, 1982] initially attempted to derive Zipf's law as the solution minimizing the average cost per unit of information conveyed by a text. George Miller seems to have found this effort amusing:

?1, 2

... the random placement of spaces which leads to Zipf's rule is actually the optimal solution. Our monkeys are doing the best possible job of encoding information word-by-word, subject to the constraints we impose on them. If we were as smart as the monkeys we, too, would generate all possible sequences of letters and so make better use of our alphabet. [Miller, 1957]

## 5.2  Dimensionality Reduction

As Section 3.5 has already suggested, our interest in matching queries and documents within a vector space can benefit greatly from other kinds of matching that have arisen in other kinds of vector spaces [Schutze, 1993]. We review several other basic features of the mathematical topic of linear algebra before applying them to the problem of FOA.

It is worth remembering that similarity information can come from many sources. For example, we will later (cf. Section 6.1) have much to say about how **citation** structure can be represented as a graph, with each document represented by a node in the graph and a directed edge going from $d_i$ to $d_j$, when $d_j$ appears in the bibliography of $d_i$. Note that the documents' citation information is entirely independent of the words they contain and can be the basis for another characterization of the topical similarity between documents:

> Two documents are about the same topic to the extent that they share the same documents in their bibliographies.

For now, such bibliometric data need only seem like a plausible, new way to analyze document content. Chapter 6 will discuss other features that we might also exploit.

Our goal in casting similarity matching of queries with documents in general mathematical terms is to make the resulting solutions sufficiently broad to handle any kind of features, keywords, or bibliographic citations.

### 5.2.1  A Simple Example

Imagine that we've collected data on the HEIGHT and WEIGHT of everyone in a classroom of $N$ students. If these are plotted, the result would be

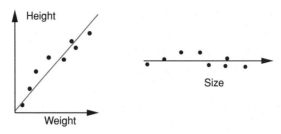

FIGURE 5.3  Weight and Height Data Reduction

something like Figure 5.3. Notice the correlation around an axis we might call something like SIZE. Students vary most along this dimension; it captures most of the information about their distribution. It is possible to capture a major source of variation across the HEIGHT/WEIGHT sample because, just as with our keywords, the two quantities are correlated.

In this section we analyze similar statistical correlations among the keywords and documents contained in the much larger vector space model first mentioned in Section 3.4. Recall that in the vector space model, the *Index* relation placing $D \equiv NDoc$ vectors corresponding to the corpus documents within the space $\Re^V$, where $V \equiv NKw$ (for vocabulary size), is defined by its keyword vocabulary.

Here we describe this in the terms of linear algebra,* where $J = Index$ is a $D \times V$ element matrix. [†]

Beyond the puny three dimensions of human existence

Attempts to reduce this large dimensional space into something smaller are called **dimensionality reduction**. There are two reasons we might be interested in reducing dimensions. The first is probably more obvious: It's a very unwieldy representation of documents' content. Individual documents will have many zeros, corresponding to the many words in the corpus $V$ not present in an individual document; the vector space matrix is very **sparse**. Dimensionality reduction is a search for a representation that is denser, more compressed.

Another reason might be to exploit what has become known as **latent semantic** relationships among these keywords. When we make each term in our vocabulary a dimension, we are effectively assuming they are **orthogonal** to one another; we expect their effects to be independent.

---

* In this language, single-letter identifiers are simplest, but that would make the *Index* relation $I$. Unfortunately, the letter $I$ already plays a useful role in linear algebra, as the identity matrix; hence, $J = Index$. For similar reasons, within this section, we will use $V \equiv NKw$ and $D \equiv NDoc$.

But many features of FOA suggest that index terms are highly dependent, highly correlated with one another. If that's the case, we can exploit that correlation by capturing only those axes of maximal variation and throwing away the rest.

## 5.2.2 Formal Notions of Similarity

Two features of the FOA problem can help us to focus on what is known as the Minkowski metric [Luenberger, 1969; Jain and Dubes, 1988]. First, the result of our calculations will be a *real-valued weight* associating a keyword with a document or query, and we can assume that this is a continuous quantity. Further, we can make the somewhat more questionable assumption that these weights make "natural" use of zero, and so index weights also fall on what is known as a "ratio" scale. With these two assumptions, the Minkowski metrics are defined as:

$$Sim(\mathbf{q}, \mathbf{d}) = \left( \sum_{k=1}^{NKw} |w_{qk} - w_{dk}|^L \right)^{1/L} \tag{5.9}$$

where $L \geq 1$. The most common version is the $L = 2$ norm, and we will use it here. The $L = 1$ ("Manhattan distance") and $L = \infty$ ("sup" norm, where $\Sigma_k$ is replaced with *max*) are also seen often.

A metric is a scalar function over pairs of points in the vector space. Minkowski metrics satisfy three critical properties:

$$Sim(x, y) \geq 0 \tag{5.10}$$

$$Sim(x, y) = Sim(y, x) \tag{5.11}$$

$$Sim(x, x) = \|x\| \tag{5.12}$$

$$\geq \arg \max_y Sim(x, y) \tag{5.13}$$

The measure $Sim(x, x)$ of a vector with itself is what we typically think of as the *length* of the vector, or more precisely, its *norm*, $\|x\|$.

Two other important features of metric spaces follow from these axioms:

1. $Sim(x, y) \leq \|x\| \cdot \|y\|$     (Cauchy-Schwarz inequality)
2. $\|x + y\| \leq \|x\| + \|y\|$     (triangle inequality)

### 5.2.3 Singular Value Decomposition

Just as students' HEIGHT and WEIGHT are correlated along the dimension SIZE, we can guess that (at least some small sets of) keywords are correlated and that the vector space representation of a document corpus (cf. Section 3.4) might be simplified in a similar way. The goal is to "reduce the dimensionality" of the documents' representation in the same way we reduced that of our students' sizes.

But although we can draw a simple picture revealing the correlational structure between two dimensions, the picture is much more complicated when we try to conceive of the full $V \approx 10^5$ space of index terms. For the $D$ vectors we seek a smaller $k < V$-dimensional solution. We still have as many documents as we had before, but we're going to use a different set of descriptors.

One of the most effective ways to characterize the correlational structure among large sets of objects is via **eigenfactor analysis**. The technique we consider is called **singular value decomposition**. This factors any rectangular matrix into three terms:

$$J = ULA^T \tag{5.14}$$

where $U$ and $A$ are each **orthonormal** and $L$ is a diagonal matrix "connecting" them.[†]

Mathematical details

As before (cf. Equation 3.39), using inner product to measure similarity, we can define $X$:

$$X = JJ^T \tag{5.15}$$

Because $J$ is a $D \times V$ matrix, $X$ is a $D \times D$ symmetric matrix capturing all $\binom{D}{2}$ interdocument similarities. Then $U$ is the system of eigenvectors of $X$, and $L$ has the square roots of the eignenvalues, $\sqrt{\lambda_i}$, along its diagonal. By convention, we order these in decreasing order:

$$L = [\sqrt{\lambda_1} \ \sqrt{\lambda_2} \ \sqrt{\lambda_3} \ \cdots \ \sqrt{\lambda_k}]$$
$$\sqrt{\lambda_1} \geq \sqrt{\lambda_2} \geq \sqrt{\lambda_3} \cdots \geq \sqrt{\lambda_k} \tag{5.16}$$

Large eigenvalues correspond to dominant correlations and so, just as looking for the SIZE dimension that captured the main interaction between HEIGHT and WEIGHT, we will rely on the first $k$ dimensions to

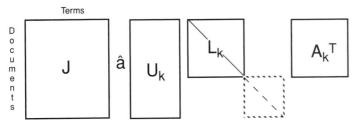

FIGURE 5.4  SVD Decomposition

capture the dominant modes of interaction in $J$:

$$J_k = U_k L_k A_k^T \qquad (5.17)$$

This operation is shown schematically in Figure 5.4.[†]

As always, whenever we throw something away (viz., the small eigen-vectors), the result must be an approximation. That is, there will be a difference between our reduced-dimension representation $J_k$ and the original $J$.

One easy way to measure this discrepancy is by referring to the $D^2$ interdocument similarities latent in the $X$ matrix and considering how different they are in the approximate matrix $X_k$

$$X_k = J_k J_k^T \qquad (5.18)$$

using the $L_2$ norm $\| \cdot \|_2$ to measure deviation. Then:

$$Err = \| X - X_k \|_2 \qquad (5.19)$$

In fact, approximating $X$ with its reduced $k$-rank SVD decomposition turns out to be optimal, in the sense that it results in minimal $Err$ over all other rank-$k$ alternatives [Bartell et al., 1992].

### 5.2.4  How Many Dimensions $k$ to Reduce To?

A central question remains: How many dimensions $k$ should be used? To date, the only answers are empirical. Early experiments suggest that using too few dimensions dramatically degrades performance.[†] The original MED corpus used in early LSI experiments [Deerwester et al., 1990; Dumais, 1991] happens to be distinguished by a particularly top-ically focused vocabulary. While a few hundred dimensions may suffice to discriminate this small set of documents, it might be necessary to use more dimensions when describing a broader domain of discourse.

*Dimensionality reduction using neural networks*

*Earlier attempts to reduce dimensionality*

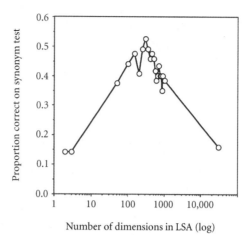

FIGURE 5.5  Retrieval Performance as Function of SVD Dimension ($k$).
From [Landauer and Dumais, 1997].
Reproduced with permission of the Association of Computing Machinery

Empirically, however, reduction to around 500 dimensions seems to provide significant improvements to even very large corpora. For example, Figure 5.5 shows one experiment [Landauer and Dumais, 1997], where $k$ is varied over four orders of magnitude. Some attempts to select $k$ theoretically, borrowing a **rank-plus-shift** method from signal processing, have also been made [Zha and Zhang, 1998]. The most satisfying answer may come from *probabilistic* models that relate the raw frequency statistics to an underlying distribution [Papadimitriou et al., 1998; Hoffman, 1999].

### 5.2.5  Other Uses of Vector Space

The same interdocument similarity information captured in the $X = JJ^T$ matrix can be used for other purposes, too. For example, Section 7.5.1 will discuss one approach to the problem of **classifying** documents known as nearest neighbor.

The *Index* captures patterns of keyword usage across a corpus of documents. The preceding sections have held the corpus constant and used this data to analyze transformations of the keyword dimensions, but the converse is also possible. For example, Section 6.3 will discuss the representation of interkeyword relationships known as **thesauri**. One simple baseline for keywords is their pairwise similarities, as captured by $J$:

$$Y = J^T J \tag{5.20}$$

This produces a $V \times V$ symmetric, square matrix capturing all $\binom{V}{2}$ interkeyword similarities, exactly analogous to the interdocument similarities of Equation 5.15.

Littman has also considered an interesting application of LSI to the problem of searching across multilingual corpora [Littman et al., 1998].

## 5.2.6  Computational Considerations

?3

All these techniques depend, of course, on being able to compute the SVD for the *Index* relation. Given the enormous size of this matrix – typically $10^4$ keywords times $10^5$ to $10^9$ documents – this is a nontrivial concern. However, the fact that these matrices are sparse (i.e., any one document vector has a relatively small fraction of keywords associated with it) means that special techniques can be used. In particular, Berry has developed methods based on Lanczos and subspace iteration methods in his **SVD-Pack**[1] implementation [Berry, 1992; Berry et al., 1994; Letsche, 1996].[†]

SVD is patentable?!

Once the document corpus has finally been compressed, another serious recurring computation must be done: Every time a user issues a query, it must be transformed from the original space of "raw" keywords into the reduced $k$-dimensional space. This means we must keep the matrix $U_k$ available to transform each query into the reduced representation.

?4

Another computational issue has to do with the effect of new documents being added to the collection, or older ones being removed. This is one particular type[†] of **drift** we might expect in FOA; Section 7.3.2 discusses several others. The addition or deletion of any one document will affect the SVD statistics of the entire corpus very slightly, especially if it is a very large corpus.

Temporal drift

?5

## 5.2.7  "Latent Semantic" Claims

Within the IR community, SVD was first applied to the *Index* matrix by Deerwester et al. [Deerwester et al., 1990; Dumais, 1991] and was called **latent semantic indexing** (LSI). The "latent semantic" claim derives from the authors' belief that the reduced dimension representation of documents in fact reveals *semantic* correlations among index terms. Further, they argue that evidence collected across entire corpora transcend individually "fallible" document instances. That is, while one document's

---

[1] www.netlib.org.svdpack

author might use the word CAR and another the synonym AUTO, the correlation of both of these with other terms like HIGHWAY, GASOLINE, and DRIVING will result in an abstracted document feature/dimension on which *queries* using either keyword, CAR or AUTO, will project equivalently. "Synonymous" retrieval has been accomplished!

Landauer and Dumais have recently extended this algebraic manipulation of the *Index* relation into an ambitious model of human memory [Landauer and Dumais, 1997]. Much of psychology is concerned with the problem of how children, those most powerful learning agents, are able to learn so much from such a "poverty of the stimulus." That is, by many forms of analysis the stimuli driving learning do not by themselves contain sufficient information to induce the elaborate conceptual structures children demonstrate.

Applying these ideas to textual corpora, Landauer and Dumais "trained" an LSI model with presentation of paragraph after paragraph drawn from more than 30,000 encyclopedia articles. Using retrieval on a standardized synonym test as their performance measure, the emerging eigenvector representation (compressed to 300 dimensions) showed a rate of improvement comparable to that of schoolchildren! Because this performance required "indirect inference" like that supported by LSI eigenvectors and beyond what could be accomplished on the basis of simple word cooccurrence alone, Landauer and Dumais suggested that LSI provides an important model of human memory. [†]

A new argument for nurture

> [S]ome domains of knowledge contain vast numbers of weak correlations that . . . can greatly amplify learning by a process of inference. . . . [A] substantial portion of the information needed . . . can be inferred from the contextual statistics of usage alone. [Landauer and Dumais, 1997]

At the very least, LSI demonstrates how traditional **associative memory** models [James, 1893; Hebb, 1949; Baddeley, 1976; Anderson and Kline, 1979] can be extended to exploit higher-order correlations.

The earlier work trying to connect a small number of factor-analytic, "semantically" meaningful dimensions [Koll, 1979; Borko and Bernick, 1963] is also interesting in this respect. Jones and Furnas have also investigated how well cosine/inner product reflects human similarity judgments [Jones and Furnas, 1987]. In any case, a cognitive interpretation of these issues promises to remain an active area of investigation.

We now consider how *RelFbk* assessments might also be used to provide document-similarity information, and how they can be used to reduce the dimensionality of documents' representations.

## 5.3  Preference Relations

### 5.3.1  Multidimensional Scaling

In many kinds of retrieval interfaces, it is easy and natural for a user to indicate a preference for one retrieved document over another. The *RelFbk* discussed in Section 4.1 is our standard characterization of this information:[†]

$$\ominus \prec \# \prec \oplus \qquad (5.21)$$

IR has historically ignored preferences

The literature on **multidimensional scaling** (MDS) was developed to deal with assessments by human subjects of the similarity or difference among multiple stimulus patterns [Borg and Lingoes, 1987]. A robust and important result from this analysis is that people can much more easily and consistently provide nonmetric assessments of the similarity than if they are forced to specify metric quantities. Rather than an experimenter *arbitrarily* imposing dimensions they believe important,

> We can ask the subjects to globally judge, without criteria provided by the experimenter, the overall similarities of different facial expressions. The *proximities* are then mapped into [MDS] *distances x*, and the configuration examined for systematic characteristics of the distribution of points. [Borg and Lingoes, 1987, p. 72, emphasis added]

The "facial expression" example is a reference to Woodworth's experiments in 1938 [Woodworth, 1938]. Imagine a hypothesis that facial expressions can be characterized in terms of two dimensions of variability. We could test this by showing human subjects pairs of pictures and asking them to judge how similar or dissimilar the two facial expressions are, in terms of "difference in emotional expression or content." Then imagine they are given some proximity $p$ scale – from $1, 2, \ldots$ $k$ – along which they are to rank the picture pairs; each pair of pictures would therefore have a proximity score $p_{ij}$. If these pictures are to be characterized in a two-dimensional plane, we can also associate with each pair of pictures a distance $d_{ij}$ according to their two-dimensional

Proximity can
capture
similarity or
dissimilar-
ity/distance

coordinates:[†]

$$p_{ij} \equiv \text{proximity (evaluation)}$$

$$d_{ij} \equiv \text{distance (in two-dimensional plane)}$$

The MDS analysis described by Borg and Lingoes (they actually prefer the term "similarity structure analysis," or SSA) is a key contribution. It is an algorithm for iteratively moving vectors corresponding to the objects of evaluation (pictures of facial expressions) within an arbitrary dimensional space so as to minimize as much as possible the **stress** they experience, relative to their pairwise proximities. We think that the pictures have been well placed if those with similar proximities are close together as measured by this distance.

Within any such space, we can replace the pairwise distances $d_{ij}$ with $d_i$ associated with each point (picture) measuring the distance of this point from the origin of the space. Proximities $p_i$ are defined in terms of the projections of these points onto the space's principal component vectors.

To quantify this notion of correspondence between humans' proximity assessments and their embedding in arbitrary spaces, Guttman has defined a measure of **monotonic correspondence** between two variables:

$$\mu_2 \equiv \frac{\sum_i \sum_j (p_i - p_j) \cdot (d_i - d_j)}{\sum_i \sum_j |p_i - p_j| \cdot |d_i - d_j|} \tag{5.22}$$

This measure captures the extent to which the placement of the items within the two-dimensional space is consistent with the proximities. This formula really is as simple as it looks: It is approximately a correlation of proximities with distances, "gated" by the comparison of differences in the numerator and absolute values of differences in the denominator. The value of $\mu_2$ is always greater than simple linear correlation, and the two quantities are exactly equal when a linear relationship holds between proximity and distance.

In the FOA retrieval situation, the obvious measure of interest is the matching function $Match(q, d)$ (cf. Section 4.3.4) score with respect to a (henceforth implicit) query $q$:

$$J \equiv \frac{\sum_{\mathbf{d}_i \succ \mathbf{d}_j} Match(\mathbf{d}_i) - Match(\mathbf{d}_j)}{\sum_{\mathbf{d}_i \succ \mathbf{d}_j} |Match(\mathbf{d}_i) - Match(\mathbf{d}_j)|} \tag{5.23}$$

The $J$ measure provides a criterion for the retrieval function $Match(\cdot)$. In experimental situations the only preferences available are that $Rel \succ \overline{Rel}$, but in natural retrieval situations, users' richer $RelFbk$ preference data can be used.

A particularly interesting use of this criterion is as part of error correction learning (cf. Section 7.3). If we assume that the ranking function $R$ has certain free variables $\Theta$, that we again have a training set of documents $T$, and that the $J$ criterion is differentiable with respect to $\Theta$, a gradient search procedure can be used to adjust $\Theta$ toward an optimal retrieval:

$$\frac{\partial J\,(Match_\Theta)}{\partial\Theta} = \sum_{\mathbf{d}\,\in\,T} \frac{\partial J\,(Match_\Theta)}{\partial Match_\Theta(\mathbf{d})} \frac{\partial Match_\Theta(\mathbf{d})}{\partial\Theta} \qquad (5.24)$$

For example, Bartell et al. [Bartell et al., 1994b; Bartell et al., 1998] consider the problem of picking a document-query similarity measure $R$ parameterized by $\Theta$ to vary across a broad range of alternatives:

$$Match_\Theta(\mathbf{d}) = Sim_\Theta(\mathbf{d}, \mathbf{q}) = \frac{\mathbf{q} \cdot \mathbf{d}}{\left(\sum_{d_i \neq 0} d_i^{\theta_1}\right)^{\theta_2}} \qquad (5.25)$$

$$\Theta = \langle\theta_1, \theta_2\rangle \qquad (5.26)$$

This characterization of similarity score includes standard inner product ($\theta_2 = 0$, $\theta_1$ can be anything), cosine ($\theta_1 = 2$, $\theta_2 = 0.5$), and pseudo-cosine ($\theta_1 = 1$, $\theta_2 = 1$) as special cases.

Through empirical testing using the CISI experimental corpus (cf. Section 4.3.9) and its binary relevance assessments for preference relations ($Rel \succ \overline{Rel}$), Bartell et al. found optimal values of $\theta_1 = 2.5$, $\theta_2 = 0.3$, a curious and nonstandard type of similarity measure indeed, but functionally quite similar to standard cosine. In fact, changing the matching function to this "optimal" value improves performance (as measured by average precision) almost not at all.

## 5.3.2  Information in *RelFbk*

Section 5.2.7 raised several important cognitive questions arising from attempts to study "semantic" interpretation of LSI/SVD dimensions. The connection to the psychologically important analysis of MDS adds even more. If we interpret *RelFbk* information as constraints about which documents a user likes, how much can we reduce dimensionality without violating the *RelFbk* constraints they are giving us? That is, how much can we reduce the representational space before we're changing somebody's order? Second, how many *RelFbk* statements do we need to accurately determine a good compression? How many people have to tell us things before we have enough information to form this reduced representation? These questions also connect to ones related to learning these representations (cf. Chapter 7) and to our mechanisms, as part of the interface or as part of a special experimental system like RAVE, for efficiently collecting large volumes of *RelFbk* (cf. Section 4.4). Most of these questions remain unanswered, but a beginning is simply counting the number of preference constraints provided by each *RelFbk* labeling of a hitlist by a user.

First note that the total number of preference statements required to completely determine $n$ elements grows very rapidly as $\left(\binom{n}{2}\right)$, corresponding to the fact that preference order information is defined over *pairs of pairs* of evaluated documents. Against this backdrop, each *RelFbk* labeling produces:

$$NPlus \equiv |\oplus| \tag{5.27}$$

$$NDCare \equiv |\#| \tag{5.28}$$

$$NMinus \equiv |\ominus| \tag{5.29}$$

$$NRetr = NPlus + NDCare + NMinus \tag{5.30}$$

$$NPref \equiv NPlus \cdot (NDCare + NMinus)$$
$$+ (NDCare \cdot NMinus) \tag{5.31}$$

When this information is used as part of error correction learning, another useful quantity is the number of documents over which the *RelFbk* preference relation and the ranked list disagree:

$$Disagree \equiv \{\langle \mathbf{d}_i, \mathbf{d}_j \rangle \,|\, (\mathbf{d}_i \prec \mathbf{d}_j) \wedge (Rank(\mathbf{d}_i) < Rank(\mathbf{d}_j))\} \tag{5.32}$$

Because this relatively small number of data points will always be dwarfed by the number of total preferences across the entire corpus, the goal becomes to constrain the application of *RelFbk* data to those subsets of the corpus possibly appropriate to a particular query. And because we intend to *learn* from the browsing users, we can afford to be patient: The documents are only written once but browsing users will continue to read them and provide *RelFbk* for some time.

### 5.3.3 Connections between MDS and LSI

Bartell et al. [Bartell et al., 1994a] have shown that any time the basis of MDS is $S$, a positive semidefinite matrix of $d$ observations of $t$ variables (cf. Equation 5.15), the LSI decomposition together with inner product similarities provides an optimal MDS scaling. That is, under reasonable conditions MDS and LSI arrive at *identical* results.

This correspondence is more than a mathematical curiosity. MDS allows generalization of the scaling to *any other source* of document-document similarity information! There are many possible sources of information regarding ways to analyze the similarity of a number of documents; bibliometric information is one practical alternative already mentioned. MDS is potentially important because it allows us to go beyond the set of static features of the corpus, to consider the unending stream of *RelFbk* generated by browsing users. Chapter 4 discussed users' *RelFbk* assessments in detail. Recall that one of the critical features of *RelFbk* information is that it is nonmetric. *MDS allows us to define optimal scalings directly from nonmetric RelFbk data.*

## 5.4 Clustering[†]

Van Rijsbergen's
long shadow

### 5.4.1 The Cluster Hypothesis

We have been talking about a measure of association between query and document, but as discussed in Section 5.2.5, we can use $X = JJ^T$ (cf. Equation 5.15) to capture similarities or differences among the documents themselves. Van Rijsbergen's **cluster hypothesis** suggests how useful this data might be:

> Closely associated documents tend to be relevant to the same request. [van Rijsbergen, p. 45]

The cluster hypothesis suggests that if we first compute a measure of distance $X$ among all the documents, we could **cluster** those documents that seem to be close to one another or seem to be <u>about</u> the same topic and retrieve them all in response to a query that matched any of them. If a query happens to match one document based on an overlap of features, then we will claim that other documents that are similar to it should also be retrieved.

As van Rijsbergen, p. 38 notes, the fact that most measures of association are monotonic with respect to one another makes it sufficient that clustering methods only respect the same *rank ordering* of their results; once again the nonmetric quality of critical FOA quantities is striking.

## 5.4.2 Clustering Algorithms

Because of its widespread application, clustering is one of the most well-studied problems within statistics and computer science [Jain and Dubes, 1988; Griffiths et al., 1986]. It can be stated in generic terms, in terms of an arbitrary similarity measure between items to be clustered. Especially in iterative applications of clustering, the relative frequency of various clustering techniques matters. The art, therefore, in applying a clustering method in a particular application depends greatly on the particular features of items to be clustered and the number of partitions within which these items are to be clustered. W. Willett has provided an excellent survey of applications of clustering applied to various aspects of the FOA task [Willett, 1988]. More recently, Zamir has considered clusterings of document "snippets" (roughly the same as the paragraph units proposed in Section 2.3) rather than on complete documents [Zamir and Etzioni, 1998].

The most typical clustering method for application within the FOA context is single-link hierarchical clustering. This is considered an **agglomerative** technique, because it begins with each data point considered to be in its own cluster and then iteratively asks which two clusters should be combined.[†]

Divisive/
partitional
clustering

The most typical method for performing this task builds a **minimum spanning tree** (MST), iteratively merging the two documents that are closest together and then including the merged nodes. The result is a tree from the finally merged root to each of the documents as a leaf. Alternatively, the complete set of interdocument similarity measures can be progressively "filtered" by a gradually increasing threshold, which is used to define whether two documents are considered connected by an edge. We can then ask for certain properties of the emerging graph, for example, stopping when all components become connected. To keep things simple and focused on robust assumptions [van Rijsbergen, p. 59], $O(n^2)$ algorithms are assumed.

One early motivation for clustering algorithms was efficient disk access: If documents were preclustered appropriately, it would be likely that a "page" of disk memory containing one document matching a query might also contain other elements of the same cluster. That is, an efficient physical disk allocation algorithm might try to ensure that clustered documents were written to the same block.

This example suggests how MST representations of the documents might also support efficient query/document matching algorithms. In brief, the MST can be interpreted as a "decision tree," with a query beginning at the root and comparing itself to a candidate representation (e.g., centroid) of each cluster.

The cluster hypothesis suggests that if a document that is similar to the query is relevant, then other documents similar to it are likely to also be relevant. By clustering neighboring documents, **nearest neighbor** documents should also be retrieved. But as Cutting et al. note, for a partitioning cluster to be useful in this application $k$ must be very near $N$ [Cutting et al., 1992]. We do not want to retrieve more than a linear constant of other documents when we retrieve one.

ScatterGather is an intereseting example of how partitional clustering can be applied in a provocative way [Cutting et al., 1992; Hearst and Pedersen, 1992]. Beginning with a clustering of the entire corpus, initial queries are posed by selecting some of the clusters. Documents identified as members of these clusters form a new subcorpus; clustering is applied across these, and so on. Evaluating the utility of such a novel browsing pattern is difficult, but the ability of the ScatterGather interface (as well as a similar effort applied to the MacOS interface called Piles [Rose et al., 1993] to improve retrieval effectiveness is quite clear. A problematic feature of the ScatterGather procedure is its sensitivity to the selection of initial "buckshot" random seeds. But Cutting doesn't necessarily see this as a bug:

> Indeed, the lack of determinism might be interpreted as a feature, since the user then had the option of discarding an unrevealing partition in favor of a fresh re-clustering. [Cutting et al., 1992, p. 324]

## 5.5 Probabilistic Retrieval

It should be clear by now that there are few logical grounds on which we could irrefutably *prove* that any document is relevant to any query. Our best hope is to retrieve relevant documents with high probability; i.e., we can only know <u>about</u> uncertainly. Beginning in the early 1970s, the most seminal thinkers within IR have attempted to connect fundamental concepts like "relevance" from within IR to probability theory (see [Cooper, 1971; Cooper, 1973; Bookstein and Swanson, 1974; Cooper and Maron, 1978; Cooper, 1983] and other references throughout this section). As typical search engines moved past simpler Boolean retrieval to ranked retrievals [Cooper, 1988], and more recently as representational languages like Bayesian networks have become widespread within artificial intelligence (cf. Section 5.5.7), a probabilistic foundation for FOA has become an increasingly central concern. The derivation of the basic components of the Bayesian decision models presented here follows van Rijsbergen, p. 115 quite closely; the ***lecture notes on probabilistic IR***[2] developed by Nobert Fuhr provide a similar treatment of this background.

## 5.5.1 Probability Ranking Principle

We begin with an important assumption called the **Probability Ranking Principle** (PRP):[†]

> Who stated
> the PRP?

> If a reference retrieval system's response to each request is a ranking of the documents in the collection in order of decreasing probability of relevance . . . the overall effectiveness of the system to its user will be the best that is obtainable. [van Rijsbergen, p. 113]

This assumption reduces the problem of building an optimal IR system to one of ordering documents in order of decreasing probability of relevance. Defining our retrieval task in these terms is optimal in the sense that it minimizes the amount of expected error in retrieval performance (cf. Section 5.5.6).[†]

> The PRP hides
> another
> assumption

There are at least two possible interpretations of precisely what a probability of relevance, $Pr(Rel)$, means, in terms of an underlying event space [Maron, 1977; Maron, 1982a; Maron and Kuhns, 1960]. The first is to imagine (again considering a particular query) that the "experiment" of showing the document to a user is repeated across multiple users. Alternatively, we can imagine that the same query/document relevance

---

[2] ls6-www.informatik.uni-dortmund.de/ir/teaching/courses/ir/kap~6.ps.gz

question is put *repeatedly to the same user*, who sometimes replies that it is relevant and sometimes that it isn't. However we interpret $Pr(Rel)$, we will focus on one particular query and compute $Pr(Rel)$ *conditionalized* by any and all **features** we might associate with the document **d**.

Consistent with previous notation (cf. Sections 4.3.4 and 5.3.1), we will define $Rank(d)$ to be a positive integer assigned to each document in the *Retr* set, in descending order of similarity with respect to a (henceforth implicit) query **q**, and using the matching function $Match(\mathbf{q}, \mathbf{d})$:

$$Match(\mathbf{q}, \mathbf{d}) \in \Re$$

$$Rank(\mathbf{d}) \in \mathcal{N}^+$$

$$Rank(\mathbf{d}_i) < Rank(\mathbf{d}_j) \iff Match(\mathbf{q}, \mathbf{d}_i) > Match(\mathbf{q}, \mathbf{d}_j) \quad (5.33)$$

According to the PRP, we can hope that our $Match(\mathbf{q}, \mathbf{d})$ function accurately reflects the probability of relevance:

$$Match(\mathbf{q}, \mathbf{d}) \propto Pr(Rel_{\mathbf{q}} | \mathbf{d}_i) \quad (5.34)$$

(Henceforth, we again restrict our attention to a single query and drop the subscript **q**.) In fact we only need to require that it reliably ranks documents (again with respect to an *implicit* query **q**):

$$Rank(\mathbf{d}_i) < Rank(\mathbf{d}_j) \iff Pr(Rel | \mathbf{d}_i) > Pr(Rel | \mathbf{d}_j) \quad (5.35)$$

Finally, to emphasize the *representation* of the document into its constituent features, as well as the sensitivity of our notions of relevance on this representation (cf. [van Rijsbergen, 1992]), the remainder of this section will change notation slightly. Let **x** be a vector of features $x_i$ describing the document. The PRP is then restated:

$$Match(\mathbf{q}, \mathbf{d}) \propto Pr(Rel | \mathbf{x}) \quad (5.36)$$

## 5.5.2 Bayesian Inversion

If we had worked hard on a particular test corpus of documents to identify (always with respect to some particular query) which documents were *Rel* and which were not, it would be possible to carefully study which features $x_i$ were reliably found in relevant documents and which were not. Collecting such statistics for each feature would then allow us to estimate:

$$Pr(\mathbf{x} | Rel)$$

the probability of any particular set of features $\mathbf{x}$, given that we know it is *Rel*. (Just which statistics we collect, and how, will be discussed in more detail in Section 7.4 as part of a more general classification task.) The retrieval question requires that we ask the converse: the probability that a document with features $\mathbf{x}$ should be considered relevant. This inversion is accomplished via the familiar Bayes rule:

$$Pr(Rel|\mathbf{x}) = \frac{Pr(\mathbf{x}|Rel)Pr(Rel)}{Pr(\mathbf{x})} \qquad (5.37)$$

### 5.5.3 Odds Calculation

Rational world    In addition to evidence the features provide to show that a document *is Rel*, $Pr(Rel|\mathbf{x})$, they may also provide evidence that it is not: $Pr(\overline{Rel}|\mathbf{x})$.[†] An *odds* calculation balances both probabilities as a ratio:

$$Odds(Rel|\mathbf{x}) \equiv \frac{Pr(Rel|\mathbf{x})}{Pr(\overline{Rel}|\mathbf{x})} \qquad (5.38)$$

The Bayes rule can also be applied to this ratio:

$$Odds(Rel|\mathbf{x}) = \frac{Pr(Rel|\mathbf{x})}{Pr(\overline{Rel}|\mathbf{x})} = \frac{Pr(Rel)}{Pr(\overline{Rel})} \cdot \frac{Pr(\mathbf{x}|Rel)}{Pr(\mathbf{x}|\overline{Rel})}$$

$$= Odds(Rel) \cdot \frac{Pr(\mathbf{x}|Rel)}{Pr(\mathbf{x}|\overline{Rel})} \qquad (5.39)$$

The first term will be small; the odds of picking a relevant versus irrelevant document independent of any features of the document are not good. Still, $Odds(Rel)$ can be expected to be a characteristic of an entire corpus or the generality of the current query but insensitive to any analysis we might perform on a particular document.

In order to calculate the second term, we need a more refined model of how documents are "constructed" from their features.

### 5.5.4 Binary Independence Model

Perhaps the simplest model proceeds by imagining binary, independent features; it is conventionally called (surprise!) the **Binary Independence Model** (BIM) [Robertson and Sparck Jones, 1976; van Rijsbergen, 1977]. First, the binary assumption is that all the features $x_i$ are binary. This is not a very restrictive assumption and is used only to simplify the derivation.

The much bigger assumption is that the documents' features occur independently of one another. We have discussed the problems with such an assumption before. Van Rijsbergen, p. 120 quotes J. H. Williams's expression of the paradox:

> The assumption of independence of words in a document is usually made as a matter of mathematical convenience. Without the assumption, many of the subsequent mathematical relations could not be expressed. With it, many of *the conclusions should be accepted with extreme caution.* [Williams, 1965, emphasis in original]

The key advantage it allows is that the probability of a feature vector **x** becomes simply the *product* of the **marginal probabilities** of the individual features:

$$Pr(\mathbf{x}|Rel) = \prod_i Pr(x_i|Rel) \qquad (5.40)$$

Very convenient – and very unrealistic.[†]

Applying this decomposition to our odds calculation gives:

Maybe this assumption isn't so bad?

$$Odds(Rel|\mathbf{x}) = Odds(Rel) \cdot \prod_i \frac{Pr(x_i|Rel)}{Pr(x_i|\overline{Rel})} \qquad (5.41)$$

It will be convenient to introduce the variables $p_i$ and $q_i$ to capture the probabilities that feature $x_i$ is present, given that a document is or is not relevant:

$$p_i \equiv Pr(x_i = 1|Rel) \qquad (5.42)$$

$$q_i \equiv Pr(x_i = 1|\overline{Rel}) \qquad (5.43)$$

The complementary probabilities concerning documents in which the feature is *absent* can also be defined easily:

$$1 - p_i = Pr(x_i = 0|Rel) \qquad (5.44)$$

$$1 - q_i = Pr(x_i = 0|\overline{Rel}) \qquad (5.45)$$

These definitions break the product into two portions, the first having to do with those features that are present in a particular document

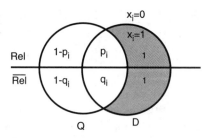

FIGURE 5.6 Random Variables Underlying Binary Independence Model

and the second with those that are not:

$$Odds(Rel \mid \mathbf{x}) = Odds(Rel) \cdot \prod_{x_i=1} \frac{p_i}{q_i} \cdot \prod_{x_i=0} \frac{1 - p_i}{1 - q_i} \qquad (5.46)$$

Recall that both queries and documents live within the same vector space defined over the features $x_i$. The *two* products of Equation 5.46 (defined in terms of presence or absence of a feature in a document) can be further broken into *four* subcases, depending on whether the features occur in the query. We next make another "background" assumption concerning all the features $x_i$ that are not in *both* the query *and* the document of current interest; we assume that the probability of these features being present in relevant and irrelevant documents is equal: $p_i = q_i$. In other words, for those terms we don't care about (because they don't affect this query/document comparison), we are happy to think that their occurrence is independent of their relevance.

Consider the sets $D$ and $Q$ shown in Figure 5.6 defined in terms of those features $x_i$ present and absent in the document and query, respectively.* Regrouping the two products of Equation 5.46 into four products created by the two sets $D$ and $Q$, the $\frac{p_i}{q_i}$ terms cancel except in the intersection of the query and document (where the feature $x_i$ is present in both) and in $Q \backslash D$, the set difference of $Q$ less $D$:

$$Odds(Rel \mid \mathbf{x}) = Odds(Rel) \cdot \prod_{x_i \in D \cap Q} \frac{p_i}{q_i} \cdot \prod_{x_i \in Q \backslash D} \frac{1 - p_i}{1 - q_i} \qquad (5.47)$$

---

* Apologies for the unfortunate overuse of the same letter 'q' for denoting both the *set Q* of features contained in the query and the *probability $q_i$* of the presence of a feature in irrelevant documents, but there is no intended, direct connection between these two quantities.

In the retrieval situation we will exploit the sparseness that makes it much more efficient to keep track of where a feature does occur ($x_i = 1$) than all the places it does not ($x_i = 0$). Since the second product is defined over all the features of $q$ except those in $d$, if we are careful to "pre-multiply" each feature in their intersection by a reciprocal, we can then safely multiply everything in the query by the same ratio:

$$Odds(Rel|\mathbf{x}) = Odds(Rel) \cdot \prod_{x_i \in Q} \frac{1 - p_i}{1 - q_i} \cdot \prod_{x_i \in D \cap Q} \frac{p_i(1 - q_i)}{q_i(1 - p_i)} \quad (5.48)$$

The next section will show the utility of separating the last term, which depends on features of the document in question, from the first two, which do not, as part of an online retrieval calculation.

But first, it is worthwhile considering how we might attempt to estimate some of the required statistics [Robertson and Sparck Jones, 1976]. Fuhr [Fuhr, 1992], for example, considers the retrospective case when we have *RelFbk* from a user who has evaluated each of the top $N$ documents in an initial retrieval and has found $R$ of these to be relevant (as well as evaluating all the $N - R$ remaining and found them to be irrelevant!). If a particular feature $x_i$ is present in $n$ of the retrieved documents with $r$ of these relevant, then this bit of *RelFbk* provides reasonable estimates for $p_i$ and $q_i$:

$$\widetilde{p}_i = \frac{r}{R} \quad (5.49)$$

$$\widetilde{q}_i = \frac{n - r}{N - R} \quad (5.50)$$

## 5.5.5 Linear Discriminators

The retrieval problem is made simpler by noting that all we really need is a simple **discrimination threshold**, above which the evidence for *Rel* is sufficient that our retrieval system elects to show a user the document as part of a hitlist. We reflect this by making the *Rank* function proportional to the odds of relevance given the document:

$$Rank(\mathbf{x}) \propto \prod_{x_i \in D \cap Q} \frac{p_i(1 - q_i)}{q_i(1 - p_i)} \quad (5.51)$$

Assuming the features $x_i$ are stochastically independent is very helpful, but manipulating the *product* of terms is still awkward. For example, we might reasonably want to **regress** (train) the feature variables against known *Rel* documents to compute weights for their relative contributions [Cooper et al., 1992; Gey, 1994]. While nonlinear regression algorithms (e.g., neural networks) do exist, regression with respect to a linear combination of features is most straightforward.

**Logarithmic** functions perform just this transformation (i.e., transforming products to sums) and are also guaranteed to be **monotonic**. Monotonicity guarantees that if $a < b$ then $log(a) < log(b)$, and the ranking scores we use to order our hitlist will not change the *relative order* of any two documents on our hitlist. The two steps of

- first comparing two probabilities in an *Odds* ratio and then
- taking logarithms to form linear combinations rather than products

Weighting evidence

arise so frequently that the two operators are often composed and considered a single *LogOdds* calculation.[†]

For our discrimination purposes, then, *LogOdds* will suffice:

$$LogOdds(Rel \mid \mathbf{x}) = LogOdds(Rel) + \sum_{x_i \in Q} \log \left( \frac{1 - p_i}{1 - q_i} \right)$$

$$+ \sum_{x_i \in D \cap Q} \log \left( \frac{p_i(1 - q_i)}{q_i(1 - p_i)} \right) \quad (5.52)$$

$LogOdds(Rel)$ reflects the *prior* probability that we are likely to find a relevant document in our corpus, independent of any features of the query/document. This could vary, for example, between very general and very specific queries, but again, it should not alter our ranking of documents pertaining to a particular query. Focusing exclusively on those factors that will be useful in discriminating one document from another, with respect to a particular query, Equation 5.52 simplifies considerably, and we come up with a *Rank* measure:

$$Rank(\mathbf{x}) = \sum_{x_i \in Q \cap D} c_i + \kappa \quad (5.53)$$

where the weight $c_i$ associated with each feature

$$c_i = \log \frac{p_i(1 - p_i)}{q_i(1 - q_i)} \quad (5.54)$$

is called the **relevance weight** (also known as **retrieval status value** (**RSV**)) of this feature, and $\kappa$ is the query-invariant constant:

$$\kappa = LogOdds(Rel) + \sum_{x_i \in Q} \frac{1 - p_i}{1 - q_i} \qquad (5.55)$$

corresponding to the log of the first two document-insensitive terms of Equation 5.52.

## 5.5.6  Cost Analysis

The discussion of Section 4.3.4 suggests that, as with most real-world decisions, there is no perfect way to select relevant documents. Even if we can accomplish the PRP and order all the documents, there remains a retrieval threshold to set. If we set the threshold too high, we will not show users some documents they might wish to see, and if we set it too low we will show them too many.

But we can capture this tension by associating two costs (a.k.a. losses) with each of two possible sources of error. The first cost $C_{RN}$ is incurred when we retrieve an irrelevant document, the second $C_{NR}$ when we don't retrieve a relevant document. To make these costs concrete, we might imagine that there is a limited resource (hitlist screen real estate, user search time), and the first cost is proportional to using up this precious resource. Similarly, the second cost might be proportional to the cost of losing a malpractice suit, when a legal case on point wasn't found but should have been!

In terms of the *LogOdds* ranking function of Equation 5.54, the trade-off between these two costs can be realized by another term added to the constant $\kappa$ of Equation 5.55:

$$\kappa' = \kappa + \log \frac{C_{RN} - C_{NR}}{C_{NR} - C_{RN}} \qquad (5.56)$$

We can easily imagine adding a knob to a browser reflecting the trade-off between these two costs [Russel et al., 1993].

## 5.5.7  Bayesian Networks

As will be discussed in great detail in Chapter 6, there are many types of information on which we might wish to base our retrieval. Most of this

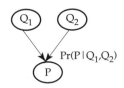

FIGURE 5.7 Interaction between Parental Influences

section has concerned probabilistic models for the crucial *Index* relation between keywords and documents, but we may wish to model other information probabilistically as well.

Bayesian networks (also known as inference or belief networks) are a modeling language within which many probabilistic relationships can be expressed as part of a common representation and used as part of a unified inference procedure [Pearl, 1988]. A Bayesian network is a graph in which nodes correspond to propositions and links correspond to conditional probabilistic dependencies between these propositions. A directed link from node $p$ to node $q$ is used to model the fact that $p$ *causes q*, although other semantics (e.g., logical implication) are sometimes also used.

When representing interactions among $n$ propositions, we must generally consider the possible dependency of each proposition on every other. To do this completely requires an exponential number of statistics, which is impractical for most situations and certainly if we attempt to model interactions between all the documents in our corpora and their keywords. Within Bayesian networks, this full set of statistics – the **joint probability distribution** – is replaced by a sparse representation only among those variables *directly* influencing one another. Interactions among indirectly related variables are then computed by propagating inference through a graph of these direct connections.

The key integration of probabilistic information across interacting variables is accomplished by specifying how each child node depends on the set of its parents' values. A table of conditional dependency probabilities specifies, for each possible value of each parent node, the probability of each of the child variable's value; see Figure 5.7. With these condiditional relationships specified for each node, querying a Bayesian network corresponds to placing prior probabilities on some elements of the network and then asking for the probability at other nodes.

One of the most comprehensive applications of Bayesian network representations to the propositions associated with FOA is due to Croft

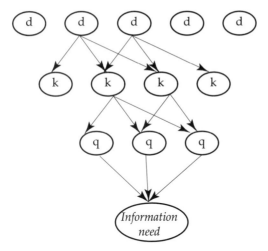

FIGURE 5.8 Bayesian Network Representation for FOA

with Turtle and other students [Turtle, 1990; Turtle and Croft, 1990; Turtle and Croft, 1991; Turtle and Croft, 1992; Callan et al., 1995] and is shown in Figure 5.8. This graph shows four types of nodes: documents, keywords, queries, and a single information need node.[†]

This graph is rooted on the document nodes. To use this representation, a single document is "instantiated," meaning that we posit that only this one document is retrieved and we ask for the probability that the information need is satisfied. Given these estimates for each document, the hitlist is formed according to the Probability Ranking Principle. Estimates for the keywords' dependencies on documents rely on the same weighting techniques discussed in Section 3.3.

Fuhr and Buckley have extended this formalism to include an additional level, which they call **relevance description** $\chi(\cdot)$ [Fuhr and Buckley, 1991]. This is an arbitrary function over terms and documents $\chi(k, \mathbf{d})$. Using this descriptive layer, rather than computing

$$Pr(Rel \mid k, \mathbf{d})$$

the probability of relevance given a particular keyword and a particular document, they propose to evaluate

$$Pr(Rel \mid \chi(k, \mathbf{d}))$$

where this is the "probability that a document will be judged relevant to an arbitrary query, given that one of the document's index terms, which

Multiple representations of the same document

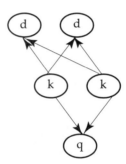

FIGURE 5.9 Concept-Matching Version of Bayesian Network

also occurs in the query, has the relevance description $\chi$." Fuhr argues that by separating the description function from the keyword and the document, a wider range of descriptions can be considered, and there is no longer a need to associate a probability of relevance with individual keywords or documents.

An alternative formulation proposed by Ribeiro and Muntz, following work by Wong and Yao, imagines the keyword vocabulary describing a universe of discourse [Ribeiro, 1995; Ribeiro and Muntz, 1996; Wong and Yao, 1995], as shown in Figure 5.9. Treating each keyword as a binary variable, any of the $2^V$ possible subsets corresponds to a concept; any query and every document can be described as a concept within this space. The goal of retrieval becomes one of **conceptual matching** of a query against that of the documents. Either $Pr(\mathbf{d}|\mathbf{q})$ or $Pr(\mathbf{q}|\mathbf{d})$ can be used to reflect the strength of the concept matching relationship. In fact, these two quantities can generally be made equivalent with proper normalization [Wong and Yao, 1995].

Note that the Bayesian network generated from this perspective inverts the causal links from those proposed by Turtle and Croft! Riberiro and Muntz argue that their formulation is superior, because it treats queries and documents symmetrically (as we would expect for a concept matching retrieval). Further, the fact that conventional cosine-similarity matching requires normalization of the document vector over all index terms creates a dependence on terms not contained in the query. Any such dependence violates a fundamental condition for Bayesian network graphs [Pearl, 1988].

A good example of modeling within the Bayesian network formalism is to show how multiple query formulations, for example, Boolean and

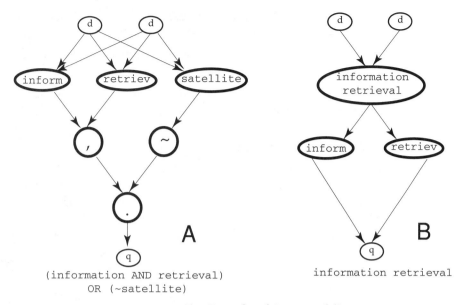

(information AND retrieval)
OR (~satellite)

information retrieval

FIGURE 5.10 Two Examples of Query Modeling

weighted vector space query strategies, can be modeled interchangeably. Figure 5.10 shows in detail two possible ways in which query nodes might be connected to particular keywords. The first shows a Boolean combination of keywords, and the second shows a network capturing dependencies between a phrase keyword and its constituent elements. Interaction among multiple queries all designed to satisfy the same information need, as discussed in terms of a query session in Section 4.2, can also be modeled.

**EXERCISE 1**    1. How much would the probability $p_6$ of a six-character word's occurrence change if case is not folded?

2. What would happen if we allowed hyphens?

3. For extra credit, discuss how the issues of capitalization and hyphenation interact (for example, in the case of politically correct schoolchildren's names, like SMITH-JONES-HARTLEY-FRANK).

4. What does this imply about the utility of **proper names** as potential index terms?

**EXERCISE 2**   On the whole, Zipf's law matches word ranking distributions extremely well, but individual words deviate from this somewhat. Derive a measure of this deviation, of a word's actual *frequency* from that predicted by Zipf's law, based strictly on character length; also consider rank-based deviation. Use it to identify those words that occur more (less) frequently than we would expect based on their length alone.

**EXERCISE 3**   The plot shown in Figure 5.5 would seem to involve a great deal of computational effort. For each $k$, compute the SVD using $k$ dimensions. Is there a way we can exploit the computation for SVD in $k$ dimensions for $k + 1$ or $k - 1$?

**EXERCISE 4**   How much memory is required to store $U_k$? What is the complexity of the computation required to compute it? Making reasonable assumptions about a query load, estimate the load this would make on a query server. Can you suggest a parallel architecture that would be especially appropriate for this purpose?

**EXERCISE 5**   As more and more documents are added, how much drift in vocabulary is likely? How much before it significantly degrades performance?

**EXERCISE 6**   Do you see any way to reconcile the models of Croft, Fuhr, Buckley, et al. with those of Muntz, Ribeiro, Wong, and Yao? Consider, for example, how *pseudo*-cosine similarity measures (cf. Equation 5.25) fare with respect to this constraint on Bayesian node independence.

## TERMS INTRODUCED IN THIS CHAPTER

| | | |
|---|---|---|
| agglomerative | conceptual matching | joint probability |
| associative memory | dimensionality | distribution |
| Binary Independence | reduction | latent semantic |
| Model | discrimination | latent semantic |
| citation | threshold | indexing |
| classifying | drift | lexicographic |
| cluster | eigenfactor analysis | trees |
| cluster hypothesis | features | logarithmic |

marginal
   probabilities
minimum spanning
   tree
monotonic
monotonic
   correspondence
multidimensional
   scaling

nearest neighbor
orthogonal
orthonormal
Probability Ranking
   Principle
proper names
rank-plus-shift
regress
relevance

description
relevance weight
retrieval status value
   (RSV)
singular value
   decomposition
sparse
stress
thesauri

# 6

# Inference beyond the *Index*

The *Index,* that critical mapping between documents and descriptive keywords, has dominated our approach to FOA in all the preceding chapters. But there is of course a larger context of available information: FOA can be accomplished by showing a user relations *among* keywords, by acquainting him or her with important authors, by pointing to important journals where relevant documents are often published, and so on. Retrieval of all these information resources, especially when structured in meaningful interfaces, can tell a user much more than a simple list of relevant documents.

This chapter is concerned with exploiting a variety of other clues we might have about documents (and keywords, authors, etc.), above and beyond the statistical, word-frequency information that has been at the heart of the *Index* relation. In all cases, these techniques identify some new source of data, represent it efficiently, and then perform some kind of inference over the representation.

AI is a subdiscipline of computer science that is centrally concerned with questions of knowledge representation and inference over those representations, especially when these algorithms arguably lead to "intelligent" behaviors. (In many ways the best characterization of the AI domain is the **extensional** one provided by the AIT corpus of Ph.D. dissertations.) We could expect, therefore, that there would be a great deal of cross-fertilization between AI methods and IR methods, both having grown up within computer science during the same period. But for complicated reasons, until recently there has been very little interaction.[†]

By and large, AI has defined its notions of inference in *logical* terms, originally based on automatic theorem-proving results. Chapter 5 discussed IR's probabilistic foundations, and one immediate axis of difference between AI and IR is the distinction between primarily logical and primarily probabilistic modes of inference. Nevertheless, some in IR perceived early on the advantages offered by AI's **knowledge representations** [Smith, 1981] and *expert systems* techniques [Fox and France, 1987; McCune et al., 1985; Fidel, 1986].

Today, the fields of AI and IR align much more closely. For example, both machine learning and natural language processing have always been considered central issues within AI. The next chapter will discuss at length machine learning techniques as they have been applied to document corpora. Section 8.2 can only sketch another large intersection, corpus-based linguistics, where natural language issues and IR techniques also merge.

The advantages of applying AI knowledge representation techniques become especially obvious when additional structured attributes are associated with documents, keywords, and authors. Early on, Kochen [Kochen, 1975] considered a broad range of these forms of information as shown in Figure 6.1. Even more inclusive lists have since been proposed [Katzer et al., 1982; Hanson, 1988].

This shows the primary *Index* relation in the larger context of other information we might have available. What all of these additional forms of information have in common is their ability to shed new light on the semantic questions of what the documents are <u>about</u>. Information on the publication details of documents, for example, the journal date or page numbers of documents, can help provide a context within which individual documents can be better understood. Much of this data-about-data document is now referred to as meta-data. This additional modeling of document structure, in languages like XML and codified in standards like the ***Dublin Core***,[1] is one of the most important ways in which database and IR technologies now interact. This constructively blurs many of the database/search engine differences mentioned earlier (cf. Section 1.6). Techniques for performing **fact extraction** – building database relations

History: AI xor IR?

---

[1] www-diglib.stanford.edu/diglib/pub/dublin.html

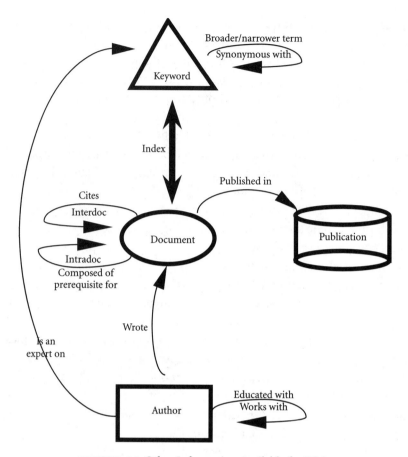

FIGURE 6.1  Other Information Available for FOA
(after [Kochen, 1975])

from analysis of textual WWW pages [Craven et al., 1998] – suggest a broad range of new ways that structured attributes may enter into the retrieval task.

Section 6.1 discusses one of the most important ways in which documents can be understood independent of their keywords. In science, in the common law tradition, more recently in email newsgroups, and now with HTML hyperlinks, the ability to link one document to another can provide vital information about how the arguments of one document relate to those contained in another.

Section 6.3 will discuss some of the special representation techniques that have been used to organize keywords in the vocabulary. It is also possible to reason about authors of documents. Section 6.4.1 discusses Ph.D. "genealogies" in which dissertation authors are related to one another by shared advisors. Coauthorship and membership in the same research institution have also been proposed as ways to provide context on a particular author's words. In some cases, characterizations of expertise of the authors, independent of the documents themselves, are available.

The chapter concludes with several suggestions of how these varied information sources can become integrated as part of next-generation FOA tools. Section 6.5 considers several "modes of inference" by which new conclusions about keywords and documents can be reached from elementary facts. Section 6.6 suggests a few of the new interface techniques that become available as richer data streams are provided by and presented back to a user. Sections 6.7 and 6.8 look at two domains of discourse in particular – the law and science surrounding molecular genetics – as examples of how such techniques can be marshaled toward particular FOA purposes. After considering all these ways that the methods of AI can be used to help with FOA, Section 6.9 concludes by speculating about how the problem of intelligence itself might be changed as we take seriously the prospect of basing it on textual representations.

## 6.1 Citation: Interdocument Links

The bibliography at the end of a scientific publication, links from one World Wide Web page to another, references in a legal brief to prior judicial opinions, and **conversational threads** connecting postings to one another within a common UseNet group may seem completely unrelated. In each case, however, the author of one document has found it useful to cite another document. Perhaps it is because the author wishes to extend a prior scientific or legal argument, or perhaps it is to attack it. It may be to pull together disjointed Web pages into a single "home page" theme. Or the citation may be designed to quiet a bunch of "newby" newsgroup discussion participants by alerting them to a FAQ (frequently asked question) answer. In all cases, a new piece of text is being woven into the larger fabric of other texts, uniting one author's contribution into the legacy of many others. The value citations can offer in supporting the FOA activity has been recognized by many [Pao and

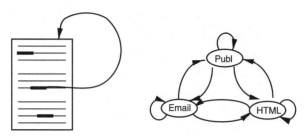

FIGURE 6.2  Basic Structure of Citations

Worthen, 1989; Salton and Bergmark, 1979] and leads to methods that allow users to capture and organize their own bibliographic materials [Belew and Holland, 1988]. As more and more scientific publishing moves to open electronic repositories, efforts such as the ***Open Citation Project***[2] are leading the way toward new standards for the exchange of this important information.

At its core, a citation is a pointer from a document to a document. We typically think of a citation pointing from one document to another document of the same type: Scientific papers cite other journal articles, email messages refer to prior messages, HTML pages point to one another. But in today's quickly changing scene, it is not uncommon to find heterogeneous forms of citation, from one document type to another, as shown in Figure 6.2.

For many publications, citations are collected at the very end of a document, in its bibliography. Often the real locus of a citation, however, is someplace earlier in the document, and many compositional styles insert an explicit bibliographic citation there. We will be interested in the **citation resolution** of both ends of the pointer: How accurately do we know the location of the citation in the citing paper, and how precisely is its pointer into the cited paper? Does it point to a particular paragraph, page, section, or the entire document?

The application of very similar citation mechanisms has been exploited in different ways in different contexts. Table 6.1 summarizes a number of dimensions across several contexts. Here we consider citations as exemplified in two particular classes of documents, generated by science and by law, which have supported social activities for a very

---

[2] journals.ecs.soton.ac.uk/x3cites/

TABLE 6.1 Comparing Citations across Document Types

|  | *Science* | *Law* | *Email/News* | *Web* |
|---|---|---|---|---|
| Purpose/ programmatics | ‡Standing on the shoulders of the giant that came before | *Stare decisis* | Many! | ?? |
| Time scale | 0 (years) | 0 (10 years) | 0 (day) | 0 (day-years) |
| Mark-up |  | Shepard's | Moderation FAQ | Topical home pages! |
| Inference | Impact Co-citation similarity Graph theoretic (Cliché = college, . . .) 'Hardness' of science!? | Impact | Public/private communication  Audience | ?? |

long time. Section 6.1.5 will report on new analyses of citation patterns observed on the WWW.


## 6.1.1 Bibliometric Analysis of Science

Most extensive analysis of citation has been in science. Long before Newton [Newton, 1776] appreciated "standing on the shoulders of the giants that came before," scientists realized that they need one another to advance. In some cases the reference is to arguments on which a new author builds; in other cases there is disagreement about hypotheses, data, or other facts.

The field of **bibliometrics** has found a great deal of interesting structure in graphs created by bibliographic citation links. That is, imagine each document in a corpus is represented by a node in a graph, and a directed edge is drawn from document $d_j$ to $d_i$, just in case $d_j$ refers to $d_i$ in its bibliography.

Figure 6.3 shows this citation structure when the references are ordered by a natural, temporal feature. In any subject area, papers can be indexed chronologically, and a dot is placed at location $\langle l, j \rangle$ just in case document $d_i$ cites document $d_j$. Because citations can only run backward in time, this graph is upper triangular.[†]

What field's literature is this?

As with many fields, this one begins with a small number of highly cross-linked papers in the upper-left corner. Strong horizontal and vertical stripes can also be seen against a more uncorrelated background.

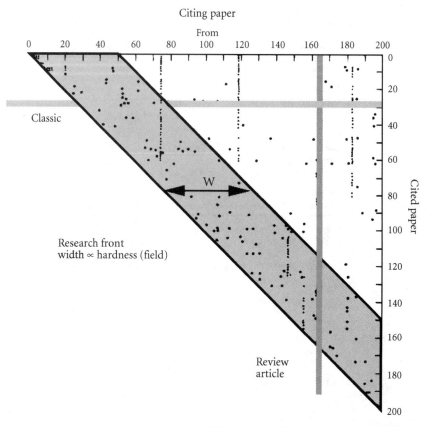

FIGURE 6.3 Temporal Structure in Citations
From [Price, 1986]. Reproduced with permission of Columbia University Press

Horizontal lines correspond to citations of **classic papers**: chestnuts that everyone includes in their bibliography. Vertical stripes are papers that have much more extensive bibliographies and that stretch much farther back in time than typical; these are often referred to as **review articles**. Note how these semantic determinations can be derived from patterns in the syntactic facts of citation. Other inferences are also possible.

Perhaps the most common use of citation graphs is **impact analysis**. In terms of the bibliographic graph, a document's importance, its effect on a field, is proportional to its **in-degree**: the number of citation links pointing to a document node. Price provides motivation for this measure:

> Flagrant violations there may be, but on the whole there is, whether we like it or not, a reasonably good correlation between

the eminence of a scientist and his productivity of papers. It takes persistence and perseverance to be a good scientist, and these are frequently reflected in a sustained production of scholarly writing. [Price, 1986, pp. 35–36]

This suggests a simple heuristic, widely used by university deans who must quickly evaluate faculty members who are up for promotion: Important authors are those with higher impact than their peers! The Institute for Scientific Information (ISI) has made an entire industry of collating bibliographic citations and inverting them. Its **Web of Science**[3] product now makes hypertext navigation of this valuable information straightforward. Similar arguments can be extended to identify important academic departments, universities, even countries. This mode of analysis, used to evaluate individuals (and, by extension, departments, colleges, universities, even countries) consistently makes news when data and politics cross paths [May, 1997].

Finally, as mentioned in Section 5.2.5, **cocitation** can be used as a basis for interdocument similarity: Two documents are similar to the extent that their bibliographies overlap. Bar-Hillel has been credited with the first suggestion of using cocitation as a similarity metric between documents [Bar-Hillel, 1957; Swanson, 1988]; Henry Small, Eugene Garfield, and others have provided some of the first empirical support for this hypothesis [Small, 1973; Garfield, 1979; Garfield, 1982; Garfield, 1986].

So-called **invisible colleges** [Merton, 1973], connecting cliques of self-referential colleagues who are relatively independent of the rest of science, also have been identified. Beyond fully isolated cliques, higher-order structure over sets of documents can also be analyzed. We can imagine that the documents of one discipline have much higher connectivity among themselves than they do with papers in other disciplines. A new paper, whose bibliography cites papers coming from more than one discipline, can therefore be imagined to be a new cutting-edge synthesis.

Bibliometrics has also made clear many dangers in using citation data. What we might call the **norm of scholarship**, the average number of citations in a document, seems to be about 10 to 20 [Price, 1986, p. 161]. Some scientific disciplines rely on much longer bibliographies

---

[3] www.webofscience.com/

than others; within a discipline, idiosyncratic author variations in bibliography length are also common.

## 6.1.2  Time Scale

Obviously bibliographic references can only go back in time, but just how far back in time a citing author reaches also tells us something. For typical journal publications, the typical time scale of references is on the order of years. A large fraction of this time has been, to date, sensitive to the production schedules of scientific journals. As the time between publication of an author's words and a reader's browsing has shrunk (e.g., in fields like physics, where the ***Los Alamos preprints Server***[4] has become a dominant mechanism of dissemination), much of the time difference is now due exclusively to delays associated with peer review, revision, etc. This delay between the time an author is finished with a document and when it reaches its public obviously provides a lower bound for **citation lag**, the time between a document's publication date and its reference by another paper's bibliography.

But independent of production schedules, there are wide varieties in how far back citations typically reach. Price sees a deep connection between the social processes underlying various scientific disciplines. First, he distinguishes between two gross types of citation, **normal aging** and the **immediacy effect**: "a special hyperactivity of the rather recent literature" [Price, 1986, p. 164]. He also defined **Price's index** to be the fraction of documents published that are cited *within five years.*

Price then uses the width of the interval to distinguish between "hard" and "soft" sciences, even "nonsciences," all based on the width of the **research front** within which most citations are typically made. He sees his Price's index as "corresponding very well with what we intuit as hard science, soft science and non-science as we descend the scale" (p. 168). Using biological metaphors, with different disciplines compared to different kinds of organisms:

> . . . pathological cases apart, it would seem that the [Price] index provides a good diagnostic for the extent to which a subject

---

[4] xxx.lanl.gov/cmp_lg/

is attempting, so to speak, to grow from the skin rather than from the body. With a low index one has a humanistic type of metabolism which the scholar has to digest all that has gone before, let it mature gently in the cellar of his wisdom, and then distill forth new words of wisdom about the same sorts of questions. In hard science the positiveness of the knowledge and its short term permanence enable one to move through the packed down past while still a student and then to emerge at the research front where interaction with one's peers is as important as the store-house of conventional wisdom. The thinner the skin of science the more orderly and crystalline the growth and the more rapid the process. (pp. 177–8)

Price also infers prescriptions from these statistics for editors of journals who are in a controlling position to influence a field:

I regard the value of this work as being not only diagnostic, but also prescriptive, so let us look in closing at what suggestions it makes for the technology of scientific information. At the personal level of the scientific writer and the editor and publisher of journals, it tells that one might well be as careful about references as we are about titles, authorships, and proper presentation of data. . . . For a research paper it should be exceptional to allow an author to eschew interaction with colleagues by citing too few references, and if he cited too many, perhaps he is writing a review paper rather than a research contribution. Similarly, if you want to make the field firm and tight and hard and crystalline you have to play with your peers and keep on the ball by citing their recent work. (p. 178)

## 6.1.3 Legal Citation

The use of citation in legal documents is interesting for a number of reasons [Rose, 1994, section 5.4]. First, the common law tradition adjudicating legal behavior is based on arguments of ***stare decisis***: Stand by previous decision.[†] The ability to reference prior judicial opinions provides the core of many forms of documents, including the judicial

U.S. courts are latitudinarian!

opinions themselves, briefs, even legislation. It is no wonder, then, that legal prose has developed an extensive system of conventions for representing how judicial opinions relate to one another.

As with scientific papers, the fact of citation – reference by one judge to the opinion of another – is never in doubt, and so some analyses like impact analysis transfer quite directly from scientific corpora. (The fact that the publishing of our courts' opinions is dependent on commercial interests means that precedent inflation [Brenner, 1992] can occur, however.[†] See Section 6.7.) But when referring to prior cases, the *relevance* of prior decisions often depends on the judge's interpretation of the *relation* holding between the two opinions.

Precedent
inflation

In fact, an entire industry exists within legal publishing to do nothing but elaborate the syntactic fact of reference to a prior ruling with an interpretation of the purpose for which the citation is made. This process is performed especially well by Shepard/Lexis. So critical are the arguments captured by these citations that the process of checking a prior ruling that a lawyer wishes to reference, to be sure that it hasn't been overruled or otherwise rendered obsolete, is known as **Sheparedizing** a case.

Table 6.2 shows the entire range of Shepard citation labels. These are broken into two categories; the first deals with the history of a case, the second with its treatment.

To make sense of this distinction, a brief digression into the purpose of legal citation is necessary. Cases, as they proceed from lower to higher courts, have basically a binary outcome: They are won or lost. There is never ambiguity as to whether a higher court agrees with or overrules the opinion of a lower court. These unambiguous statements are captured as the history of a case.

But in a common law tradition, a much larger number of citations refer to cases and decisions in those cases by other judges. The relationship between these cases and the one before the author-judge is less clear. But as Figure 6.4 makes explicit, the two cases (citing and cited) have at least two important dimensions along which they may be similar or dissimilar. First, the set of facts associated with one case may be very close to those in the other, or they may be very different. Second, the rules of law that are to be applied may be consistent between one judge and the other, or they may be contrary. Figure 6.4 shows these two dimensions and orders Shepard's treatment labels roughly along dimensions of this two-dimensional similarity space.

TABLE 6.2 Shepard Citation Labels
From [Rose, 1994]. Reproduced with permission of Lawrence Erlbaum

| Code | Description | Comments |
|---|---|---|
| | | **HISTORY OF CASE** |
| A | Affirmed | Same case affirmed on appeal |
| CC | Connected case | Different case from cited case but arising out of same subject matter or intimately connected therewith |
| CF | Certiorari filed | |
| DE | Denied | |
| DM | Dismissed | Appeal from same case dismissed |
| GR | Granted | |
| IN | US cert denied | Certiorari denied by U.S. Supreme Court |
| | US cert dismissed | Certiorari dismissed by U.S. Supreme Court |
| | US reh denied | Rehearing denied by U.S. Supreme Court |
| | US reh dismissed | Rehearing dismissed by U.S. Supreme Court |
| M | Modified | Same case modified on appeal |
| MI | Mandate issued | |
| NP | Not published | |
| PD | Petition denied | |
| PG | Petition granted | |
| R | Reversed | Same case reversed on appeal |
| S | Superseded | Substitution for former opinion |
| SC | Same case | |
| V | Vacated | Same case vacated |
| | | **TREATMENT OF CASE** |
| C | Criticized | Soundness of decision or reasoning in cited case criticized |
| D | Distinguished | Case at bar different either in law or fact from case cited |
| E | Explained | Statement of import of decision in cited case |
| EX | Examiner's decision | Not merely a restatement of the facts |
| F | Followed | Cited as controlling |
| H | Harmonized | Apparent inconsistency explained and shown not to exist |
| J | Dissenting | Citation in dissenting opinion |
| L | Limited | Refusal to extend decision of cited case beyond precise issues involved |
| O | Overruled | Ruling in cited case expressly overruled |
| P | Parallel | Citing case substantially alike ("on all fours") with cited case in its law or facts |
| Q | Questioned | Soundness of decision or reasoning in cited case questioned |

## 6.1.4 Citations and Arguments

Expository documents are arguments: attempts to convince an audience that some set of propositions are true. Depending on the type of

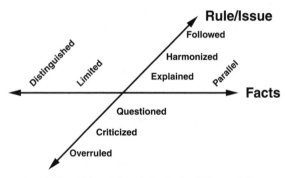

FIGURE 6.4 Rose's Two-Dimensional Analysis of Shepard Treatment Codes

document and the type of audience, the argument may be more or less formally structured.

Perhaps the most structured kinds of documents are mathematical papers. Mathematical arguments typically depend on, indeed are defined by, theorem proving, which connects new propositions to previously established results. Even in the case of mathematical papers, however, it is interesting to observe the crucial role natural language text continues to play in providing a context for formal theoretical results. Readers can be persuaded that assumptions are reasonable, that mathematical definitions capture intuitive relationships, etc. Citations in a mathematical paper typically point to papers containing theorems that were used as part of the current proof.

In a scientific paper, the form of the argument often has to do with the discipline. There is often data to present, methodology to describe, and so on. Many of the citations are typically gathered in a section relating the current piece of work to prior literature. This prior literature may be referenced for at least two, very different, purposes. Most typically the prior work is used much as theorems in mathematical papers: to establish a result from which the current work proceeds. The current author points to the work of a prior author as providing validation for a proposition they both believe to be true. Another potential reason for citation is the opposite. In this case, the current author is interested in debating a position put forward by the cited work.

This polarity, reflecting whether the cited work and its conclusions are positively or negatively correlated with those in the citing work, will be termed the **polarity** of the citation. Here legal documents provide a good example for what might be possible in scientific writing. Every law student learns proper legal syntax for codifying references as they learn to write **legal briefs**, the structured memos provided to judges that are often incorporated into the ultimate opinion[Harvard Law Review Association, 1995]. One feature of legal briefs is the special syntax used to refer to statutory law (e.g., 17 U.S.C 101 refers to a section of the U.S. Code) or case law (e.g., West Pub. Co. v. Mead Data Cent., Inc., 616 F.Supp 1571) in a conventional fashion. A more interesting aspect of legal brief style is the explicit syntactic marking of the relation of the cited case to the argument being made in the brief: Reference to a supporting legal precedent is marked by cf., while potentially antagonistic arguments are marked with but cf.!

Note the importance of the syntactic localization of both the source and destination of a citation pointer to the two documents' semantic purposes. Localization helps to anchor the author's purpose in using the citation to the document's larger argument. Most papers make many points and attempt to establish a number of propositions. The ability to point to particular conclusions within the cited paper is therefore important. The citing paper's argument structure is simultaneously being extended, and so reference to a prior argument at a particular location in the current argument can be more persuasive than if all cites aren't localized.   ?3, 4, 5

One reason citation has been less exploited in FOA applications than it might otherwise be is due to the expense of obtaining this data. In the context of the WWW, however, it turns out that the indices built by Web crawlers can be quite easily extended to capture information on *cited* pages, which can be easily inverted to maintain information on *citing* pages as well (cf. Section 8.1).

## 6.1.5 Analyzing WWW Adjacency

To a computer scientist, the WWW looks much like the directed graphs (digraph) we have studied in data structure classes for decades. It's big, it's dynamic, we have special questions about it, etc., but many of the same analyses we would apply to any digraph are good starting points for the WWW. A useful first step is to define the **adjacency matrix** $A$ connecting all the documents $d_i$ of the WWW:

$$A_{ij} = 1 \quad \text{if } d_i \text{ cites } d_j \tag{6.1}$$

$$A_{ij} = 0 \quad \text{otherwise} \tag{6.2}$$

For example, the *Google search engine*[5] imagines the WWW graph as the basis of a **Markov process**, where the probability of jumping from one page is uniform across all of its anchor/citations.

If $\epsilon$ is defined to be this (small) probability, the **stationary distribution** of this Markov process provides some insight into how likely a browsing user would be to find him or herself on a particular page. NEC's *CiteSeer*[6] is another example of how useful citation information can be as part of a tool for searching computer science literature.

A more extensive analysis [Chakrabarti et al., 1998b; Kleinberg, 1998] has analyzed the WWW, looking especially for methods that extract **authoritative** pages from the vast numbers of other pages the WWW also contains. The first component of this method corresponds approximately to the notion of **impact** discussed in Section 6.1.1.

> ... the fundamental difficulty lies in what could be called the Abundance Problem: The number of pages that could reasonably be returned as "relevant" is far too large for a human user to digest. Thus, to provide effective methods for automated search under these constraints, one does not necessarily need stronger versions of classical information retrieval notions such as relevance; rather one needs a method of providing a user, from a large set of relevant pages, a small collection of the most "authoritative" or "definitive" ones. ...
>
> Unfortunately, "authority" is perhaps an even more nebulous concept than "relevance," again highly subject to human judgment. ...
>
> We claim that an environment such as the WWW is explicitly annotated with precisely the type of human judgment that we need in order to formulate a notion of authority. Specifically, the creation of a link in the WWW represents a concrete indication of the following type of judgment: the creator of page $p$, by including a link to page $q$, has in some measure conferred authority on $q$. [Chakrabarti et al., 1998b, p. 2]

Second, they define **hub** documents to be ones that are particularly exhaustive in their reference to other pages. This is roughly analogous to review papers also mentioned in Section 6.1.1. To a first approximation,

---

[5] www.google.com/

[6] citeseer.nj.nec.com/cs

authoritative pages are those with high in-degree while hubs are those with high out-degree. But Kleinberg imposes an important additional constraint: A **community** of hubs and authority pages must be mutually self-referential. The thinking underlying Kleinberg's method is provocative:

> Authoritative pages relevant to the initial query should not only have large in-degree; since they are all authorities on a common topic, there should also be considerable overlap in the sets of pages that point to them. Thus, in addition to highly authoritative pages, we expect to find what could be called hub pages: these are pages that have links to multiple relevant authoritative pages. It is these hub pages that "pull together" authorities on a common topic, and allow us to throw out unrelated pages of large in-degree. Hubs and authorities exhibit what could be called a mutually reinforcing relationship: a good hub is a page that points to many good authorities; a good authority is a page that is pointed to by many good hubs. [Kleinberg, 1998, p. 4]

Two quantities, **x** and **y**, are associated with each document, corresponding to how good an authority or hub, respectively, the document is, based on the adjacency matrix $A$:

$$x_i \equiv \text{Authority}(d_i) \tag{6.3}$$

$$y_i \equiv \text{Hubness}(d_i) \tag{6.4}$$

$$\mathbf{x} \equiv \langle x_i \rangle \tag{6.5}$$

$$\mathbf{y} \equiv \langle y_i \rangle \tag{6.6}$$

**x** and **y** values are iteratively updated by premultiplication with the adjacency matrix or its transpose:

$$\mathbf{x}^{t+1} = A^T \mathbf{y}^t \tag{6.7}$$

$$\mathbf{y}^{t+1} = A \mathbf{x}^t \tag{6.8}$$

It is also important to renormalize these vectors to unit length after each update.

Under reasonable assumptions, this update procedure is guaranteed to converge on values with $\mathbf{x}^*$ being the principal eigenvector of $A^T A$

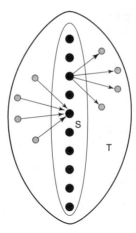

FIGURE 6.5  Citation-Expanded Hitlist

and $\mathbf{y}^*$ the principal eigenvector of $AA^T$:

$$\mathbf{x}^* = \omega_1(A^TA) \tag{6.9}$$

$$\mathbf{y}^* = \omega_1(AA^T) \tag{6.10}$$

Using this notation, the similarity of documents $d_i$ and $d_j$ can be conveniently measured in terms of cocitation as the $\langle i, j \rangle$ entry of $AA^T$.*

While we can *conceive of* applying these techniques to the graph corresponding to the entire WWW, the computational time and space required still makes such an analysis intractable. Kleinberg et al. typically recommend applying this adjacency analysis to a subset of pages pulled together by a query against some search engine. In their experiments, they augment this initial hitlist with documents that either point to or are pointed to from documents in the hitlist itself, as shown in Figure 6.5.

Note that the values for authority and hub on which this analysis converges correspond to the first, primary eigenvector. Using these values to identify high hub and anchor nodes gives rise to the first, primary community of documents in the graph. Another interesting application of adjacency analysis is to consider communities other than the one corresponding to the first, largest eigenvalue. A particularly striking application of this analysis concerns bimodal queries: Consider results arising from a query ABORTION, shown in Table 6.3. After first identifying

---

* Kleinberg also notes that the complementary measure $A^TA$ corresponds to the earlier, bibliometric construct of bibliographic coupling [Kessler, 1963].

TABLE 6.3  Authority Nodes Elicited by **ABORTION** Query, Associated with
Second Eigenvector

| $x_2$ | URL | Title |
|---|---|---|
| .321 | www.caral.org/abortion.html | Abortion and Reproductive Rights Internet Resources |
| .219 | www.plannedparenthood.org/ | Welcome to Planned Parenthood |
| .195 | www.gynpages.com/ | Abortion Clinics OnLine |
| .172 | www.oneworld.org/ippf/ | IPPF Home Page |
| .162 | www.prochoice.org/naf/ | The National Abortion Federation |
| .161 | www.lm.com/Imann/femirnst/abortion.html | |
| −.197 | www.awinc.com/partners/bc/commpass/lifenet/ lifenet.htm | Life WEB |
| −.169 | www.worldvillage.com/wv/square/chapel/xwalk/html/ peter.htm | Healing after Abortion |
| −.164 | www.nebula.net/maeve/hfelink.html | |
| −.150 | members.aol.com/pladvocate/ | |
| −.144 | www.clark.net/pub/jeffd/factbot.html | The Right Side of the Web |
| −.144 | www.catholic.net/HyperNews/get/abortion.html | |

a community of pages extensively citing both pro-choice and pro-life
documents, the second eigenvector $\omega_2$ clearly separates pages associated
with pro-choice organizations (with relatively high positive values) and
pro-life (with negative values).*

Another important feature of this analysis is that it depends on only
first-order adjacency information. That is, while it is always easy to find all
of the documents pointed to by a target document simply by inspecting
the document for its anchors, the in-neighborhood of a document can be
identified through direct inspection of other documents. This means, for
example, that search engine crawlers that look at every single document
can, as part of their normal search, simultaneously collect this adjacency
data.

## 6.2  Hypertext, Intradocument Links

Since the very first papyrus scrolls were used to capture written language,
it has become natural to conceive of text as a single, linear, and continuous

---

* Of course, the fact that one happens to be positive values and the other negative is
  completely circumstantial!

thread, authored and then read as a single stream. But as books became longer, tables of contents were prepended, indices were appended, and the opportunities for traversing the text in fundamentally *nonlinear* ways became more common. We are becoming interested in other kinds of documents, many of which bring their own special structures and writing conventions, for example, the abstract paragraph, introductions, and conclusions of longer papers and the "methods" sections in scientific papers. In news reporting, **spiral exposition** is often used; a news item is summarized in the first paragraph, then treated in more detail in the paragraphs that fit on page 1 or "above the fold" of the newspaper, and in still more detail in the body of the article.

The attempt to analyze, support, and create such nonlinear hypertext relations among documents began long before the WWW made hypertext links commonplace; *Vannevar Bush's "As We May Think"*[7] article (published in 1945!) [Bush, 1945] and Ted Nelson's revolutionary *Xanadu*[8] project [Nelson, 1987] are often mentioned as seminal works. Mice and graphical interfaces made clicking on one textual passage, to jump to another, second nature. Hypertext conferences focusing on these new issues began in the mid-1980s and have taken on new energy as the HTTP protocols and HTML authoring languages made it easy to support many kinds of intra- and interdocument relations [Conklin, 1987; Conklin and Begman, 1988; Agosti et al., 1992; Agosti and Marchetti, 1992; Bruza and Weide, 1992; Egan et al., 1991]. In the process, many types of linkages between documents have been proposed. The following sections mention some of the most common and useful, sometimes using this FOA text (self-referentially!) as examples.

## 6.2.1  Footnotes, Hyperfootnotes, and cf.

Footnote text embellishes a primary text. It provide a more detailed treatment of terms or concepts used in the primary text. A lexical token, typically smaller in size,* creates a correspondence between the primary text and the annotation on it.

Perhaps the most direct claim of hypertext authors is that the standard linear presentation of text does violence to the more networked way

---

* This footnote doesn't do much to amplify, but it does create a small example:).

[7] www.theatlantic.com/unbound/flashbks/computer/bushf.htm

[8] jefferson.village.virginia.edu/elab/hfl0155.html

in which we naturally conceive of the concepts being discussed. At the same time, the conventional sequential flow through text mandated by printed media does a great deal to support a **rhetorical argument**. For this reason, this FOA text was written first as a traditional book, assuming a basically linear flow. On this linear spine, two hypertext extensions have been added (cf. Section 8.2.1).

For example, the primary purpose of the last paragraph was to move (the primary, linear course of the textbook) from a discussion of the syntactic conventions of footnoting to a consideration of communication's ultimate purposes. Because these issues are covered in more depth in Section 8.2.1, a parenthetical cf. reference to this other section was made. The cf. relation is best viewed as an opportunity (offered by the author to a reader) to compare the two passages.[†]

cf. for *confer*

In this FOA text I have also chosen to distinguish between standard footnotes and **hyperfootnotes**, which are used to capture more extended digressions. The last paragraph allows readers with access to the CD-ROM version of *FOA* who are interested in the Latin etymology of the cf. token to poke into that. Hyperfootnotes include a caption, providing a clue to what additional information lies on the other end of the hyperjump; standard footnotes are referenced by a simple asterisk.

## 6.2.2  Hierarchic Containment

One of the most common features of all document types is that as larger and larger portions are aggregated, an explicit hierarchic structure is used to organize the text. For example, this textbook is broken into chapters, which are broken into sections and subsections, and so on. This is basically a **containment** relationship, with shorter passages aggregated to form larger ones, but with short textual **rubrics** providing useful summaries of the themes of the smaller units. Typical atomic units of text can be a few sentences [Salton et al., 1993; Salton et al., 1994], but typically they are paragraphs [Hearst and Plaunt, 1993].

A provocative picture of how the containment relation can be exploited is shown from Salton et al.'s analysis of encyclopedia text in Figure 6.6. This shows the encyclopedia text ordered sequentially around a ring. In the top figure, individual pages of the encyclopedia are treated as separate documents, and in the bottom figure larger sections are aggregated. In both cases, links between documents are created when their similarity

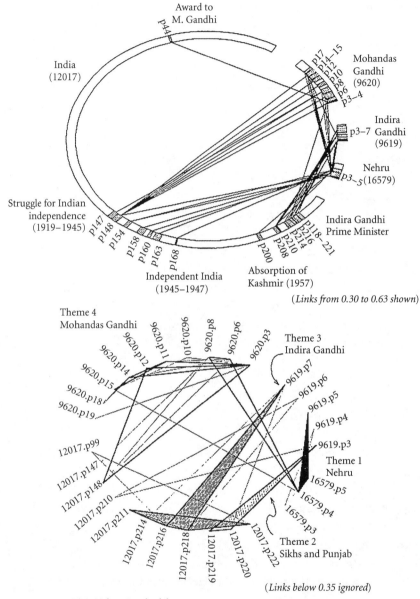

FIGURE 6.6 Containment and Document References
From [Salton et al., 1994]. Reproduced with permission of American Association
for the Advancement of Science

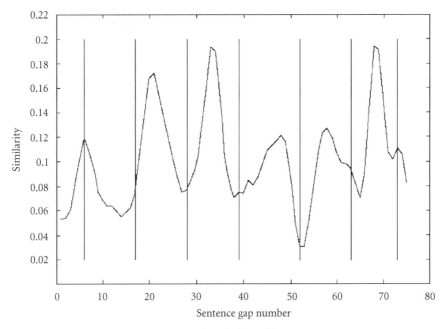

FIGURE 6.7  Correlation of Passages
From [Hearst and Plaunt, 1993]. Reproduced with permission

(as measured according to their vector space representations; cf Section 3.4) exceeds a threshold. As Chapter 3 explained in detail, a vector space representation of document content is very sensitive to length. Salton investigated the use of inclusion to aggregate text into larger units (in the bottom of Figure 6.6) and various "global" versus "local" weighting schemes to manipulate the effects of length normalization. Note also how co-reference to similar topical themes can be seen at different scales within the containment hierarchy.

When considering constituent passages of the same document, it becomes possible to ask how much the **topic** of the prose changes as it goes from one passage to the next. Hearst [Hearst and Plaunt, 1993] analyzed how *similarity (using TF-IDF weighting and cosine similarity) varies across passages.*[9] The result is the wave of Figure 6.7. Also shown in this figure are vertical bars where a human judge has determined that a topical shift has occurred.

---

[9] www.sims.berkeley.edu/hearst/tb-example.html

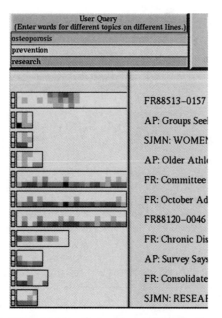

FIGURE 6.8 Visualizing Topical Distributions
From [Hearst, 1999]. Reproduced with permission of Addison-Wesley

Having isolated individual passages as part of retrieval, it becomes important to show the user this additional level of analysis as part of the retrieval of the "documents." Figure 6.8 shows **topical tiling**, another visualization technique Hearst developed to highlight shifts in topical focus from one passage to the next. By increasing the resolution of document analysis, users can see which passages match particular keywords or combinations of keywords in their query.

Containment relations among documents may also be useful in supporting queries of widely varying generality (cf. Section 4.3.4). If a user issues a very broad query, it may mean he or she seeks documents with an equally broad overview or level of treatment. One reasonable hypothesis would be that broader queries should correspond to the retrieval of large sections and narrower queries to smaller sections, but only if the assumption that documents in general obey something like a uniform level of treatment. Such an assumption would not be unreasonable for the encyclopedia text considered by Salton et al., because we expect (and encyclopedia editors attempt to ensure) that there is some document <u>about</u> every topic.

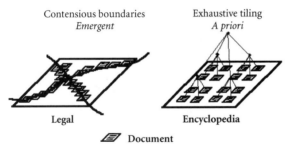

FIGURE 6.9 Topical Document Distributions

Figure 6.9 contrasts the encyclopedia's top-down coherent topical tiling with another (hypothetical) document distribution, generated by bottom-up organic case law. People don't go to court unless they disagree, and so what judges must write <u>about</u> are contentious legal issues defining the *borders* of legal disputes. As courts work out a legal issue (for example, the intellectual property status of software or whether genes can be patented), we can expect many opinions to cover very similar topical ground.

## 6.2.3  Argument Relations

A central purpose of many documents is to persuade. Especially interesting, then, are relations among documents that reveal the *arguments* relating among the documents [Sitter and Maier, 1992]. The law provides several interesting examples, as shown in Figure 6.10 (taken from Rose, 1994, Figure 7.4). Rose enumerates four relations often found in legal documents, from simple reference to more elaborate logical relations such as exception.

While less explicit than within legal documents, educational materials also have implicit or explicit **prerequisite** relationships assumed by a text's author. Figure 6.11 shows dependencies among this book's chapters. In interdisciplinary papers, it is common to have several introductory sections, providing background for experts in one field who may not have the requisite background in another. When taken across many texts, such a prerequisite structure imposes a lattice, which can be exploited to help a reader/browsing user find just those components of the document that are most important to them.

| Link Type | Example |
|---|---|
| contains, contained-in | (Chapter 1 contains §101) |
| refers-to, referred-to-by | "The works specified in §§102 and 103..." |
| subject-to, governs | "Subject to §§107 through 118..." |
| excepts, excepted-by | "Except as provided in §810 of this title..." |
| despite, ignored-by | "Notwithstanding the provisions of §106..." |

Sec. 104: Subject matter of copyright: National origin
(a) Unpublished works. -- The works specified by
section 102 and 103, while unpublished, are subject
to protection...

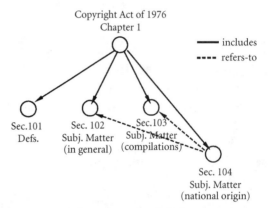

FIGURE 6.10  Intradocument Relations
From [Rose, 1994]. Reproduced with permission of Lawrence Erlbaum

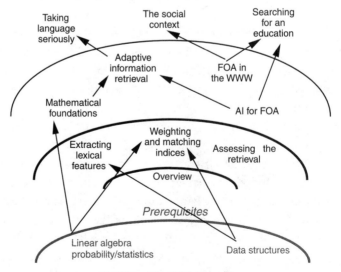

FIGURE 6.11  FOA Overview

## 6.2.4  Intra- versus Interdocument Relations

It is interesting to see how similar many conventions for relating textual passages *within* a single document are to those used to traditionally refer *across* documents. In part this reflects circumstantial features of a document's production – whether it was printed on newsprint, archival paper, in a journal or book, or a WWW page – that will disappear as a common technology underlies them all. At the same time, integrating new technologies into the publication process makes it clear how certain features will remain true only *within* a single document.

This can be described in terms of a "membrane" that functionally defines what we will continue to consider the document. The defining membrane in this case has to do with a notion of **authorship**. The words expressed are the creation/opinion of a single author or multiple authors, each of whom has signed his or her name. For example, when one paragraph of a legal document* refers to another passage within the same document:

> Except as provided in the case of certain unauthorized signatures (§8-205), lack of genuineness of a certificated security or an initial transaction statement is a complete defense. . . .

we can be assured that the document's authors were thinking about both passages and commit to a particular relation between them. Interdocument citations, on the other hand, reflect a new opinion about some preexisting document.

The Talmud, arguably one of the world's first legal documents, is most commonly published as a single volume. But extensive typographical conventions (as shown in Figure 6.12) are used to isolate individual voices and relations among commentaries; a more WWW-conventional approximation is shown in Figure 6.13, taken from an *HTML Version of the Talmud*.[10] In the common law tradition, the connection between implicit and explicit meanings becomes similarly fused. The "primary" text, secondary commentary on this, commentary on the commentary,

---

* §8-202.3 of part 2 of the Uniform Commercial Code. Here the "authors" are literally hundreds of lawyers, judges, and scholars.

[10] www.acs.ucalgary.ca/elsegal/TalmudPage.html

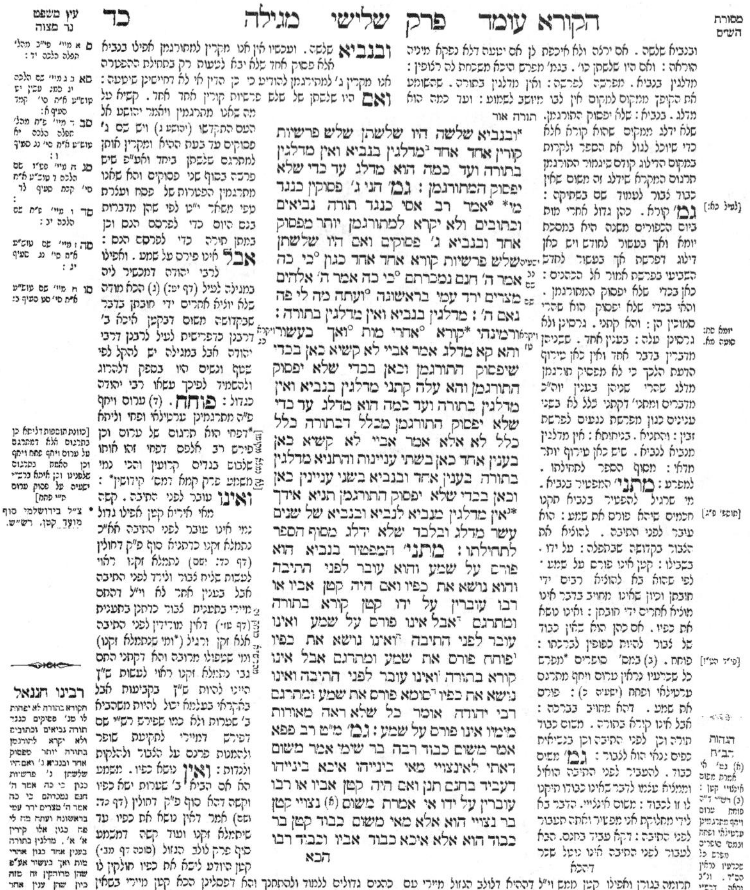

FIGURE 6.12 Typography Used to Isolate Talmudic Voices

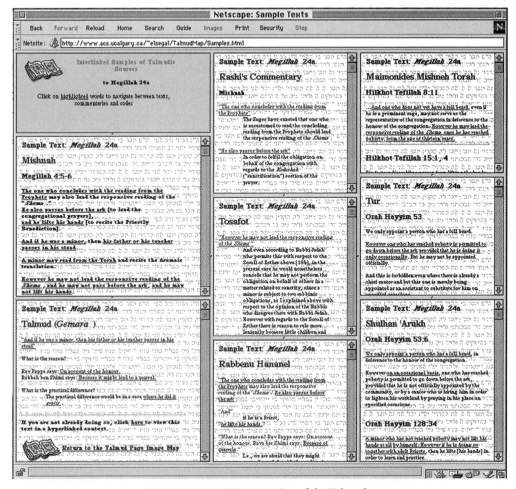

FIGURE 6.13  HTML Version of the Talmud

and so on become fused into a single unified work written by multiple authors who may have never met.[†]

What the Talmud says about Web sites

## 6.2.5 Beyond Unary *About (k)* Predicates

Our discussion of FOA has generally assumed that we are attempting to find the topic or topics that a document is <u>about</u>. In the language of logic, we can talk about this as applying a unary predicate *About(k)*. That is, the determination that a document is <u>about</u> keyword *k* depends on only one argument, a single keyword. But no piece of writing deals with only a single topic, at least for more than a moment. Good writing connects topics. It discusses a *relation* among those topics.

Within the paragraph-size textual passages that have been our focus, this relational aspect of language has not been too troubling. But it should make us especially interested in the transitions in topical focus as we move from one paragraph to the next within the same document. Passage-level analysis like this was mentioned earlier (cf. Section 6.2.2).

As we move to larger documents, an additional source of information is citations from one to another. Assuming that we have characterized the topical area of each document independently, an analysis of the citations, placed by one author relating another document to the author's topic, is an explicit indication of the relationships between these topics.

All three levels of analysis – within-paragraph relations among topics, paragraph-to-paragraph topical progression, and interdocument relations reflected by citations – are some of the clues we can exploit when suggesting potential browsing directions for users trying to FOA.

## 6.3 Keyword Structures

Most of what we have said about the *Index* relation (e.g., as part of the vector space model) assumes that keywords are simply a set of features. But beyond simply providing access to the retrieval of documents, the fact that keywords are <u>meaning</u>-ful objects in their own right means that we can analyze relationships among keywords directly.

Thesauri are structured representations of relations among keywords. Common relations represented in thesauri include:

- **broader term/narrower term (BT/NT)**; these capture hierarchic relations, generally between a kind of semantics, sometimes a part-whole relation.
- **related term (RT)**, capturing synonym or quasi-synonym relationships.
- **use for (UF)**, capturing a preferred, conventional, or authoritative term over possible alternatives.

One of the most extensive examples of such a representation is the MeSH (Medical Subject Headings) thesaurus, part of the National Library of Medicine's extensive PubMed system. Figure 6.14 shows the term LYMPHOMA within the MeSH thesaurus.* Example hierarchic BT/NT relations are shown as indentation. Because this thesaurus allows a single keyword to fit in multiple places in the hierarchy (e.g., treating LYMPHOMA as a kind of NEOPLASM as well as a kind of IMMUNOLOGIC DISEASE), this browser shows the term as part of three separate paths; note that the children (narrower terms) of LYMPHOMA are repeated in each location.

## 6.3.1 Automatic Thesaurus Construction

Before considering WordNet, another elaborate thesaurus, it is useful to relate these manually constructed representations with automatic, statistically derived analogs. Such comparisons have been part of IR research since its beginnings [Joyce and Needham, 1958; Dennis, 1964; Soergel, 1974]. Section 5.2.5 has discussed how the same information used to cluster documents can be used with keywords. The semantics of relations based strictly on cooccurrence frequencies are not obvious [van Rijsbergen, 1977] but seem to provide evidence for the **RT** (related term, or synonymy relation) discussed earlier.

Using this information to construct hierarchic relations among keywords corresponds to (hierarchic) clustering techniques. Thesaurus-specific techniques generally exploit a heuristic that high-frequency keywords correspond to broad, general terms while low-frequency keywords correspond to narrow, specific ones [Srinivasan, 1992]. This heuristic can be used to organize keywords into levels of a taxonomy, with the hierarchic parent/child relation formed between those keywords with similar document distributions. *RelFbk* can also be used to provide thesaurus structure[Guntzer et al., 1989]. Whether constructed manually or automatically, thesuarus structures support many new forms of navigation [Rada and Bicknell, 1989; McMath et al., 1989].

---

* Ellipses are used to elide some parts of this display: other types of LYMPHOMA, NON-HODGKIN and the redundant children of LYMPHOMA expanded in the second two tree locations.

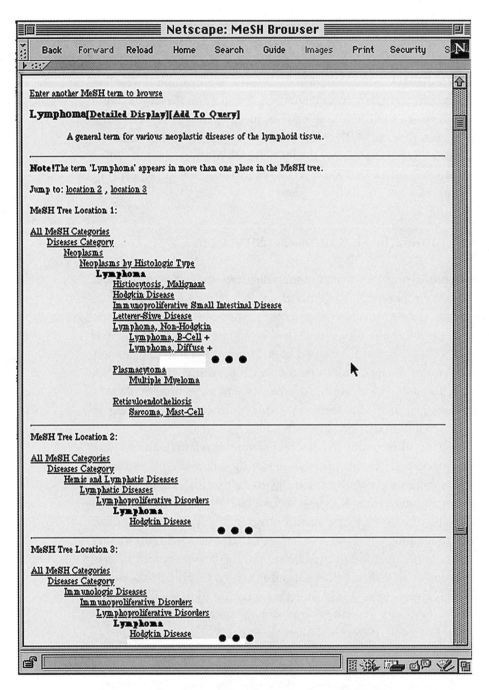

FIGURE 6.14  Example of the Term LYMPHOMA within the MeSH Keyword Thesaurus
Reproduced with permission of National Library of Medicine

## 6.3.2  Corpus-Based Linguistics and WordNet

Linguistics has traditionally focused on the phenomena of *spoken* language, and since Chomsky [Chomsky, 1965; Chomsky, 1972] it has further focused on *syntactic* rules describing the generation and understanding of individual sentences. But as more large samples of written text have become available, **corpus-based linguistics** has become an increasingly active area of research. D. D. Lewis and E. D. Liddy have collected a useful *bibliography and resource list on NLP for IR*,[11] and R. Futrelle and X. Zhang have collected large-scale persistent object systems for *Corpus Linguistics and Information Retrieval.*[12] Stuart Shieber maintains the *The Computation and Language Archive*[13] as part of the LANL reprint server.

The sophistication of syntactic analysis of computational linguistics provides a striking contrast to IR's typical **bag-of-words** approach, which aggressively ignores any ordering effects. Conversely, IR's central concerns with semantic issues of meaning and the ultimate pragmatics of using language to find relevant documents go beyond the myopic concern with isolated sentences that is typical of linguistics. The range of potential interactions between these perspectives is only beginning to be explored, but it includes the introduction of parsing techniques with IR retrieval systems [Smeaton, 1992; Strzalkowski, 1994], as well as using statistical methods to identify **phrases** that are a first step from a simple bag-of-words to syntactically well-formed sentences [Lewis, 1992; Krovetz, 1993; Church and Hanks, 1989; Steier, 1994; Steier and Belew, 1994a]. Another important direction of interaction is the use of IR methods across multilingual corpora, for example, arising from the integration of the European Community [Hull and Grefenstette, 1996; Sheridan and Ballerini, 1996].

From a syntactic perspective, the only way to get issues of real meaning into language is via the **lexicon**: a dictionary of all words and their meanings. Our present concern, interkeyword structures, becomes an issue of **lexical semantics** [Cruse, 1986], and it is no surprise that linguists have also developed representational systems for interword relationships. An influential and widely used example of a keyword

---

[11] ftp://ciir-ftp.cs.umass.edu/pub/papers/lewis/nlirbib93.ps.Z

[12] atg1.wustl.edu/DL94/paper/futrelle.html

[13] xxx.lanl.gov/cmp-lg/

TABLE 6.4 WordNet Vocabulary
Distribution by Lexical Category

| Category | Forms | Meanings (SynSets) |
|---|---|---|
| Nouns | 57,000 | 48,800 |
| Adjectives | 19,500 | 10,000 |
| Verbs | 21,000 | 8,400 |
| Total | 95,600 | 70,100 |

A wide-ranging psychologist thesaurus is the **WordNet**[14] system developed by George Miller[†] and colleagues [Fellbaum, 1998].

One obvious distinction of WordNet is simply the size of its vocabulary: It contains almost 100,000 distinct word forms, divided into lexical categories as shown in Table 6.4. Central to the lexical approach to semantics is distinguishing between lexical items and the "concepts" they are meant to invoke:

> "Word form" will be used here to refer to the physical utterance or inscription and "word meaning" to refer to the lexicalized concept that a form can be used to express. Then the starting point for lexical semantics can be said to be the mapping between forms and meanings. [Fellbaum, 1998, p. 4]

The relations connecting words in WordNet are similar – but not identical – to those used within thesauri. The first and most important relation is **synonymy**. This has a special role in WordNet, pulling multiple word forms together into a **synonym set**, which, by definition, all have the same meaning:

> According to one definition (usually attributed to Leibniz) two expressions are synonymous if the substitution of one for the other never changes the truth value of a sentence in which the substitution is made. . . . A weakened version of this definition would make synonymy relative to a context: two expressions are synonymous in a linguistic context C if the substitution of one for the other in C does not alter the truth value. [Fellbaum, 1998, p. 6]

---

[14] www.cogsci.princeton.edu/wn/

TABLE 6.5 WordNet's Top-Level
Noun Categories

| | |
|---|---|
| act, action, activity | natural object |
| animal, fauna | natural phenomenon |
| artifact | person, human being |
| attribute, property | plant, flora |
| body, corpus | possession |
| cognition, knowledge | process |
| communication | quantity, amount |
| event, happening | relation |
| feeling, emotion | shape |
| food | state, condition |
| group, collection | substance |
| location, place | time |
| motive | |

The BT/NT relation in standard thesauri is refined in WordNet into two types of relations, **hypernymy** and **meronymy**. The former relation plays a dominant role, allowing **inheritance** of various properties of parent words by their children:

> Much attention has been devoted to hyponymy/hypernymy (variously called subordination/superordination, subset/superset, or the ISA relation).... A hyponym inherits all the features of the more generic concept and adds at least one feature that distinguishes it from its superordinate and from any other hyponyms of that superordinate. This convention provides the central organizing principle for the nouns in WordNet. [Fellbaum, 1998, p. 8]

This hypernymy relation connects virtually all the words into a forest of trees rooted on a very restricted set of "unique beginners." In the case of nouns, the top-level categories are those shown in Table 6.5; those for verbs are Table 6.6.

The final category of **stative verbs** is used to capture the distinction between the majority of **active verbs** and those (e.g., SUFFICE, BELONG, RESEMBLE) reflecting state characteristics.

WordNet also represents roughly the opposite of the synonym relation with the **antonymy** relation. Defining this logically proves more

TABLE 6.6 WordNet's Top-Level
Verb Categories

| | |
|---|---|
| bodily care and functions | creation |
| change | emotion |
| cognition | motion |
| communication | perception |
| competition | possession |
| consumption | social interaction |
| contact | weather |
| stative | |

difficult, and Miller is forced to simply equate it with human subjects'
typical responses:

> Antonymy is a lexical relation between word forms, not a se-
> mantic relation between word meanings. . . . The strongest psy-
> cholinguistic indication that two words are antonyms is that
> each is given on a word association test as the most common re-
> sponse to the other. For example, if people are asked for the first
> word they think of (other than the probe word itself) when
> they hear VICTORY, most will respond DEFEAT; when they
> hear DEFEAT most will respond VICTORY. [Fellbaum, 1998,
> pp. 7, 24]

The use of the antonymy relation in WordNet is particularly interesting when applied to adjectives:

> The semantic organization of descriptive adjectives is entirely
> different from that of nouns. Nothing like the hyponymic rela-
> tion that generates nominal hierarchies is available for adjec-
> tives. . . . The semantic organization of adjectives is more nat-
> urally thought of as an abstract hyperspace of $N$ dimensions
> rather than as a hierarchical tree. [Fellbaum, 1998, p. 27]

First, WordNet distinguishes the bulk of adjectives, which are
called **descriptive adjectives** (such as BIG, INTERESTING, POSSI-
BLE), from **relational adjectives** (PRESIDENTIAL, NUCLEAR) and

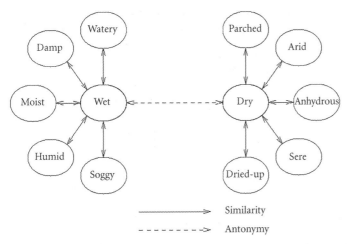

FIGURE 6.15 Bipolar Organization of Adjectives in WordNet
From [Fellbaum, 1998]. Reproduced with permission of MIT Press

**reference-modifying adjectives** (FORMER, ALLEGED). They then
find:

> All descriptive adjectives have antonyms; those lacking direct
> antonyms have indirect antonyms, i.e., are synonyms of adjec-
> tives that have direct antonyms. [Fellbaum, 1998, p. 28]

An example of the resulting dumbbell-shaped **bipolar** organization is
shown in Figure 6.15.

Voorhees was one of the first to explore how WordNet data can be
harnessed as part of a search engine [Voorhees, 1993].

## 6.3.3 Taxonomies

As their central role in WordNet suggests, the hierarchic BT/NT, or
hypernymy, relations are especially important. Because of the constant
analytic pressure of the Western intellectual tradition, topics continue
to be refined into smaller topics, which the next generation of scholars
immediately refines further. This has led to a wide range of classification taxonomies associated with various social groups of scholars and
scientists.

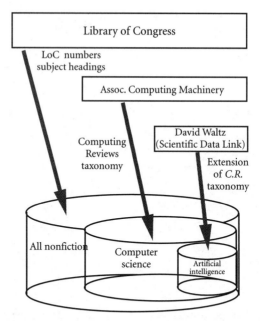

FIGURE 6.16 Nesting Taxonomies from Various Sources

Figure 6.16 shows several different sources from which indexing information might be obtained. The single most important source of subject indexing is the Library of Congress (LoC). Its indexing system is the basis of most large libraries because it covers all disciplines. For exactly the same reason, however, the indexers at the LoC have too much to do, and the resulting indices are admittedly crude. Partly as a response to the lack of adequate indexing structures, various professional groups have developed their own taxonomies to help organize the information within their particular technical specialty. For example, the Association of Computing Machinery has developed the ***ACM Computing Reviews Classification***[15] for use by its *Computing Reviews* publication [ACM, 1986]. This taxonomy is much more specific, and therefore more widely used by computer specialists. However, it lacks many of the advantages of the LoC system. In general, the keywords are assigned by the authors rather than by trained librarians. The system is rarely, if ever, integrated into the operations of libraries. And although the indexing structure is

---

[15] ls6-www.informatik.uni-dortmund.de/CRclass.html

much more refined than that of the LoC, it is still too crude for most research currently going on in any subspecialty. This has caused some practitioners in various subspecialties to develop their own extensions. For example, David Waltz was commissioned by Scientific Data-Link to extend the ACM's *Computing Reviews* taxonomy for the sub-specialty of artificial intelligence [Waltz, 1985]. Waltz's extension is extremely refined and helpful to AI practitioners. At the same time, it is even more ad hoc, its "sponsoring institution" has less impact, and consequently it is even less well accepted within libraries.

All three of these indexing systems are examples of **top-down knowledge structures.** That is, they are developed by various social institutions as prescriptive languages used to represent the consensus opinion as to how information is to be organized. Such "consensual" knowledge structures are critical if individuals are to *share* information. Each indexing system represents a compromise between increased scope and diminished resolution. Increased scope brings along with it broader acceptance and adherence. These advantages occur at the expense of acceptance by users actively involved in technical specialties.

The central role of hierarchic BT/NT relations in organizing keyword vocabularies should make us especially concerned with a precise semantics for this relationship. Most would agree that if B is a broader term than A, then A "is a" B. But as knowledge engineers within AI have known for a long time, the ubiquitous IS_A relation admits a number of interpretations, which can support different types of inference [Brachman, 1979; Brachman, 1983]. In general, the BT/NT relation seems to correspond most closely to the "a kind of" implication relating predicates A and B:

$$(\forall x)\, B(x) \rightarrow A(x) \qquad\qquad (6.11)$$

Earlier generations of Internet users participated in the construction of the extensive *UseNet hierarchy*[16] of discussion boards, on topics from ALT.SEX.FETISH.ROBOTS to COMP.SYS.MAC.OOP.TCL; see Section 7.5.5 for an example of the use of this hierarchy in text classification tasks. These days the most widely known taxonomies are

---

[16] ftp://rtfm.mit.edu/pub/usenet-by-hierarchy/

**WWW directories** such as *Yahoo!*,[17] whose employees have constructed a hierarchy, primarily of places to spend money. One of the most exciting recent developments is the development of **collaborative classification** efforts such as the ***Open Directory Project (DMOZ)***,[18] which involves large communities of experts, each working to make sense within his or her own area of expertise.

## 6.4 Social Relations among Authors

Another potential source of information about documents that we can use to augment statistial keywords is "cultural" information, capturing some features of the *social* relationships among authors in a field. Most of our discussion of documents has treated them as if they were completely dead artifacts. But documents are written by *people*, authors who write from a particular perspective. When their writing is in science or the law, or any other tradition within which they participate, we can make reasonable guesses about some aspects of what it is they are trying to say.

An author's education, in particular, offers clues as to how we can interpret their words. Work and writing in many fields requires extensive graduate education. Students are soon moved from common "core" curricula to more advanced material. Kuhn and others have analyzed the central role textbooks play as part of the social process of codifying a discipline [Kuhn, 1970]. As students move beyond common textbooks to specialized training, their approach to the problem often resembles that of their teachers (at least as long as they are around the teacher). By knowing something about the author's education, and especially about his or her dissertation advisor, we may have a basis for interpreting the writing. The importance of dissertations as an academic resource was recognized as early as 1940 by University Microfilms Inc. (UMI), as copies of virtually every dissertation published by many universities were microfilmed. UMI (now the Information and Learning division of Bell & Howell) makes its ***Dissertation Abstracts***[19] corpus available for WWW searching.

---

[17] www.yahoo.com

[18] dmoz.org/about.html

[19] wwwlib.umi.com/dissertations

## 6.4.1 AI Genealogy

The AI Genealogy project (AIG) is an attempt to collect information relating authors in artificial intelligence to one another through shared advisors. In analogy to genealogical family trees, we can treat the advisor as a parent to the advisee. Students of students become grandchildren, and so on. A subset of this data is shown in Figure 6.17.

As an example of how this additional information about authors can be exploited to understand more about the words used in documents, Steier has analyzed word-pair cooccurrence data as a means of finding potential index phrases [Steier and Belew, 1994b]. Take, for example, the phrase CASE-BASED REASONING. This phrase has a high degree of phrasal information content (using mutual information statistics to identify statistically dependent word pairs) when these statistics are collected across the entire AIT document corpus.

But a statistically significant different distribution is observed within dissertations coming from a particular set of universities: Yale, Georgia Tech, and the University of Massachusetts. Within these particular university contexts, the constituent concepts of CASE-BASED and REASONING are examined in detail and independently. Not only do these words occur together as CASE-BASED REASONING, but they often occur separately (e.g., CASE-BASED PLANNING, CASE-BASED ARGUMENT, CASE-BASED PROBLEM, SCHEMA-BASED REASONING, ANALOGICAL REASONING, COMMONSENSE REASONING). Within the limited context of these subcorpora, the keywords occur more independently and hence are considered less phraselike. As this phrase is "exported" into the general AI vocabulary, the semantic nuances are left behind, and the dominant use of the constituent words is as part of the phrase.

What is it that makes language use so different at Yale, Georgia Tech, and the University of Massachusetts? Perhaps it is merely coincidence, but our hypothesis is that it is the common lineage traced to Roger Schank! Work across these geographically distant research institutions is pulled together by an intellectual tradition captured by the AIG data.

Part of what is interesting about the AIT corpus is its demonstration within a single corpus of many of the representations discussed in this chapter. The AI genealogy captures some of the intellectual linkage due

McCulloch, W. S.
   ---- Minsky, Marvin                        ----
     ---- Winston, Patrick H.                   ----
       1973 Waltz, David L.                   ----
         1980 Finin, Timothy W.          THE SEMANTIC INTERPRETATION...
           1988 Kass, Robert John      ACQUIRING A MODEL OF THE...
           1989 Klein, David A.           SEE CO-ADV SHORTLIFFE, TED
         1987 Pollack, Jordan B.        ON CONNECTIONST MODELS OF...
         1993 Angeline, Peter           EVOLUTIONARY ALGORITHMS AND...
         1994 Kolen, John              COMPUTATION IN RECURRENT...

Mey, Jacob
     1969 Schank, Roger C.           A CONCEPTUAL DEPENDENCY...
     ---- Kolodner, Janet L.          ----
       1989 Shinn, Hong Shik         A UNIFIED APPROACH TO...
       1989 Turner, Roy Marvin       A SCHEMA-BASED MODEL OF...
       1991 Hinrichs, Thomas Ryland  PROBLEM-SOLVING IN OPEN...
       1992 Redmond, Michael Albert LEARNING BY OBSERVING AND...
     ---- Dejong, Gerald Francis     ----
       1987 Segre, Alberto Maria    EXPLANATION-BASED LEARNING...
       1988 Shavlik, Jude William   GENERALIZING THE STRUCTURE...
         1991 Towell, Geoffrey Gilmer SYMBOLIC KNOWLEDGE AND...
       1988 Mooney, Raymond Joseph A GENERAL EXPLANATION-BASED...
         1992 Ng, Hwee Tou          A GENERAL ABDUCTIVE SYSTEM...
       1989 Rajamoney, Shankar Anand EXPLANATION-BASED THEORY...
     ---- Lehnert, Wendy G.          ----
       1983 Dyer, Michael G.        IN-DEPTH UNDERSTANDING: A...
         1987 Mueller, Eric           DAYDREAMING AND COMPUTATION:...
         1987 Zernik, Uri            STRATEGIES IN LANGUAGE...
         1988 Pazzani, Michael John   LEARNING CAUSAL...
         1988 Gasser, Michael        SEE CO-ADV HATCH, EVELYN
         1989 Dolan, Charles Patrick  TENSOR MANIPULATION...
         1989 Alvarado, Sergio Jose   UNDERSTANDING EDITORIAL...
         1989 Dolan, Charles        THE USE AND ACQUISITION OF...
         1991 Lee, Geunbae           DISTRIBUTED SEMANTIC...
         1991 Reeves, John Fairbanks  COMPUTATIONAL MORALITY: A...
         1991 Nenov, Valeriy Iliev   PERCEPTUALLY GROUNDED...
         1991 Quilici, Alexander Eric  THE CORRECTION MACHINE: A...
         1993 Turner, Scott R.        MINSTREL: A COMPUTER MODEL...
       1990 Williams, Robert Stuart LEARNING PLAN SCHEMAS FROM...
     1976 Meehan, James R.        THE METANOVEL: WRITING...
     1978 Wilensky, Robert        UNDERSTANDING GOAL-BASED...
       1985 Jacobs, Paul           A KNOWLEDGE-BASED APPROACH...
       1986 Norvig, Peter          A UNIFIED THEORY OF...
       1986 Arens, Yigal            CLUSTER: AN APPORACH TO...
       1987 Chin, David Ngi         INTELLIGENT AGENTS AS A...
       1992 Wu, Dekai              AUTOMATIC INFERENCE: A...
     1978 Carbonell, Jaime G.      SUBJECTIVE UNDERSTANDING:...
       1988 Minton, Steven        LEARNING EFFECTIVE SEARCH...
       1989 Lehman, Jill Fain      ADAPTIVE PARSING:...
       1991 Perlin, Mark W.        AUTOMATING THE CONSTRUCTION...
       1991 Hauptmann, Alexander Georg MEANING FROM STRUCTURE IN...
       1992 Veloso, Manuela M.    LEARNING BY ANALOGICAL...
     1980 Lebowitz, Michael      GENERALIZATION AND MEMORY IN...
     1987 Hovy, Eduard Hendrik    GENERATING NATURAL LANUGAGE...
     1988 Hunter, Lawrence E.     GAINING EXPERTISE THROUGH...
     1989 Ram, Ashwin           QUESTION-DRIVEN...
     1989 Dehn, Natalie Jane      COMPUTER STORY-WRITING: THE...
     1990 Leake, David Browder   EVALUATING EXPLANATIONS
     1992 Domeshek, Eric Andrew   DO THE RIGHT THING: A...
     1993 Edelson, Daniel Choy    LEARNING FROM STORIES:...

FIGURE 6.17  A Sample of the AI Genealogical Record

to the Ph.D. advisor/advisee relationship. David Waltz's taxonomy of AI provides an excellent initial thesaurus over keywords [Waltz, 1985.]

## 6.4.2  An Empirical Foundation for a Philosophy of Science

One advantage of studying a focused corpus like the AIT is that we have an especially good chance of understanding some of these social relations. A history of AI often begins with a seminal conference that took place at Dartmouth in 1956 [McCorduck, 1985; Russell and Norvig, 1995].[†] If we treat the attendees at that meeting as "founding fathers" (in a population genetic sense!), we can attempt to track their "genetic" impact on the current field of AI.

Alternate histories

?6

In an attempt to capture other significant intellectual influences beyond the advisor, the AIG questionnaire asks for committee members other than the chairman. The role of committee members varies a great deal from department to department and from campus to campus. But all of these numbers can be expected to exert some intellectual influence. Asking for committee members is a step toward other nonadvisor influencers, and it is also a matter of record. Research institutions are another way to capture intellectual interactions among collaborators.

Even if and when the AI-Ph.D. family tree is completed, it will certainly *not* have captured all of what we mean by "artificial intelligence research." For example:

- The Dartmouth "founding fathers" probably provide (direct) lineage for a *minority* of AI Ph.D.s currently working in the field.
- Ph.D. theses themselves are probably some of the *worst* examples of research, in AI and elsewhere. By definition, we are talking about students who are doing some of their first work. They had *better* improve with time!
- Ph.D.s account for only a fraction of AI research.

Nevertheless, science is primarily concerned with *accumulating* knowledge, at least as much as it is about its initial discovery. A primary argument for interest in the AIG is that traditional academic relationships, as embodied by Ph.D. genealogies, form a sort of "skeleton" around which the rest of scientific knowledge coalesces. Certainly, individuals can pursue their own research program, and corporations can fund extended investigations into areas that are not represented in academia whatsoever. But it is hard to imagine extended research programs (like that "fathered" by Roger Schank, for example) that do not involve multiple "generations" of investigators; academia is almost certainly the most successful system for such propagation. Further, clear demonstrations of intellectual lineages like this promise much more concrete evidence for **memes** – the hypothetical analogs of biological genes in cultural systems [Dawkins, 1976] – than analyses of text alone [Best, 2000] can ever provide.

Kuhnian [Kuhn, 1970] and post-Kuhnian [Hull, 1988; Latour, 1987] analyses highlight the importance of the *social* aspects of science. "Paradigms" are extremely appealing constructs, but they're also amorphous. For all of its faults, the AI-Ph.D. tree represents incontrovertible *facts*, just as word frequencies do.

## 6.5 Modes of Inference

If deduction is the process of proceeding from a set of rules to the implications of those rules, and if induction is the process of forming rules based on patterns across many examples, and if abduction is the process of forming hypotheses worthy of asking, FOA can also be viewed as an inference process: the process of forming questions that elicit desirable answers.

### 6.5.1 Theorem-Proving Models
###       for Relevance

Imagine the current state of knowledge possessed by a browsing user as a set of axioms $\Sigma$. Then we can model their information need as a question: Can we infer that a theorem $\tau$ is true or false from our current knowledge?

$$\Sigma \overset{?}{\models} \tau \tag{6.12}$$

The fact that the user has an information need can be taken as an assumption that there must be additional knowledge, contained in some documents, that together with his of her current knowledge base does allow $\tau$ (or $\neg \tau$) to be proven. Relevant documents are exactly those that support such an inference:

$$Rel \equiv \{d \,|\, \Sigma \cup d \models \tau\} \qquad (6.13)$$

Practically speaking, of course, this model is impossible. It would demand a complete and consistent *logical* description of the user's cognitive state. It also requires that the full set of *all possible logical facts* contained in *each and every document* be similarly encoded. (And then, of course, there is the minor problem of searching for the minimal set of documents that satisfy this inference!)[†]                                        Late Winograd

Still, this basic conception of existing knowledge being extended by new facts and new inferences becoming possible as new facts become known is a provocative metaphor at the least. Sperber and Wilson's notion of "connected" information corresponds exactly to such new inferences (cf. Section 8.2.2).

Van Rijsbergen has talked about this strong notion of relevance as **objective relevance** [van Rijsbergen, p. 147]. In more recent work, he has extended this basic model to a full **relevance logic**, based on a four-valued semantics over $2^{\{T, F\}}$ [van Rijsbergen, 1986].

## 6.5.2 Spreading Activation Search

The facts that keywords can be associated with documents or with one another, that documents become associated by citations, and so on led early IR pioneers such as Doyle and Stiles to adopt simple *association* as a unifying relation connecting many objects of the FOA inquiry [Doyle, 1960; Doyle, 1961; Doyle, 1962; Stiles, 1961; Maron, 1982b; Giuliano, 1963; Findler, 1979]. Integrating information across **semantic networks** of such associative relations has been an important example of knowledge representation within AI since the memory models of Collins and Qullian [Collins and Quillian, 1972]. In its simplest form, a simple quantity known as **activity** is allowed to propagate through a network like that shown in Figure 6.18 from several sources. **Spreading**

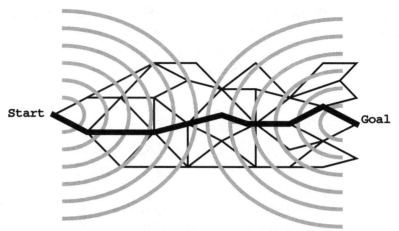

FIGURE 6.18 Spreading Activation Search

**activation search** is the name for a broad range of techniques that find solutions (for example, a path from Start to Goal in Figure 6.18) by controlling the propagation of activity through associative networks like this [Preece, 1981; Salton and Buckley, 1988a; Cohen and Kjeldsen, 1987].

The Adaptive Information Retrieval (AIR) system was a prototype search engine built as part of my dissertation at the University of Michigan in the mid-1980s [Belew, 1986; Belew, 1989]. This research was one of several systems applying **connectionist** (neural network) learning methods to the IR search engine problem [Mozer, 1988; Bein and Smolensky, 1988; Doszkocs et al., 1990; Belew, 1987b].

### Basic Representation

In AIR, each new document first causes a corresponding document node to be generated. An author node is then generated (if it doesn't already exist) for each author of the document. Two links are then created between the document and each of its keywords (one in each direction), and two more between the document and each of its authors. Weights are assigned to these links according to an inverse frequency weighting scheme: The sum of the weights on all links going out of a node is forced to be a constant; in our system that constant is one. Figure 6.19 shows the subnet corresponding to the book *Parallel Models of Associative*

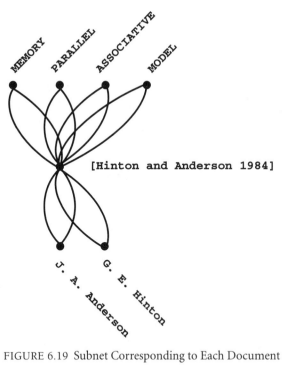

MEMORY PARALLEL ASSOCIATIVE MODEL

[Hinton and Anderson 1984]

J. A. Anderson G. E. Hinton

FIGURE 6.19 Subnet Corresponding to Each Document

*Memory,* by G. E. Hinton and J. A. Anderson [Hinton and Anderson, 1984].

The initial network is constructed from the superposition of many such documents' representations. Most of the experiments described in this report used a network constructed from 1600 documents, forming a network of approximately 5000 nodes. This is a trivial corpus that uses relatively crude lexical analysis and keyword weighting ideas. However, AIR requires only that the initial automatic indexing assign *some* weighted set of tentative keywords to each document.

There is one property of the inverse weighting scheme on which AIR does depend, however. A network built using this keyword weighting scheme, together with similar constraints on the weights assigned to author links, has the satisfying property of *conserving activity.* That is, if a unit of activity is put into a node and the total outgoing associativity from that node is one, the amount of activity in the system will neither increase nor diminish. This is helpful in controlling the spreading activation dynamics of the network during querying.

### Querying and Retrieval

Users begin a session with AIR by describing their information need, using a very simple query language. An initial query is composed of one or more clauses. Each clause can refer to one of the three types of "features" represented in AIR's network: keywords, documents, or authors, and all but the first clause can be negated. This query causes activity to be placed on nodes in AIR's network corresponding to the features named in the query. This activity is allowed to propagate throughout the network, and the system's response is the set of nodes that become most active during this propagation.

The traditional result of a query is only documents. AIR also provides keywords and authors. Keywords retrieved in this manner are considered **related terms** that users may use to pursue their searches. Retrieved authors are considered to be closely linked to the subject of interest. There are many ways in which a user might find related terms and centrally involved authors, a valuable information product in their own right.

Figure 6.20 shows AIR's response to a typical query:

```
(((:TERM "ASSOCIATIVE")(:AUTH "ANDERSON,J.A.")))
```

This is the network of keywords, documents, and authors considered relevant to this query. The nodes are drawn as a tripartite graph with keywords on the top level, documents in the middle, and authors on the bottom. Associative links that helped to cause a node to become retrieved (and only those links) are also displayed. Heavier lines imply stronger associative weights. AIR uses directed links, and this directionality is represented by the concavity of the arcs; a clockwise convention is used. For example, a link from a document node (in the middle level) to a keyword node (in the top level) goes clockwise, around to the left.

Actually, this is only a picture of the final state of the system's retrieval. The network is actually drawn *incrementally*, with the first nodes to become significantly active being drawn first and in the middle of the pane. As additional nodes become active at significant levels, they are drawn farther out along the three horizontal axes and the links through which they became active are drawn as well. This dynamic display has at

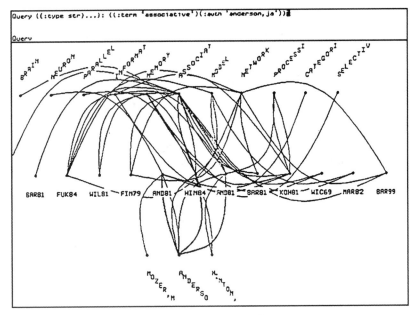

FIGURE 6.20  AIR Interface

least two real advantages. First, the fact that AIR provides the first part of its retrieval almost immediately means that the user is not impatiently waiting for the retrieval to complete (typically 5 to 10 seconds in this implementation). Second, displaying the query's dynamics helps to give the user a tangible feeling of "direct manipulation"[Rose and Belew, 1990]; the user "prods" the network in a certain place and then watches as waves of activity flow outward from that place.

## *RelFbk* in AIR

Queries subsequent to the first are performed differently. After AIR has retrieved the network of features, the user responds with *RelFbk*, indicating which features are considered (by that user) relevant to the query and which are not. Using a mouse, the user marks features with the symbols: $\oplus\oplus$, $\oplus$, $\ominus$, and $\ominus\ominus$, indicating that the feature was Very Relevant, Relevant, Irrelevant, or Very Irrelevant, respectively. Not all features need be commented on (cf. Section 4.1.1).

The system constructs a new query directly from this feedback. First, terms from the previous query are retained. Positively marked features are added to this query, as are the negated versions of features marked negatively. Equal weight is placed on each of these features, except that features marked Very Relevant or Very Irrelevant are counted double.

From the perspective of retrieval, this *RelFbk* becomes a form of *browsing*: Positively marked features are directions the user wants to pursue, and negatively marked features are directions that should be pruned from the search. From the perspective of learning, this *RelFbk* is exactly the training signal AIR needs to modify its representations through learning. This unification of learning (i.e., changing representations) and doing (i.e., browsing) was a central component of AIR's design. It means that the collection of feedback is not an additional onerous task for the user, but rather is a natural part of the retrieval process.

## Learning in AIR

Nodes marked by the user with positive or negative feedback act as sources of a signal that then propagates backwards along the weighted links. A local learning rule then modifies the weight on links directly or indirectly involved in the query process. Several learning rules were investigated; the experiments reported here used a learning rule that correlated the activity of the **presynaptic** $node_i$ with the feedback signal experienced by the **postsynaptic** $node_j$:

$$w_{ij} \propto Corr(n_i\ active,\ n_j\ relevant)$$

$$= \frac{\mu_{a_i \cdot r_j} - \mu_{a_i} \cdot \mu r_j}{\sigma_{a_i} \cdot \sigma_{r_j}}$$

$$= \frac{\Sigma(a_i \cdot r_j) - \frac{\Sigma a_i \Sigma r_j}{N}}{\sqrt{\Sigma a_i^2 - \frac{(\Sigma a_i)^2}{N}} \sqrt{\Sigma r_j^2 - \frac{(\Sigma r_j)^2}{N}}}$$

AIR makes a most direct correspondence between the connectionist notion of *activity* and the IR notion of *Pr(Rel)* 5.5):

*The activity level of nodes at the end of the propagation phase is considered to be a prediction of the probability that this node will be judged relevant to the query presented by the user.*

This interpretation constrained the AIR system design in several ways (e.g., activity is a real number bounded between zero and one, query nodes are activated fully). AIR also allows negative activity, which is interpreted as the probability that a node is *not* relevant. The next step of the argument is to consider a link weight $w_{AB}$ to be the conditional probability that $Node_B$ is relevant given that $Node_A$ is relevant. Next, this definition must be extended inductively to include indirect transitive paths that AIR uses extensively for its retrievals.

The system's interactions with users are then considered experiments. Given a query, AIR predicts which nodes will be considered relevant and the user confirms or disconfirms this prediction. These results update the system's weights (conditional probabilities) to reflect the system's updated estimates. Thus, AIR's representation results from the combination of two completely different sources of evidence: the word frequency statistics underlying its initial indexing and the opinions of its users.

A straightforward mechanism exists to incrementally introduce new documents into AIR's database. Links are established from the new document to all of its initial keywords and to its authors; new keyword and author nodes are created as necessary. The weights on these links are distributed evenly so that they sum to a constant. Because the sum of the (outgoing) weights for all nodes is to remain constant, any associative weight to the new document must come from existing link weights. A new parameter (*CONSERVATIVE*) is introduced to control the weight given these new links at the expense of existing ones. If the network is untrained by users, this parameter can be set to zero to make the effect of an incremental addition exactly the same as if the new document had been part of the initial collection. In a trained network, setting *CONSERVATIVE* near unity ensures that the system's experience incorporated in existing link weights is not sacrificed to make the new connections. Also, note that the computation required to place the new document is strictly local: Only the links directly adjacent to the new document's immediate neighbors must be changed. The major observation about the inclusion of new documents, however, is that there is an immediate "place" for new documents in AIR's existing representation.

A second source of new information to the AIR system comes from users' queries. If a query contains a term unknown to AIR, this term is held in abeyance and AIR executes the query based on the remaining terms. Then, after the user has designated which of AIR's responses are relevant to this query, a new node corresponding to the new query term is created and becomes subjected to the same learning rule used for all other nodes.

Although easily incorporating new documents and new query terms is a valuable property for any IR system, from the perspective of machine learning these are examples of simple rote learning, and they are necessarily dependent on the specifics of the IR task domain. The main focus of the AIR system is the use of general-purpose connectionist learning techniques that, once the initial document network is constructed, are quite independent of the IR task.

## Generalized Representation

The standard, interkeyword and interdocument associations typically evaluated as part of keyword and document clustering are part of the broader context of the associative representation used by AIR. The system extends these pairwise clustering relations and the fundamental keyword-document *Index* relation to include higher-order *transitive* relations as well. That is, if node A is associated with node B and node B is associated with node C, then node A is also considered to be associated with node C, but to a lesser extent.

Obviously, this transitive assumption is not always valid, and this may be why most IR research does not consider this extension. But AIR is an adaptive system, and one of the critical problems facing any learning system is the generation of *plausible hypotheses*, i.e., theories that stand a better than average chance of being correct. Transitivity is considered a default assumption, the consequences of which will be subjected to adaptations that favor appropriate transitivities and cull out inappropriate ones.

It is interesting to contrast the adaptive changes made by AIR in response to *RelFbk* with the document modification strategies of G. Salton and his students [Friedman et al., 1967; Brauen, 1969] mentioned in Section 4.2.7 (and returned to in Section 7.3). The query-document matches used as the basis of their changes consider only direct, keyword-to-document associations while AIR makes use of a much wider web of indirect associations. To a first approximation the changes made by AIR to direct keyword-to-document associations are not unlike those proposed by Salton and Brauen (if I'd only known!), but AIR also makes other changes, to more indirect associations.

Salton and Buckley have analyzed the spreading activation search used in some of these systems and concluded that it is inferior to more traditional retrieval methods [Salton and Buckley, 1988a; Salton and Buckley, 1988b]. They point out:

> . . . the relationships between terms or documents are speci-
> fied by *labeled* links between the nodes . . . . the effectiveness
> of the procedure is crucially dependent on the *availability* of
> a representative node association map. (pp. 4, 5, emphasis
> added)

In a weighted, associative representation of the *semantics* of index-ing, interdocument and interkeyword clustering links are dropped in favor of a single, homogeneous **associative relation**. AIR treats all three types of weighted links equally. For example, if interdocument citation data had been available, this information could naturally be included as well; again the semantics of these relations would have been dropped in favor of a simple associative weight. The contrast between the use of spreading activation search in *connectionist* networks with its use in *semantic* networks is admittedly a subtle one, but it is also critically im-portant [Rose and Belew, 1989]. One clear difference is that semantic networks typically make logical, deterministic use of labeled links, while connectionist networks like AIR rely on weighted links for probabilistic computations.

Figure 6.21 shows how many of the features discussed here can inter-act as part of a single retrieval system. This figure comes from Dan Rose's SCALIR (Symbolic and Connectionist Approach to Legal Information Retrieval) system, which was built to investigate the use of both logical, "symbolic" modes of inference and probabalistic, "subsymbolic" ones. This figure shows containment relations between document elements (like those shown in more detail in Figure 6.10), topical connections between keywords, and interdocument citations, all mixed and used as part of spreading activation-based inference.

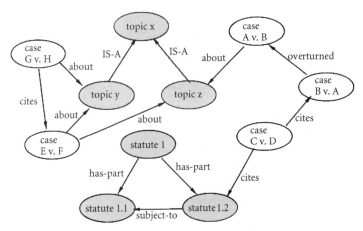

FIGURE 6.21 Semantic Net of Legal Document Relations
From [Rose, 1994]. Reproduced with permission of Lawrence Erlbaum

## 6.5.3 Discovering Latent Knowledge within a Corpus

Nothing is more frustrating than spending many hours on a technical problem, unless it is finding out later that someone else had *previously solved* the same problem! One of the motivations shared by many people working on search engine technology is the hope that we can reduce the number of times the same wheel is reinvented.

D. R. Swanson has concentrated on the scientific and medical literature and viewed it as "a potential source of new knowledge" [Swanson, 1990; Swanson and Smalheiser, 1997]. Each new medical report contains new knowledge about some particular disease or treatment. But Swanson has taken the next step: to imagine what modes of inference might be most appropriate across a *network* of such papers, each of which describes potential causal relations:

Each scientific article contributes to a web of logical connections that interlace the literature of science. Some of these connections are made explicit through references from one article to another, citations that reflect, among other things, authors' perceptions of how their own work is related to that of others and how it fits into the scheme of existing knowledge. However, there may exist many implicit logical interarticle connections that are unintended and not marked by citations; such implicit links are the focus of this paper. (The word "logical" here is used informally; a "logical connection" is formed by statements that are related by any process of scientific reasoning or argument.)

Scientific articles can be seen as clustering into more or less independent sets or "literatures." Within each set, common problems are addressed, common arguments are advanced, and articles "interact" by citing one another. Distinct literatures that are essentially unrelated are in general "noninteractive" in that they do not cite or refer directly to each other, have no articles in common, and are not cited together by other articles. On the other hand, if two literatures are linked by arguments that they respectively put forward – that is, are "logically" related or connected – one would expect them to cite each other. If they do not, then the logical connections between them would be of great interest, for such connections may be unintended, unnoticed, and unknown – therefore potential sources of new knowledge. . . .

The number of possible pairs of literatures (that might be connected) increases very nearly as the square of the number of literatures; the number of possible connections increases at even a greater rate if triple or higher combinations are taken into account rather than just pairs. From this perspective, the significance of the "information explosion" may lie not in an explosion of quantity per se, but in an incalculably greater combinatorial explosion of unnoticed *logical* connections. (pp. 29, 35)

Swanson's first and most well-known example of new knowledge discovered in this fashion identified fish oil as a treatment for Raynaud's syndrome, a circulatory problem resulting in poor blood supply to the extremities. Figure 6.22 shows a second example of Swanson's method. Beginning with a syndrome like migraine headaches, Swanson searches the literature for features mentioned in the context of migraines that have also been mentioned in a second, disjoint, "mutually oblivious" literature. Working backwards from the syndrome to be explained, a query is formed against a medical corpus like Medline. The resulting set of

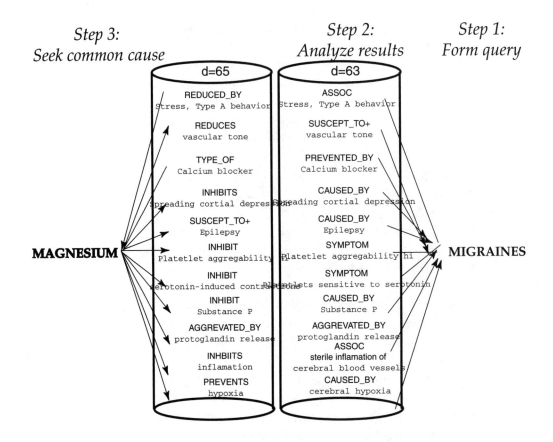

FIGURE 6.22 Swanson's Search for Latent Knowledge

(in this case 63) documents is then analyzed and clustered into related sets; it is in this clustering that Swanson's *manual*, intellectual effort is most obvious. The clusters are used to suggest new additional queries. Finally, the single common "cause" of **magnesium** is identified. Figure 6.22 also shows an attempt to classify the relationship between common phrases in the retrieved literature and the relation to the syndrome. Further, the relationship between these same phrases (or lexical variations on them!) and the common cause magnesium is also forced into structured relationships.

It is hard to imagine a more exciting prospect for the analysis of all literature. The identification of such "undiscovered public knowledge" is almost certainly possible in many other situations. The question becomes how we might algorithmically search for all of them. Note especially the liberties taken in interpreting the literature and phrases used consistently within it as they have been transformed into the *structured relations* of Figure 6.22. These relations are meant to suggest more formal and powerful modes of inference between causes and effects mentioned within each paper. Some of the arrowheads show suggested causal relationships; some relationships (e.g., associated_with) are neutral with respect to correlation versus causation; others (type_of) suggest hierarchic relations between classes.

Swanson is aware of these difficulties:

> ... [the] form and structure of logically connected arguments are in general recognizable by scientists irrespective of their specialty, a point that may have implications for research on futuristic, more fully automated systems. However, the simple structure of the syllogistic model does not in many respects reflect the depth or range of actual problems that would be encountered if one tried to build a database of logical connections. ...
>
> The objective, moreover, is not simply to draw mechanistic logical inferences, but rather to determine whether certain plausible connections or hypotheses appear to be worth testing. Most articles harbor, either explicitly or implicitly, an enormous number of logical connections. Which connections are relevant and important can be determined only in the light of a specific context, hypothesis, problem, or question; but such contexts and questions are always changing. The degree to which one can hope to encode logical connections in any form suitable for all future uses may therefore be quite limited. [Swanson, 1990, p. 35]

Recognizing that even if fully automatic discovery of new facts is currently too hard, Gordon and Lindsey have investigated forms of "discovery support" [Gordon and Lindsay, 1996]. Gordon and Dumais have also explored the use of LSI techniques (cf. Section 5.2.3) as part of the literature-based discovery process [Gordon and Dumais, 1998]. The formation of an SVD, eigenstructure analysis of the relationship between a query and documents (step 2), and then the analysis of these intermediate literatures and ultimate causes (step 3) is an important extension beyond the manual investigations originally proposed by Swanson.

## 6.6 Deep Interfaces

Probably because interface technology did not support rich graphical presentations and pointing devices until late in the development of computer science, the human-computer interface (HCI) is often an afterthought in software engineering. This bias remains today in search engine designs, which assume the indexing and match algorithms can be separated from the presentation of results [Harman, 1992b; Rose and Belew, 1990].

Sometimes interface design is approached as a data visualization task [Veerasamy and Belkin, 1996]. Korfhage's VIBE presentation [Korfhage, 1995] highlights a user's and author's perspectives on topical areas. Rather than assuming that there is one absolute preferred perspective on keywords, Korfhage considers what the words look like from the perspective of users and authors, respectively.

In terms of the vector space model, we can think of these as projections. The huge dimensional space of keywords, or even the still large reduced dimension representation, is still far more than we can visualize on a two-dimensional computer screen. We can try to impose other dimensions (e.g., color or size), but we still must pick some projected subspace of the larger data set. Norman and Schneiderman have written extensively on the design of interfaces that are deeply connected to the user's underlying task [Norman, 1988; Schneiderman, 1992]; Marchianoni has focused particularly on interfaces for the "information seeking" task [Marchianoni, 1995]. As part of the Xerox PARC group, Hearst has explored a number of visualization techniques (cf. Figure 6.8); she has also recently provided an extensive survey of interface technologies [Hearst, 1999].

### 6.6.1 Geographical Hitlists

Singular tokens are those proper nouns – people, places, events – that have a unique reference in the world. They are distinguished from **general** terms, which refer to **categories** of objects in the world.

Distinctions like this have been a part of linguistic analysis since the beginning [Searle, 1980], and many with a background in AI will recall Ron Brachman's CLYDE_THE_ELEPHANT example [Brachman and Levesque, 1985; Brachman and McGuinness, 1988].

In FOA the distinction initially arose out of practical considerations. The basic morphological process of folding case – Porter's stemmer and similar tools – is designed primarily to deal with what we could, in the current context, call **general terms** only. Conversely, proper names (e.g., family and place names) rarely observe morphological transformation names. The capitalization that often flags singular proper nouns is thrown away rather than actually helping to ease the task of automatically identifying and parsing them.

It is no wonder, then, that **name-tagging** techniques that deal intelligently with singular tokens were an early area of search engine development [Rau, 1988; Jacobs, 1987]. Identifying the subclass of *people* singulars is an especially active area. Relatively small dictionaries of the "movers and shakers" of the modern world – politicians, captains of industry, artists, etc. – can provide an especially informative and commercially valuable set of additional indexing tokens in applications such as financial news services.

Chris Needham has proposed an interesting strategy for progressively applying stronger models of representation based on various classes of singulars (personal communication). Working on a representation for *Encyclopædia Britannica's* editors, the procedure Needham and his group hit upon was to

1. first describe *places* in the world;
2. then describe *people* who live (are born, travel through, and then die) in these places; and
3. finally to describe *events* involving people at locations.

Specification of one layer of terminology provided a concrete frame of reference for the next: Events involve people, who are associated with places. This suggests one argument for focusing on place-related singulars first. However, modeling even this "simplest" class of proper names quickly required even tighter focus onto **physical places** about which it was quite easy to give very concrete references and distinguished from **political places** whose names and extents can vary dramatically. As editors of the *Encyclopædia Britannica*, these designers were especially aware of how historically and culturally sensitive resolving political place names could be.

At least for physical locations, the emergence of **global positioning system** (GPS) technologies that allow users to know their position within a single, reconciled geographic frame has helped to drive a growing market for **geographical information systems** (GIS) software, and the development of worldwide **authority lists** of place names (e.g., *The U. S. Board on Geographic Names (BGS)*[20] and the earlier *Federal Information Processing Standards (FIPS)*[21] "Countries, Dependencies, Areas of Special Sovereignty, and Their Principal Administrative Divisions" list). Like people's names, place information is important.

Further, human cognition has evolved to live in a three-dimensional world. We each have deep psychological commitments to basic features of our physical space and orientation with respect to a spatial frame of reference [Shepard, 1981; Kosslyn, 1980]. In contrast to all the other abstract, disembodied dimensions along which information often barrages a user's screen, place information is special. Our experience of time is the other important experiential dimension, as demonstrated by representations like the **time line**. The orientation provided by such concrete frames can be critical.

Consider, for example, the query CIVIL WAR BATTLE and its conventional retrieval, as shown in Figure 6.23. We should be able to see these retrieved items in the geographical frame they naturally suggest, as shown in Figure 6.24.

Note the steps this required: First the textual hitlist was parsed for geographical tokens. Next, the map coordinates for each of these WiW entries are collected, and a **convex hull** (bounding polygon) for at least a majority of them is computed. Finally the map that best contains this region is identified, zoomed into, and shifted to best fit.

Within this same frame, a user also immediately knows how to **draw queries**, for example, restricting a search to only those battles near the East Coast or along a particular river. With modern graphical techniques, animation of these battles as a timeline slider is slid back and forth is almost trivial. But the additional power to browsing users of visualization

---

[20] 164.214.2.59/gns/html/BGN.html
[21] 164.214.2.59/gns/html/FIPS/FIP10-4.html

```
Britannica ® CD

civil war battle

Britannica CD contains at least 40 items relevant to this query....

• Missionary Ridge, Battle of (699 bytes)
in the American Civil War, battle that ended the Confederate siege of
Union troops at Chattanooga, Tenn. See Chattanooga, Battle of.

• Carthage (1,225 bytes)
city, seat of Jasper county, southwestern Missouri, U.S. It lies along
Spring River, just east of Joplin. Established in 1842, it was named
for ancient Carthage. During the Civil War, it was a centre of border
warfare and was destroyed by Confederate guerrillas in 1863; it was
rebuilt in 1866. Carthage is an agricultural-trade centre . . .

• South Mountain (783 bytes)
northernmost section of the Blue Ridge in the Appalachian Mountains,
extending southwestward for 65 miles (105 km) from southern
Pennsylvania to northern Virginia, U.S. Quirauk Mountain (2,145 feet
[654 m]) in Maryland is the highest point. It is crossed by the
Appalachian Trail (for hikers). The American Civil War Battle of South
Mountain . . .

• Rappahannock River (980 bytes)
river in Virginia, U.S. It rises near Chester Gap in the Blue Ridge
Mountains east of Front Royal and flows southeastward past
Fredericksburg (head of navigation and of tidewater) to enter
Chesapeake Bay after a course of 184 miles (296 km). Its chief
tributary is the Rapidan, which joins it above Fredericksburg. A number
of American Civil . . .

• Gordon, John Brown (2,667 bytes)
(b. Feb. 6, 1832, Upson county, Ga., U.S.--d. Jan. 9, 1904, Miami,
Fla.), Confederate military leader and post-American Civil War
politician who symbolized the shift from agrarian to commercial ideals
in the Reconstruction South.

• Spanish Civil War (7,585 bytes)
(1936-39), military revolt against the Republican government of Spain,
supported by conservative elements within the country. When an initial
military coup failed to win control of the entire country, a bloody
civil war ensued, fought with great ferocity on both sides. The
Nationalists, as the rebels were called, received aid from Fascist . .
.
```

FIGURE 6.23 CIVIL WAR BATTLE Query, Standard Textual Hitlist

and **direct manipulation** interface techniques [Rose and Belew, 1990] such as these is enormous. The important thing is that this additional functionality does not come at the expense of a much more complex interface of commands or menu items. People already know what space <u>means</u>, how to interpret it, and how to work within it.

FIGURE 6.24 CIVIL WAR BATTLE Query, Geographical Presentation

## 6.7 FOA (The Law)

The careful reader will have noticed that there have been an unusually large number of examples drawn from the legal domain. There are a number of things it can teach us about general principles of FOA [Belew, 1987a]. The common law tradition is very old and has been connected to an organized corpus of documents in free text for a very long time. As the Doonesbury cartoon (part of Gary Trudeau's bicentennial series) in Figure 6.25 suggests, legal documents help to demonstrate just how long prose can live beyond its drafting. Hafner was one of the first to recognize this, manually representing a wide range of attributes for a small number of documents in the legal domain [Hafner, 1978]. This work has now become a part of a larger effort within AI to model the legal reasoning process (e.g., reasoning by analogy [Ashley, 1990]). Here

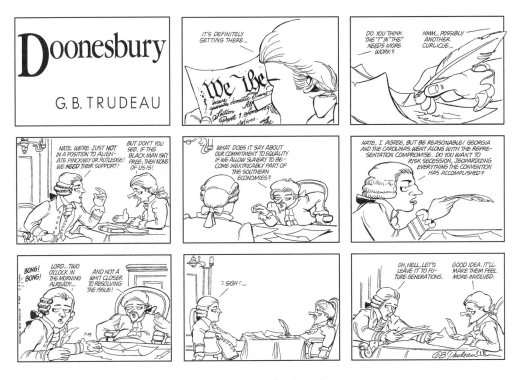

FIGURE 6.25 The Long Life of Legal Documents
Doonesbury © 1987 G. B. Trudeau. Reprinted with permission of Universal
Press Syndicate. All Rights Reserved

we are most concerned with what we can learn from lawyers who have FOA the law, which might generalize to other corpora and searchers.

First, the fact that judicial opinions have been written for so long and in such a particular "voice" has meant that it is also possible to consider special linguistic characteristics of this legal genre [Goodrich, 1987; Levi, 1982].

Second, notions of citation are especially well used within this corpus. Simple concepts like impact have been described [Shapiro, 1985], and theories of legal citation proposed [Merryman, 1977; Tapper, 1980; Ogden, 1993]. Obviously, manipulation of access to the legal printed record (for example, by controlling which judges' opinions are made available!) has enormous political ramifications [Brenner, 1992]. This became even more true because recent consolidation of the media industry means that one or two corporations effectively control the entire process of legal publication.

Third, the backbone of the legal process is an adversarial argument. This dialectic is often explicit, for example, as marked by the cf. and but cf. citation conventions (cf. Section 6.1). The presence of such syntactic markers makes it conceivable to analyze polarization across an entire legal literature. Of course, the arguments contained in briefs and opinions have a great deal more structure than simple opposition. The analysis of legal **argument structures**, in conjunction with the textual foundations of common law, is perhaps the most important feature of the legal domain to FOA. On the one hand, it is possible to model individual documents and their *logical* features so as to reason about them [Hafner, 1978; McCarty, 1980]. Special **deontic logics** have been developed especially to deal with the concepts of "rights" and "obligations" that are at the heart of many legal relations [Lowe, 1985].

*Statistical* analyses of large document corpora may seem contrary to *logical* analyses of the arguments contained in each of them, and in fact this chasm runs very deep. Not only does it suggest different technology bases from the arsenal of (roughly inductive versus deductive) AI techniques, but it also reflects a tension within the law itself. Rose [Rose, 1994, p. 95] refers to a spectrum of legal philosophies ranging from "formalism" to "realism." On the one hand, many legal documents certainly seem to function logically, with careful definitions and reasoning that Langdell [Langdell, 1887] has idealized as "mechanical jurisprudence." At the same time, analyses such as the Critical Legal Studies [Unger, 1983] have helped to demonstrate that the law is just another social process.

It is exactly this dual nature of the law, and hence of legal texts, that makes it especially interesting as an example of FOA [Nerhot, 1991]. Individual applications include litigation support systems, which allow lawyers to search through the truckloads of documents involved in extended trials. On a much larger scale, systems like West Group's *West-Law*[22] and Reed Elsevier's *LEXIS*[23] systems provide access to the bulk of statutory and case law to all practicing lawyers [Cohen, 1991; Bing, 1987].

---

[22] www.westlaw.com/

[23] www.lexis.com

## 6.8 FOA (Evolution)

For some time the study of evolution has demanded an especially interdisciplinary approach, so it is no wonder that profound difficulties in
communication arise as scientists trained in paradigms as varied as biology, psychology, and computer science attempt to communicate with
one another [Belew and Mitchell, 1996]. Now, of course, theories of
evolution are increasingly informed by huge volumes of concrete data,
generated by the Human Genome Project and related efforts. Serendip-
itously, the field of molecular biology is also one of the first (but quite
certainly not the last) disciplines to undergo a qualitative change because of the WWW. The nearly simultaneous growth of the WWW and
genomic databases has meant that computational biology as a science
has grown up with a very advanced notion of publication. Beyond formal publication channels, even beyond informal email and discussion
groups, the genomic databases at the heart of molecular biology today
may point to forms of communication among scientists that are arguably,
like image-based WWW traffic, **post-verbal**.

   The flood of biological sequence data – nucleic acid, proteins, and
now gene expression networks and metabolic pathways – into sequence
databases, with the related flood of molecular biology literature, represents an unprecedented opportunity to investigate how concepts learned
automatically from various data sets relate to the words and phrases used
by scientists to describe them. Learning this linkage – between molecular biology *concepts* and the *genomic data* relating to them – can be
described as *annotating* the data. It is now possible to learn many of
these correspondences automatically, guided by the *RelFbk* of practicing
scientists, as a natural by-product of their browsing through genome
data and publications related to them. *RelFbk* provides a key additional
piece of information to learning algorithms, beyond the statistical correlations that may exist within the genome data or textual corpora treated
independently: It captures the fact that a scientist who understands both
the sequence data and the journal articles deeply does (or does not) believe that a particular sequence and particular keyword/concept share a
common referent. Sequences are posted, annotations are often automatically constructed based on **homologous** relations to other sequences
found in the databases. A different variety of "sequence search engines,"
specially developed to look for similarities among sequences rather than

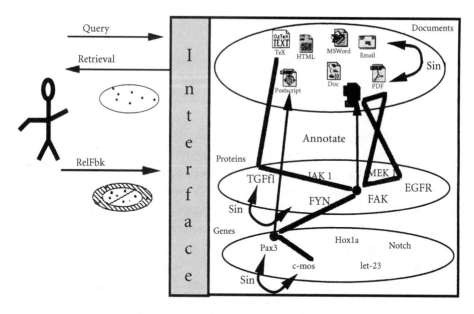

FIGURE 6.26  The Annotation Relation between Text and Sequence Data

among documents, has become the basis for retrievals. These retrievals can – and often do – connect the work of one scientist to that of another without a single verbal expression passing between them.

Figure 6.26 sketches the basic relations. On the bottom are the most fundamental classes of molecular data, namely, gene and protein sequences. On the top is a set of scientific documents, such as those found in MEDLINE. The primary relation connecting the raw genetic data and textual corpora are **annotation** links that scientists have (manually) established between articles and sequences that are both significant and useful. They are significant because they help to establish the construction of the genome as a piece of the scientific enterprise, linking it to the traditions of academic publication. They are also useful to many scientists who, for example, are interested in a particular gene or protein and want to find out all that others might know about it. But annotation is not done consistently by all participating scientists, nor has a precise semantics for what exactly an annotation should mean been established. The **Entrez**[24] interface to MEDLINE makes it convenient for a user with

---

[24] www.ncbi.nlm.gov/ Entrez

a particular sequence in mind to find its corresponding publication, and vice versa. Together with the MESH thesaurus of medical terms (cf. Section 6.3), these features make the National Library of Medicine's resource one of the most advanced on the WWW.

In addition to expediting the searches of scientists and doctors, the identification of significant patterns in one modality (i.e., in text or in sequence data) can be used to suggest hypotheses in the other (similar to suggestions made by Swanson (cf. Section 6.5.3)). Also shown in Figure 6.26 are *Sim* arcs relating "similar" data. In the case of genetic or protein sequence data, these similarity measures are typically based on a notion of "edit distance" generated by string-matching tools such as BLAST and FastA, but the investigation of new methods for this problem is one of the most active areas within machine learning (cf. [Glasgow et al., 1996]). The investigation of interdocument similarities has been an important problem within the field of information retrieval (IR) for many decades. Most document similarity measures are based on correlations between "keywords" contained by pairs of documents, but other methods (e.g., those based on a bibliometric analysis of shared entries in the documents' bibliographies) have also received considerable attention.

## 6.9 Text-Based Intelligence

Knowledge representation has always been a central issue for AI, and as a subdiscipline within computer science its primary contribution is probably the beginnings of a computational theory of knowledge. Although it is still too early to speak of such a theory, some key aspects of good knowledge representation are becoming clear [Belew and Forrest, 1988].

The text captured in document corpora was not entered with the *intention* of being part of a knowledge base. These are documents written by someone as part of a natural communication process, and any search engine technology simply gives this document added life. Alternatively, we can say that the document *was* intended to become part of a "knowledge base," but one that predates (at least the AI) use of that term: People publish their documents with the explicit hope that their ideas can become part of our collective wisdom and be used by others.

Note the ease with which an author–as–knowledge engineer can express his or her knowledge. Hypertext knowledge bases are accessible to every writer. In this view, hypertext solves the key AI problem of the **knowledge acquisition bottleneck**, providing a knowledge representation language with the ease, flexibility, and expressiveness of natural language – by actually using natural language! The cost paid is the weakness of the inferences that can be made from a textual foundation: Contrast the strong theorem-proving notions of inference of Section 6.5.1 with the many confounded associations that arise in Swanson's analysis of latent knowledge in Section 6.5.3.

## Grounding Symbols in Texts

According to Harnad's grounding hypothesis, if computers are ever to understand natural language as fully as humans, they must have an equally vast corpus of experience from which to draw [Harnad, 1987]. We propose that the huge volumes of natural language text managed by hypertext systems provide exactly the corpus of "experience" needed for such understanding. Each word in every document in a hypertext system constitutes a separate experiential "data point" about what that word <u>means</u>. The exciting prospect of using search engines as a basis for natural language–understanding systems is that their understanding of words, and concepts built from these words, will reflect the richness of this huge base of textual "experience." There are, of course, differences between the text-based "experience" and first-person, human experience, and these imply fundamental limits on language understanding derived from this source.

In this view, the computer's experience of the world is secondhand, from documents written by people about the world and subsequently through users' queries of the system. The "trick" is to learn what words <u>mean</u> by interacting with users who already know what the words <u>mean</u>, with the documents of the textual corpus forming the common referential base of experience.

The hypertext itself is in fact only the first source of information, viz., how authors use and juxtapose words. The second, ongoing source of experience is the subsequent interactions with users, a new population of people who use these same words and then react positively or negatively to the system's interpretation of them. Both the original authors and the browsing users function as the text-based intelligent system's "eyes" into the real world and how it looks to humans. That insight is something no video camera will ever give any robot.

---

**EXERCISE 1**   Characterize the distinction between those publications that typically localize citations within a document's text and those that collect all citations at the document's end. How does this vary across types of publication and across topical areas?

**EXERCISE 2**   Imagine you are an assistant professor. You realize that you will be evaluated for tenure soon and that your citation index (the number of citations to your papers) will be a major factor in the decision. One strategy might be to find a famous person in your field and criticize a central tenet of one of his or her major papers. Even if you're wrong, you are almost guaranteed to have many replies to your (specious) argument. Although it may be embarrassing, your citation count should go through the roof!

Estimate the research front width for your field, and compute how far ahead of time you would need to begin this strategy for it to count in your tenure decision.

**EXERCISE 3**   Construct a Boolean function $SameName(Name_1, Name_2)$ that returns 1 if the two people's proper names should be treated as equivalent references and 0 otherwise.

First, try constructing your best manual solution.

Next, try to *learn* this function. Ideally it should be trained with pairs of names for which you have made the correspondences yourself (as well as "negative" examples of nonmatching names). See what happens if you use your manually constructed solution as a training signal.

Finally, extend the function to a $BestName(Name_1, Name_2)$ that still returns a 0 if the names are not the same, but a merged $Name_{1+2}$ that combines the best features of both (e.g., if one has a full versus abbreviated first name and the other has a middle initial).

**EXERCISE 4**   Repeat Exercise 3 but with *bibliographic citations* rather than people's names. (Note, however, the dependence of the bibliographic solution on the $SameName(Name_1, Name_2)$ function.)

Page numbers
are worth real
money

**EXERCISE 5**    One estimate (offered by someone familiar with the industry) of the value of West's page numbers[†] over legal citations without them was $400M. Use this estimate together with an estimate of the average case length per page to give a per-page estimate of the additional value of this higher precision.

**EXERCISE 6**    A good test of coverage is provided by a sample of papers in a proceedings of the major AI conference, AAAI. Using the data set of file AAAI94-submissions.t, determine what fraction of current AI work can be traced back to the 1954 founding fathers.

**EXERCISE 7**    Names like JOHNSON purportedly began as names to describe sons of John. Suggest rules like those used in Porter's stemmer to exploit systematic variations in family names such as this.

TERMS INTRODUCED IN THIS CHAPTER

active verbs
activity
adjacency matrix
annotation
antonymy
argument
   structures
associative relation
authoritative
authority lists
authorship
bag-of-words
bibliometrics
bipolar
categories
citation lag
citation resolution
classic papers
cocitation
collaborative

classification
community
connectionist
containment
conversational
   threads
convex hull
corpus-based
   linguistics
deontic logics
descriptive adjectives
direct manipulation
draw queries
extensional
fact extraction
general
general terms
geographical
   information
   systems

global positioning
   system
homologous
hub
hyperfootnotes
hypernymy
immediacy effect
impact
impact analysis
in-degree
inheritance
invisible colleges
knowledge
   acquisition
   bottleneck
knowledge
   representations
legal briefs
lexical semantics
lexicon

# 7

# Adaptive Information Retrieval

## 7.1 Background

Most of the techniques described in the last chapter built on representational and inference methods originally developed within AI in the 1970s and '80s. Today, these methods are sometimes called **Good Old-Fashioned AI** (GOFAI), to distinguish them from more recent advances. There are many ways to characterize this change (see Russell and Norvig's text for an alternative account [Russell and Norvig, 1995, p. 827] and cf. Sections 6.9 and 7.8), but the most important is: AI is now centrally concerned with *learning* the representations it uses rather than assuming that some smart **knowledge engineer** has entered it manually.

To be concrete, imagine that you are to act as a librarian with respect to your own email. We have assumed at several points that you are collecting vast amounts of email, but perhaps are only now starting to think how it should be classified for subsequent retrieval. If we hire a librarian, we can reasonably expect him or her to bring certain useful skills to this new job and to continue to *learn* ways of doing it better. As their boss we must provide regular feedback that points out both good and bad aspects of their work. If this person was having their first annual review and they were no better at finding useful information than the day they were hired, we would have reason for concern.

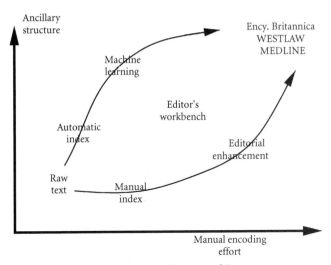

FIGURE 7.1  Learning Conceptual Structures

The preceding chapters have surveyed a number of techniques for supporting the FOA task, but their utility is immediately apparent and we do not expect it to improve. This chapter is concerned with **adaptive** techniques: those that improve their performance over time, in response to **feedback** they receive on prior performance. We can idealize our goal for the learning system in terms of a person – a clever, resourceful, *adaptive* librarian.

Figure 7.1 gives an overview of how machine learning fits into the space of existing IR techniques. The horizontal axis is meant to indicate the amount of manual effort expended to improve the corpus. These activities may include constructing a controlled vocabulary, forming good lexical index terms, including phrases, building thesauri relating the keywords to one another, etc. The vertical axis attempts to capture something like ease of use for FOA. Such ease-of-use metrics are notoriously difficult to quantify, but some indicators may include search time to find a known item.

Prior to the widespread application of search engine technologies, brought on by efforts like B. Kahle's Wide Area Information System (WAIS) and G. Salton's SMART system, to search text meant to grep across textual fields. Because grep and related search methods rely on regular expressions for queries, and because regular expressions can't be conveniently composed with Boolean operators, early search systems provided only these search techniques.

But with the introduction of search engine technologies, the goal became to build an index, much like a librarian might construct for a collection of books or documents. These indices have been at the core of our FOA discussion.

Figure 7.1 extends this progression further. While it is rare to have any textual corpus receive manual attention from a librarian or editor, and so there are very few manual indices, a very few corpora have received even more extensive editorial enhancement. *The Encyclopædia Britannica*, Westlaw, and Medline are examples of just how much the FOA activity can be supported by rich representations.

This becomes the goal for our machine learning techniques. They will turn out to form a natural extension of the statistical techniques underlying automatic index construction. Peter Turney maintains a useful bibliography of **Machine Learning Applied to Information Retrieval**[1] references generally, and of **Text Classification Resources**[2] in particular.

Finally, it is always a mistake to view the relationship between algorithmic (artificially intelligent) methods and the natural, human intelligent behaviors they mimic as an opposition. The most constructive systems we can build are ones that leverage editorial capabilities with new computational tools. The **editor's workbench** is a good metaphor for such designs.

## 7.1.1 Training against Manual Indices

We will be especially concerned with corpora that have benefited from extensive manual indexing. For example, the articles in the *Encyclopædia Britannica* have benefited from man-centuries of effort that have been applied to organize these textual passages into coherent indices, thesauri, and taxonomies. This manual attention provides two advantages in the context of machine learning.

First, the manual classification of documents to categories can be used as training data in the context of supervised learning (see

---

[1] www.iit.nrc.ca/bibliographies/ml-applied-to-ir.html

[2] www.iit.nrc.ca/II_public/Classification/resources.html

Section 7.4). Second, manually constructed representations provide a kind of upper bound on what we can hope our automatic learning techniques can build. Ultimately, however, we can expect that the most successful applications will not oppose manual, editorial enhancement with automatic induction but rather will integrate learning into the editorial process. Machine learning can already do much of the job that has traditionally been done by human editors; and yet, many aspects of the editorial function will remain beyond our learning techniques for the foreseeable future. Harnessing machine learning as part of an editor's workbench promises to leverage this scarce resource most effectively.

Of course, corpora that have benefited from such careful manual attention are few and far between. Much more typical is the textual corpus without any manual indexing whatsoever. The third advantage, then, of those special corpora that do have attending editorial enhancements is that if our learning techniques can generate analogous structures on these special collections, we can realistically expect the same techniques to generate useful structure on other collections as well.

## 7.1.2 Alternative Tasks for Learning

One obvious task we might ask of a learning algorithm is that it learn the *Rank*( ) function. Following the Probability Ranking Principle (Section 5.5.1), we might attempt to learn the probability that a document is relevant, given a set of features it contains. Recall from Section 4.2.1 how *RelFbk* information can be used to modify a query vector so as to move it closer to those documents a user has marked as relevant. As discussed in Section 4.2.2, the same technique can be used to move documents toward the query! The radically different consequence of this change is that while query modification is only useful once to the user benefiting from it, document modification changes the document's representation for all subsequent users' queries.

We will also be concerned with another task. Rather than assigning a single real number to each document ( *Pr*(*Relevance*), for example), we shall attempt (using the same set of document features) to *classify* a document into one of a small number of potential categories. Most simply, we may be interested in **binary** classification of documents into one of two categories. An obvious use of binary classification would be to classify into Relevant and Nonrelevant classes. More complex classifications into one of $C$ different classes are also possible. For example, imagine that you would like to have your email client automatically sort your incoming email into various mail folders you have used historically. Having decided how many classes to use, we must also determine whether our **assignment** to these classes is binary or if we should provide the probability that it belongs to a specific class. Classification techniques are discussed in Section 7.4.

### 7.1.3  Sources of Feedback

Two distinct classes of machine learning techniques can be applied to the FOA problem. These can be distinguished on the basis of the type of training *feedback* given to the learning system. The most powerful and best-understood are **supervised** learning methods, where every training instance given to the learning system comes with an explicit label as to what the learning system should do. Using an email example, suppose we want talk announcements to consistently go into one folder, mail from our family to go in another, and spam to be deleted. In terms of supervised learning, this regime requires that we first provide a **training set** (cf. Section 7.4). In our case, the training set would consist of email messages and the $C$ mail categories we have used to classify them in the past. After training on this data set, we hope that our classifier generalizes to new, previously unseen messages and classifies them correctly as well.

A second class of machine learning techniques makes weaker assumptions concerning the availability of training feedback. **Reinforcement** learning assumes only that a positive/negative signal tells the learning system when it is doing a good/bad job. In the FOA process, for example, *RelFbk* generates a reinforcement signal (saying whether it was a good or bad thing that a document was retrieved).

Note that *RelFbk* does not count as supervised learning; in general, we do not know all of the documents that should have been retrieved with respect to a particular query. Supervised training provides more information in the sense that every aspect of the learner's action (retrieval) can be contrasted with corresponding features of the correct action. Reinforcement information, on the other hand, aggregates all of these features into a single measure of performance.

The difference between these two kinds of learning is especially stark in the FOA context. To provide reinforcement information, users need

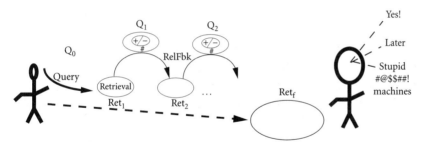

FIGURE 7.2  Browsing across Queries in Same Session

only react to each document and say whether they are happy or sad it was retrieved. In order to do supervised training, the user would need to identify the perfect retrieval, requiring the user to evaluate each and every document in the corpus!                                                    ?2

The distinction between the supervised retrieval and that shaped by *RelFbk* highlights the need to be explicit about which kinds of feedback are hard for the user and which are easier. The discussion of RAVE made some of our assumptions concerning cognitive overhead clear (Section 4.4), but this is another important area for further study. Here we will continue to assume that *RelFbk* is easy to acquire.                               ?3

## Learning from the Entire Session

Note that each iteration of the FOA conversation is but a link in the larger dialog leading from the users' initial information need to the end of their search; cf. Figure 7.2.

First, the continuity of the same search pursuing the same information need from iteration of the FOA dialog to the next iteration helps to constrain interpretations of the users' *RelFbk*; we know which documents they have seen previously, we may know something about how a document retrieved in iteration $i + 1$ is related to one from iteration $i$ and why it was retrieved, and so on. But perhaps the most important reason to model multiple queries as part of a single session is that it is the total, *aggregate* difference between their cognitive states at the beginning of the session and at the end of the session that should most concern us. Users begin the search with their best characterization of what it is they want to FOA, and they leave for one of a number of potential reasons:

- because they ran out of time (but would like to continue this same session at a later time),
- because they found what they were looking for,
- because they reached ultimate frustration, etc.

Our interpretation of what the system could or should learn from this termination will be radically different, and so determining which of these reasons pertains becomes particularly important to establish.

### Distributions over Learning Instances

Anyone familiar with basic statistics will appreciate how sensitive our estimate of an average is on the set of examples we happen to select for our sample. Learning methods are similarly sensitive to the amount and distribution of training data. For example, the ratio of the number of features to the number of instances can affect learning performance significantly [Moulinier et al., 1996; Dagan et al., 1997].

Define a **positive training instance** $\oplus$ to be one that has been identified as a member of a class and a **negative training instance** $\ominus$ to be one that is identified as not a member of that class.

It is less obvious that the ratio of positive to negative training instances is also important. In binary classification tasks we can expect an even number of positive and negative training instances. But when classifying into a larger number of categories, it is common to treat each training instance as a positive instance of one class and a negative instance of all the others. Continuing our email classification example, we can expect that every classified message in our training set corresponds to a positive instance of one classification and simultaneously as a negative example of all the others. This makes efficient use of the training data, but also generates a $\frac{1}{C-1}$ skew to the positive versus negative training instance distribution.

## 7.2 Building Hypotheses about Documents

We will talk about competing "hypotheses," for example, rules that successfully separate our spam email from our family's email. If only very simple hypotheses are to be considered, a relatively small amount of data can be used to select between them. For example, if our hypothesis is that spam email always contains the phrase $$$$ BIG MONEY $$$$$, a small amount of training data is sufficient to confirm or disconfirm this rule [Sahami et al., 1998]. But if we wish to consider elaborate discrimination rules, for example, including many keywords and/or date information, it takes much more data to tease apart all the alternatives. The volume of training data available, then, provides a very real constraint on how complex the hypotheses we can consider can be and how statistically reliable we expect rules to perform on unseen test data.

## 7.2.1  Feature Selection

When you are thinking about how you classifiy your email, keywords contained in your email are almost certainly some of the features you think of first. Recall, however, that the keyword vocabulary can be very large. Using this feature space, then, individual document representations will be very sparse. In terms of the vector space model of Section 3.4, many of the vector elements will be zero. To use Littlestone's lovely expression, "Irrelevant attributes abound" [Littlestone, 1988], and so it should come as no surprise that his learning techniques are especially appropriate in the FOA learning applications discussed in Section 7.5.3.

Efforts to control the keyword vocabulary and make the lexical features as meaningful as possible are therefore important preconditions for good classification performance. For example, name-tagging techniques (cf. Section 6.6.1) that reliably identify proper names can provide valuable classification features. A proper name tagger would be one that was especially sophisticated about capitalization, name order, and abbreviation conventions. When both people's proper names and institutional names (government agencies, universities, corporations, etc.) are capitalized, the recognition of complex, multitoken phrases becomes possible.

In part because of the difficult issues lexical, keyword-based representations entail, it is worth thinking briefly about some of the alternatives. There are also less-obvious features we might use to classify documents. Meta-data associated with the document, for example, information about its date and place of publication, is one possibility. Geographic place information associated with a document can also be useful; cf. Section 6.6.1. Finally, recall the bibliographic citations that many documents contain (cf. Section 6.1). The set of references one document makes to others (representable as links in a graph) can be used as the basis of classification in much the same way as its keywords.

In summary, while keywords provide the most obvious set of features on which classifications can be based, these result in very large and sparse learning problems. Other features are also available and may be more useful. It is important to note, however, that careful Bayesian reasoning about dependencies among keyword features is a very difficult problem, as discussed in Section 5.5.7. Attempting to extend this inference to include other heterogeneous types of features must be done carefully.

## Distribution-Based Selection

Because our typical assumption has been that keywords occur independently, it should come as no surprise that when we try to reduce from the full set of all keywords in the *Vocab* to a smaller set, a good way to decide which features are most useful is to pick those that are most independent of any others. That is, we can hope that two keywords that are statistically dependent can be merged into a single one.

As mentioned in Section 3.3.6, **entropy** captures the amount of randomness in (or uncertainty about) some random variable:

$$H(X) = -\sum_x Pr(X = x) \log (Pr(x)) \qquad (7.1)$$

When the distribution of a random variable $X$ is conditionally dependent on that of a second random variable $Y$, the **conditional entropy** of $X$ on $Y$ (a.k.a. **post-Y entropy** of $X$) can be similarly defined [Papoulis, 1991, pp. 549–54]:

$$H(X \mid Y) = -\sum_{X=x, Y=y} Pr(x \mid y) \log(Pr(X = x \mid Y = y)) \qquad (7.2)$$

If knowledge of values of $Y$ reduces our uncertainty about the distribution of $X$, it is natural to think that Y *informs* us about X. **Mutual information** $I$ captures this notion:

$$I(X, Y) = H(X) - H(X \mid Y)$$
$$= -\sum_x Pr(x) \log (Pr(x)) + \sum_{x,y} Pr(x \mid y) \log(Pr(x \mid y)) \qquad (7.3)$$

This information is mutual in the sense that it is a symmetric relation between the two variables; $Y$ tells us as much about $X$ as $X$ does about $Y$: $I(X, Y) = I(Y, X)$.

If the mutual information $I(k_i, k_j)$ between all pairs of keywords in $K$ is known, van Rijsbergen, p. 123 recommends selecting the **maximum spanning tree**, which maximizes the total information across all edges of the tree:

> the MST . . . incorporates the most significant of the dependen-
> cies between the variables subject to the global constraint that
> the sum of them should be a maximum. [van Rijsbergen, p. 123]

Note, however, that the mutual information statistic has an intrinsic bias toward keyword pairs $k_i$, $k_j$ in which the individual keyword frequencies $f_i$ and $f_j$ are intermediate. The post-Y entropy of X can only reduce it [Papoulis, 1991]:

$$H(X \mid Y) \leq H(X) \qquad (7.4)$$

In terms of keyword frequencies, then, the mutual information of a pair of keywords is limited by their marginal entropies. This implies that very rare and very common keywords are "penalized" with respect to the mutual information measure. For this reason, it is worthwhile considering the relation between mutual information as a measure of keyword interdependencies and the eigenstructure analysis (cf. Section 5.2.3) of the keyword cross-correlation matrix $J$.

Mutual information considers the full joint probability between the two keywords, while methods like singular value decomposition (SVD) and principal component analysis (PCA) consider only the cross-correlation matrix. When random variables happen to fit a normal distribution, these correlation statistics are sufficient, but that is unlikely in the case of our keywords. A second important difference is that correlation-based methods construct new feature variables, out of linear combinations of the initial keyword tokens. Mutual information–based methods (or at least van Rijsbergen, p. 123's MST-based construction) select the best variables from a constant set.

## Selection Based on "Fit" to a Classification Task

Rather than using distributional statistics among the keywords them-selves as the basis for feature selection, it is also possible to look for those features that are most "fit" with respect to some classification task [Lewis and Hayes, 1994] (cf. Section 7.4).

Both mutual information and correlation statistics can be used in either supervised or unsupervised learning situations, considering either the mutual information $I(k, c)$ of each keyword $k$ with respect to the class $c$ in the former case or Fisher's **linear discriminant** [Duda and Hart, 1973, p. 114] in the latter.

Using the classification performance criterion, Yang and Pederson considered a wide range of potential measures and found that simply measuring $f_k$, the document frequency of keyword $k$, provided an effective measure over potential keyword features [Yang and Pedersen, 1997]. In fact, using document frequency as a criterion, they were able to remove 98 percent of all keywords while retaining (even improving slightly!?) classification performance. Given the efficient way in which $f_k$ can be collected (relative to $MI$, $\chi^2$, and other potential measures), the level of performance maintained by such **aggressive dimensionality reduction** is indeed striking. But because the features selected are sensitive to the particular classification task considered, their utility for other purposes may be suspect. Distribution-based selection methods may therefore be more robust.

## 7.2.2 Hypothesis Spaces

However they are selected, the features discussed in the previous section must now be composed into hypotheses concerning how we might describe documents. There is an extraordinary range of alternatives represented here. Some of these are shown in Figure 7.3.

Decision trees are formed by asking a question about individual features and using the answers to these questions to navigate through a series of tests until documents are ultimately classified at the leaves. Weighted, linear combinations of the features can also be formed. Neural networks are best viewed as nonlinear compositions of weighted features [Crestani, 1993; Crestani, 1994; Gallant, 1991; Kwok, 1995; Wong et al., 1993]. Boolean formulas can be formed from sentences using simple conjunctive or disjunctive combinations. Our focus here will be on Bayesian networks, which attempt to represent probabilistic relationships among the features.

In any of these cases, machine learning techniques must be sensitive to their inductive bias. That is, given a fixed amount of data, we must

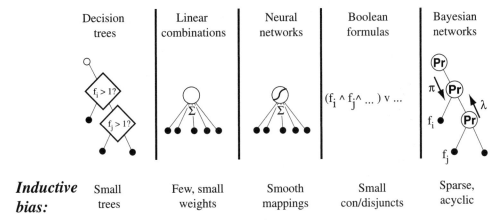

| Decision trees | Linear combinations | Neural networks | Boolean formulas | Bayesian networks |
|---|---|---|---|---|

*Inductive bias:*

| Small trees | Few, small weights | Smooth mappings | Small con/disjuncts | Sparse, acyclic |
|---|---|---|---|---|

FIGURE 7.3 Inductive Bias

have some a priori preference for some kinds of hypotheses over others. For example, decision tree learning algorithms [Quinlan, 1993] prefer small trees and neural networks prefer smooth mappings [Mitchell, 1997].

A common feature of all of these learning algorithms is a general preference for parsimony, or simplicity. This preference is typically attributed first to William of Occam (ca. 1330). **Occam's Razor** has been used since then to cleave simpler hypotheses from more complex ones.

Another motivation for the parsimony bias has been realized more recently within machine learning: Simple hypotheses are more likely to accurately go beyond the data used to train them to classify other unseen data. That is, very complicated hypotheses have a tendency to **over-fit** to the training data given a learning algorithm, but the good fit they can accomplish on this set is not matched when the same classification is done on new data. The issues involved in evaluating a classifier's performance are an important topic within machine learning [Mitchell, 1997].

## 7.3 Learning Which Documents to Route

Arguably, the first use of *RelFbk* information in an adaptive IR context came out of the SMART group led by Gerald Salton. As was discussed in Section 4.2.2, Salton's vector space model lends itself to a representation of documents and queries that suggest ways of producing better matches, as shown in Figure 7.4.

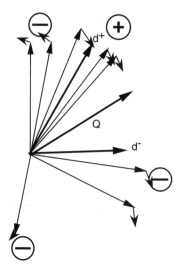

FIGURE 7.4  Document Modifications due to *RelFbk*

Rocchio's characterization of the task is best described as routing: We imagine that a stream of all the world's news is available to some institution (for example, a corporation), and many members of this institution (employees) are expected to build long-standing queries characterizing their interests. These queries are passed against the incoming stream of documents, and those matching a particular employee's query are **routed** to him or her [Schutze et al., 1995a].

From this employee's point of view, he or she will be receiving a stream of documents, all of which are of interest to him or her. If he or she identifies those documents that are not relevant, the resulting corpus can be viewed as a training set and used to adjust the filter. This is a concrete application of the binary classification technology.

Brauen, in particular, considered "document vector modifications," resulting in "dynamic" document spaces [Brauen, 1969]. Documents marked as relevant can be moved closer to the query that successfully retrieved them in several ways. First and most obviously, features shared by query and document can have their weight increased. Features in the document but not in the query can have their weight decreased, and terms in the query but not in the document can be added to the document's representation with small initial weights.

From the perspective of modern machine learning, Brauen's method would be considered a type of **gradient descent** learning algorithm:

The disparity between document and query creates a gradient along which small changes are made. One difference, however, is that Brauen imagined a **batch** learning scenario, with the entire set of labeled documents available simultaneously. **Online** learning algorithms, on the other hand, make small, incremental adaptive changes in immediate response to every learning instance (document). Each individual step of learning (e.g., weight update in neural networks) must be very small, in order to guarantee convergence toward the globally optimal value. The size of the small change is controlled by $\eta$, typically known as the **learning rate**. Stochastic approximation theory suggests that this constant should be relatively small for online learning so that the weights are small enough to allow convergence [White, 1989]. Online learning is generally preferred to avoid time delay and data collection complications.

Idealizing our learning task to produce a perfect match (i.e., the dot product of query and document is 1.0) on relevant documents and no match on irrelevant documents, we can treat this behavior as the target for our error correction learning. Let $R_d$ stand for this Boolean relevant/not relevant classification of each document. Then (as discussed further in Section 7.4), we can hope to have available a training set $T$ of documents that have been labeled a priori as $R_d = 0$ or $R_d = 1$, specifying whether they are considered relevant. With such evidence as to what documents we do and don't consider relevant, we can define precisely how well we have learned. A typical **error measure** or **loss function** can be defined as the squared difference between the actual vector match and the target $R_d^\dagger$:

$$Error \equiv \sum_{\mathbf{d} \in T} (\mathbf{d} \cdot \mathbf{q} - R_d)^2 \qquad (7.5)$$

The **q/d** gradient runs in both directions

## 7.3.1 Widrow-Hoff

The **Widrow-Hoff** (a.k.a. **least mean squared (LMS)**) algorithm is the best-understood and principled approach to training a linear system to minimize this squared error loss [Widrow and Hoff, 1960]. It does this by making a small move (scaled by the parameter $\eta$) in the direction of the gradient of error. This gradient is defined exactly by the derivative of Equation 7.5 with respect to the document vector:

$$\Delta \mathbf{q} = -2\eta (\mathbf{q} \cdot \mathbf{d} - R_d) \mathbf{d} \qquad (7.6)$$

It is also important to remember that changes made to a single document in response to a single query can make no guarantees about improved performance with respect to other documents and other queries. For example, two documents might both be moved closer to a query (as proposed by Brauen and Rocchio) but their relative rankings may not change at all!

## 7.3.2  User Drift and Event Tracking

One interesting feature of the training set generated by the routing task is the odd distribution of positive and negative examples it generates. Initially, we can imagine that this filter is very inaccurate; i.e., we are likely to see many negative examples. Later, when we hope it is better trained, the filter has nearly perfect performance and the system gets very few negative examples.

Further, no user's interests remain static. As discussed in the next chapter, one common purpose for the FOA activity is to become educated (cf. Section 8.3.4), and this is an elusive, ever-changing goal. The world changes, and what users read changes their opinions of what needs to be done and what the new questions are. In brief, documents they used to find relevant become irrelevant. This has been called **concept drift** [Klinkenberg and Renz, 1998]. When the world changes, this corresponds to documents, and the news they contain changes too. This side of the dynamic is called **topic tracking** [Allan et al., 1998; Baker et al., 1999]. Jaime Carbonell's (of CMU) approach is to first identify that a concept change has occurred and then to adjust a time window on the stream of incoming training data over which a new invariant is then identified (personal communication).

The distribution of *RelFbk* generated by the filtering task, where a standing query is allowed to adapt to a stream of *RelFbk* generated by users who receive and evaluate routed documents (cf. Section 4.3.9), provides an especially interesting form of learning task, because of its **temporal dimension**. Initially, the set of documents routed to users must depend on the same fundamental matching function shared by other search engine tasks. But as *RelFbk*, in response to the first retrievals, comes to affect the users' characterizations of interest, only a skewed sample (relative to the initial distribution) of potential documents is shown to the users, and only these can be the basis of subsequent *RelFbk*.

This tension between **exploration** of the universe of potentially relevant documents and **exploitation** of those documents that prior *RelFbk* makes it seem are most likely to be perceived as relevant by the users is familiar to other **reinforcement learning** situations [Sutton and Barto, 1998].

## 7.4  Classification

The classification task is . . . classic:), and a wide range of technologies for accomplishing it have been developed [Duda and Hart, 1973; Carlin and Louis, 1996]. Even in the relatively recent context of text-based domains, many techniques have been applied [Lewis and Hayes, 1994]. Here we will focus primarily on extending the probabilistic approach of Section 5.5, but we'll consider other alternatives in Section 7.5. Andrew McCallum and colleagues have developed a software suite called *RAINBOW*[3] that is very useful for experiments into text classification.

We begin by assuming that we have been given a set of classes $\mathcal{C} = \{c_1, c_2, \ldots c_C\}$ and have been asked to produce a function that **classifies** a new document into one of these classes. McCallum gives a good overview of the Bayesian approach applied to text:

> This approach assumes that the text data was generated by a parametric model, and uses training data to calculate the Bayes-optimal estimates of the model parameters. Then, equipped with these estimates, it classifies new documents using Bayes' rule to *turn the generative model around* and calculate the posterior probability that a class would have generated the test document in question. [McCallum and Nigam, 1998, p. 42, emphasis added]

The major features of the training regime are shown in Figure 7.5. During the first phase, a correspondence has been established *manually* between each example document $\mathbf{d}_i$ and some classification $c_i$ in the training set $T$:

$$T \equiv \{\langle \mathbf{d}_i, c_i \rangle\} \tag{7.7}$$

---

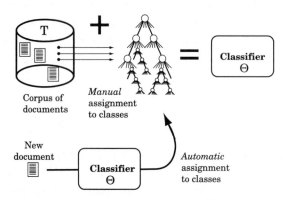

FIGURE 7.5  Training a Classifier

(In Figure 7.5, the classifications are imagined to be part of a hierarchical classification system, as will be discussed in detail in Section 7.5.5.) These data are used somehow (for now it's okay to think of it as magic) to tune the set of parameters $\Theta$ specifying a particular classifier. The second and dominant phase is then to use this classifier to *automatically* assign documents to classes in an analogous manner to those manually classified in the training set.

We seek the **posterior probability** of a particular class, given the evidence provided by a new document, $Pr(c \mid d)$. The second step is then, given these probabilities for all classes, to return the one that maximizes this likelihood. Bayes' rule is typically invoked in such situations to "invert" this conditional dependency:

$$Pr(c \mid \mathbf{d}) = \frac{Pr(\mathbf{d} \mid c)Pr(c)}{\sum_{c} Pr(\mathbf{d} \mid c)Pr(c)} \qquad (7.8)$$

The likelihood $Pr(d \mid c)$ can be more easily estimated if we assume classes are represented as **mixtures** of the documents' features. We can think of hypothetical documents (that we imagine belong to the class) as generated by some model, the parameters $\Theta$ of which we hope to discover. Assuming that a document is generated by first picking a particular class and then using its parameters to select features,* the likelihood of

---

* More general models are also possible [McCallum and Nigam, 1998].

a document being selected can be computed by considering the prior probability of each class $Pr(c \mid \Theta)$ and its distribution $Pr(\mathbf{d} \mid c; \Theta)$:

$$Pr(\mathbf{d} \mid \Theta) = \sum_{c} Pr(c \mid \Theta) \cdot Pr(\mathbf{d} \mid c; \Theta) \qquad (7.9)$$

These measures allow us to precisely state how well a learned model captures regularities found in the training set: The model is doing a good job if it applies the same classifications as observed in the training data. But this criterion also highlights the dependence of any learning method on the training data $T$ used to construct it, which cannot be overemphasized. Independent of the range of hypotheses considered, and of the learning methods used to build the best possible model, our ability to **inductively generalize** from the training data to new examples (e.g., unclassified documents) depends entirely on how typical the training data are. Within **computational learning theory** this dependence is captured by the assumption that training data and subsequent trials are drawn from the same distribution [Valiant, 1984; Kearns and Vazirani, 1994].

In practice, performance of a classifier on the training set is bound to be an optimistic overestimate of how well it can generalize to previously unseen data. The most common way to guard against such overestimates is to artificially **hold out** some of the training set as a separate **test set**. Training proceeds as before on all the training data but not on the test set, and then the system is evaluated on the test set, which provides a more reasonable estimate as to how the system will fare. More sophisticated **cross-validation** procedures begin by partitioning the available training data into $k$ subsets. Iteratively, each partition is used as the holdout set while the remaining $\frac{k-1}{k}$ balance of $T$ is used for training. The average performance across all $k$ tests is then used as a more statistically reliable estimate of true performance. The statistical validity derived by cross-validation and related techniques becomes especially important when the total amount of training data is small; given the time and effort required to produce manual classifications, this is often the case.

## 7.4.1 Modeling Documents

The general framework of empirical Bayesian estimation is broad and powerful enough that it has been applied in many contexts. The hard work comes, however, in specifying just how the parametric model $\Theta$ is to be constructed from a set of individual parameters $\theta_i$ and how these can be estimated from the training data. Principled approaches to the text classification problem require specification of explicit models of how documents are generated. Two models of the **event space** underlying our construction of hypothetical documents have been proposed [McCallum and Nigam, 1998], and we consider each of these below.

One critical, simplifying assumption shared by both models is that the features occur *independently* in the documents. As we have discussed a number of times, any such **naïve Bayesian** model will miss a great many of the interactions arising among real words in real documents. It is somewhat curious, then, that such naïve classifiers do as well as they do [Domingos and Pazzani, 1997].

## Multivariate Bernoulli

Arguably the simplest model captures only the presence or absence of words in the document. That is, the document is modeled as the composition of $k$ keywords drawn from the *Vocab* as so many independent Bernoulli trials. We imagine that a document **d** is constructed by repeatedly selecting $|\mathbf{d}|$ words for each position in the document.[†]

Ordered sequence

If we associate a biased coin with each keyword $k$, we can decompose the desired model $\Theta$ into two sets of parameters:

$$\theta_c \equiv Pr(c) \tag{7.10}$$

$$\theta_{ck} \equiv Pr(k\,|\,c) \tag{7.11}$$

i.e., the prior probability of each class $c$ and the probability that a keyword is present given that we know a document containing it is in class $c$. Then the naïve Bayesian assumption allows us to assume that the keywords occur at each positional location independently of one another:

$$Pr(\mathbf{d}\,|\,c) = \prod_{k=1}^{|\mathbf{d}|} \theta_{ck} \tag{7.12}$$

## Multinomial

An alternative model of document generation is as repeated draws from an **urn of words** containing all the keywords in the *Vocab*. This gives rise to a multinomial model that is sensitive to the *frequency* $f_{dk}$ of keywords' occurrence in $d$, rather than just their presence or absence:*

$$Pr(\mathbf{d}\,|c) = Pr(|\mathbf{d}|) \cdot (|\mathbf{d}|)! \prod_{k \in Vocab} \frac{\theta_{ck}^{f_{dk}}}{f_{dk}!} \qquad (7.13)$$

## 7.4.2 Training a Classifier

The parameters $\Theta$ controlling the classifier could come from many places, but of course here we are concerned with *learning* them. In terms of the training set $T$:

$$T \equiv \{\langle d_i, c_i \rangle\} \qquad (7.14)$$

we seek the parameters $\Theta$ with the highest probability of having produced $T$. Depending on the model we employ, how we decompose $\Theta$ into its constituent parameters $\theta_i$ will differ.

One piece of this is easy to estimate: The **prior probability** of the class $Pr(c)$ is how frequently one classification is observed in $T$ relative to the others. Using a "twiddle" hat to distinguish estimates $\widetilde{\theta}$ of the probabilities from their true values $\theta$:

$$\widetilde{\theta}_c = \frac{f_c}{|T|} \qquad (7.15)$$

Estimating $\widetilde{\theta_{ck}}$ is more complicated. The fact that both the multivariate Bernoulli and the multinomial models of document generation involve the *product* of the keywords' $\widetilde{\theta_{ck}}$ should make it obvious that our cumulative estimate will be very sensitive to any one of these values; consider, for example, what happens if even one of these terms is zero!

Within the Bayesian framework,[†] these statistical sensitivities are addressed by providing **priors** for the underlying word-events of document generation.

Probabilists' religious wars

---

* For simplicity, we assume that the documents' lengths are independent of the classes, i.e., that knowing a document's length tells us little about which class it should be in.

### 7.4.3 Priors

When we are attempting to estimate $\theta_{ck}$, the most common prior applied within text classification is the **m-estimate** [Mitchell, 1997, p. 179]. This corresponds to pretending that the actual training data in $T$ are augmented by $NKw \equiv |Vocab|$ pseudo-trials uniformly distributed across all the keywords in $Vocab$. Operationally, this simply means that all keyword counters are "primed" (initialized to) one before real statistics are collected. With the priors specified, we can estimate $\theta_{ck}$ under each of the two models discussed in Section 7.4.1.

Recall that the multivariate Bernoulli model associates a single biased coin $\theta_{ck}$ with each keyword used by a class. The Bernoulli assumption is then that a document in the class will contain at least one occurrence of the keyword with probability $\theta_{ck}$ but also with probability $1 - \theta_{ck}$ that it will *not* contain any instances of the keyword. Using a Boolean **indicator function** $B_{dk}$ to signal the presence or absence of a keyword in a document and another $B_{cd}$ to signal whether the document is classified with respect to class $c$:*

$$\widetilde{\theta_{ck}} = \frac{1 + \sum_{d \in T} B_{dk} B_{dc}}{2 + \sum_{d \in T} B_{dc}} \qquad (7.16)$$

Note that in this statistic the "nonoccurrence" of keywords *not* present in the document also affects our estimate. This somewhat odd **Mark of Zero** [Lewis et al., 1996] should make us feel less sanguine about what is captured by any Bernoulli model.

The multinomial alternatives (assuming the same priors as before) for these estimates are:

$$\widetilde{\theta_{ck}} = \frac{1 + \sum_{d \in T} f_{cd} B_{dc}}{NKw + \sum_{k \in V} \sum_{d \in T} f_{cd} B_{dc}} \qquad (7.17)$$

Empirically, the multinomial model seems to support better classification performance, especially when larger vocabulary sizes are considered [McCallum and Nigam, 1998].

---

* $B_{dk} = 1$ if $k$ occurs at least once in $d$ and is zero otherwise; $B_{cd} = 1$ if $d$ is classified as an instance of class $c$ and is zero otherwise.

$$
\text{``Ireland''} \quad \leftrightarrow \quad \begin{aligned} &\text{IRELAND} \vee \\ &(\text{IRA} \wedge \text{KILLED}) \vee \\ &(\text{IRA} \wedge \text{SHOT}) \vee \\ &\cdots \\ &(\text{IRA} \wedge \text{OUT}) \end{aligned}
$$

FIGURE 7.6 RIPPER Classification Rule

## 7.5 Other Approaches to Classification

### 7.5.1 Nearest-Neighbor Matching

One of the most straightforward ways to classify documents is to make a rote memory of the training set $T$ and retrieve those documents from $T$ that are most similar to a new document to be classified [Cost and Salzberg, 1993; Larkey and Croft, 1996; Yang and Pedersen, 1997; Larkey, 1998a]. This corresponds to using the $|d \cdot d|$ similarity metric discussed in Section 5.2. A weighted sum of the $k$ most similar documents' classifications can be used to pick the best match.

### 7.5.2 Boolean Predicates

A different approach to the text classification task has been proposed by Cohen in his RIPPER system [Cohen, 1996a; Cohen, 1996b]. The space of hypothesis considered by RIPPER is a set of Boolean rules composed over a space of keywords. A simple example is shown in Figure 7.6, which extends the obvious definition of IRELAND to include documents that mention violent IRA activities. Like decision lists, RIPPER's rule sets are easier for human experts to interpret than a large system of Bayesian probabilities.

   RIPPER is an example of a "covering" learning algorithm; cf. Figure 7.7. This means that it iteratively forms conjunctions of Boolean predicates that "cover" some of the positive instances of a Boolean classification while excluding all the negative instances. In the next iteration, the positive instances, which were covered previously, are removed from the training set, and a new conjunctive clause is formed, which again covers some more positive instances while excluding all negative ones. Ultimately, then, the rule set will be in **disjunctive normal form** (DNF).

   RIPPER also includes optimizations to simplify rules by removing conditions that do not affect performance and by picking conditions

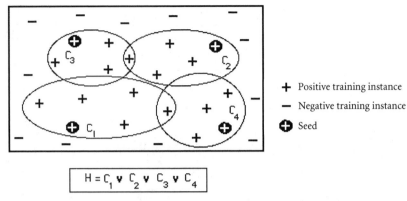

FIGURE 7.7  Covering Algorithms

that provide the most information gain [Quinlan, 1993]. Finally, Cohen adapted these rule learning techniques to the text domain by adding "set-valued attributes." These special attributes collapse a document's representation to be simply the set of words it contains. RIPPER's rules can then include tests for sets of words, rather than having to test the presence or absence of each word individually.

## 7.5.3  When Irrelevant Attributes Abound

In documents where "irrelevant attributes abound" [Littlestone, 1988] (e.g., when any one document contains a small fraction of the full vocabulary but still more than are important in a classifier), the rapid "winnowing" of features is critical. One approach is to use **boosting** methods, which begin with many very weak hypotheses but focus in on the most successful [Schapire et al., 1998].

Kivinen and Warmuth's exponentiated gradient EG algorithm extends from Winnow's binary features and output to real-valued quantities [Warmuth, 1997]. The result shares much with the Widrow-Hoff model (cf. Section 7.3.1), but rather than having weight changes making an *additive* change in the direction of the gradient, EG recommends making a *multiplicative* change to each element of the document vector. Using $R_\mathbf{d}$ as in Equation 7.6:

$$\mathbf{d}' = \mathbf{d}\frac{\exp(-2\eta(\mathbf{d} \cdot \mathbf{q} - R_\mathbf{d})\mathbf{q})}{|\mathbf{d}''|} \qquad (7.18)$$

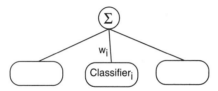

FIGURE 7.8 Combining Experts

where $\mathbf{d}'$ is the updated document vector and $|\mathbf{d}''|$ is the length of the document vector after all weights have been updated. That is, weights are always *renormalized* so that their sum remains one (and nonnegative). Renormalization is an important feature of EG, which, in conjunction with the multiplicative increases in those "relevant" features that are shared with a query, results in quick (i.e., exponentially fast) reduction to zero for irrelevant weights [Lewis et al., 1996]. Callan has also found that rather than training the EG classifier with zero for incorrect classifications and unity for correct ones, using more moderate target values pegged to the minimum and maximum feature values is more successful [Callan, 1998].

Another very recent approach is to apply Vapnik's **support vector machines** (SVM) [Vapnik, 1995]. Rather than searching for dichotomizing planes within a representational space that has been predefined (e.g., the hyperplanes that gradient descent methods adjust), SVMs search in the "dual" space defined by the set of training instances for **kernels** (representations) wherein the classes can be conveniently separated! As Joachims [Joachims, 1998] recently emphasized, the way in which these techniques avoid searching the vast space of potential keyword features seems to make SVM a very appropriate technology for this application.

## 7.5.4 Combining Classifiers

The preceding chapters have described a wide range of potentially useful retrieval techniques. A very reasonable response is to ask if perhaps the best possible retrieval system isn't some sort of mixture of these various techniques. For example, Bartell [Bartell et al., 1994a] has considered simple linear combinations of experts like those shown in Figure 7.8. His experiments considered two experts, one that used a set of simple words as features and a second that did more elaborate phrase extraction.

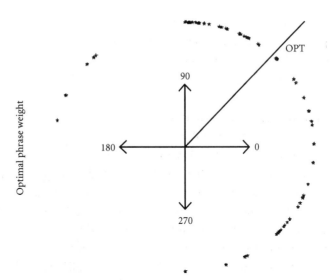

Optimal term weight
(weights normalized to unit circle)

FIGURE 7.9  Optimal Weightings Distribution
From [Bartell et al., 1994b]

Holding the sum of the two experts' contributions constant, their relative contribution describes a circle of fixed radius. Figure 7.9 shows a set of 228 test queries and the optimal weighting of phrase and term experts for each. That is, for a particular query, the optimal contribution of ranking information from the phrase and term expert is determined. Also shown is a line corresponding to the optimal balance between phrase and term expert across all queries. In general, the phrase expert was not very useful. On some queries, however, it was able to improve performance significantly. The way in which individual queries make special demands of the retrieval system is perhaps the most striking feature of these results.

As search engine technologies have developed, the composition of hybrid systems involving multiple systems has required a more "black box" composition. That is, rather than manipulating a single feature of the retrieval system (e.g., term versus phrase features), the combination has been of a system's net ranking [Thompson, 1990a; Thompson, 1990b].

**Collection fusion** refers to the problem of combining results coming from disjoint corpora [Towell et al., 1995; Yager and Rybalov, 1998]. (In the emerging environment of combined corpora and primarily *publisher-driven* search engines, corpora have become confounded with the search engines allowed to search them.) Diamond (personal communication) has hypothesized several effects we might imagine from **fusing** multiple search engines:

> **Skimming effect** . . . [when] retrieval approaches that represent [documents] differently may retrieve different relevant items, so that a combination method that takes the top-ranked items from each of the retrieval approaches will "push" non-relevant items down in the ranking.
>
> **Chorus effect** . . . when several retrieval approaches (each representing the *query* differently) suggest that an item is relevant to a query, this tends to be stronger evidence for relevance than a single approach doing so. Thus, allowing several independent retrieval approaches to "vote" on the relevance of an item should enable a sharper distinction between relevant and non-relevant items. [Diamond, personal communication]

Note how the first of these focuses on differences in the systems-based treatment of *documents* and the second on *queries* (cf. Section 3.3.3).[†]

Dark Horse effect, too

In some ways, this combination of classifiers is reminiscent of earlier work using multiple query representations [Belkin et al., 1993]. Vogt has recently performed an exhaustive analysis of linear combinations for all 61 search engines submitted to the TREC5 competition [Vogt and Cottrell, 1998]. His primary conclusion, following Lee [Lee, 1997], is that two systems are best combined linearly when there is a great deal of overlap in the set of relevant documents they identify, while their retrieval of nonrelevant documents is nearly disjoint. In terms of Diamond's qualitative expectations, linear combinations are best able to support the "chorus" effect. Schutze et al. and Larkey have considered combining various types of special-function classifiers [Schutze et al., 1995b; Larkey and Croft, 1996].

## 7.5.5  Hierarchic Classification

In many areas of careful scholarship, classification labels are not merely members of a big set, but rather they are organized hierarchically into

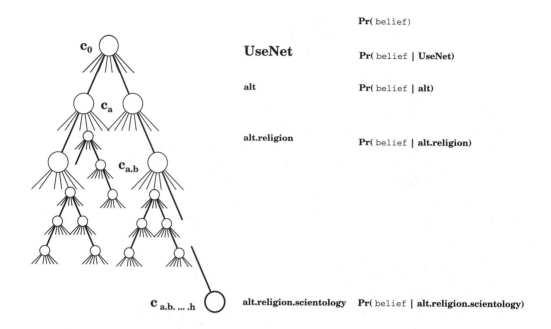

| | $\mathbf{Pr}(\texttt{belief})$ |
| --- | --- |
| **UseNet** | $\mathbf{Pr}(\texttt{belief} \mid \textbf{UseNet})$ |
| alt | $\mathbf{Pr}(\texttt{belief} \mid \textbf{alt})$ |
| alt.religion | $\mathbf{Pr}(\texttt{belief} \mid \textbf{alt.religion})$ |
| alt.religion.scientology | $\mathbf{Pr}(\texttt{belief} \mid \textbf{alt.religion.scientology})$ |

FIGURE 7.10  Hierarchic Classification

systems of BT/NT hypernymy (cf. Section 6.3). For example, the U.S. Patent Office has 400 top-level classifications with 135,000 subclasses [Larkey, 1998b]. These classes are part of a hierarchic tree going down 15 levels. A simple example suggested by Mitchell and others' use of the UseNet newsgroup hierarchy [Mitchell, 1997; McCallum et al., 1998] is shown in Figure 7.10. Here the probability of the keyword BELIEFS is conditionalized with respect to a series of increasingly specific newsgroups.

Let $c_h$ be a **hierarchic classification**, meaning that it is part of a taxonomy rooted at $c_0$ and connected via a path of **ancestor** classifications $\oplus c_h$:

$$\oplus c_h \equiv \{c_0, c_a, c_{a.b}, \ldots, c_{a.b.c\ldots h}\} \tag{7.19}$$

This notation is meant to capture the relationship shown in Figure 7.11.

McCallum et al. creatively applied the statistical technique known as **shrinkage** to the problem of text classification [McCallum et al., 1998]. Parameter estimates of child classes, which will have very few

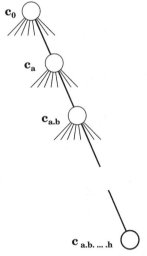

FIGURE 7.11 Ancestors of a Class

data instances, can be "shrunk" toward the data-rich ancestor's, and the contributions of each ancestor's classification are then linearly combined:    ?4

$$\theta_{kc_h} = \sum_{i \in \oplus c_h} w_i Pr(k \,|\, c_i) \qquad (7.20)$$

## 7.6 Information-Seeking Agents

### 7.6.1 Exploiting Linkage for Context*

All samples of language, including the documents indexed by Web search engines, depend heavily on *shared context* for comprehension. A document's author makes assumptions, often tacit, about the intended audience, and when this document appears in a "traditional" medium (conference proceedings, academic journal, etc.), it is likely that typical readers will understand it as intended. But one of the many things the Web changes is the huge new audience it brings to documents, many of whom will *not* share the author's intended context.

But because most search engines attempt to index indiscriminately across the entire WWW, the *global* word frequency statistics they collect can only reflect gross averages. The utility of an index term, as a

---

* Portions previously published in [Menczer and Belew, 2000].

discriminator of relevant from irrelevant items, can become a muddy average of its application across multiple distinct subcorpora within which these words have more focused meaning [Steier and Belew, 1994a; Steier and Belew, 1994b].

Querying for
link topology

Hypertext information environments like the Web contain additional structure information [Chakrabarti et al., 1998a].[†] This linkage information is typically exploited by browsing users. But **linkage topology** – the "spatial" structure imposed over documents by their hypertext links to one another – can be used to generate a concrete notion of context within which each document is understood: Two documents and the words they contain are imagined to be in the same context if they are close together in this space. Even in unstructured portions of the Web, authors tend to cluster documents about related topics by letting them point to each other via links. Such linkage topology is useful inasmuch as browsers have a better-than-random expectation that following links can provide them with guidance. If this were not the case, browsing would be a waste of time.

This suggests that **agents** (infobots, spiders, etc.) that navigate over such structural links might be able to discover this context. For example, agents browsing through pages about ROCK CLIMBING and ROCK 'N ROLL should attribute different weights to the word ROCK, depending on whether the query they are trying to satisfy is about music or sports. Where an agent is situated in an "environment" (neighborhood of highly interlinked documents) provides it with the *local context* within which to analyze word meanings – a structured, situated approach to polisemy. The words that surround links in a document provide an agent with valuable information to evaluate links and thus guide its path decisions – a statistical approach to action selection.

The idea of decentralizing the index-building process is not new. Dividing the task into localized indexing, performed by a set of *gatherers,* and centralized searching, performed by a set of *brokers,* has been suggested since the early days of the Web by the Harvest project [Bowman et al., 1994]. WebWatcher [Armstrong et al., 1995] and Letizia [Lieberman, 1997] are agents that learn to mimic the user by looking over his or her shoulder while browsing. Then they perform look-ahead searches and make real-time suggestions for pages that might interest the user. Fab [Balabanovic, 1997] and Amalthaea [Moukas and Zacharia, 1997] are multiagent adaptive filtering systems inspired by genetic algorithms, artificial life, and market models. Term weighting and relevance feedback are used to adapt a matching between a set of discovery agents (typically search engine parasites) and a set of user profiles (corresponding to single- or multiple-user interests).

Here we focus on InfoSpiders, a multiagent system developed by Fillipo Menczer [Menczer et al., 1995; Menczer, 1997; Menczer and Belew, 1998; Menczer, 1998; Menczer and Belew, 2000]. In InfoSpiders an evolving population of many agents is maintained, with each agent browsing from document to document online, making autonomous decisions about which links to follow and adjusting its strategy. Population-wide dynamics bias the search toward more promising areas and control the total amount of computing resources devoted to the search activity. Basic features of the algorithm are discussed, and then an example of how these agents perform as searchers through a hypertext version of the *Encyclopædia Britannica* are presented herein.

## 7.6.2 The InfoSpiders Algorithm

InfoSpiders searches online for information relevant to the user by making autonomous decisions about what links to follow. Algorithm 7.1 is the InfoSpiders implementation of the local selection algorithm. A central part of the system is the use of *optional* relevance feedback. The user may assess the relevance of (some of) the documents visited by InfoSpiders up to a certain point. Such relevance assessments take place asynchronously with respect to the online search and alter the subsequent behaviors of agents online by changing the energy landscape of the environment. The process is akin to the replenishment of environmental resources; the user interacts with the environment to bias the search process. Let us first overview the algorithm at a high level; representation-dependent details will be given in the following subsections and experimental parameter values in the next section.

The user initially provides a list of keywords and a list of starting points, in the form of a bookmark file.* The search is initialized by prefetching the starting documents. Each agent is "positioned" at one of these documents and given a random behavior (depending on the representation of agents) and an initial reservoir of energy.

---

* This list would typically be obtained by consulting a search engine.

---

**Algorithm 7.1 An Evolutionary Algorithm
for Distributed Information Agents**

initialize $p_0$ agents, each with energy $E = \theta/2$
*loop:*
    *foreach* alive agent $a$:
        pick link from current document
        fetch new document $D$
        $E_a \leftarrow E_a - c(D) + e(D)$
        Q-learn with reinforcement signal $e(D)$
        *if* $(E_a \geq \theta)$
            $a' \leftarrow mutate(recombine(clone(a)))$
            $E_a, E_{a'} \leftarrow E_a/2$
        *elseif* $(E_a! \leq 0)$
            $die(a)$
    process optional relevance feedback from user

---

Each agent "senses" its local neighborhood by analyzing the text of the document where it is currently situated. This way, the relevance of all neighboring documents – those pointed to by the hyperlinks in the current document – is estimated. Based on these link relevance estimates, the agent "moves" by choosing and following one of the links from the current document.

Next, the agent's energy is updated. Energy is needed to survive and move, i.e., to continue to visit documents on behalf of the user. Agents are rewarded with energy if the visited documents appear to be relevant. The $e()$ function is used by an agent to evaluate the relevance of documents. If a document has previously been visited and assessed by the user, the user's assessment is used; if the document has not been visited before, its relevance must be estimated. This mechanism is implemented via a cache, which also speeds up the process by minimizing duplicate transfers of documents. While in the current, client-based implementation of InfoSpiders this poses no problem; caching is a form of communication and thus is a bottleneck for the performance of distributed agents. In a distributed implementation, we imagine that agents would have local caches. When using the current implementation to simulate the performance of distributed InfoSpiders, we will simply set the cache size to zero.

Agents are charged energy costs for the network load incurred by transferring documents. The cost function $c()$ should depend on used resources, for example, transfer latency or document size. For simplicity we will assume a constant cost for accessing any new document and a (possibly smaller) constant cost for accessing the cache; this way stationary behaviors, such as going back and forth between a pair of documents, are discouraged.

Just as for graph search, instantaneous changes of energy are used as reward and penalty signals. This way agents adapt during their lifetime by Q-learning. This adaptive process allows an agent to modify its behavior based on prior experience by learning to predict which are the best links to follow.

Depending on its current energy level, an agent may be killed or selected for reproduction. In the latter case, offspring are recombined through the use of *local crossover*, whereby an agent can only recombine with agents residing on the same document, if there are any. Offspring are also mutated, providing the variation necessary for adapting agents by way of evolution.

Finally, the user may provide the system with relevance feedback. It is important to stress that this process is entirely optional – InfoSpiders can search in a completely unsupervised fashion once it is given a query and a set of starting points. Relevance feedback takes place without direct online interactions between user and agents. The user may assess any visited document $D$ with feedback $\phi(D) \in \{-1, 0, +1\}$. All the words in the document are automatically assessed by updating a "feedback list" of encountered words. Each word in this list, $k$, is associated with a signed integer $\omega_k$ that is initialized with 0 and updated each time any document is assessed by the user:

$$\forall k \in D : \omega_k \leftarrow \omega_k + \phi(D)$$

The word feedback list is maintained to keep a global profile of which words are relevant to the user.

The ultimate output of the algorithm is a flux of links to documents ranked according to some relevance estimate – modulo relevance assessments by the user. The algorithm terminates when the population becomes extinct for lack of relevant information resources or when it is terminated by the user.

## 7.6.3  Adapting to "Spatial" Context

In order to test InfoSpiders, agents were allowed to breed in a controlled test environment previously used by Steier [Steier and Belew, 1994a; Steier, 1994]: a portion of the *Encyclopædia Britannica*. The advantage is that we can make use of readily available relevant sets of articles associated with a large number of queries. The subset corresponds to the HUMAN SOCIETY topic, roughly one-tenth of the entire encyclopedia. Links to other parts of the *EB* are removed, along with any terminal documents produced as a result. The final environment is made of $N = 19,427$ pages, organized in a hypertext graph (the *EB* is already in HTML format). Of these pages, 7859 are full articles constituting the *Micropædia*. These, together with 10,585 Index pages (containing links to articles and pointed to by links in articles), form a graph with many connected components. The remaining 983 nodes form a hierarchical topical tree, called *Propædia*. These nodes contain topic titles and links to children nodes, ancestor nodes, and articles. Micropædia articles also have links to Propædia nodes. Propædia and index pages are included in the search set to ensure a connected graph and to be faithful to the *EB* information architecture – an actual subset of the Web.

Now consider two agents, A and B, born at the same time and attempting to satisfy the same query, but in different "places" within this hypergraph of *EB* document pages.

As Table 7.1 shows, the original query words were displaced from their top positions and replaced by new terms. For example, PRIVAT and ALLEVI had relatively low weights, while FOUNDAT appeared to have the highest correlation with relevance feedback at this time.

A's and B's keyword vectors are shown in Table 7.2. In the course of the evolution leading to A and B through their ancestors, some query terms were lost from both genotypes. A was a third-generation agent; its parent lost ALLEVI through a mutation in favor of HULL. At A's birth, PRIVAT was mutated into TH. B was a second-generation agent; at its birth, both ALLEVI and PRIVAT were replaced by HULL and ADDAM, respectively, via mutation and crossover. These keyword vectors demonstrate how environmental features correlated with relevance were internalized into the agents' behaviors.

The difference between A and B can be attributed to their evolutionary adaptation to spatially local context. A and B were born at documents

TABLE 7.1  Part of the Word Feedback
List and Weights at Time 550

| Rank | New | $k$ | $I_k$ |
|------|-----|-----|-------|
| 1 | ★ | FOUNDAT | 0.335 |
| 2 | ★ | RED | 0.310 |
| 3 | ★ | MISSION | 0.249 |
| 4 |  | SOCIAL | 0.223 |
| 5 | ★ | CROSS | 0.197 |
| 6 | ★ | HULL | 0.184 |
| 7 | ★ | HOUS | 0.183 |
| 8 |  | ORGAN | 0.161 |
| 15 |  | SERVIC | 0.114 |
| 16 |  | ACTIV | 0.112 |
| 23 | ★ | TH | 0.094 |
| 30 |  | PUBLIC | 0.087 |
| 32 | ★ | ADDAM | 0.079 |
| 37 |  | HUMAN | 0.075 |
| 41 |  | PRIVAT | 0.067 |
| 44 |  | ALLEVI | 0.065 |

*Note:* Stars mark new terms not present in the original query. Note that TH does not correspond to the
article the, which is a noise word and thus is removed from all documents; rather, it corresponds
to the th used for ordinal numbers and often associated with centuries.

TABLE 7.2  Keyword Vectors
for Agents A and B

| A | B |
|---|---|
| ORGAN | ORGAN |
| PUBLIC | PUBLIC |
| TH | ADDAM |
| SERVIC | SERVIC |
| SOCIAL | SOCIAL |
| HUMAN | HUMAN |
| ACTIV | ACTIV |
| HULL | HULL |

$D_A$ and $D_B$, respectively, whose word frequency distributions are partly
shown in Table 7.3. TH represented well the place where A was born, being the second most frequent term there; and ADDAM represented well
the place where B was born, being the third most frequent term there.

TABLE 7.3 Most Frequent Terms in the Documents where Agents
A and B were Born

| $rank_{D_A}$ | $k$ | $freq(k, D_A)$ | $rank_{D_B}$ | $k$ | $freq(k, D_B)$ |
|---|---|---|---|---|---|
| 1 | WORKHOUS | 0.076 | 1 | HOUS | 0.043 |
| 2 | TH | 0.038 | 1 | HULL | 0.043 |
| 2 | POOR | 0.038 | 3 | ADDAM | 0.025 |
| 4 | SOCIAL | 0.030 | | | |
| 4 | CENTURI | 0.030 | 38 | AMERICAN | 0.004 |

*Note:* Word frequencies are normalized by the total number of words in each document.

By internalizing these words, the two situated agents are better suited to
their respective spatial contexts.

## 7.7 Other Learning Applications and Issues

This chapter has focused primarily on applications of classification techniques that are among the most successful with machine learning. There
are, however, a wide range of other ways that adaptive mechanisms have
been incorporated within the FOA context [Bono, 1972]. For example,
Gordon has applied genetic algorithm optimization to the construction
of effective queries [Gordon, 1988]. The success of social **collaborative
filtering**, where adaptation in response to the activities of one user is
extrapolated to other users [Shardaanand and Miaes, 1995], promises to
become an important part of the WWW industry (as recently demonstrated by Microsoft's purchase of Firefly, for example). Learning to extract structured, database-like relations from the vast WWW of unstructured documents is another important new direction [Howe and
Dreilinger, 1997; Craven et al., 1998]. Here we mention several other ways
that adaptation mechanisms can be exploited and some new problems
arising from this dynamism.

### 7.7.1 Adaptive Lenses

A discussion of the routing or filtering task should make it clear that
learning technology can be placed at many levels within the FOA system.
A personal classification tool can be very useful to a single individual
organizing his or her own email. These categories need not make any

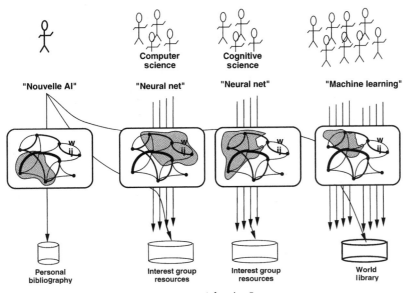

FIGURE 7.12  Adaptive Lens

sense to or be consistent with those used by anyone else. But when multiple users all browse through shared corpora, it becomes possible for one person's browsing experience to benefit another's. Of course, interuser consistency in *RelFbk* will help to determine just how statistically correlated these training signals are. But if users are clustered as part of socially cohesive groups (for example, a research lab full of students and faculty pursuing the same research questions) and they are searching documents of shared interests (for example, reprints they have all collected on topics of mutual interest, as part of a journal club perhaps), it is not unreasonable to believe that their assessments will be very similar indeed. Figure 7.12 shows a single individual with a classification system on his or her own machine. But their searches often go through a second classifier or "adaptive lens" that they share with other members of a computer science group. The figure also shows two different social groups of users, for example, computer scientists and cognitive scientists, each learning different connotations for the phrase NEURAL NETWORK, perhaps computationally and physiologically skewed, respectively. Finally, these smaller groups are merged into progressively larger groups of users over which *RelFbk* assessments are pooled.

## 7.7.2  Adapting to Fluid Language Use

The advantages of my benefiting from your experience training a system are obvious. Just as obvious, though, are ways in which you and I might differ in our notions of relevant documents. Even this comparison is only possible if we each evaluate exactly the same query, and how often will that happen?!

If we are to change our representations of documents based on users' opinions, should we value "expert" opinions over those of "novices"? Common sense would suggest that if we could ascertain that one user was indeed expert in a particular topical area, then their assessments of relevance should perhaps carry more weight. But based at least on the experience of lawyers searching case law [Cohen, 1991; Sprowl, 1976] experts are less likely to search in their own area of expertise, probably because they already know what they will find there. The typical user searches in areas they know less about. In that respect, perhaps the novice's *RelFbk* is, in fact, a better characterization of what we should attempt to satisfy.

Once the index representation is allowed to change in response to users' *RelFbk*, we are faced with the question of how fast this change should occur. Some of these questions were mentioned in terms of conceptual drift by users and topic tracking in news sources (cf. Section 7.3.2). Adopting the longer-term archival perspective of a librarian perhaps, how quickly should we want our adaptive system to track current trendy terms? (cf. *Wired* magazine's ***Tired/Wired Memes***[4] feature). When old terms of art have been rendered obsolete, how can we nevertheless maintain an archival record of this previous

ETHOLOGY    terminology?[†]

## 7.8  Symbolic and Subsymbolic Learning

Most of the learning applications we have discussed apply to the *Index* relation between keywords and documents. But there are many other syntactic clues associated with documents from which we can also learn.

---

[4] www.wired.com/wired/archive/4.10/tiredwired.html

Chapter 6 discussed a number of these heterogeneous data sources. But as we attempt to learn with and across both structured attributes and statistical features (recall the distinction of Section 1.6), it is important to keep several key differences in mind.

The distinction between **symbolic** features of each document (e.g., date and place of publication or author), which represent unambiguous features of the world that human experts can reliably program directly, and the much larger set of **subsymbolic** features from which we hope to compose our induced representation [Rose and Belew, 1989] becomes especially important as we attempt to combine both manually programmed and automatically learned knowledge as part of the same system [Belew and Forrest, 1988]. Even among these attributes, however, there is room for learning about their <u>meaning</u>. For example, while a scientific paper may have many nominal authors, it is often only one or two to whom most readers will attribute significant intellectual contribution. While papers often have extensive bibliographies, some of these also are more significant than others and can be considered supporting or antagonistic (see Section 6.1).

For all these reasons, FOA is an especially ripe area for AI and machine learning. The fact that documents are composed of semantically meaningful tokens allows us to make especially strong hypotheses about how they should be classified. One fundamentally important feature of the FOA activity (unless the WWW alters our world entirely!) is that there will always be more instances of document readings than of document writings. That is, while we can imagine spending a huge effort analyzing any text, there are fundamental limits to how much we can learn about it from only the features it contains. But each time a document is retrieved and read by a reader, we can potentially learn something new about the <u>meaning</u> of this document from this new person's perspective. Machine learning techniques are mandatory if we are to exploit the information provided by this unending stream of queries.

As discussed in Chapter 6, the histories of IR and AI have crossed many times in the past, generally in head-on collisions rather than constructively. But as AI has moved from a concern with manually constructed knowledge representations to machine learning, and as IR has begun to consider how indexing structures can change with use, these two methodologies can be expected to increasingly overlap.

**EXERCISE 1**   *EB*, Westlaw, and Medline are not the only examples of editorial enhancement. Find another example of an information resource on the Web. Describe the raw corpus and then the editorial enhancement used in this instance. How would you argue that it makes searching more efficient or effective?

**EXERCISE 2**   Clearly, having each user evaluate whether every document retrieved for every query is relevant is excessive. What approximations to this notion of "correct" answer might be useful?

**EXERCISE 3**   What other feedback might we reliably and easily be able to elicit? Can users reliably react that a retrieved document is too general or specific? Too theoretic or applied? How could such information be exploited by a learning system?

**EXERCISE 4**   Many new issues arise when classifications are organized hierarchically. Must all classifications occur only at the leaves? Is a document classified at a leaf an instance only of this subclass or of all ancestor classifications as well? Discuss the consequences to a classifier of each of these questions.

## TERMS INTRODUCED IN THIS CHAPTER

| | | |
|---|---|---|
| adaptive | collaborative | entropy |
| agents | filtering | error measure |
| aggressive | collection fusion | event space |
| dimensionality | computational | exploitation |
| reduction | learning | exploration |
| ancestor | theory | feedback |
| assignment | concept drift | fusing |
| batch | conditional entropy | Good Old-Fashioned |
| binary | cross-validation | AI |
| boosting | disjunctive normal | gradient descent |
| chorus effect | form | hierarchic |
| classifies | editor's workbench | classification |

# 8

# Conclusions and Future Directions

The important thing is not to stop questioning. Curiosity has its own reason for existing. One cannot help but be in awe when he contemplates the mysteries of eternity, of life, of the marvelous structure of reality. It is enough if one tries to comprehend a little of this mystery every day. – *Albert Einstein* [Einstein, 1955]

## 8.1  Things that Are Changing

Alta Vista was, in 1995, arguably the first search engine offered for general use, so ***Alta Vista's history***[1] is especially interesting. At that time, Alta Vista was developed by Digital Equipment Corporation to primarily demonstrate how powerful its new Alpha architecture was, especially its then-novel 64-bit addressing and the consequentially vast data spaces. Indexing all the WWW's pages and providing a useful service to many was simply good publicity.

Since that time Digital Equipment has been acquired by Compaq, and Alta vista has been spun off to CMGI. As searching newly authored pages on the WWW has become increasingly profitable, similar

---

[1] doc.altavista.com/company_info/about_av/background.shtml

search technologies have been applied to existing, traditionally published corpora to form the next generation of **digital libraries** [Fox and Marchionini, 1998; Paepcke et al., 1998]. It is amazing how closely they resemble the vision H. G. Wells had of what a "World Encyclopedia" might mean, as early as 1938 [Wells, 1938]!

As the Internet reaches a mass audience and these new search engine users begin to FOA in earnest, important new data are becoming available about how these real users (as opposed to most IR experimental subjects; cf. Section 4.3.1) behave. Silverstein et al. report on their analysis of approximately one billion ($10^9$) queries issued against the Alta Vista search engine during six weeks in August and September 1998 [Silverstein et al., 1999]. Another important qualification on this preliminary study is that no attempt was made to discriminate "real," human-generated queries from automatic queries generated by robots. Still, several features of this study are significant.

First, fully 15% of the queries were entirely empty; they contained no keywords! Two-thirds of these empty queries were generated within Alta Vista's "advanced query" interface. Clearly, good interface design and user education remains a fundamental issue for effective search engine design.

Second, WWW searches use *very short*, simple queries, averaging only 2.3 keywords/query (not including the zero-length queries in this average). Only 12.6 percent of queries used more than three keywords. Of course, the fact that Alta Vista's interface does not easily support longer *RelFbk* queries (cf. Section 3.6) keeps these from occurring. Most users also avoid query syntax and issue simple queries: Only 20 percent of queries used any of Alta Vista's query operators (+, –, and, or, not, near); half of these used only one operator.

These findings are especially significant because they paint a different picture of the "typical user" from what IR has traditionally held. When IR systems were first developed, the target audience was primarily reference librarians, **search intermediates** who helped library patrons find what they were seeking from sophisticated systems such as DIALOG. These librarians were specially educated, in particular in the subtleties of Boolean query operators and other sophisticated techniques for constructing exactly the right "magic bullet" query for a particular corpus. IR system design and theory therefore generally assumed that queries were fairly rich, structured expressions. At least at the moment, these assumptions do not seem to hold for most Web searching.

But despite the relatively simple form of most queries, the third interesting fact is that Web queries are rarely repeated. Even folding case and ignoring word order, only one third of queries appeared more than once in the billion queries; only 14 percent occurred more than three times.[†] These statistics are especially significant in the face of new services such as *Ask Jeeves*,[2] which focus on providing especially relevant answers for a restricted set of anticipated queries.

Finally, Silverstein et al. attempted to analyze query sessions. Knowing when a query is part of a session is notoriously difficult, especially when some queries are being generated by robots; this study used a combination of server-set cookies and a five-minute time window to capture coherent searches by the same user. It appears that 78 percent of query sessions involve only a single query and that an average session involves only two queries! These data are preliminary, but they provide an interesting contrast to the power law, Zipfian distribution of Web surfing behavior reported by Huberman et al. [Huberman et al., 1998] (cf. Section 3.2.5).

The primary extension of the search engine technology developed so far in this text is the **crawling** function that must harvest Web pages prior to their indexing. The design of Web crawlers is now one of the most active areas of computer science research; we provide only a few basic references here.

*We mostly ask about SEX*

## 8.1.1  WWW Crawling

One important way in which Web search engines extend beyond the notions of FOA presented here concerns the crawlers that feed them. In all of our discussions, the corpus was imagined to be a static object. For WWW search engines, the underlying set of documents that are to be indexed and made available to users is constantly changing. Further, the task of quickly, reliably, and exhaustively visiting all WWW-linked pages is a fundamental task in and of itself. One good, accessible example of

---

[2] askjeeves.com/

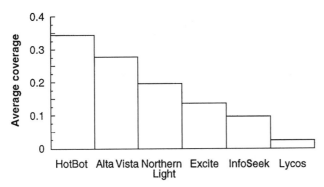

FIGURE 8.1 Crawler Coverage. From [Lowrence and Giles, 1998].
Reproduced with permission of American Association for the
Advancement of Science

crawler code is provided by the ***LibWWW Robot***,[3] part of the **WWW Consortium** (W3C) LibWWW distribution. A Perl-based ***crawler interface***[4] has also been developed by Gisle Aas; ***ParallelUserAgent***,[5] developed by Marc Langheinrich, is another Perl alternative.

Naïve WWW users often seem to have the tacit belief that every Web crawler is aware of (i.e., has indexed) every document on the Web. More sophisticated users know that there is a certain lag time between the posting of a new page and its inclusion in the Web search engine's index. But the fundamental omissions by most search engine crawlers are still underappreciated. The most concrete data in this respect is due to a recent experiment done by Lawrence and Giles [Lawrence and Giles, 1998], shown in Figure 8.1. Using a statistical extrapolation from the mismatch of documents found by one of the six most important search engines suggests that at that time the Web contained approximately 320 million pages. Of this total, even the best search engine was able to capture only about a third of those documents.

The ecology of these various search engines and their co-evolutionary technological responses to one another create an extremely dynamic situation. Danny Sullivan edits an excellent newsletter, ***Search Engine Watch***,[6] that does nothing but track changes in the volatile

---

[3] www.w3.org/Robot/

[4] www.linpro.no/lwp/

[5] http://www.inf.ethz.ch/~langhein/ParallelUA/

[6] www.searchenginewatch.com

marketplace of search engines and portals. The search engine business and supporting technologies can be expected to continue to foment for some time to come. In asymptote, however, current notions of search engines will go extinct for two basic reasons: Their methods do not scale to the Internet, and they only get in the way.

### Search Engines Don't Scale

Scalability is a major issue limiting the effectiveness of search engines. The factors contributing to the problem are the large size of the WWW, its rapid growth, and its highly dynamic nature. In order to keep indexes up to date, **crawlers** periodically revisit every indexed document to see what has been changed, moved, or deleted. Heuristics are used to estimate how frequently a document is changed and needs to be revisited, but the accuracy of such statistics is highly volatile. Moreover, crawlers attempt to find newly added documents either exhaustively or based on user-supplied URLs. Yet Lawrence and Giles have shown that the coverage achieved by search engines is at best around 33 percent, and that coverage is anticorrelated with currency – the more complete an index, the staler the links [Lawrence and Giles, 1998]. More importantly, such disappointing performance comes at high costs in terms of the load imposed on the Net [Eichmann, 1994].

This becomes an important reason for investigating search agents for the WWW like those described in Section 7.6 . *Online* agents do not have a scale problem because they search through the *current* environment and therefore do not run into stale information. On the other hand, they are less efficient than search engines because they cannot amortize the cost of a search over many queries.

### Disintermediation

Section 8.2.1 will discuss FOA as a particular type of "language game." In brief, the FOA language game is played by three players: the text's author, its readers, and the search engine. Authors have something to say and an audience they are trying to say it to. They attempt to characterize their content to intermediates (book publishers, journal editors, WWW search engines) in ways that capture "markets" for what they have to say. Readers have an information need and some ideas about where to look for writings that might satisfy it. These readers sometimes (and now much more often than in the past) characterize their information need to intermediates (librarians, paralegals, WWW search engines) in hopes of being shown documents likely to be relevant to their information needs.

The second fundamental flaw of current search engines, then, is that they are and will forever be only *mediators*; they neither produce content nor consume it directly. The search engine is caught in the middle of the other two players. It must somehow make the correspondence between the languages used by writers and readers. If it plays its part of the FOA language game well, it reliably connects readers with writers.

Said another way, search engines are simply noise in the channel between author and reader. If they are doing their jobs effectively, they should disappear as transparent background to facilitate easy communication of rich messages. The difficulty browsing users currently experience as they attempt to FOA documents on the WWW makes it clear just how far current search engines are from this ideal.

Traditionally, authors have made conventional assumptions about how their readers would find them. They would sell their book to a publisher, and part of this economic relationship involved the publisher putting its distribution channels at the services of the author. For magazine and newspaper reporters, as well as for fiction authors, periodical publications provided a regular audience for a magazine of contributions. Textbook authors would favor publishers with extensive connections with educational institutions. Scientists would submit articles to peer review under the supervision of editors for professional societies. In every case, multiple levels of mediation between the author and the reader are assumed by the author.

Even if the WWW were only a new technological substrate on which all of these conventional activities occurred, we might expect the level of confusion now present as search engines cross everyone's wires. But it seems likely that the change is even more fundamental: **The number of content-producers (writers) is rapidly approaching the number of content-consumers (readers)!** Never before has the machinery of producing and distributing media been as widely available as it is today. Our collective expectations as to just what documents are "out there," not to mention the care and authority with which they have been authored, are in terrific flux.

Authors trying to be heard through this cacophony must fundamentally rethink their assumptions of how their content will be published. The most obvious examples of this are author-created keyword **meta-tags**. A wide range of meta-tags are now in use – ranging from ones that carry intellectual property information to ones that carry "decency" ratings; the HTML standard in fact allows an open-ended set of such tags to support any number of additional attributes of the document. Two meta-tags, however, are especially important from the perspective of FOA. The KEYWORDS meta-tag is designed to contain (the author's recommendation for) content descriptors, and the DESCRIPTION meta-tag to provide a proxy string. Both provide explicit mechanisms for authors to convey additional <u>meaning</u> in their writings, beyond words that happen to be in the text of the document itself. They have the additional advantage of being free of any morphological and weighting heuristics used by a particular search engine. Of course, this additional expressive power on the part of authors also makes it at least possible for them (or their Web masters) to attempt to **spoof** search engines with meta-tags designed simply to draw users to the page. Like much of the law concerning the WWW, exactly what constitutes "good faith" use of meta-tags is a matter of great debate (a recent example is *Playboy v. Terri Welles*[7]).

Whether in good faith or not, attempts by authors to express themselves clearly are currently compromised by the refusal of search engines to *publicly commit* to some basic standards of crawling and indexing behavior. Their wide variety in operation, compounded by opaque descriptions of how each works, currently makes articulate expression by an author impossible.[†] It is no wonder that searching users become confused.

Just how do Alta Vista, HotBot, . . . work?!

## 8.2  Things that Stay the Same

While some features of FOA change as quickly as Internet stock prices, others are as old as language itself. To characterize current search engines as noise on a communication channel between author and reader is an attempt to reconsider what we'd like to have happen with WWW communications.

---

[7] www.terriwelles.com/dismissal.html

## 8.2.1 The FOA Language Game

Lurking at the core of the entire FOA enterprise is the fundamental question of **semantics**: What do the words in our language <u>mean</u>? Computer scientists are most familiar with artificial languages (formal grammars, programming languages, etc.) for which precise semantics in terms of a particular machine are absolutely necessary. Many philosophers of language, notably Frege and Ludwig Wittgenstein, have advocated that a similarly precise semantics of natural language is also possible. Words are predicates about states of the world: Either they apply or they don't.

An alternative point of view says that such a precise and abstract semantics can never be achieved. What language <u>means</u> is what it <u>means</u> to us, the language users. That is, words' <u>meaning</u> cannot be separated from the forms of life of which they are a part. As it happens the same Ludwig Wittgenstein has argued forcefully on this side of the debate too![†]

One of Wittgenstein's most useful devices for getting across his theory of language was his notion of the **language game** (*Sprachspiele* in German) [Wittgenstein, 1953]. Wittgenstein gives many varieties of language games, from chidren's games as simple as "ring-around-the-rosy" [Wittgenstein, 1953, Section 7] to such "adult" games as:

*Early versus late Wittgenstein*

- forming and testing hypotheses;
- making up a story and reading it; and
- asking questions.

It is interesting to compare the multiplicity of the tools in language and of the ways they are used [Wittgenstein, 1953, Section 23]. Certainly FOA counts as another example of a language game, but one with special rules.

Another interesting aspect of Wittgenstein's theory is how well it anticipates the models of language <u>meaning</u> arising from modern machine learning techniques. The common cause is that Wittgenstein was centrally concerned with *learning* by children. This is evident in his "ring-around-the-rosy" example, and in his explicit attention to consequences of learning that apply equally well to our algorithms:

> [Consider] two pictures, one of which consists of colour patches with vague contours, and the other of patches... with clear contours. The degree to which the sharp picture *can* resemble

the blurred one depends on the latter's degree of vague-ness.... Won't you then have to say: "Anything and nothing is right." And this is the position you are in if you look for the definition corresponding to our concepts in aesthetics or ethics.

In such a difficulty always ask yourself: How did we *learn* the meaning of this word [vague]? From what sort of examples? In what language games? Then it will be easier for you to see that the word must have a family of meanings. [Wittgenstein 1953, Sections 76, 77]

Our current versions of the FOA language games are tied to the technologies by which we are currently allowed to communicate with one another. For now, centralized search engines are in the center of this dialog. Authors write and sometimes try to influence the audiences their documents reach. Later, readers use a few of the first words that come to mind to tease out some possible answers. Search engines do their best to connect these two vocabularies.

Reading and writing are the primitive language games on which FOA is based. The tools available to help writers and readers are currently strong constraints in the FOA rules. People can only express what they are allowed to express. If only simple query languages are available, only simple questions will be asked. If all documents are treated interchangeably, as context-free samples of text, then the tacit context assumed by the author is not available.

And so, our abilities to automatically *learn* what the words really do <u>mean</u> to authors and to readers will change as the evidence in the WWW dialogs changes. Especially unclear are guarantees about **communication privacy and security**: If we believe all our words are for everyone's ears, then many things will never be said via the Net. If search engines watch over our shoulders as we browse, should we be grateful because it will understand what we <u>mean</u>, or should we send them a bill for the valuable training data we have provided? As companies like *Amazon.com*[8] use *new technologies that allow them to "eavesdrop" on commercial transactions*,[9] consumers must ultimately decide what their privacy and more effective indexing are worth to them personally.

---

[8] Amazon.com

[9] news.cnet.com/news/0-1007-200-1517791.html

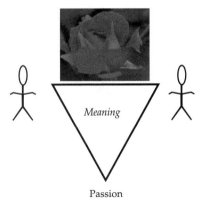

Passion

FIGURE 8.2 The Semiotic View

## Semiotics

The next step toward a theory of what the FOA language game might mean involves semiotics, the subfield of linguistics centrally concerned with the ability of signs to convey meaning. Dating back at least to the American pragmatist philosopher C. S. Peirce and the French linguist Saussure, semiotics is now often associated with Umberto Eco (most famous for his popular novel *Name of the Rose* [Eco, 1983]). David Blair has written an excellent overview of the field [Blair, 1990, chapter 4].

In order to get away from using words as communicative signs, semi-oticists often use other symbols, such as the ROSE shown in Figure 8.2 In brief, semiotic theory imagines meaning being trapped by the triad of signifier, signified, and sign. Hawkes (quoted from Blair) uses a gift of ROSES as an example of how meaning can be conveyed:

> ... a BUNCH OF ROSES can be used to signify passion. When it does so, the BUNCH OF ROSES is the signifier, the passion the signified. The relation between the two (the associative to-tal) produces the third term, the BUNCH OF ROSES as a sign. And, as a sign it is important to understand that the BUNCH OF ROSES is quite a different thing from the BUNCH OF ROSES as a signifier, that is, as a horticultural entity. As a signifier, the BUNCH OF ROSES is empty, as a sign it is full. What has filled it (with signification) is a combination of my intent and the na-ture of society's conventional modes and channels which offer me a range of vehicles for the purpose. The range is extensive,

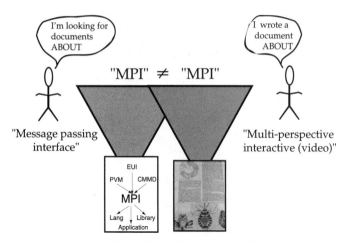

FIGURE 8.3 A Semiotic Analysis of Keyword Mismatch

but conventionalized and so finite, and it offers a complex system of ways, of signing. [Hawkes, 1977, p. 131, quoted from Blair, 1990, monospace font not in original]

That is, in a successful communicative act, the sign of ROSES successfully unites what the signifier was trying to express with what the receiving listener thinks they are pointing at, i.e., the content of the sign.

Figure 8.3 applies this analysis to the case when a mediating search engine stands between linguistic sign users. When a keyword like MPI is used as part of a query by a user intent on the features of the MESSAGE PASSING INTERFACE (a communication standard used by parallel computers and language compilers), it is confounded with documents authored by people who use MPI to mean MULTI-PERSPECTIVE INTERACTIVE (video). The same signifier MPI points to two different significations. If a specialist in PARALLEL COMPUTING has MULTIMEDIA VIDEO documents returned by the search engine, the communication of a unifying sign has *not* been accomplished.

## Speech Acts

Certainly the communication going on between sender and receiver of flowers is different from that between WWW author and browser. One important difference is that flowers, like spoken **oral language**, happen in the moment between two people who know one another. The WWW,

1. Quantity
>   1.1. Make your contribution as informative as required.
>   1.2. Do not make your contribution more informative than is required.
2. Quality
>   2.1. Do not say what you believe to be false.
>   2.2. Do not say that for which you lack adequate evidence.
3. Relation
>   3.1. Be relevant.
4. Manner
>   4.1. Avoid obscurity of expression.
>   4.2. Avoid ambiguity.
>   4.3. Be brief.
>   4.4. Be orderly.

FIGURE 8.4  Grice's Maxims
From [Grice, 1975]. Reproduced with permission of Academic Press

like libraries, contains **written language**, which communicates between readers and writers separated by arbitrary amounts of time and space. Differences between **orality** and **literacy** are some of the most important to understand if FOA is to become a part of traditional linguistics [Ong, 1982].

An important dimension of the difference between oral and literate communication concerns the **attentional focus** of sender and receiver and how and when it is given. Before any symbols can be exchanged, the sender must apply attention to the construction of a message, and before a receiver can understand it he or she must be "listening." Communication is a demand for attention by the author and of a reader.

Grice has defined what he calls the **cooperative principle** to make explicit the co-dependence of sender and receiver's communicative tasks [Grice, 1957; Grice, 1975]. **Grice's maxims** (see Figure 8.4) help to codify ways in which this tacit contract can lead to <u>meaningful</u> communication or be broken.[†] Although these were drafted with oral communication in mind, they remain (with Strunk and White's *Elements of Style* [Strunk and White, 1979]) excellent advice to authors on how to write clearly.

*Star Trek* script generator

A second important difference between oral and written communication is its intimacy. Spoken language is imagined to be a quiet act, between a particular speaker and a listener. The FOA communicative acts with which we are most concerned involve much more public displays of language. In 1975, Saracevic [Saracevic, 1975] talked about this as communicating **public knowledge**, a concept "as pertinent now as when it was written" [Sparck Jones and Willett, 1997, p. 86].

The author had an intended audience in mind when he or she wrote, but once the document is written and published, it is (like graffiti!) there for all to read. Search engines connect huge sets of authors with vast audiences of readers. The language used in queries and indexing vocabularies is bound to be loud and broad.

## 8.2.2 Sperber and Wilson's "Relevance"

The notion of relevance has been at the heart of much of the FOA enterprise, particularly its evaluation (cf. Chapter 4). By making connections to foundational theories of language games and speech acts, Sperber and Wilson offer one of the soundest definitions of what "relevance" might mean [Sperber and Wilson, 1986].

Their **principle of relevance** puts the onus on the communicator: Ostensive behaviors (i.e., those in which there is a manifest intention to inform another) should be taken as guarantees that the sender believes them to be relevant to the receiver. They then provide a **pragmatics** for the communication, i.e., *why* a reader or listener should pay attention: viz., to improve their knowledge. Then the most relevant information we might convey has two properties: It must be new, or we have not improved the state of knowledge. But it also must be *connected* to other information, or this new factoid really adds almost nothing.

The value of connected information can be made most clear in terms of a logical theorem-proving model (cf. Section 6.5). Assuming again that the user already "knows" the contents of an intitial knowledge base $\Sigma$ and has a question whether the proposition $\tau$ is true or false, relevant documents are those that most extend what they know. Sperber and Wilson's notion of connected information corresponds exactly to the set of new inferences that are now allowed.

Sperber and Wilson also draw our attention to the importance of the context within which any communicative act occurs. One aspect of this context is the **mutual knowledge** that sender and receiver must have in order for communication to proceed efficiently:

$$MutualKnow(I, U) \equiv \{k \mid Know(I, k) \leftrightarrow Know(U, k)\} \qquad (8.1)$$

Mutual knowledge is that knowledge $k$ that if I know it, you know it too. This deep knowing what you mean, and your knowing that I know, and my knowing that you know that I know, etc., is what we seek in eye contact, in email responses, and in "active" listening. Relevance feedback is the fundamental communicative act that this text proposes for the process of assuring mutual knowledge.

The context within which any particular communicative act occurs has many other dimensions, too. As the earlier MPI example suggested, one of the fundamental issues in WWW searching is the confounding of contexts. The author of a journal article from the multimedia community can use MPI with his colleagues and students without any problem or confusion, because they share the same context. But when these journal articles are mingled with those from the parallel computing community, using MPI as a sign causes it to straddle two different contexts.

In summary, then, the FOA language game seems to propose a ternary predicate about connecting keywords and a document with a person who believes that the relation holds.

## 8.2.3 Argument Structures

Another important notion of context surrounding any particular document is the system of argumentation within which it participates.

The tendency of search engines to slice and dice documents into salads of their constituent words has been called the bag-of-words phenomenon. It is typically used in contrast to syntactic parsing methods, which place these words as part of well-structured, grammatical constructs. But there is another level of violence done to language when word frequency counts are collected, and that has to do with the argument structures by which sentences are strung together to form persuasive communicative acts.

Many of modern cultures' most well-documented communications involve the use of language as a persuasive device. Mathematical theorem proving, legal opinions, scientific papers, Op-Ed newspaper and magazine pages, artistic criticism, all have in common the fundamental purpose of convincing an audience.

A mathematical paper (purportedly!)[†] convinces by proving theorems. In legal corpora, the fundamental principle of *stare decisis* on which the common law tradition is based has already been mentioned. Within science, varying disciplines have wildly differing standards for what constitutes a convincing argument. Political and artistic forms of

Math proofs are more informal than you may think!

persuasion are being changed as they move from the media of newspapers and magazines to the WWW.

While the modes of argument supporting each of these social activities have diverged, there remains a common thread connecting all such documents, viz., their common heritage as written artifacts. Since long strips of papyrus were first rolled onto scrolls, our expectations about a fundamentally linear progression through a text have held. The Greeks' theories of **narrative** and rhetoric, analyzing how good stories and persuasive arguments are constructed, are still worth knowing today. Clearly these theories were shaped by the **linear media** of scrolls and books that then conveyed culture. The fundamentally **nonlinear** capabilities of hypertext media seem to open the door to radically different notions of argument. On the other hand, many modern theories of cognition continue to highlight the fundamentally linear and sequential flow of human attention [Newell, 1990]; we can only think about one thing at a time, no matter how fast we click. It will probably be artists, using new forms of media and hypertext authorship, who teach us the most about how these new technologies can be used most expressively. It is still too early to tell how our existing social institutions will absorb these technological changes. Attempts to index musical content offer some glimpses of the future [Bakhmutova et al., 1997; Foote, 1997; Ghias et al., 1995; Wold et al., 1996].

### 8.2.4  User as Portal

How could we possibly know so much about the story or argument an author is attempting to get across?! Or about just what question a user has in mind, and why they want the answer?! In fact, more and more evidence is making itself available to make just such determinations. Virtually every author now composes using a word processor, and even if they are only interested in *ultimately* producing a paper document, it generally carries with it much of the intra- and interdocument structure discussed in Chapter 6. Further, it may be possible to infer even more of their thinking if the *process* of word processing is allowed to leave a trace with the document.[†]

The editor's dual representation of a document

Similarly, browsers retain more and more state (i.e., permanent changes to the local computer's files that exist after the browser program is no longer running) all the time. **Bookmark lists** and **search history**

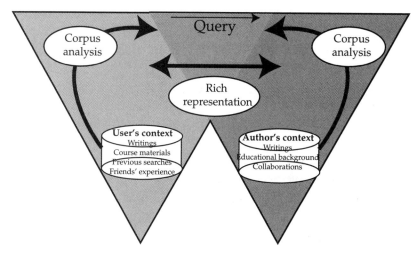

FIGURE 8.5  Query as Portal, Connecting Corpora

files are the most obvious examples. Less obvious to most users are the **cookies** left by WWW servers on the user's client, to better identify when they come to visit.

The point is that there are actually fairly rich streams of information available about both author and user, above and beyond the query and document text with which we have been primarily concerned in this book. Of course, there are some computations over these two data sets that can be done a priori, before any search commences. But the more interesting computations are those that can only be done on the occasion of a particular query. A sketch of this perspective is shown in Figure 8.5, with the user and his active seeking behaviors creating a **portal** through which corpora can interact.

Here we propose that in fact each user's query, each bit of *RelFbk*, and each move from one document to another effectively create the *opportunity* to juxtapose two corpora in ways that, until that moment, had never been analyzed in that way before.

## 8.3  Who Needs to FOA

In attempting to survey both the most dynamic aspects of FOA and its most classic aspects, the preceding chapters have jumped over a wide range of topics. We conclude with a much more personal (Al Franken)–mode of analysis: Just why are the issues discussed in this text important to *you*? This question is addressed from the perspective of four special-interest user groups especially involved in FOA language games: scientists, publishers, and (as befits a textbook!) teachers and students.

## 8.3.1  Authors

Note first the new precision/recall-like trade-offs facing authors: If they are aggressively selling their documents, then putting spam-like descriptors on them will make them be retrieved in the most possible situations. Getting your document into the hands of only those readers you anticipate finding it relevant means anticipating their queries and how they'll describe their information need. Who is the audience? What words are familiar to this audience? What words in this document will be unfamiliar to them? How might you describe the unfamiliar concepts using familiar words? At their core, these questions are no different from what authors have needed to ask since the beginning.

The tendency of authors to oversell their documents is exactly what makes checkpoints in the publication process valuable. We value news editors, publishers, reviewers, and all others whose profession it is to apply discretion.

Authors should think about FOA because they need to have their documents found. Publishers have traditionally helped with this process, but only for those authors they choose to publish. The WWW opens a much larger number of useful communication channels to potential authors. Not all of this authoring activity is healthy, however. Moderation of newsgroups and the peer review process are two important checks on the flow of information that have worked traditionally in UseNet and scientific exchanges.

Authors need to know how to write to be found. The ability to separate documents explicitly with meta-data about the documents means that there is no need to compromise the work itself to publicize it to an audience. It is true, of course, that the most effective ways of automatically producing meta-descriptions of a document still involve FOA-style statistical keyword analysis. But many authors are willing to manually add useful keywords or connect their documents to relevant Web pages or search engines. For many authors and artists this explicit analysis of potential readerships is an important part of their art.

Of course, authors may or may not be aware of all of the ways potential readers might be interested in their work. This is where a third-party editorial role becomes most valuable. Good editors are able to span the gap between what an author is trying to say and what an audience is interested in hearing.

## 8.3.2  Scientists

Scientifically constructed knowledge can take many forms, especially in the modern age of genomic data, hypertexts, and multimedia. **Knowledge networks** is a term used (e.g., by the National Science Foundation) to refer to an even wider range of interconnections, among both the scientists who have created them and the representations themselves. In the new science occurring on the WWW, the speed with which a manuscript can go from author to reader has been accelerated dramatically.

Perhaps because the physical installations required to do modern physics (high-energy accelerators, telescopes, etc.) required them to come to the same geographical location (CERN, Livermore, Los Alamos), physicists have long been aware of how useful informal "preprint" communication channels can be [Latour, 1987]. This may be one reason why the server begun by P. Ginsparg at Los Alamos National Labs has been a leader in exploring how scientific publication can occur. This system, originally developed for only physicists, has been so wildly successful that it now houses many documents from many disciplines. The National Institute of Health has recently proposed extending this example with *PubMed Central,*[10] which would disseminate research reports, both with and without peer review.

As might be expected, computer scientists have a particularly wide range of resources for searching their own literature, including:

- *The Computing Research Repository*[11] (CoRR);
- *CORA,*[12] a search engine developed especially for computer science research;
- *NCSTRL*[13] (pronounced "ancestral"), a system for sharing archives of technical reports in computer science.

---

[10] http://www.nih.gov/about/director/pubmedcentral.htm

[11] xxx.lanl.gov/archive/cs/intro.html

[12] www.cora.justresearch.com/

[13] www.ncstrl.org/

One ugly truth of science is that the primary task of scientists is to disagree with one another. The scientific process works because it effectively weeds out flawed arguments. One scientist can gain fame by claiming something new is true; a second scientist can gain fame by showing that it is not. If the question is sufficiently important, a third, scholarly scientist can do useful work by enumerating the many people who said all the things that were neither new nor true, as well as the very few publications that are both.

The printed record of science must contain all aspects of this ongoing debate, but the channel is not wide enough to contain all debates among all scientists, and so only some aspects of the debate can be published. Reviewers play a critical role in deciding what is worthy of publication. Searching for journal articles is only a part of what scientists must do. They are planning experiments and executing them, they may be teaching, they may be relating their basic findings to the development of a product, etc.

The browsing behaviors of scientists contribute to a philosophy of how science is actually prosecuted, but only if it deals with the larger realm of scientists' activities. A great deal has been said about the small fraction of a typical scientist's day that is in fact reflected in their publication record [Latour, 1987]. But the WWW and email suggest a new characterization of scientists' activities that includes traditional publication channels and informal artifacts similar to the letters and correspondence that have traditionally been the mainstay of historians of science [Rudwick, 1985].

Logical positivists aside, most current philosophy of science acknowledges the tremendous burden carried by the *language* used as scientists muddle toward a common understanding. This point has been made especially clear in biology by Keller and Lloyd's *Keywords in Evolutionary Biology* [Keller and Lloyd, 1992]. For these philosophers, the word "keyword" is not being used as it has in this text, as an element of an automatically assigned indexing vocabulary. Rather, they are interested in those *key words* that scientists use to talk to one another. As parts of scientific theories expressed in natural language, keywords

> . . . serve as conduits for unacknowledged, unbidden, and often unwelcome traffic between worlds. Words also have memories; they can insinuate theoretical or cultural past into the present. Finally, they have force. Upon examination, their multiple shadows

and memories can be seen to perform real conceptual work, in science as in ordinary language. [Keller and Lloyd, 1992, p. 2]

Indeed, it is precisely because of the large overlap between forms of scientific thought and forms of societal thought that "keywords" – terms whose meanings chronically and insistently traverse the boundaries between ordinary and technical discourse – can serve not simply as indicators of either social meanings and social change *or* scientific meaning and scientific change, but as indicators of the ongoing traffic *between* social and scientific meaning and, accordingly, between social and scientific change. [Keller and Lloyd, 1992, pp. 4–5, emphasis in original]

As suggested by Section 6.8, the emergence of vast data sets like those surrounding the Human Genome Project point to qualitatively different relationships between the keywords used as part of natural language by scientists and the data and theories to which they are meant to refer.

## 8.3.3  The Changing Economics of Publishing

Every aspect of the publishing business is undergoing radical transformation:

- the costs of production, creating bits rather than applying ink to paper;
- the means of distribution, permitting a file versus trucking pallets of books;
- even the fundamental social interactions, schmoozing with your agent over lunch versus contracting with someone you've never met;
- having all of these things occur in hours and days rather than months and years.

In such turbulent times, economic models that encompass many forms of interaction among readers, writers, editors, and publishers are very useful. M. Wellman provides one useful analysis of *digital library economics*.[14]

---

[14] ai.eecs.umich.edu/people/wellman/UMecon.html

One easy dimension is the contrast between *product* and *service*. When a magazine is something you buy once a month at the grocery store, it is easiest to imagine it as a product. But when a personalized newspaper appears on your computer screen every morning, it seems more like a service.

Stefik has characterized the processing of content in terms of a refinery model [Stefik, 1995; Belew, 1985]. Crude, raw data are produced in large volumes (e.g., by satellites, video cameras, and so on). People who watch these data streams, and now automatic data mining algorithms, find interesting correlations and report on them. Individual observations and correlations are integrated into larger stories, related to prior work, and the like. At each stage of refining, the raw number of bits diminishes, but the *information*, and thus the knowledge (perhaps even the *wisdom*?!), is increased as the individual facts become integrated into more meaningful accounts. Along with each change comes increased economic value.

Another model for interaction comes from the **open source** model of software development. The best metaphor for this may be the hippies' notion of co-ops: Everyone contributes a little bit, so that a valuable resource is available to many. This model is most often applied to software development, but fine-grained "clipping services" and moderation-for-hire newsgroups are very similar. More and more business models for such interactions are already being explored, with some paid for by members and others filling more informal roles.[†]

*Computists is a good example*

If publishers are to have a role in the future, the **editorial enhancement** and other added value they provide beyond the authors' original content must be significant. For example, a key feature of publishing in academic journals is the authority conferred to a publication by the process of **peer review**. An article published in a major journal is not only made available to a wide audience, but it comes with a "seal of approval" of external validation by recognized experts in the field (viz., the editorial board and referees of their choosing) that the document represents significant work. The increased speed and reduced cost promised by electronic communication associated with electronic journals will not be realized unless social mechanisms such as these can be successfully transferred from the printed communication channel.

Another traditional distinction that electronically produced hypertext tends to blur is between the rough working notes and drafts that an author maintains personally and the polished prose that is typically published. When two documents were both typed from scratch, there was every reason that they should be as different as possible. But as word processing technologies have allowed us to cut and paste, it seems that different versions of approximately the same document wind up being published independently. It is sometimes worthwhile saying the same thing more than once (e.g., with different audiences in mind), and in some fields it is common to first publish a shorter, in-progress report in a conference proceedings, with a more thorough and refined version of the same text appearing subsequently in a journal. But viewed cynically, the pressure on academics to "publish or perish," together with the increasing number of more and less formal publication channels, makes the ease of such self-plagiarism an issue. Just as funding agencies like the National Science Foundation now limit the number of publications that can be mentioned (in support of grant proposals or as part of an investigator's vita), publishers and professional societies may find it necessary to limit the raw *quantity* of publications in order to preserve their *quality*.

Obviously, this text itself is an example of an experiment in electronic publishing, and hence in publishing economics. For more details about how the economics is intended to play out, see the final "(Active) Colophon."

## 8.3.4 Teachers and Students

"Finding out about" describes an activity from the perspective of the searcher, someone actively educating him- or herself. Note how similar activities like **computer-aided education** and **distance learning** are to FOA. They too present many documents to a user/student toward a similar educational goal. The critical difference is who is "driving" the educational process: In most educational settings we expect there is a teacher present, and the onus of the educational dialog is on the teacher.

In the semiotic terms of the last section, teachers and students (and sometimes authors and their readers) are involved in a special form of language game that might be called a **tell/ask duality** (see Figure 8.6). As author and reader, or teacher and student, become engaged in a conversation, they alternatively cede control of their shared attentional focus. A teacher explains by telling a story that takes some time to

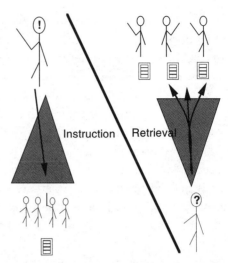

FIGURE 8.6 The Tell/Ask Duality

complete. Some of these stories are relatively self-contained, but most are only pieces of much larger stories. There must be opportunities for students to ask questions in this exchange, even as these necessarily interrupt the flow of the story.

Another way to appreciate the value of this pedagogical structure is to consider what happens when it is removed: When a query is asked of a search engine, the resulting hitlist is missing just this pedagogical structure. When trying to characterize what is most missing from hitlists, imagining a lecture that explains their relationships is one good characterization.

Our image of the classroom typically has a single teacher at the front and many, perhaps 30, students remaining quiet to hear the lecture. The teacher has prepared readings and made these available (and maybe the students have even read them:). The lecture is part of a larger curriculum, and the readings help to relate the current lecture to a larger question.

It is likely that there are simultaneously other teachers in other educational institutions teaching similar courses. For example, the NSF has sponsored the construction of a repository for **Computer Science curricula.**[15] In every subject, there are texts other than the one selected

---

[15] www.education.siggraph.org/nsfcscr/nsfcscr.home.html

by a particular instructor. The student, especially the good student, may check out these other sources of information, but they must be on their guard to give special emphasis to those materials most likely to affect the *grade* they will ultimately receive from this teacher!

Now consider the serious (in the sense that they are there to be informed, not entertained) WWW surfer. They have a question in mind and hope that somewhere on the WWW they will find their answer. Their question is almost certainly much smaller than the question around which a course is defined. This surfer may choose, if he or she has many questions in a related area, to take the course, but the point is that one of the pieces of information this surfer may well see in his search is the curriculum for a course like the one just described.

There are many important questions about just how curricular materials available via the WWW can and should be used. They range from intellectual property issues (who owns them, the institution or the faculty?), to presentation media choices, to a reconsideration of exactly what is the importance of face-to-face meetings in the classroom.

Here we concentrate on the fundamental exchange of information: Who is attempting to learn what? In the class situation, the teacher is charged with presenting information that most efficiently allows these students to learn the concepts the instructor thinks are important. The surfer, on the other hand, is trying to make sense of the almost random set of documents in their hitlist. As we've discussed, if the browsing user really knew the answer of their information need precisely, they wouldn't be surfing! Literate, intelligent surfers have remarkable skill at identifying documents that are likely to contain the answer to their question. In this sense they are both learner and teacher, trying to teach themselves.

Especially once they are beyond (compulsory, K–12) elementary education, the WWW is an excellent place for active students to construct their education. There are choices to be made between educational institutions and then between teachers of the same class. Students must pick a major discipline. Then there may be graduate school, and the process repeats itself. As the workforce becomes more involved in *continuing* education, as distance learning becomes more possible and fashionable, as lifelong learning becomes a political objective, students will be actively seeking curricular units of all different sizes and scopes. Many of these questions resolve ultimately in economic issues: How much is a master's degree worth? How much is tuition at two different schools? How much larger a salary can I earn if I have a certain education?

These changes go hand in hand with the changing institutional pressures on public and private educational systems. For example, corporations such as the Educational Testing Service (ETS) are being pressed to incorporate more holistic essay questions in place of easier-to-grade multiple-choice questions. As a consequence, textual classification techniques like those considered in Section 7.4 are being used to explore algorithmic *e-rater*[16] computer grading of ETS essay questions [Larkey, 1998a]!

From the publisher's point of view, K–12 curricula are being divided into smaller curricular units. No longer is it necessary to buy an entire curriculum (grades K–6, mathematics) and have it adopted in toto by a school board. State guidelines have many facets, and publishers can equate units to these facets at a very fine grain of detail. Local curricular goals and teacher preferences can help to assemble units taken from various publishers and assembled like beads on strings. For the entrepreneurial teacher this provides an excellent opportunity to write curricula themselves, because they are in an excellent position to suggest ways that topics can be connected to guidelines.

As we build more and more autonomous agents (cf. Section 7.6), this interplay between teacher and student (now both software entities!) must transform our notions of who is controlling the dialog to one of **mixed initiatives**. Within the field of machine learning, we typically make the assumption that the learner is extremely passive. More recent analysis extends this to situations of **active learning**, where a large part of the problem is how informative the exemplars selected can be so as to most quickly learn.

## 8.4  Summary

And so we come full circle: This is a textbook about how to write a textbook. In writing it, I was writing the book I wished I read when I wrote my dissertation, 12 years too late.

For now, I leave you with this incomplete version. We have touched on many themes, too many to do real justice to any but the most

---

[16] www.ets.org/research/erater.html

important. As the Einstein quote beginning this chapter suggests, in FOA it is not really the documents retrieved that matter, but the journey to them. The reader is encouraged to follow the bibliographic citations, and the more active pointers collected on the **FOA WWW page**,[17] in order to really FOA (Find Out About).

## TERMS INTRODUCED IN THIS CHAPTER

active learning
attentional focus
bookmark lists
communication
    privacy and
    security
computer-aided
    education
cookies
cooperative
    principle
crawlers
crawling
digital libraries
distance learning

editorial
    enhancement
Grice's maxims
knowledge
    networks
language game
linear media
literacy
meta-tags
mixed initiatives
mutual knowledge
narrative
nonlinear
open source
oral language

orality
peer review
portal
pragmatics
principle of
    relevance
public knowledge
search history
search
    intermediates
semantics
spoof
tell/ask duality
written language
WWW Consortium

---

[17] www.cse.ulsd.edu/~rik/FOA

# (Active) Colophon

Production of this book would have been impossible without the use of a number of tools. Many of these were provided by their developers free of charge or as shareware. These include:

- the emacs editor and related tools from Gnu Project;
- the LaTeX and TeX formatting systems, and the OzTex port to MacOS;
- the gimp image manipulation package; and
- the Linux operating system,

to name only a few. Said another way, this text should be considered a beneficiary of the Open Source movement, as recently enunciated by E. S. Raymond's *Cathedral and the Bazaar*[1] and earlier by *GNU Manifesto*[2] by R. Stallman.

I firmly believe in the future importance of the Open Source model and would like to express my appreciation in a more active way than simply listing the tools I've used. Cambridge University Press seems to believe there is at least some chance that *FOA* will make more money than it cost to produce; I'll believe that when I see it. Should that come

---

[1] www.tuxedo.org/esr/writings/cathedralbazaar/

[2] www.gnu.org/gnu/the-gnu-project.html

to pass, however, it is because you (the reader) bought it, and I think you should get some of the credit! I therefore propose the following, admittedly unusual, procedure:

After expenses directly related to producing *FOA*, I hereby commit to passing on 50 percent of all royalties I receive from *FOA* to organizations who have produced the tools listed above (and others). If you go to the *FOA Web site*[3] and register your copy of the text, you will then be allowed to "vote" on which of these worthy organizations you'd like the money to go to; the Web page will contain full details.

---

[3] http://www.cse.ucsd.edu/~rik/FOA/

# Bibliography

[Abbott, 1952]  Abbott, E. (1952). *Flatland*. Dover.

[Abiteboul et al., 1995]  Abiteboul, S., Hull, R., and Vianu, V. (1995). *Foundations of Databases*. Addison-Wesley.

[ACM, 1986]  ACM. (1986). *Computing Review's* classification. *Computing Reviews*, 27(1).

[Agosti et al., 1992]  Agosti, M., Gradenigo, G., and Marchetti, P. (1992). A hypertext environment for interacting with large databases. *Information Processing & Mgmt.*, 28:371–87.

[Agosti and Marchetti, 1992]  Agosti, M., and Marchetti, P. G. (1992). User navigation in the IRS conceptual structure through a semantic association function. *The Computer Journal*, 35:194–9.

[Allan, 1996]  Allan, J. (1996). Incremental relevance feedback for information filtering. In *Proc. 19th Annual Intl. ACM SIGIR Conf. on R&D in Information Retrieval*.

[Allan et al., 1998]  Allan, J., Papka, R., and Lavrenko, V. (1998). On-line new event detection and tracking. In *Proc. 21st Annual Intl. ACM SIGIR Conf. on R&D in Information Retrieval*.

[Allen, 1992]  Allen, B. (1992). Cognitive differences in end user searching of a CD-ROM index. In *Proc. 15th Annual Intl. ACM SIGIR Conf. on R&D in Information Retrieval*.

[Allen, 1980]  Allen, L. (1980). Language, law and logic: Plain legal drafting for the modern age. In Niblett, B., editor, *Computer Science and Law*, pp. 75–100. Cambridge University Press.

[Anderson and Kline, 1979]  Anderson, J., and Kline, P. (1979). A general learning theory and its application to schema abstraction. In *Psychology of Learning and Motivation*, pp. 277–318.

[Armstrong et al., 1995]  Armstrong, R., Freitag, D., Joachims, T., and Mitchele, T. (1995). Webwatcher: A learning apprentice for the World Wide Web. In *AAAI Spring Symposium on Information Gathering from Heterogeneous, Distributed Environments*.

[Ashley, 1990]  Ashley, K. D. (1990). *Modeling Legal Argument: Reasoning*. MIT Press.

[Baddeley, 1976]  Baddeley, A. (1976). *The Psychology of Memory*. Basic Books.

[Baeza-Yates and Ribeiro, 1999]  Baeza-Yates, R., and Ribeiro, B. editors (1999). *Modern Information Retrieval*. Addison-Wesley.

[Baker et al., 1999]  Baker, L. D., Hofmann, T., McCallum, A. K., and Yang, Y. (1999). A hierarchical probabilistic model for novelty detection in text. In *Neural Information Processing Systems 1999*.

[Bakhmutova et al., 1997]  Bakhmutova, I. V., Gusev, V. D., and Titkova, T. N. (1997). The search for adaptations in song melodies. *Computer Music Journal*, 21(1):58–67.

[Balabanovic, 1997]  Balabanovic, M. (1997). An adaptive Web page recommendation service. In *Proceedings of the 1st International Conference on Autonomous Agents*.

[Bar-Hillel, 1957]  Bar-Hillel, Y. (1957). A logician's reaction to recent theorizing on information search systems. *American Documentation*, 8(2):103–13.

[Barry, 1994]  Barry, C. L. (1994). User-defined relevance criteria: An exploratory study. *Journal of the American Society for Information Science*, 45(3).

[Bartell et al., 1992]  Bartell, B. T., Cottrell, G. W., and Belew, R. K. (1992). Latent semantic indexing is an optimal special case of multidimensional scaling. In Belkin, N., editor, *Proc. 15th Annual Intl. ACM SIGIR Conf. on R&D in Information Retrieval*.

[Bartell et al., 1994a]  Bartell, B. T., Cottrell, G. W., and Belew, R. K. (1994a). Automatic combination of multiple ranked retrieval systems. In *Proc. 17th Annual Intl. ACM SIGIR Conf. on R&D in Information Retrieval*.

[Bartell et al., 1994b]  Bartell, B. T., Cottrell, G. W., and Belew, R. K. (1994b). Learning the optimal parameters in a ranked retrieval system using multi-query relevance feedback. In *Proceedings of the Symposium on Document Analysis and Information Retrieval*.

[Bartell et al., 1998]  Bartell, B. T., Cottrell, G. W., and Belew, R. K. (1998). Optimizing similarity using relveance feedback. *Journal of the American Society for Information Science*, 49(8):742–61.

[Bates, 1986]  Bates, M. J. (1986). Subject access in online catalogs: A design model. *Journal of the American Society for Information Science*, 37(6).

[Bates, 1989]  Bates, M. J. (1989). The design of browsing and berry-picking techniques for the online search interface. *Online Review*, 13(5):407–24.

[Bateson, 1973]  Bateson, G. (1973). *Steps to an Ecology of Mind*. Paladin.

[Bayerman, 1988]   Bayerman, C. (1988). *Shaping Written Knowledge*. Univ. Wisconsin Press.

[Bein and Smolensky, 1988]   Bein, J., and Smolensky, P. (1988). Application of the interactive activation model to document retrieval. Technical Report CU-CS-405-88, Dept. Computer Science, Univ. Colorado, Boulder.

[Belew, 1985]   Belew, R. (1985). Evolutionary decision support systems: An architecture based on information structure. In Methlie, L. B., and Sprague, R. H., editors, *Knowledge Representation for Decision Support Systems*, pp. 147–60. North-Holland.

[Belew, 1986]   Belew, R. (1986). *Adaptive Information Retrieval: Machine Learning in Associative Networks*. Ph.D. thesis, Univ. Michigan, Ann Arbor.

[Belew, 1987a]   Belew, R. (1987a). A connectionist approach to conceptual information retrieval. In *Proc. First Intl. Conf. on AI and Law*, pp. 116–26, ACM Press.

[Belew, 1987b]   Belew, R. (1987b). Designing appropriate learning rules for connectionist systems. In *Proc. IEEE Intl. Conf. on Neural Networks*.

[Belew and Forrest, 1988]   Belew, R., and Forrest, S. (1988). Learning and programming in the classifier system. *Machine Learning*, 3(2).

[Belew and Holland, 1988]   Belew, R., and Holland, M. (1988). BIBLIO: A computer system designed to support the near-library user of information retrieval. *Microcomputers for Info. Mgmt.*, 5(3):147–67.

[Belew and Hatton, 1996]   Belew, R. K., and Hatton, J. (1996). Rave reviews: Acquiring relevance assessments from multiple users. In Hearst, M., and Hirsh, H., editors, *Machine Learning in Information Access*. AAAI Spring Symposia.

[Belew and Mitchell, 1996]   Belew, R. K., and Mitchell, M. (1996). *Adaptive Individuals in Evolving Populations: Models and Algorithms*, volume XXVI of *Santa Fe Institute Studies in the Science of Complexity*. Addison-Wesley.

[Belew and Rentzepis, 1990]   Belew, R. K., and Rentzepis, J. (1990). HyperMail: Treating electronic mail as literature. In *Proc. Conf. on Office Information Systems*. Association of Computing Machinery, Cambridge, MA.

[Belkin et al., 1982]   Belkin, N. J., Oddy, R., and Brooks, H. (1982). Ask for information retrieval. Part 1: Background and theory. *Journal of Documentation*, 38:61–71.

[Belkin et al., 1993]   Belkin, N., Cool, C., Croft, W., and Callan, J. (1993). Effect of multiple query representations on information retrieval system performance. In *Proc. 16th Annual Intl. ACM SIGIR Conf. on R&D in Information Retrieval*.

[Belkin and Croft, 1987]   Belkin, N. J., and Croft, W. B. (1987). Retrieval techniques. In *Annual Review of Information Science and Technology*. Elsevier Science Publishers.

[Berry, 1992]   Berry, M. (1992). Large scale singular value computations. *Intl. J. Supercomputer Applications*, 6(1):13–49.

[Berry et al., 1994]   Berry, M., Dumais, S., and O'Brien, G. (1994). The computational complexity of alternative updating approaches for an svd-encoded indexing scheme. In *SIAM Conference on Parallel Processing for Scientific Computing*.

[Best, 2000]  Best, M. (2000). *Microevolutionary Language Theory*. Ph.D. thesis, MIT Media Lab.

[Bing, 1987]  Bing, J. (1987). Performance of legal text retrieval systems: The curse of Boole. *Law Library*, 79(2):187–202.

[Blair, 1990]  Blair, D. (1990). *Language and Representation in Information Retrieval*. Elsevier.

[Blair, 1984]  Blair, D. C. (1984). The data-document distinction in information retrieval. *Communications of the ACM*, 27.

[Blair, 1992]  Blair, D. C. (1992). Information retrieval and the philosophy of language. *The Computer Journal*, 35:200–7.

[Blair and Maron, 1985]  Blair, D. C., and Maron, M. E. (1985). An evaluation of retrieval effectiveness for a full-text document retrieval system. *Communications of the ACM*, 28(3):289–99.

[Bonhoeffer et al., 1996]  Bonhoeffer, S., Herz, A. V. M., Boerlijst, M. C., Nee, S., Nowak, M. A., and May, R. M. (1996). No signs of hidden language in noncoding dna. *Physical Review Letters*, 76(11):1977.

[Bono, 1972]  Bono, P. (1972). *Adaptive Procedures for Automatic Document Retrieval*. Ph.D. thesis, CCS Dept., Univ. Michigan, Ann Arbor, MI.

[Bookstein and Kraft, 1977]  Bookstein, A., and Kraft, D. (1977). Operations research applied to document indexing and retrieval decisions. *Journal of the Association for Computing Machinery*, 24(3):418–427.

[Bookstein and Swanson, 1974]  Bookstein, A., and Swanson, D. R. (1974). Probabilistic models for automatic indexing. *Journal of the American Society for Information Science*, 25:312–319.

[Borg and Lingoes, 1987]  Borg, I., and Lingoes, J. (1987). *Multidimensional Similarity Structure Analysis*. Springer-Verlag.

[Borko and Bernick, 1963]  Borko, H. and Bernick, M. D. (1963). Automatic document classification. *Journal of the Association for Computing Machinery*, 10:1151–1162.

[Bowman et al., 1994]  Bowman, C., Danzig, P., Manber, U., and Schwartz, M. (1994). Scalable internet resource discovery: Research problems and approaches. *Communications of the ACM*, 37(8):98–107.

[Brachman, 1979]  Brachman, R. (1979). On the epistemological status of semantic networks. In Findler, N., editor, *Associative Networks: Representation and Use of Knowledge by Computers*, pages 3–50.

[Brachman, 1983]  Brachman, R. (1983). What ISA is and isn't: An analysis of taxonomic links in semantic nets. *Computer*, 16:30–36.

[Brachman and Levesque, 1985]  Brachman, R., and Levesque, H. (1985). *Readings in knowledge representation*. Morgan Kaufmann, Los Altos, CA.

[Brachman and McGuinness, 1988]  Brachman, R., and McGuinness, D. (1988). Knowledge representation, connectionism, and conceptual retrieval. In *Proc. 11th Intl. Conf. on Research and Development in Info. Retrieval*.

[Brauen, 1969] Brauen, T. (1969). Document vector modification. In Salton, G., editor, *The SMART Retrieval System*, chapter 24. Prentice-Hall, New Jersey.

[Brenner, 1992] Brenner, S. W. (1992). *Precedent Inflation*. Transaction Publishers.

[Brower, 1994] Brower, D. (1994). Splay trees. In *Software Solutions in C*. AP Professional.

[Bruza and Weide, 1992] Bruza, P. D., and Weide, T. P. V. D. (1992). Stratified hypermedia structures for information disclosure. *The Computer Journal*, 35:208–220.

[Buckley, 1985] Buckley, C. (1985). Implementation of the SMART information retrieval system. Technical Report 85-686, Cornell University.

[Buckley and Lewit, 1985] Buckley, C., and Lewit, A. F. (1985). Optimization of inverted vector searches. In *Proc. 8th Annual Intl. ACM SIGIR Conf. on R&D in Information Retrieval*, pages 97–110.

[Buckley and Salton, 1995] Buckley, C., and Salton, G. (1995). Optimization of relevance feedback weights. In *Proc. 18th Annual Intl. ACM SIGIR Conf. on R&D in Information Retrieval*.

[Buckley et al., 1994] Buckley, C., Salton, G., and Allan, J. (1994). The effect of adding relevance information in a relevance feedback environment. In *Proc. 17th Annual Intl. ACM SIGIR Conf. on R&D in Information Retrieval*.

[Bush, 1945] Bush, V. (1945). As we may think. *Atlantic Monthly*.

[Callan, 1998] Callan, J. (1998). Learning while filtering documents. In *Proc. 21st Annual Intl. ACM SIGIR Conf. on R&D in Information Retrieval*, pages 224–231.

[Callan et al., 1995] Callan, J., Croft, W., and Broglio, J. (1995). Trec and tipster experiments with inquiry. *Information Processing & Mgmt.*, 31:327–343.

[Carlin and Louis, 1996] Carlin, B. and Louis, T. (1996). *Bayes and Empirical Bayes Methods for Data Analysis*. Chapman & Hall.

[Cawsey et al., 1992] Cawsey, A., Galliers, J., Reece, S., and Jones, K. S. (1992). Automating the librarian: Belief revision as a base for system action and communication with the user. *The Computer Journal*, 35:221–232.

[Chakrabarti et al., 1998a] Chakrabarti, S., Dom, B., and Indyk, P. (1998a). Enhanced hypertext categorization using hyperlinks. In *Proceedings of the ACM SIGMOD*.

[Chakrabarti et al., 1998b] Chakrabarti, S., Dom, B., Raghavan, P., Rajagopalan, S., Gibson, D., and Kleinberg, J. (1998b). Automatic resource compilation by analyzing hyperlink structure and associated text. In *World Wide Web Conference 7*.

[Charniak, 1993] Charniak, E. (1993). *Statistical Language Learning*. MIT Press, Cambridge, MA.

[Chomsky, 1965] Chomsky, N. (1965). *Aspects of the Theory of Syntax*. MIT Press, Cambridge, MA.

[Chomsky, 1972] Chomsky, N. (1972). *Language and Mind*. Harcourt Brace Jovanovich, New York.

[Church and Hanks, 1989]  Church, K. W., and Hanks, P. (1989). Word association, norms, mutual information, and lexicography. In *Proceedings of the 27th Annual Meeting of the Association for Computational Linguistics*, pages 76–83.

[Cleverdon and Mills, 1963]  Cleverdon, C., and Mills, J. (1963). The testing of index language devices. *Aslib Proceedings*, 15(4):106–130.

[Cohen, 1991]  Cohen, M. L. (1991). The legal publishing industry. In Woxland, T. A., editor, *Symposium of Law Publishers*.

[Cohen and Kjeldsen, 1987]  Cohen, P., and Kjeldsen, R. (1987). Information retrieval by constrained spreading activation in semantic networks. *Information Processing & Mgmt.*, 23(4):255–268.

[Cohen, 1996a]  Cohen, W. W. (1996a). Context-sensitive learning methods for text categorization. In *Proc. 19th Annual Intl. ACM SIGIR Conf. on R&D in Information Retrieval*, pages 307–315.

[Cohen, 1996b]  Cohen, W. W. (1996b). Learning trees and rules with set-valued features. In *Proc. 13th Conf. on AI*, pages 709–716.

[Cole and Zuckerman, 1984]  Cole, J. and Zuckerman, H. (1984). The productivity puzzle: persistence and change in patterns of publication in men and women scientists. In Steinkamp, M. W., and Maehr, M. L., editors, *Women in Science*. JAI Press, Greenwich, CN.

[Collins and Quillian, 1972]  Collins, A., and Quillian, M. (1972). *Experiments on Semantic Memory and Language Comprehension*.

[Conklin, 1987]  Conklin, J. (1987). Hypertext: An introduction and survey. *Computer*, 20(9).

[Conklin and Begman, 1988]  Conklin, J., and Begman, M. L. (1988). gIBIS: A hypertext tool for exploratory policy discussion. *ACM Transactions on Information Systems*, 6:303–331.

[Cooper, 1971]  Cooper, W. (1971). A definition of relevance for information retrieval. *Information Storage & Retrieval*, 7:19–37.

[Cooper, 1973]  Cooper, W. (1973). On selecting a measure of retrieval effectiveness, part 1. *Journal of the American Society for Information Science*, 24:87–100.

[Cooper, 1983]  Cooper, W. (1983). Exploiting the maximum entropy principle to increase retrieval effectiveness. *Journal of the American Society for Information Science*, 34(1):31–39.

[Cooper, 1988]  Cooper, W. (1988). Getting beyond boole. *Information Processing & Mgmt.*, 24:243–248.

[Cooper, 1994]  Cooper, W. (1994). The formalism of probability theory in IR: A foundation or an encumbrance? In *Proc. 17th Annual Intl. ACM SIGIR Conf. on R&D in Information Retrieval*.

[Cooper et al., 1992]  Cooper, W., Gey, F., and Dabney, D. (1992). Probabilistic retrieval based on staged logistic regression. In *Proc. 15th Annual Intl. ACM SIGIR Conf. on R&D in Information Retrieval*.

[Cooper, 1968]  Cooper, W. S. (1968). *Journal of the American Society for Information Science*, 19:30–41.

[Cooper and Maron, 1978]  Cooper, W. S., and Maron, M. E. (1978). Foundations of probabilistic and utility-theoretic indexing. *Journal of the Association for Computing Machinery*, 25(1):67–80.

[Cost and Salzberg, 1993] Cost, S., and Salzberg, S. (1993). A weighted nearest neighbor algorithm for learning with symbolic features. *Machine Learning*, 10:57–78.

[Craven et al., 1998] Craven, M., DiPasquo, D., Freitag, D., McCallum, A., Mitchell, T., Nigam, K., and Slattery, S. (1998). Learning to extract symbolic knowledge from the World Wide Web. In *AAAI-98*.

[Crestani, 1993] Crestani, F. (1993). Learning strategies for an adaptive information retrieval system using neural networks. *1993 IEEE International Conference on Neural Networks*, 1:244–249.

[Crestani, 1994] Crestani, F. (1994). Comparing neural and probabilistic relevance feedback in an interactive information retrieval system. *1994 IEEE International Conference on Neural Networks*, 5:3426–30.

[Croft and Harper, 1979] Croft, W., and Harper, D. (1979). Using probabilistic models of document retrieval without relevance information. *Journal of Documentation*, 35:285–295.

[Cruse, 1986] Cruse, D. (1986). *Lexical Semantics*. Cambridge Univ. Press, Cambridge.

[Cutting et al., 1992] Cutting, D. R., Larger, D. R., Pedersen, J. O., and Tukey, J. W. (1992). Scatter/gather: A cluster-based approach to browsing document collections. In *Proc. 15th Annual Intl. ACM SIGIR Conf. on R&D in Information Retrieval*, pages 318–329.

[Cutting and Pedersen, 1997] Cutting, D. R., and Pedersen, J. O. (1997). Space optimizations for total ranking. In *Actes: Recherche d'Informations Assistée par Ordinateur*, pages 401–412.

[Dagan et al., 1997] Dagan, I., Karov, Y., and Roth, D. (1997). Mistake-driven learning in text categorization. In *In EMNLP-97, The Second Conference on Empirical Methods in Natural Language Processing*, pages 55–63.

[Daniels et al., 1985] Daniels, P., Brooks, H., and Belkin, N. (1985). Using problem structures for driving human-computer dialogues. In *Actes: Recherche d'Informations Assistée par Ordinateur*, pages 645–660. RIAO-85, France: IMAG.

[Dawkins, 1976] Dawkins, R. (1976). *The Selfish Gene*. Oxford Univ. Press, New York.

[Deerwester et al., 1990] Deerwester, S., Dumais, S., Furnas, G., Landauer, T., and Harshman, R. (1990). Indexing by latent semantic analysis. *Journal of the American Society for Information Science*, 41(16):391–407.

[DeMers and Cottrell, 1993] DeMers, D., and Cottrell, G. (1993). Nonlinear dimensionality reduction. In Hanson, S., Cowan, J., and Giles, L., editors, *Advances in Neural Information Processing Systems 5*, pages 580–587. San Mateo, CA. Morgan Kaufmann.

[Dennis, 1964] Dennis, S. F. (1964). The construction of a thesaurus automatically from a sample of text. In *National Bureau of Standards Publication 269*.

[Dennis, 1967] Dennis, S. F. (1967). The design and testing of a fully automatic indexing-searching system for documents consisting of expository text. In Schecter, G., editor, *Information Retrieval: A Critical Review*, pages 67–94. Thompson Book Co., Washington, D.C.

[Dewey, 1929]  Dewey, J. (1929). *Experience and Nature*. Open Court Pub. Co., La Salle, Ill., 2d edition.

[Domingos and Pazzani, 1997]  Domingos, P., and Pazzani, M. (1997). Beyond independence: Conditions for the optimality of the simple Bayesian classifier. *Machine Learning*, pages 103–130.

[Doszkocs et al., 1990]  Doszkocs, T. E., Reggia, J., and Lin, X. (1990). Connectionist models and information retrieval. *Annual Review of Information Science & Technology*, 25:209–260.

[Doyle, 1960]  Doyle, L. (1960). Semantic road maps for literature searchers. *Journal of the Association for Computing Machinery*, 8:553–578.

[Doyle, 1962]  Doyle, L. (1962). Indexing and abstracting by association, part 1. Technical Report SP-718/001/00, System Development Corporation @Unisys Corporation, Santa Monica, CA.

[Doyle, 1961]  Doyle, L. B. (1961). Semantic road maps for literature searchers. *Journal of the Association for Computing Machinery*, 8:553–578.

[Drosnin, 1997]  Drosnin, M. (1997). *The Bible Code*. Simon & Schuster.

[Duda and Hart, 1973]  Duda, R., and Hart, P. (1973). *Pattern Classification and Scene Analysis*. John Wiley & Sons, New York, NY.

[Dumais, 1991]  Dumais, S. (1991). Enhancing performance in LSI retrieval. Technical Report 91/09/17, Bellcore.

[Eco, 1983]  Eco, U. (1983). *Name of the Rose*. Harcourt Brace. Translated by W. Weaver.

[Egan et al., 1991]  Egan, D. E., Lesk, M. E., Ketchum, R. D., Lochbaum, C. C., and Remde, J. R. (1991). Hypertext for the electronic library? core sample results. In *Proceedings of the ACM Hypertext Conference*.

[Eichmann, 1994]  Eichmann, D. (1994). The RBSE spider: Balancing effective search against web load. In *Proceedings of the 1st International World Wide Web Conference*.

[Einstein, 1955]  Einstein, A. (1955). (interview). *Life Magazine*.

[Elman et al., 1996]  Elman, J., Bates, E., Johnson, M., Karmiloff-Smith, A., Parisi, D., and Plunkett, K. (1996). *Rethinking Innateness – A Connectionist Perspective on Development*. The MIT Press.

[Fellbaum, 1998]  Fellbaum, C. (1998). *WordNet: An Electronic Lexical Database*. MIT Press.

[Fidel, 1986]  Fidel, R. (1986). Towards expert systems for the selection of search keys. *Journal of the American Society for Information Science*, 37(1):37–44.

[Findler, 1979]  Findler, N. V. (1979). A heuristic information retrieval system based on associative networks. In *Associative Networks: Representation and Use of Knowledge by Computers*. Academic Press.

[Foote, 1997]  Foote, J. T. (1997). Content-based retrieval of music and audio. In *Proc. SPIE*, volume 3229, pages 138–147.

[Fox, 1990]  Fox, C. (1990). *SIGIR Forum*, 24(1–2).

[Fox, 1992]  Fox, C. (1992). Lexical analysis and stoplists. In Frakes, W. B., and Baeza-Yates, R., editors, *Information Retrieval: Data Structures and Algorithms*, chapter 7. Prentice-Hall, Englewood Cliffs, New Jersey.

[Fox and France, 1987]  Fox, E., and France, R. (1987). Architecture of an expert system for composite document analysis, representation, and retrieval. *Journal of Approximate Reasoning*, 1:151–175.

[Fox and Marchionini, 1998]  Fox, E. A., and Marchionini, G. (1998). Toward a worldwide digital library. *Communications of the ACM*, 41(4):28–32.

[Frakes, 1992]  Frakes, W. B. (1992). *Stemming Algorithms*, chapter 8. Prentice-Hall, Englewood Cliffs, New Jersey.

[Frakes and Baeza-Yates, 1992]  Frakes, W. B., and Baeza-Yates, R., editors (1992). *Information Retrieval: Data Structures and Algorithms*. Prentice-Hall, Englewood Cliffs, New Jersey.

[Francis and Kucera, 1982]  Francis, W., and Kucera, H. (1982). *Frequency Analysis of English Usage*. Houghton Mifflin, New York.

[Friedman et al., 1967]  Friedman, S., Maceyak, J., and Weiss, S. (1967). A relevance feedback system based on document transformations. In Salton, G., editor, *The SMART retrieval system*, chapter 23. Prentice-Hall, New Jersey.

[Froehlich, 1994]  Froehlich, T. J. (1994). Relevance reconsidered – towards an agenda for 21st centry: Introduction. *Journal of the American Society for Information Science*, 45(3).

[Fuhr, 1992]  Fuhr, N. (1992). Probabilistic models in information retrieval. *The Computer Journal*, 35:243–255.

[Fuhr and Buckley, 1991]  Fuhr, N., and Buckley, C. (1991). A probabilistic learning approach for document indexing. *ACM Transactions on Information Systems*, 9(3):223–248.

[Fujii and Croft, 1993]  Fujii, H., and Croft, W. B. (1993). A comparison of indexing techniques for Japanese text retrieval. In *Proc. 16th Annual Intl. ACM SIGIR Conf. on R&D in Information Retrieval*.

[Furnas et al., 1987]  Furnas, G., Landauer, T., Gomez, L., and Dumais, S. T. (1987). The vocabulary problem in human-system communication. *Communications of the ACM*, 30(11):964–971.

[Gallant, 1991]  Gallant, S. I. (1991). A practical approach for representing context and for performing word sense disambiguation using neural nets. *Neural Computation*, 3:293–309.

[Garfield, 1979]  Garfield, E. (1979). *Citation Indexing – Its Theory and Applications in Science, Technology, and Humanities*. John Wiley, New York.

[Garfield, 1982]  Garfield, E. (1982). Computer-aided historiography: How ISI uses cluster tracking to monitor the 'vital signs' of sciences. *Current Contents*, 14:5–15.

[Garfield, 1986]  Garfield, E. (1986). *Essays of an Information Scientist*. ISI Press, Philadelphia, PA.

[Gey, 1994]  Gey, F. (1994). Inferring probability of relevance using the method of logistic regression. In *Proc. 17th Annual Intl. ACM SIGIR Conf. on R&D in Information Retrieval*.

[Ghias et al., 1995]  Ghias, A., Logan, H., Chamberlin, D., and Smith, B. C. (1995). Query by humming: musical information retrieval in an audio database. In *Proc. Third Intl. Conference on Multimedia*, pages 231–236.

[Giuliano, 1963]  Giuliano, V. E. (1963). Analog networks for word association. *IEEE Transactions on Military Electronics*, MIL-7:221–225.

[Glasgow et al., 1996]  Glasgow, J., Littlejohn, T., Major, F., Lathrop, R., Sankoff, D., and Sensen, C., editors (1996). *Proceedings of the Sixth International Conference on Intelligent Systems for Molecular Biology*. AAAI Press.

[Goldberg, 1995]  Goldberg, E. (1995). The problem of citation: West's stronghold of the electronic publishing arena.

[Gonnet et al., 1992]  Gonnet, G. H., Baeza-Yates, R. A., and Snider, T. (1992). *New indices for text: PAT trees and PAT arrays*, chapter 5. Prentice-Hall, Englewood Cliffs, NJ.

[Goodrich, 1987]  Goodrich, P. (1987). *Legal Discourse: Studies in Linguistics, Rhetoric and Legal Analysis*. Macmillan, London.

[Gordon, 1988]  Gordon, M. (1988). Probabilistic and genetic algorithms in document retrieval. *Communications of the ACM*, 31(10).

[Gordon and Dumais, 1998]  Gordon, M. D., and Dumais, S. (1998). Using latent semantic indexing for literature-based discovery. *Journal of the American Society for Information Science*.

[Gordon and Lindsay, 1996]  Gordon, M. D., and Lindsay, R. K. (1996). Toward discovery support systems: A replication, re-examination, and extension of Swanson's work on literature-based discovery of a connection between Raynaud's Disease and fish oil. *Journal of the American Society for Information Science*, 47(2):116–128.

[Gove, 1993]  Gove, P. B., editor (1993). *Webster's Third New International Dictionary*. Merriam-Webster.

[Grice, 1957]  Grice, H. P. (1957). Meaning. *Philosophical Review*, 66:377–388.

[Grice, 1975]  Grice, H. P. (1975). Logic and conversation. In Cole, P., and Morgan, J., editors, *Syntax and Semantics 3: Speech Acts*, pages 41–58. Academic Press, New York.

[Griffiths et al., 1986]  Griffiths, A., Luckhurst, H., and Willett, P. (1986). Using interdocument similarity information in document retrieval systems. *Journal of the American Society for Information Science*, 37:3–11.

[Guntzer et al., 1989]  Guntzer, U. G., et al. (1989). Thesaurus construction from relevance feedback. *Information Processing & Mgmt*.

[Guttman, 1978]  Guttman, L. (1978). What is not what in statistics. *The Statistician*, 26:81–107.

[Gwyn, 1994]  Gwyn, D. A. (1994). Portable directory access. In *Software Solutions in C*. AP Professional.

[Hafner, 1978]  Hafner, C. (1978). *An Information Retrieval System Based on a Computer Model of Legal Knowledge*. Ph.D. thesis, University of Michigan.

[Hanson, 1988] Hanson, R. (1988). Toward hypertext publishing: issues and choices in database design. *SIGIR Forum*, 22(1):9–26.

[Harman, 1992a] Harman, D. (1992a). *Ranking Algorithms*, chapter 14. Prentice-Hall, Englewood Cliffs, New Jersey.

[Harman, 1992b] Harman, D. (1992b). User-friendly systems instead of user-friendly front-ends. *Journal of the American Society for Information Science*, 43:164–174.

[Harman, 1995] Harman, D. (1995). The trec conferences. In *Proceedings of Hypertext, Information Retrival, Multimedia*, pages 9–28.

[Harman and Candela, 1990] Harman, D., and Candela, G. (1990). Retrieving records from a gigabyte of text on a minicomputer using statistical ranking. *Journal of the American Society for Information Science*, 41(8):581–589.

[Harnad, 1987] Harnad, S. (1987). *Categorical Perception: The Groundwork of Cognition*. Cambridge Univ. Press, Cambridge.

[Harper and Walker, 1992] Harper, J. D., and Walker, A. D. M. (1992). Eclair: an extensible class library for information retrieval. *The Computer Journal*, 35:256–267.

[Harvard Law Review Association, 1995] Harvard Law Review Association (1995). *The Bluebook: A Uniform System of Citations (15th edition)*. Harvard Law Review Association.

[Hawkes, 1977] Hawkes, T. (1977). *Structuralism and Semiotics*. Univ. California Press.

[Hearst, 1999] Hearst, M. (1999). User interfaces and visualization. In Baeza-Yates, R., and Ribeiro-Neto, B., editors, *Modern Information Retrieval*. Addison-Wesley.

[Hearst and Plaunt, 1993] Hearst, M., and Plaunt, C. (1993). Subtopic structuring for full-length document access. In *Proc. 16th Annual Intl. ACM SIGIR Conf. on R&D in Information Retrieval*.

[Hearst and Pedersen, 1992] Hearst, M. A., and Pedersen, J. O. (1992). Reconsidering the cluster hypothesis: Scatter/gather on retrieval results. In *Proc. 15th Annual Intl. ACM SIGIR Conf. on R&D in Information Retrieval*, pages 318–329.

[Hebb, 1949] Hebb, D. (1949). *Organization of Behavior: A Neuropsychological Theory*. John Wiley & Sons, New York, NY.

[Hersh, 1994] Hersh, W. (1994). Ohsumed: An interactive retrieval evaluation and new large test collection for research. In *Proc. 17th Annual Intl. ACM SIGIR Conf. on R&D in Information Retrieval*.

[Hill, 1970] Hill, B. M. (1970). Zipf's law and prior distributions for the composition of a population. *Journal of the American Statistical Association*, 65(331):1220–1232.

[Hill, 1974] Hill, B. M. (1974). The rank-frequency form of Zipf's law. *Journal of the American Statistical Association*, 69(348):1017–1026.

[Hinton and Anderson, 1984] Hinton, G., and Anderson, J. (1984). *Parallel Models of Associative Memory*. Lawrence Erlbaum Assoc., Hillsdale, NJ.

[Hoffman, 1999]  Hoffman, T. (1999). Probabilistic latent semantic indexing. In *Proc. 22nd Annual Intl. ACM SIGIR Conf. on R&D in Information Retrieval*, pages 50–57.

[Howe and Dreilinger, 1997]  Howe, A., and Dreilinger, D. (1997). Savvysearch: A metasearch engine that learns which search engines to query. *AI Magazine*, 18(2):19–25.

[Huberman et al., 1998]  Huberman, B. A., Pirolli, P. L., Pitkow, J. E., and Lukose, R. M. (1998). Strong regularities in World Wide Web surfing. *Science*, 280:95–97.

[Hull, 1993]  Hull, D. (1993). Using statistical testing in the evaluation of retrieval experiments. In *Proc. 16th Annual Intl. ACM SIGIR Conf. on R&D in Information Retrieval*.

[Hull and Grefenstette, 1996]  Hull, D., and Grefenstette, G. (1996). Querying across languages: A dictionary-based approach to multilingual information retrieval. In *Proc. 19th Annual Intl. ACM SIGIR Conf. on R&D in Information Retrieval*.

[Hull, 1988]  Hull, D. L. (1988). *Science as a Process*. Univ. Chicago Press, Chicago.

[Hutchins, 1978]  Hutchins, W. (1978). The concept of "aboutness" in subject indexing. *Aslib Proceedings*, 30:172–181.

[Jacobs, 1987]  Jacobs, P. S. (1987). Knowledge-intensive natural language generation. *Artificial Intelligence*, 33:325–378.

[Jain and Dubes, 1988]  Jain, A., and Dubes, R. (1988). *Algorithms for Clustering Data*. Prentice-Hall.

[James, 1893]  James, W. (1893). *Psychology (Briefer Course)*. Collier Books, New York.

[Jardine and van Rijsbergen, 1971]  Jardine, N., and van Rijsbergen, C. J. (1971). The use of hierarchic clustering in information retrieval. *Information Storage & Retrieval*, 7:217–240.

[Joachims, 1998]  Joachims, T. (1998). Text categorization with support vector machines. In Ndellec, C., and Rouveirol, C., editors, *European Conf. on Machine Learning (ECML-98)*, volume 1398 of *Lecture Notes in Artificial Intelligence*. Springer-Verlag.

[Jones and Furnas, 1987]  Jones, W. P., and Furnas, G. W. (1987). Pictures of relevance: A geometric analysis of similarity measures. *Journal of the American Society for Information Science*, 38(6):420–442.

[Joyce and Needham, 1958]  Joyce, T., and Needham, R. M. (1958). The thesaurus approach to information retrieval. *American Documentation*, 9:192–197.

[Karlgren, 1996]  Karlgren, J. (1996). Poster abstract: Assessed relevance and stylistic variation. In *Proc. 19th Annual Intl. ACM SIGIR Conf. on R&D in Information Retrieval*.

[Katzer et al., 1982]  Katzer, J., McGill, M. J., Tessier, J. A., Frakes, W., and DasGupta, P. (1982). A study of the overlap among document representations. *Information Technology: Research and Development*, 2:261–274.

[Kearns and Vazirani, 1994]  Kearns, M. J. and Vazirani, U. V. (1994). *An Introduction to Computational Learning Theory*. MIT Press, Cambridge, MA.

[Keen, 1992] Keen, E. (1992). Presenting results of experimental retrieval comparisons. *Information Processing & Mgmt.*, 28:491–502.

[Keller and Lloyd, 1992] Keller, E. F., and Lloyd, E. A., editors (1992). *Keywords in Evolutionary Biology*. Harvard Univ. Press, Cambridge, MA.

[Kent et al., 1955] Kent, A., Berry, M., Leuhrs, F. U., and Perry, J. W. (1955). Machine literature searching VIII: Operational criteria for designing information retrieval systems. *American Documentation*, 6(2):93–101.

[Kessler, 1963] Kessler, M. M. (1963). Bibliographic coupling between scientific papers. *American Documentation*, 14:10–25.

[Kleinberg, 1998] Kleinberg, J. (1998). Authoritative sources in a hyperlinked environment. In *ACM-SIAM Symposium on Discrete Algorithms*.

[Klinkenberg and Renz, 1998] Klinkenberg, R., and Renz, I. (1998). Adaptive information filtering: Learning in the presence of concept drifts. In *AAAI-98 Workshop on Learning for Text Categorization*.

[Knuth, 1990] Knuth, D. E. (1990). *3:16 Bible Texts Illuminated*. A-R Editions, Inc, Madison, Wisconsin. ISBN 0-89579-252-4; A-R Editions, Inc. (phone 608-836-9000).

[Kochen, 1975] Kochen, M. (1975). *Principles of Information Retrieval*. Melville, Los Angeles, CA.

[Koenemann and Belkin, 1996] Koenemann, J., and Belkin, N. J. (1996). A study of interactive information retrieval behavior and effectiveness. In *Proceedings of ACM/CHI*, pages 205–212.

[Koll, 1979] Koll, M. (1979). An approach to concept-based information retrieval. *ACM Special Interest Group on Information Retrieval Forum*, 13:32–50.

[Korfhage, 1995] Korfhage, R. (1995). Vibe: Visual information browsing environment. In *Proc. 18th Annual Intl. ACM SIGIR Conf. on R&D in Information Retrieval*, page 363.

[Korfhage, 1997] Korfhage, R. R. (1997). *Information Storage and Retrieval*.

[Kosslyn, 1980] Kosslyn, S. M. (1980). *Image and Mind*. Harvard Univ. Press, Cambridge, MA.

[Krovetz, 1993] Krovetz, R. (1993). Viewing morphology as an inference process. In *Proc. 16th Annual Intl. ACM SIGIR Conf. on R&D in Information Retrieval*.

[Kruskal, 1977a] Kruskal, J. B. (1977a). Multidimensional scaling and other methods for discovering structure. In *Statistical Methods for Digital Computers*, pages 296–339. John Wiley & Sons, Inc.

[Kruskal, 1977b] Kruskal, J. B. (1977b). The relationship between multidimensional scaling and clustering. In *Classification and Clustering*, pages 7–44. Academic Press, Inc.

[Kuhn, 1970] Kuhn, T. (1970). *The Structure of Scientific Revolutions (second edition)*. University of Chicago Press, Chicago, IL.

[Kwok, 1995] Kwok, K. (1995). A network approach to probabilistic information retrieval. *ACM Transactions on Information Systems*, 13(3):324–353.

[Lancaster, 1969] Lancaster, F. (1969). Medlars: Report on the evaluation of its operating efficiency. *American Documentation*, 20:119–142.

[Lancaster, 1968] Lancaster, F. W. (1968). *Information Retrieval Systems: Characteristics, Testing and Evaluation.* J. Wiley.

[Landauer and Dumais, 1997] Landauer, T., and Dumais, S. (1997). A solution to Plato's problem: The latent semantic analysis theory of acquisition, induction, and representation of knowledge. *Psychological Review*, 104(2):211–240.

[Langdell, 1887] Langdell, C. C. (1887). *Law Quarterly Review*, 3.

[Larkey and Croft, 1996] Larkey, L., and Croft, W. (1996). Combining classifiers in text categorization. In *Proc. 19th Annual Intl. ACM SIGIR Conf. on R&D in Information Retrieval*.

[Larkey, 1998a] Larkey, L. S. (1998a). Automatic essay grading using text classification techniques. In *Proc. 21st Annual Intl. ACM SIGIR Conf. on R&D in Information Retrieval*, pages 90–95.

[Larkey, 1998b] Larkey, L. S. (1998b). Some issues in the automatic classification of U.S. patents. In Sahami, M., editor, *Learning for Text Categorization*, number WS-98-05, pages 87–90. AAAI Press.

[Larson, 1996] Larson, R. R. (1996). Chesire II: Designing a next-generation online catalog. *Journal of the American Society for Information Science*, 47(7):555–567.

[Latour, 1987] Latour, B. (1987). *Science in Action.* Harvard University Press, Cambridge, MA.

[Lawrence and Giles, 1998] Lawrence, S., and Giles, C. L. (1998). Strong regularities in World Wide Web surfing. *Science*, 280:98–100.

[Lee, 1997] Lee, J. (1997). Analyses of multiple evidence combination. In *Proc. 20th Annual Intl. ACM SIGIR Conf. on R&D in Information Retrieval*.

[Letsche, 1996] Letsche, T. A. (1996). Toward large-scale information retrieval using latent semantic indexing. Master's thesis, Univ. Tennessee, Knoxville.

[Levi, 1982] Levi, J. N. (1982). *Linguistics, Language and Law: A Topical Bibliography.* Indiana University Linguistics Club, Bloomington, Ind.

[Lewis and Gale, 1994] Lewis, D., and Gale, W. (1994). A sequential algorithm for training text classifiers. In *Proc. 17th Annual Intl. ACM SIGIR Conf. on R&D in Information Retrieval*, pages 3–12.

[Lewis, 1992] Lewis, D. D. (1992). An evaluation of phrasal and clustered representations on a text categorization task. In *Proc. 18th Annual Intl. ACM SIGIR Conf. on R&D in Information Retrieval*, pages 37–50.

[Lewis and Hayes, 1994] Lewis, D. D., and Hayes, P. H. (1994). Special issue on text classification (guest editorial). *ACM Transactions on Information Systems*, 12(3):231.

[Lewis et al., 1996] Lewis, D. D., Schapire, R. E., Callan, J. P., and Papka, R. (1996). Training algorithms for linear text classifiers. In *Proc. 19th Annual Intl. ACM SIGIR Conf. on R&D in Information Retrieval*, pages 298–306.

[Li, 1992] Li, W. (1992). Random texts exhibit Zipf's-law-like word frequency distribution. *IEEE Transactions on Information Theory*, 38(6):1842–1845.

[Lieberman, 1997] Lieberman, H. (1997). Autonomous interface agents. In *Proceedings of the ACM Conference on Computers and Human Interface*.

[Littlestone, 1988] Littlestone, N. (1988). Learning quickly when irrelevant attributes abound. *Machine Learning*, 2(4):285–318.

[Littman et al., 1998] Littman, M. L., Jiang, F., and Keim, G. A. (1998). Learning a language-independent representation for terms from a partially aligned corpus. In *Proceedings of the Fifteenth International Conference on Machine Learning*, pages 314–322.

[Lovins, 1968] Lovins, J. B. (1968). Development of a stemming algorithm. *Mechanical Translation and Computational Linguistics*, 11(1–2):22–31.

[Lowe, 1985] Lowe, D. (1985). Cooperative structuring of information: the representation of reasoning and debate. *Intl. J. of Man-Machine Studies*, 23:97–111.

[Luenberger, 1969] Luenberger, D. G. (1969). *Optimization by Vector Space Methods*. J. Wiley.

[Luhn, 1961] Luhn, H. (1961). *The Automatic Derivation of Information Retrieval Encodements from Machine-Readable Texts*, chapter 3, pages 1021–1028. New York: Interscience Publication.

[Luhn, 1957] Luhn, H. P. (1957). A statistical approach to mechanized encoding and searching of literary information. *IBM Journal of Research and Development*, 1(4).

[Malcolm, 1967] Malcolm, N. (1967). L. J. J. Wittgenstein. In Edwards, P., editor, *The Encyclopedia of Philosophy*, pages 327–340. Macmillan, New York.

[Mandelbrot, 1953] Mandelbrot, B. (1953). An informational theory of the statistical structure of language. In Jackson, W., editor, *Symp. Applied Communications Theory*, pages 486–500.

[Mandelbrot, 1982] Mandelbrot, B. (1982). *Fractal Geometry of Nature*. Freeman.

[Manning and Schütze, 1999] Manning, C. D., and Schütze, H. (1999). *Foundations of Statistical Natural Language Processing*. MIT Press.

[Mantegna et al., 1994] Mantegna, R. N., Buldyrev, S. V., Goldberger, A. L., Havlin, S., Peng, C.-K., Simons, M., and Stanley, H. E. (1994). Linguistic features of noncoding DNA sequences. *Physical Review Letters*, 73(23):3169–3172.

[Marchionini, 1995] Marchionini, G. (1995). *Information Seeking in Electronic Environments*. Cambridge Univ. Press.

[Maron, 1977] Maron, M. (1977). On indexing, retrieval and the meaning of about. *Journal of the American Society for Information Science*, 28.

[Maron, 1982a] Maron, M. (1982a). Associative search techniques versus probabilistic retrieval models. *J. Amer. Society for Information Science*, 33:308–310.

[Maron and Kuhns, 1960] Maron, M. and Kuhns, J. (1960). On relevance, probabilistic indexing and information retrieval. *Journal of the ACM*, 7(3):216–244.

[Maron, 1982b] Maron, M. E. (1982b). Associative search techniques versus probabilistic retrieval models. *Journal of the American Society for Information Science*, pages 308–310.

[May, 1997] May, R. M. (1997). The scientific wealth of nations. *Science*, 275:793–796 (in Policy Forum).

[McCallum and Nigam, 1998] McCallum, A., and Nigam, K. (1998). A comparison event model for naive Bayes text classification. In Sahami, M., editor, *Learning for Text Categorization*, number WS-98-05, pages 41–48. AAAI Press.

[McCallum et al., 1998] McCallum, A., Rosenfeld, R., Mitchell, T., and Ng, A. Y. (1998). Improving text classification by shrinkage in a hierarchy of classes. In *Proc. 15th Intl. Conf. on Machine Learning*, number WS-98-05, pages 359–367.

[McCarty, 1980] McCarty, L. (1980). The taxman project: towards a cognitive theory of legal argument. In Niblett, B., editor, *Computer Science and Law*, pages 23–43. Cambridge University Press, Cambridge, England.

[McCorduck, 1985] McCorduck, P. (1985). *The Universal Machine: Confessions of a Technological Optimist*. McGraw-Hill, New York.

[McCune et al., 1985] McCune, B., Tong, R., and Dean, J. (1985). Rubric, a system for rule-based information retrieval. *IEEE Transactions on Software Engineering*, 11:939–944.

[McFadden and Hoffer, 1994] McFadden, F., and Hoffer, J. (1994). *Modern Database Management*. Benjamin Cummings Publishers, fourth edition.

[McMath et al., 1989] McMath, C. F., Tamaru, R. S., and Rada, R. (1989). A graphical thesaurus-based information retrieval system. *Intl. J. Man-Machine Studies*, 31:121–147.

[Menaud, 1996] Menaud, L. (1996). Is the 'Bible Code' this year's Ouija board? *New Yorker*, page 35.

[Menczer, 1997] Menczer, F. (1997). ARACHNID: Adaptive retrieval agents choosing heuristic neighborhoods for information discovery. In Fisher, D., editor, *Machine Learning: Proceedings of the 14th International Conference (ICML97)*, San Francisco, CA. Morgan Kaufmann.

[Menczer, 1998] Menczer, F. (1998). *Life-like Agents: Internalizing Local Cues for Reinforcement Learning and Evolution*. Ph.D. thesis, Computer Science & Engr. Dept., Univ. Calif., San Diego.

[Menczer and Belew, 1998] Menczer, F., and Belew, R. K. (1998). Adaptive information agents in distributed textual environments. In *Proc. 2nd International Conference on Autonomous Agents*, Minneapolis, MN.

[Menczer and Belew, 2000] Menczer, F., and Belew, R. K. (2000). Adaptive retrieval agents: Internalizing local context and scaling up to the Web. *Machine Learning*, 29(2–3).

[Menczer et al., 1995] Menczer, F., Belew, R. K., and Willuhn, W. (1995). Artificial life applied to adaptive information agents. In Knowblock, C., Levy, A., Chen, S.-S., and Wiederhold, G., editors, *AAAI Spring Symposium Series: Information Gathering from Heterogeneous, Distributed Environments*. AAAI.

[Merryman, 1977] Merryman, J. H. (1977). Toward a theory of citations: An empirical studynof the citation practice of the California supreme court in 1950, 1960, and 1970. *So. California Legal Review*, 50:381.

[Merton, 1973] Merton, R. (1973). *The Sociology of Science*. Univ. Chicago Press, Chicago.

[Miller, 1956]  Miller, G. (1956). The magic number seven, plus or minus two. *Psychological Review*, 63(21):81–97.

[Miller, 1957]  Miller, G. (1957). Some effects of intermittent silence. *American Journal of Psychology*, 70:311–314.

[Mitchell, 1997]  Mitchell, T. (1997). *Machine Learning*. Addison-Wesley.

[Moukas and Zacharia, 1997]  Moukas, A., and Zacharia, G. (1997). Evolving a multi-agent information gathering solution in amalthaea. In *Proceedings of the 1st International Conference on Autonomous Agents*.

[Moulinier et al., 1996]  Moulinier, I., Raskinis, G., and Ganascia, J. (1996). Text categorization: A symbolic approach. In *Annual Symposium on Document Analysis and Information Retrieval (SDAIR)*.

[Mozer, 1988]  Mozer, M. C. (1988). The perception of multiple objects: A parallel distributed processing approach. Technical report, University of California, San Diego, Institute for Cognitive Science, La Jolla, CA.

[Nelson, 1987]  Nelson, T. H. (1987). *Literary Machines: The Report on, and of, Project XANADU Concerning Word Processing, Electronic Publishing, Hypertext, Thinkertoys, Tomorrow's Intellectual Revolution, and Certain Other Topics Including Knowledge, Education and Freedom*. Self.

[Nerhot, 1991]  Nerhot, P., editor (1991). *Legal Knowledge and Analogy: Fragments of Legal Epistemology, Hermeneutics, and Linguistics*. Kluwer Academic Publishers, Dordrecht, The Netherlands.

[Newell, 1990]  Newell, A. (1990). *Unified Theories of Cognition*. Harvard University Press.

[Newton, 1776]  Newton, I. (1776). (Letter to Robert Hooke). "If I had seen further (than you and Descartes) it is by standing upon the shoulders of giants."

[Norman, 1988]  Norman, D. (1988). *The Psychology of Everyday Things*. Basic Books.

[O'Day and Jeffries, 1993]  O'Day, V. L., and Jeffries, R. (1993). Orienteering in an information landscape: How information seekers get from here to there. In *Proceedings of ACM/InterCHI '93*.

[Oddy, 1977]  Oddy, R. (1977). Information retrieval through man-machine dialogue. *Journal of Documentation*, 33:1–14.

[Oddy et al., 1992]  Oddy, R. N., et al. (1992). Towards the use of situational information in information retrieval. In *Journal of Documentation*.

[Ogden, 1993]  Ogden, P. (1993). 'Mastering the lawless science of our law': A story of legal citation indexes. *Law Library Journal*, 85(1 (Winter)):1–48.

[Ong, 1982]  Ong, W. J. (1982). *Orality and Literacy: The Technologizing of the Word*. Methuen, New York. UCSD Call # P35 .O5 1982 (Central).

[Paepcke et al., 1998]  Paepcke, A., Chang, C.-C. K., Garcia-Molina, H., and Winograd, T. (1998). Interoperability for digital libraries worldwide. *Communications of the ACM*, 41(4):33–43.

[Pao and Worthen, 1989]  Pao, M. L., and Worthen, D. B. (1989). Retrieval effectiveness by semantic and citation searching. *Journal of the American Society for Information Science*, 40:226.

[Papadimitriou et al., 1998] Papadimitriou, C. H., Raghavan, P., Tamaki, H., and Vempala, S. (1998). Latent semantic indexing: A probabilistic analysis. *Proceedings of the Seventeenth ACM SIGACT-SIGMOD-SIGART Symposium on Principles of Database Systems.*

[Papoulis, 1991] Papoulis, A. (1991). *Probability, Random Variables and Stochastic Processes.* McGraw-Hill.

[Pearl, 1988] Pearl, J. (1988). *Probabilistic Reasoning in Intelligent Systems.* Morgan Kaufmann, San Mateo, CA.

[Persin, 1994] Persin, M. (1994). Document filtering for fast ranking. In Croft, W. B., and van Rijsbergen, C. J., editors, *Proc. 17th Annual Intl. ACM SIGIR Conf. on R&D in Information Retrieval*, pages 339–348. Springer-Verlag.

[Piattelli-Palmarini, 1980] Piattelli-Palmarini, M. (1980). *Language and Learning: The Debate between Jean Piaget and Noam Chomsky.* Harvard University Press, Cambridge, MA.

[Pinker, 1994] Pinker, S. (1994). *The Language Instinct – How the Mind Creates Language.* Harper Collins.

[Pirolli and Card, 1997] Pirolli, P., and Card, S. (1997). The evolutionary ecology of information foraging. Technical Report UIR-R97-01, Palo Alto Research Center.

[Pollack, 1968] Pollack, S. M. (1968). *American Documentation*, 19(4):387–397.

[Porter, 1980] Porter, M. (1980). An algorithm for suffix stripping. *Program*, 14:130–137.

[Preece, 1981] Preece, S. (1981). *A Spreading Activation Network Model for Information Retrieval.* Ph.D. thesis, CS Dept., Univ. Illinois, Urbana, IL.

[Price, 1986] Price, D. J. (1986). *Little Science, Big Science...and Beyond.* Columbia University Press.

[Pugh, 1990] Pugh, W. (1990). Skip lists: A probabilistic alternative to balanced trees. *Communications of the ACM*, 33(6):668–677.

[Quinlan, 1993] Quinlan, J. R. (1993). *C4.5: Programs for Machine Learning.* Morgan Kaufmann.

[Rada and Bicknell, 1989] Rada, R., and Bicknell, E. (1989). Ranking documents with a thesaurus. *JASIS*, 40(5):304–310.

[Rau, 1988] Rau, L. F. (1988). Conceptual information extraction and retrieval from natural language input. In *Actes: Recherche d'Informations Assistée par Ordinateur*, pages 423–437. Centre des Hautes Etudes Internationales d'Informatique Documentaire.

[Ribeiro, 1995] Ribeiro, B. (1995). *Approximate Answers in Intelligent Systems.* Ph.D. thesis, Univ. California – Los Angeles.

[Ribeiro and Muntz, 1996] Ribeiro, B., and Muntz, R. (1996). A belief network model for ir. In *SIGIR96*, pages 253–260.

[Robertson and Walker, 1994] Robertson, S. and Walker, S. (1994). Some simple effective approximations to the 2-Poisson model for probabilistic weighted retrieval. In Croft, W., and van Rijsbergen, C., editors, *Proc. 17th Annual Intl. ACM SIGIR Conf. on R&D in Information Retrieval*, pages 232–241. Association of Computing Machinery, Inc.

[Robertson, 1969]  Robertson, S. E. (1969). The parameter description of retrieval tests part I: The basic parameters. *Journal of Documentation*, 25:1–27.

[Robertson and Sparck Jones, 1976]  Robertson, S. E., and Sparck Jones, K. (1976). Relevance weighting of search terms. *Journal of the American Society for Information Science*, 27(3):129–146.

[Rocchio, 1966]  Rocchio, J. J. (1966). *Document Retrieval Systems – Optimization and Evaluation*. Ph.D. thesis, Harvard University.

[Rosch, 1977]  Rosch, E. (1977). Classification of real-world objects: origins and representations in cognition. In Johnson-Laird, P. N., and Wason, P. C., editors, *Thinking: Readings in Cognitive Science*. Cambridge Univ. Press.

[Rosch and Mervis, 1975]  Rosch, E., and Mervis, C. (1975). Family resemblances: Studies in the internal. *Cognitive Psychology*, 7:573–605.

[Rose and Belew, 1989]  Rose, D., and Belew, R. (1989). A case for symbolic/sub-symbolic hybrids. In *Proc. Cognitive Science Society*, pages 844–851.

[Rose and Belew, 1990]  Rose, D. and Belew, R. (1990). Toward a direct-manipulation interface for conceptual information retrieval. In Dillon, M., editor, *Interfaces in Information Retrieval*. Greenwood Press, Westport, CT.

[Rose et al., 1993]  Rose, D., Mander, R., Oren, T., Ponceleon, D., Salomon, G., and Wong, Y. (1993). Content awareness in a file system interface: Implementing the 'pile' metaphor for organizing information. In *Proc. 16th Annual Intl. ACM SIGIR Conf. on R&D in Information Retrieval*.

[Rose, 1994]  Rose, D. E. (1994). *A Symbolic and Connectionist Approach to Legal Information Retrieval*. Lawrence Erlbaum, Hillsdale, NJ.

[Ross, 1953]  Ross, A. S. C. (1953). Discussion of 'an informational theory of the statistical structure of language', by B. Mandelbrot. In Jackson, W., editor, *Symp. Applied Communications Theory*, pages 500–501.

[Rudwick, 1985]  Rudwick, M. (1985). *The Great Devonian Controversy: The Shaping of Scientific Knowledge among Gentlemanly Specialists*. University of Chicago Press.

[Russel et al., 1993]  Russel, D. M., et al. (1993). The cost structure of sensemaking. In *Proceedings of ACM/InterCHI '93*.

[Russell and Norvig, 1995]  Russell, S., and Norvig, P. (1995). *Artificial Intelligence: A Modern Approach*. Prentice-Hall.

[Sahami et al., 1998]  Sahami, M., Dumais, S., Heckerman, D., and Horvitz, E. (1998). A bayesian approach to filtering junk e-mail. In Sahami, M., editor, *Learning for Text Categorization*, number WS-98-05, pages 55–62. AAAI Press.

[Salton, 1971]  Salton, G. (1971). *The SMART Retrieval System – Experiments in Automatic Document Processing*. Prentice-Hall, Englewood Cliffs, NJ.

[Salton, 1972]  Salton, G. (1972). Dynamic document processing. *Communications of the ACM*, 15(7):658–668.

[Salton, 1989]  Salton, G. (1989). *Automatic Text Process*. Addison-Wesley, Reading, MA.

[Salton et al., 1993]  Salton, G., Allan, J., and Buckley, C. (1993). Approaches to passage retrieval in full text information systems. In *Proc. 16th Annual Intl. ACM SIGIR Conf. on R&D in Information Retrieval.*

[Salton et al., 1994]  Salton, G., Allan, J., Buckley, C., and Singhal, A. (1994). Automatic analysis, theme generation, and summarization of machine-readable texts. *Science*, 264:1421–1426.

[Salton and Bergmark, 1979]  Salton, G., and Bergmark, D. (1979). A citation study of computer science literature. *IEEE Transactions on Professional Communication*, 22(3):146–58.

[Salton and Buckley, 1988a]  Salton, G., and Buckley, C. (1988a). On the use of spreading activation methods in automatic information retrieval. Technical Report 88-907, Dept. Computer Science, Cornell Univ., Ithaca, NY.

[Salton and Buckley, 1988b]  Salton, G., and Buckley, C. (1988b). On the use of spreading activation methods in automatic information retrieval. *Proc. 11th Annual Intl. ACM SIGIR Conf. on R&D in Information Retrieval*, 1:147–160. Ithaca, New York.

[Salton and Buckley, 1988c]  Salton, G., and Buckley, C. (1988c). Parallel text search methods. *Communications of the ACM*, 31(2).

[Salton and Buckley, 1988d]  Salton, G., and Buckley, C. (1988d). Term-weighting approaches in automatic text retrieval. *Information Processing & Mgmt.*, 24:513–523.

[Salton and Buckley, 1990]  Salton, G., and Buckley, C. (1990). Improving retrieval performance by relevance feedback. *Journal of the American Society for Information Science*, 41(4):288–297.

[Salton and Lesk, 1968]  Salton, G., and Lesk, M. (1968). Computer evaluation of indexing and text processing. *Journal of the Association for Computing Machinery*, 15:8–36. Association of Computing Machinery, Inc. Reprinted by permission.

[Salton and Lesk, 1971]  Salton, G., and Lesk, M. (1971). Information analysis and dictionary construction. In Salton, G., editor, *The SMART Retrieval System*, chapter 6. Prentice-Hall, New Jersey.

[Salton and McGill, 1983]  Salton, G. and McGill, M. J. (1983). *Introduction to Information Retrieval.* McGraw-Hill, Inc., New York, NY.

[Salton et al., 1975]  Salton, G., Wong, A., and Yang, C. (1975). A vector space model for automatic indexing. *Communications of the ACM*, 18:613–620. Association of Computing Machinery, Inc.

[Saracevic, 1975]  Saracevic, T. (1975). Relevance: A review of and a framework for the thinking on the notion in information science. *Journal of the American Society for Information Science*, November-December:321–343.

[Saracevic et al., 1988]  Saracevic, T., Kantor, P., Chamis, A., and Trivison, D. (1988). A study of information seeking and retrieving. 1. Background and methodology. *Journal of the American Society for Information Science*, 39:161–176.

[Schapire et al., 1998]  Schapire, R., Singer, Y., and Singhal, A. (1998). Boosting and rocchio applied to text filtering. In *Proc. 21st Annual Intl. ACM SIGIR Conf. on R&D in Information Retrieval.*

[Schutze, 1993]  Schutze, H. (1993). *Advances in Neural Information Processing Systems 5*. Morgan Kaufmann.

[Schutze et al., 1995a]  Schutze, H., Hull, D. A., and Pedersen, J. O. (1995a). A comparison of classifiers and document representations for the routing problem. In *Proc. 18th Annual Intl. ACM SIGIR Conf. of R&D in Information Retrieval*, pages 229–237.

[Schutze et al., 1995b]  Schutze, H., Pedersen, J. O., and Hearst, M. A. (1995b). Xerox trec 3 report: Combining exact and fuzzy predictors. NIST Special Publication 500-226.

[Searle, 1980]  Searle, J. (1980). Minds, brains and programs. *Brain and Behavioral Sciences*, 3:450–464.

[Sereno, 1991]  Sereno, M. (1991). Four analogies between biological and cultural/linguistic evolution. *Journal of Theoretical Biology*, 151:467–507.

[Shafer and Pearl, 1990]  Shafer, G., and Pearl, J., editors (1990). *Readings in Uncertain Reasoning*. Morgan Kaufmann.

[Shapiro, 1985]  Shapiro, F. R. (1985). The most-cited law review articles. *California Law Review*, 73:1540.

[Shardaanand and Miaes, 1995]  Shardaanand, U., and Miaes, P. (1995). Social information filtering: Algorithms for automating "word of mouth." In *Proceedings of ACM/CHI*, pages 210–217.

[Shepard, 1981]  Shepard, R. (1981). Psychophysical complementarity. In Kubovy, M., and Pomerantz, J., editors, *Perceptual Organization*, pages 279–341. Lawrence Erlbaum Assoc., Hillsdale, NJ.

[Shepard et al., 1972]  Shepard, R., Romney, A., and Nerlove, S. (1972). *Multidimensional Scaling: Theory and Applications in Behavioral Sciences*. Seminar Press, New York.

[Sheridan and Ballerini, 1996]  Sheridan, P., and Ballerini, J. P. (1996). Experiments in multilingual information retrieval using the spider system. In *Proc. 19th Annual Intl. ACM SIGIR Conf. on R&D in Information Retrieval*.

[Schneiderman, 1992]  Shneiderman, B. (1992). *Designing the User Interface: Strategies for Effective Human-Computer Interaction*. Addison-Wesley, 2d. edition.

[Silverstein et al., 1999]  Silverstein, C., Henzinger, M., Marais, H., and Morica, M. (1999). Analysis of a very large web search engine query log. *SIGIR Forum*, 33(1):6–12.

[Simon, 1955]  Simon, H. (1955). On a class of skew distribution functions. *Biometrika*, 42:425–440.

[Singhal et al., 1996]  Singhal, A., Buckley, C., and Mitra, M. (1996). Pivoted document length normalization. In *Proc. 19th Annual Intl. ACM SIGIR Conf. on R&D in Information Retrieval*.

[Sitter and Maier, 1992]  Sitter, S., and Maier, E. (1992). Rhetorical relations in a model of information-seeking dialogues. In *ECAI 92, 10th European Conference on Artificial Intelligence*.

[Sleator and Tarjan, 1985]  Sleator, D. D. K., and Tarjan, R. E. (1985). Amortized efficiency of list update and paging rules. *Communications of the ACM*, 28(2).

[Small, 1973] Small, H. (1973). Co-citation in the scientific literature. *Journal of the American Society for Information Science*, 24(4):265–269.

[Smeaton, 1992] Smeaton, A. F. (1992). Progress in the application of natural language processing to information retrieval tasks. *The Computer Journal*, 35:268–279.

[Smith, 1981] Smith, L. (1981). Representation issues in information retrieval system design. *Proc. Information Storage and Retrieval*, 19(1):100–105.

[Snow, 1961] Snow, C. P. (1961). *The Two Cultures and the Scientific Revolution (The Rede Lecture)*. Cambridge Univ. Press.

[Soergel, 1974] Soergel, D. (1974). *Indexing Languages and Thesauri: Construction and Maintenance*. Melville Publishing Company.

[Sparck Jones, 1972] Sparck Jones, K. (1972). A statistical interpretation of term specificity and its application to retrieval. *Journal of Documentation*, 28:11–21.

[Sparck Jones, 1973] Sparck Jones, K. (1973). *Linguistics and Information Science*. Academic Press, New York.

[Sparck Jones, 1979a] Sparck Jones, K. (1979a). Experiments in relevance weighting of search terms. *Information Processing & Mgmt.*, 15(3):133–44.

[Sparck Jones, 1979b] Sparck Jones, K. (1979b). Search term relevance weighting given little relevance information. *Journal of Documentation*, 35:30–48.

[Sparck Jones, 1986] Sparck Jones, K. (1986). *Synonymy and semantic classification*. Edinburgh Univ. Press.

[Sparck Jones et al., 1996] Sparck Jones., K., Jones, G., Foote, J., and Young, S. (1996). Experiments in spoken document retrieval. *Information Processing & Mgmt.*, 32:399–419.

[Sparck Jones and van Rijsbergen, 1976] Sparck Jones, K., and van Rijsbergen, C. J. (1976). Information retrieval test collections. *Journal of Documentation*, 32(1):59–75.

[Sparck Jones and Willett, 1997] Sparck Jones, K., and Willett, P., editors (1997). *Readings in Information Retrieval*. Morgan Kaufmann.

[Sperber and Wilson, 1986] Sperber, D., and Wilson, D. (1986). *Relevance – Communication and Cognition*. Harvard University Press.

[Sprowl, 1976] Sprowl, J. (1976). Computer-assisted legal retrieval: an analysis of full-text information retrieval. *A.B.F. Research Journal*, 175.

[Srinivasan, 1992] Srinivasan, P. (1992). *Thesaurus Construction*, chapter 9. Prentice-Hall.

[Stanfill and Kahle, 1986a] Stanfill, C., and Kahle, B. (1986a). Parallel free-text search on the connection machine system. *Communications of the ACM*, 29(12):1229–1239.

[Stanfill and Kahle, 1986b] Stanfill, C., and Kahle, B. (1986b). Parallel free-text search on the connection machine system. *Communications of the ACM*, 29(12):1229–1239.

[Stefik, 1995]  Stefik, M. (1995). *Introduction to Knowledge Systems*. Academic Press/Morgan Kaufmann.

[Steier, 1994]  Steier, A. M. (1994). *Statistical Semantics of Phrases in Hierarchical Contexts*. Ph.D. thesis, Computer Science & Engr. Dept., Univ. Calif., San Diego.

[Steier and Belew, 1994a]  Steier, A. M., and Belew, R. K. (1994a). Exporting phrases: A statistical analysis of topical language. In Casey, R., and Croft, B., editors, *2nd Symposium on Document Analysis and Information Retrieval*.

[Steier and Belew, 1994b]  Steier, A. M., and Belew, R. K. (1994b). Talking about AI: Socially-defined linguistic subcontexts in AI. In *Proc. 15th Amer. Assoc. for Artificial Intelligence*, pages 715–720.

[Stiles, 1961]  Stiles, H. (1961). The association factor in information retrieval. *Journal of the ACM*, 8:271–279.

[Stone, 1987]  Stone, H. S. (1987). Parallel querying of large databases: A case study. *Computer*.

[Strunk and White, 1979]  W. Strunk, W. Jr., and White, E. B. (1979). *The Elements of Style*. Macmillan.

[Strzalkowski, 1994]  Strzalkowski, T. (1994). Robust text processing in automated information retrieval. In *Proceedings of the 4th Conference on Applied Natural Language Processing*, pages 168–173. Stuttgart, Germany: Association for Computational Linguistics.

[Sutton and Barto, 1998]  Sutton, R. S., and Barto, A. G. (1998). *Reinforcement Learning: An Introduction*. MIT Press, Cambridge, MA.

[Svenonius, 1986]  Svenonius, E. (1986). Unanswered questions in the design of controlled vocabularies. *Journal of the American Society for Information Science*, 37(5):331–340.

[Swanson, 1988]  Swanson, D. (1988). Historical note: information retrieval and the future of an illusion. *Journal of the American Society for Information Science*, 39:92–98.

[Swanson, 1990]  Swanson, D. R. (1990). Medical literature as a potential source of new knowledge. *Bulletin of the Medical Library Assoc.*, 78(1):29–37.

[Swanson and Smalheiser, 1997]  Swanson, D. R., and Smalheiser, N. R. (1997). An interactive system for finding complementary literatures: a stimulus to scientific discovery. *Artificial Intelligence*, 91(2):183–203.

[Swets, 1963]  Swets, J. A. (1963). Information retrieval systems. *Science*, 141:245–250.

[Tague-Sutcliffe, 1992]  Tague-Sutcliffe, J. (1992). The pragmatics of information retrieval experimentation, revisited. *Information Processing & Mgmt.*, 28:467–490.

[Tapper, 1980]  Tapper, C. (1980). Citations as a tool for searching the law by computer. In Niblett, B., editor, *Computer Science and Law*, pages 209–217. Cambridge University Press.

[Thompson, 1990a]  Thompson, P. (1990a). A combination of expert opinion approach to probabilistic information retrieval, part 1: The conceptual model. *Information Processing & Mgmt.*, 26(3):371–382.

[Thompson, 1990b] Thompson, P. (1990b). A combination of expert opinion approach to probabilistic information retrieval, part 2: Mathematical treatment of CEO model 3. *Information Processing & Mgmt.*, 26(3):383–394.

[Thorndike, 1937] Thorndike, E. L. (1937). On the number of words of any given frequency. *Psycholological Record*, 1:399.

[Towell et al., 1995] Towell, G., Voorhees, E. M., Gupta, N. K., and Johnson-Laird, B. (1995). Learning collection fusion strategies for information retrieval. *Proceedings of the Twelfth Annual Machine Learning Conference.*

[Turtle and Croft, 1991] Turtle, H., and Croft, B. (1991). Evaluation of an inference network-based retrieval model. *ACM Transactions on Information Systems*, 9(3):187–222.

[Turtle and Croft, 1990] Turtle, H., and Croft, W. (1990). Inference networks for document retrieval. In Vidick, J., editor, *Proc. 13th Annual Intl. ACM SIGIR Conf. on R&D in Information Retrieval*, pages 1–24. New York: Association for Computing Machinery. Association of Computing Machinery, Inc.

[Turtle, 1990] Turtle, H. R. (1990). *Inference Networks for Document Retrieval.* Ph.D. thesis, University of Massachusetts.

[Turtle and Croft, 1992] Turtle, H. R., and Croft, W. B. (1992). A comparison of text retrieval models. *The Computer Journal*, 35:279–290.

[Unger, 1983] Unger, R. M. (1983). *The Critical Legal Studies Movement.* Harvard Univ. Press.

[Valiant, 1984] Valiant, L. (1984). A theory of the learnable. *Communications of the ACM*, 27(11):1134–1142.

[van Rijsbergen, 1986] van Rijsbergen, C. (1986). A non-classical logic for information retrieval. *Computer Journal*, 29:481–485.

[van Rijsbergen, 1973] van Rijsbergen, C. J. (1973). Note on evaluation (letter to the editor). *Information Storage & Retrieval*, 9:473.

[van Rijsbergen, 1977] van Rijsbergen, C. J. (1977). A theoretical basis for the use of co-occurrence data in information retrieval. *Journal of Documentation*, 27:106–119.

[van Rijsbergen, 1979] van Rijsbergen, C. J. (1979). *Information Retrieval.* Butterworths, London.

[van Rijsbergen, 1992] van Rijsbergen, C. J. (1992). Probabilistic retrieval revisited. *The Computer Journal*, 35:291–299.

[Vapnik, 1995] Vapnik, V. N. (1995). *The Nature of Statistical Learning Theory.* Springer.

[Veerasamy and Belkin, 1996] Veerasamy, A., and Belkin, N. (1996). Evaluation of a tool for visualization of information retrieval results. In *Proc. 19th Annual Intl. ACM SIGIR Conf. on R&D in Information Retrieval.*

[Vogt and Cottrell, 1998] Vogt, C. C., and Cottrell, G. W. (1998). Predicting the performance of linearly combined IR systems. In *Proc. 21st Annual Intl. ACM SIGIR Conf. on R&D in Information Retrieval*, pages 190–196.

[Voorhees, 1993] Voorhees, E. (1993). Using wordnet to disambiguate word senses for text retrieval. In *Proc. 16th Annual Intl. ACM SIGIR Conf. on R&D in Information Retrieval.*

[Voorhees, 1998]  Voorhees, E. (1998). Variations in relevance judgements and the measurement of retrieval effectiveness. In *Proc. 21st Annual Intl. ACM SIGIR Conf. on R&D in Information Retrieval*.

[Voorhees et al., 1995]  Voorhees, E., Gupta, N., and Johnson-Laird, B. (1995). Learning collection fusion strategies. In *Proc. 18th Annual Intl. ACM SIGIR Conf. on R&D in Information Retrieval*.

[Walker, 1989]  Walker, S. (1989). *The Online Catalogue-Developments and Directions*, pages 84–106. Library Association, London.

[Waltz, 1985]  Waltz, D. (1985). Scientific datalink's artificial intelligence classification scheme. *The AI Magazine*, 6(1):58–63.

[Wang et al., 1992]  Wang, Z., Wong, S., and Yao, Y. (1992). An analysis of vector space models based on computational geometry. In *Proc. 15th Annual Intl. ACM SIGIR Conf. on R&D in Information Retrieval*.

[Warmuth, 1997]  Warmuth, M. (1997). Additive versus exponentiated gradient updates for linear prediction. *Journal of Information and Computation*, 132(1):1–64.

[Watson and Crick, 1953]  Watson, J. D., and Crick, F. H. C. (1953). Molecular structure of nucleic acids: A structure for deoxyribose nucleic acid. *Nature*, 171:737–738.

[Wells, 1938]  Wells, H. G. (1938). *World Encyclopaedia*, pages 3–35. Doubleday, Doran & Co., Inc.

[Welsh, 1988]  Welsh, D. (1988). *Codes and Cryptography*. Oxford University Press.

[White, 1989]  White, H. (1989). Some asymptotic results for learning in single hidden layer feedforward network models. *Journal of the American Statistical Association*, 84:1003–1013.

[Widrow and Hoff, 1960]  Widrow, B., and Hoff, M. E. (1960). Adaptive switching circuits. In *IRE WESTCON Connection Record*, volume 4, pages 96–104. Reprinted in [Anderson 1988].

[Wilbur, 1998]  Wilbur, W. (1998). The knowledge in multiple human relevance judgments. *ACM Transactions on Information Systems*, 16(2):101–126.

[Willet, 1988]  Willet, P. (1988). Recent trends in hierarchical document clustering: A critical review. *Information Processing & Mgmt.*, 24:577–597.

[Williams, 1965]  Williams, J. H. (1965). Results of classifying documents with multiple discrimination functions. In Stevens, editor, *Statistical Association Methods for Mechanized Documentation*, pages 217–224, Washington, D.C. U.S. National Bureau of Standards.

[Wilson, 1973]  Wilson, P. (1973). Situational relevance. *Information Storage & Retrieval*, 9:457–471.

[Winograd, 1983]  Winograd, T. (1983). *Language as a Cognitive Process – Syntax*, volume 1. Addison-Wesley, Reading, MA.

[Winograd and Flores, 1986]  Winograd, T., and Flores, F. (1986). *Understanding Computers and Cognition: A New Foundation for Design*. Ablex Pub. Corp, Norwood, N.J.

[Wittgenstein, 1922]  Wittgenstein, L. (1922). *Tractatus Logico-Philosophicus*.

Routledge, London, with an introduction by Bertrand Russell; translated from the German by C. K. Ogden; originally published 1922.

[Wittgenstein, 1953] Wittgenstein, L. (1953). *Philosophical Investigations (3d edition)*. Macmillan, New York.

[Witztum et al., 1994] Witztum, D., Rips, E., and Rosenberg, Y. (1994). Equidistant letter sequences in the Book of Genesis. *Statistical Science*, 9(3):429–438.

[Wold et al., 1996] Wold, E., Blum, T., Keisler, D., and Wheaton, J. (1996). Content-based classification, search and retrieval of audio. *IEEE Multimedia*, 3(3):27–36.

[Wong et al., 1993] Wong, S., Cai, Y., and Yao, Y. (1993). Computation of term associations by a neural network. In *Proc. 16th Annual Intl. ACM SIGIR Conf. on R&D in Information Retrieval*, pages 107–115.

[Wong and Yao, 1995] Wong, S., and Yao, Y. (1995). On modeling information retrieval with probabilistic inference. *ACM Transactions on Information Systems*, pages 39–68.

[Woodworth, 1938] Woodworth, R. (1938). *Experimental Psychology*. Holt, New York.

[Yager and Rybalov, 1998] Yager, R. R., and Rybalov, A. (1998). On the fusion of documents from multiple collection information retrieval systems. *Journal of the American Society for Information Science*, 49(13):1177–1184.

[Yang and Pedersen, 1997] Yang, Y., and Pedersen, J. (1997). A comparative study on feature selection in text categorization. In *International Conference on Machine Learning*.

[Yule, 1924] Yule, G. U. (1924). A mathematical theory of evolution, based on the conclusions of Dr. J. Willis, F.R.S. *Philosophical Transactions B.*, 213:21.

[Zamir and Etzioni, 1998] Zamir, O., and Etzioni, O. (1998). Web document clustering: A feasibility demonstration. In *Proc. 21st Annual Intl. ACM SIGIR Conf. on R&D in Information Retrieval*.

[Zha and Zhang, 1998] Zha, H., and Zhang, Z. (1998). On matrices with low-rank-plus-shift structures: Partial SVD and latent semantic indexing. Technical Report CSE-98-002, Department of Computer Science and Engineering, Pennsylvania State University.

[Zipf, 1949] Zipf, H. (1949). *Human Behavior and the Principle of Least Effort*. Addison-Wesley, Cambridge, MA.

# Index

11-point average, 99, **131**

Abiteboul, S., 29
abstracting, automatic, 14
accumulator, **98**, 100, 101
accuracy classification. *See* classification,
    accuracy
ACM, 218
active verb. *See* verb, active / stative
ad hoc retrieval. *See* retrieval, ad hoc
adaptive, 1, 113, **252**, 280, 283, 284
adjacency matrix. *See* matrix, adjacency
adjective
    descriptive, **216**
    relational / reference-modifying, **216**
agents, 111, **280**, 296, 316
agglomerative cluster. *See* cluster, agglomerative
aging citation. *See* citation, aging
Agosti, M., 200
alienation, point, **134**, 142, 146
Allan, J., 114, 266
Allen, B., 119
Allen, L., 22
alphabet, marked, **16**
analysis, level of, 40, 61, 101, 203, 210
ancestor, **278**, 284
Anderson, J., 160
annotation, 185, 196, 200, 245, **246**,
    311

antonymy, **215**
argument, 18, 184, 185, 187, 189, 194, 205, 234,
    244, 299, 305, 310
    rhetorical, **200**, 306
    structure, 193, 237, **244**, 305, 306
Armstrong, R., 280
artificial intelligence (AI), 182, 221
    Good old-fashioned (GOFAI), **252**
    thesis (AIT) corpus, 76
Ashley, K. D., 242
association
    measure. *See* measure, association
    associative memory, **160**
    associative relation, 215, 225, **233**
attentional focus, 24, **303**, 313
attribute, 19, 30, 106, 242, 259, 297
    structured, 19, 30, **49**, 183, 288
audience, **4**, 12, 13, 193, 279, 296, 304, 305, 308,
    312
author, **4**, 12, 17, 21, 27, 50, 60, 64, 67, 74, 82,
    101, 184, 187, 189, 195, 199, 205, **207**,
    220, 279, 296–8, 300, 303, 304, 306, 308,
    312
authority, **32**, 196, 240, **312**
    citation. *See* citation, authority
    list. *See* list, authority

Baddeley, A., 160
bag-of-words, **213**, **305**

347